OFF THE TRACKS

Cautionary Tales About the Derailing of Mental Health Care

OFF THE TRACKS

Cautionary Tales About the Derailing of Mental Health Care

VOLUME 1

Sexual and Nonsexual Boundary Violations

Jeffrey Berman and Paul W. Mosher

IPBOOKS.net
International Psychoanalytic Books

International Psychoanalytic Books (IPBooks)
New York • http://www.IPBooks.net

Published by IP Books 2019

Disclaimer

Book cover design and formatting services by BookCoverCafe.com

www.ipbooks.net

ISBN:
978-1-949093-15-5 (pbk)

Contents

Introduction

Psychiatry has much in common with the irresistible little girl Henry Wadsworth Longfellow immortalized in a poem that became a household nursery rhyme: "When she was good, she was very good indeed, / But when she was bad she was horrid." The same can be said for the mental health profession.

Despite numerous advances in the past century, the treatment of mental disorders is still in a rudimentary state due to our fundamental lack of understanding of the complex causes of some of its daunting problems. Most mental health professionals now believe that both psychological (psychodynamic) and physical (inherited or biomedical) factors combine in varying proportions to undermine a person's state of emotional well-being. Most experts also believe that an optimal combination of psychological and physical treatments will provide for many patients the best chance of recovery. Across this wide spectrum of possible combinations, the one factor that appears to be most crucial to recovery is the *treatment relationship*.

Many studies of purely psychological treatments have shown that the treatment relationship is the single most important variable in determining therapy outcome. "The therapy relationship accounts for why clients improve—or fail to improve—as much as the particular treatment method," a major review of "Evidence-Based Therapy Relationships" concludes. Thousands of qualitative and quantitative studies have demonstrated that about 75–80% of patients who enter psychotherapy show improvement, a treatment outcome well above that of many medical procedures. It is self-evident, then, that the treatment relationship must be a powerful force in and of itself. Like any powerful force, the management or mismanagement of the treatment relationship can bring great benefit or harm to the patient.

Off the Tracks: Cautionary Tales About the Derailing of Mental Health Care presents dramatic examples, across a broad range of theoretical approaches to mental health care, where the treatment relationship was mismanaged in such a way as to harm mentally ill patients. We are not presenting these examples to condemn psychoanalytic, psychiatric or psychological treatments, but rather to show how these cautionary tales indicate the necessity of self-monitoring and self-regulation by members of the mental health profession. Because we speak here of a *relationship*, the extent to which the personality of the therapist is implicated makes the requirements of the therapist unique in the world of health care. We are not limiting ourselves only to the role of the therapist in purely psychological treatments. In the realm of predominantly physical treatments of mental disorders, clinicians delivering the treatment are psychotherapists as well. Clinicians' judgments in choosing a physical approach or a pharmacological agent, determining its frequency or dose, or even deciding how often they see their patients, are clearly related to the relationship as much as to the underlying scientific theory supposedly governing such choices.

PART 1

SEXUAL BOUNDARY VIOLATIONS

CHAPTER 1

A Brief History of Sexual Boundary Violations

In the film *Lovesick*, a 1983 romantic comedy made shortly past the end of the so-called "Golden Age" of psychoanalysis in the United States, Dudley Moore portrays a typical Manhattan psychoanalyst, Saul Benjamin, who falls in love with a patient, Chloe Allen, a young, talented, magically appealing but not overtly seductive playwright portrayed by Elizabeth McGovern at an early stage of her career. They become involved in a romantic and sexual relationship. Despite its relative obscurity, the film is notable for its spot on portrayal of New York psychoanalysts of that era, including the appearance of their offices, their decor, dress and pretentiousness, the officious behavior of their "committees" and their flirtations with the arts. The ghost of Sigmund Freud, played by Alec Guinness, appears now and then to offer wise and sarcastic comments about Dr. Benjamin's behavior. In his

February 18, 1983 review of *Lovesick* in the *New York Times*, Vincent Canby wrote that the film "may be the most indigenously New York comedy since Woody Allen's *Manhattan*."

Lovesick is at its best in portraying and parodying a patient's infatuation with her analyst and the latter's reciprocal if guilty passion. "I had the weirdest dream last night," Chloe confesses to Dr. Benjamin, "It's kind of intimate—a sex dream." The analyst can hardly restrain his curiosity, and when she hesitates to elaborate on the details of the dream, he invites her to lie on his couch. "I was in a strange new place," she continues, "with a strange man who was very wise and gentle and kind." In the dream, the stranger is making love to her, giving her great pleasure. "His name was Herzog," Chloe recalls, adding, "I don't know anyone of that name." Dr. Benjamin asks her to free associate on the name, and she suddenly remembers a novel called *Herzog* written by Bellow, whose first name she has forgotten. "The author's first name is Saul, Saul Bellow," Dr. Saul Benjamin replies with a straight face, to which she exclaims, "Oh boy!"

As entertaining to some as *Lovesick* might have been, however, the story is illustrative, if not typical, of a serious problem that has haunted the psychotherapy professions from the earliest era of Freud himself down to the present day. Sexual involvement between therapists and patients is sufficiently common that modern day psychotherapists are no longer surprised by reports of colleagues who have taken the misstep of crossing the line in what is primly called in the profession a "sexual boundary violation," but what has been more recently called in the law and by regulatory authorities "sexual misconduct," "professional misconduct," "assault," "malpractice," "unethical behavior," or even "rape." Because of *Lovesick*'s depiction of a romantic relationship with a happy ending, the film was criticized by many mental health professionals. "It can be argued," Krin Gabbard and Glen O. Gabbard observe in

Psychiatry and the Cinema, "that *Lovesick* is the most insidious depiction of a psychiatrist acting on erotic countertransference feelings that has ever appeared on film" (149). In *Hollywood on the Couch*, Stephen Farber and Marc Green characterize *Lovesick* as "one of the most incendiary of all cinematic treatments of psychiatry" (197).

Space does not permit us to review the extensive studies that have illuminated sex in the patient-therapist relationship, but a few statistics suggest the dimensions of the problem. Citing a dozen different studies from 1973 to 2001, Andrea Celenza states in *Sexual Boundary Violations* (2007) that the number of therapists who admitted to sexual contact with one or more patients in the United States ranged from 7–12% (6). Most of these studies involve psychotherapists who responded to questionnaires asking whether they had erotic contact with patients. Several self-reporting surveys reveal—according to Linda Jorgenson, Steven B. Bisbing, and Pamela K. Sutherland in a 1992 study—that the incidence of therapists who engaged in some form of erotic contact with one or more patients was nearly 14% (596). According to Celenza, "male practitioners account for over 80% of the incidences [i.e. perpetrators]" (7). One might wonder if sexual boundary violations are unique to psychotherapists, since instances of such misconduct have been reported in a number of professions and medical specialties. However, a 1998 review of state disciplinary actions makes clear that of all the medical specialties, psychiatrists had been involved in such misconduct in numbers grossly out of proportion to their representation among the specialties, comprising about 28% of such cases from a pool of medical practitioners in which psychiatrists were 6.3% of the overall medical profession (Dehlendorf and Wolfe). This is a 4.4 fold overrepresentation and is statistically a highly significant finding. At the time of the 1998 review, there was some evidence that the rate of such misconduct among psychiatrists was slowly decreasing, partly because many psychiatrists were abandoning psychotherapy as a treatment modality and turning to psychopharmaceuticals and other somatic treatments, and partly because a gradually increasing number of psychiatrists are women.

The extent of this problem comes to light in the compilations of documented cases assembled by some seemingly or even admittedly "antipsychiatry" websites that devote much energy to—and seem to take glee in—assembling their depressing lists. Some of these websites serve a more positive role, however, in allowing victims to locate help and support from experts in the profession, feel validated, find therapists, receive educational materials and learn about their legal rights. The website "Psychiatric & Mental Health Rape Reporter" has assembled 330 documented examples since 2009 (psychrapereporter.wordpress. com). Furthermore, growing public awareness of this issue is shown in N. M. Gharaibeh's 2005 study of American films about psychiatrists. Of 106 such films, a highly disproportionate 45% showed boundary violations of one sort or another; approximately half of these, a total of 26, were sexual violations.

Transference

To understand the phenomenon of "lovesickness" in psychotherapy and how it might lead to sexual boundary violations, we must first understand the related phenomena of transference, transference-love and countertransference. Freud's most complete discussion of transference appears in *An Autobiographical Study* (1925), where he vividly captures its fraught complexity and significance:

> In every analytic treatment there arises, without the physician's agency, an intense emotional relationship between the patient

and the analyst which is not to be accounted for by the actual situation. It can be of a positive or of a negative character and can vary between the extremes of a passionate, completely sensual love and the unbridled expression of an embittered defiance and hatred. This *transference*—to give it its short name—soon replaces in the patient's mind the desire to be cured, and, so long as it is affectionate and moderate, becomes the agent of the physician's influence and neither more nor less than the mainspring of the joint work of analysis. Later on, when it has become passionate or has been converted into hostility, it becomes the principal tool of the resistance. It may then happen that it will paralyse the patient's powers of associating and endanger the success of the treatment. Yet it would be senseless to try to evade it; for an analysis without transference is an impossibility. (*SE*, vol. 20, 42)

One of Freud's greatest discoveries, transference involves a person's largely unconscious projective tendencies, a phenomenon intensified through psychoanalysis. The patient sees in the analyst, Freud remarks in *An Outline of Psycho-Analysis* (1940), "the return, the reincarnation, of some important figure out of his childhood or past, and consequently transfers on to him feelings and reactions which undoubtedly applied to this prototype. This fact of transference soon proves to be a factor of undreamt-of importance, on the one hand an instrument of irreplaceable value and on the other hand a source of serious dangers" (*SE*, vol. 23, 174–175).

Transference-Love

We could make believe I love you
Only make believe that you love me
Others find peace of mind in pretending
Couldn't you? Couldn't I? Couldn't we?

Make believe, our lips are blending
In a phantom kiss or two or three
Might as well, make believe I love you
For to tell the truth, I do.

—Oscar Hammerstein, "Make Believe," from the musical *Show Boat*,
https://www.youtube.com/watch?v=1VvpDE87b7E&t=3m29s

One of the most serious dangers of transference, as Freud reveals in
"Observations on Transference-Love" (1915), occurs when patients fall
in love with their analysts. "This situation has its distressing and comical
aspects, as well as its serious ones. It is also determined by so many and
such complicated factors, it is so unavoidable and so difficult to clear
up, that a discussion of it to meet a vital need of analytic technique has
long been overdue. But since we who laugh at other people's failings are
not always free from them ourselves, we have not so far been precisely
in a hurry to fulfil this task" (*SE*, vol. 12, 159).

Freud was the first to acknowledge the many ambiguities of transference-
love. After noting in "Observations on Transference-Love" that it is
created by the analytic situation and that the "outbreak of a passionate
demand for love is largely the work of resistance" (162), he concedes that
transference–love "consists of new editions of old traits and that it repeats
infantile reactions. But this is the essential character of every state of being
in love" (168). Nevertheless, Freud concludes, an element of unreality
surrounds transference-love that distinguishes it from "normal" love.

In one of his first letters to Jung, written in December 6, 1906 at the
beginning of their seven-year friendship, Freud emphasized the importance of
transference in the therapeutic process. "Essentially, one might say, the cure is
effected by love. And actually transference provides the most cogent, indeed,
the only unassailable proof that neuroses are determined by the individual's love

life" (McGuire, 12–13). This passage has been widely quoted and sometimes misleadingly translated as "Psychoanalysis is in essence a cure through love." There is no ambiguity, however, over the meaning of Freud's words: he was referring to the patient's transference-love, not the analyst's countertransference.

What should analysts do when patients fall in love with them? It seems to a "layman," Freud points out in "Observations on Transference-Love," that there are only two options. "One, which happens comparatively rarely, is that all the circumstances allow of a permanent legal union between them; the other, which is more frequent, is that the doctor and the patient part and give up the work they have begun which was to have led to her recovery, as though it had been interrupted by some elemental phenomenon." There is, he concedes, a third choice, for analyst and therapist to enter into an illicit and temporary union. This is impossible, Freud emphatically asserts, because of "conventional morality and professional standards" (160).

How, then, should analysts respond to transference-love? To begin with, the phenomenon "signifies a valuable piece of enlightenment and a useful warning against any tendency to a counter-transference which may be present in his own mind" (160). Freud was reluctant to write about countertransference, the analyst's projective tendencies, because he feared opponents of psychoanalysis would use the concept to call attention to the analyst's subjectivity. He first referred to countertransference in "The Future Prospects of Psycho-Analytic Therapy" (1910), where he makes the noteworthy statement that "no psycho-analyst goes further than his own complexes and internal resistances permit" (*SE*, vol. 11, 145). Psychoanalytic organizations were so reluctant to call attention to countertransference that it was not until 1984 that the American Psychoanalytic Association was willing to discuss this troubling concept during one of its annual meetings.

Countertransference remains one of the most vexing issues in psychoanalytic training. Analysts must undergo a long training analysis to become aware of their own projective tendencies, the inclination to project onto a patient the feelings and desires they have toward the key people in their own lives. Analysts must recognize—Freud adds with wry, self-deprecating humor—that the "patient's falling in love is induced by the analytic situation and is not to be attributed to the charms of his own person; so that he has no grounds whatever for being proud of such a 'conquest,' as it would be called outside analysis" (160–161).

Transference-love is one of the most bedeviling clinical phenomena, and it is "just as disastrous for the analysis if the patient's craving for love is gratified as if it is suppressed." The situation is perilous because analysts have no model in life to help them. They must steer a course between the Scylla of gratification and the Charybdis of suppression of their patients' transference-love. "He must keep firm hold of the transference-love, but treat it as something unreal, as a situation which has to be gone through in the treatment and traced back to its unconscious origins and which must assist in bringing all that is most deeply hidden in the patient's erotic life into her consciousness and therefore under her control" (166). Freud never underestimated the potential danger of transference-love. "The psycho-analyst knows that he is working with highly explosive forces and that he needs to proceed with as much caution and conscientiousness as a chemist" (170).

Freud's technical papers on the dynamics of transference emphasize the ease with which positive and negative transference dissolve into each other and the extent to which both may represent resistance to cure. As James Strachey, the general editor of the *Standard Edition*, points out, the first time Freud mentions the word *ambivalence*, coined by the Swiss psychiatrist Eugen Bleuler, is in "The Dynamics of Transference" (*SE*, vol. 12, 106, n.1).

Freud concludes "Observations on Transference-Love" with one of the most prescient paragraphs found anywhere in his writings. "The analytic psychotherapist thus has a threefold battle to wage in his own mind against the forces which seek to drag him down from the analytic level; outside the analysis, against opponents who dispute the importance he attaches to the sexual instinctual forces and hinder him from making use of them in his scientific technique; and inside the analysis, against his patients, who at first behave like opponents but later on reveal the overvaluation of sexual life which dominates them, and who try to make him captive to their socially untamed passion" (170).

Transference is one of Freud's greatest discoveries, but it is also enveloped with great ambiguities, as Thomas Szasz observed in 1963:

> Transference is the pivot upon which the entire structure of psycho-analytic treatment rests. It is an inspired and indispensable concept; yet it also harbours the seeds, not only of its own destruction, but of the destruction of psycho-analysis itself. Why? Because it tends to place the person of the analyst beyond the reality testing of patients, colleagues, and self. This hazard must be frankly recognized. Neither professionalization, nor the "raising of standards," nor coerced training analyses can protect us from this danger. Only the integrity of the analyst and of the analytic situation can safeguard from extinction the unique dialogue between analysand and analyst. (443)

Early Sexual Involvements Between Analysts and Patients

From the earliest days of psychoanalysis, sexual involvements between psychoanalysts and their patients, either during the analysis or after the treatment ended, were reported. As Glen O. Gabbard and Eva P. Lester point out, Carl Jung became involved in "a tempestuous love affair" with a former analysand (his first analytic patient), Sabina Spielrein, in 1906.

"The relationship between Jung and Spielrein is a cogent illustration of why so many 'post-termination' romantic relationships present the same difficulties as those that are concurrent with analysis. Although the treatment had officially ended, the transference and countertransference dimensions of the relationship continued with a life of their own outside the formal confines of treatment" (72).

The Freud-Jung correspondence over the Spielrein "affair" doesn't prove conclusively that Jung had a sexual relationship with his former patient—he remains evasive over what actually happened between them—but it reveals his ambiguous guilt, a "piece of knavery" that he felt he had to "confess" to Freud "as my father" (236). The correspondence also shows the male analysts' anxiety over "seductive" women. "She has kicked up a vile scandal solely because I denied myself the pleasure of giving her a child," Jung wrote to Freud on March 7, 1909. Claiming that he has always "acted the gentleman towards her," Jung nevertheless admits that he doesn't "feel clean," adding, "you know how it is—the devil can use even the best of things for the fabrication of filth." Jung learned a painful lesson: "until now I had a totally inadequate idea of my polygamous components despite my self-analysis" (McGuire, 207).

Freud, to whom Spielrein had earlier written a letter sharing some details about her relationship with Jung, sent off a reassuring note to Jung two days later, implying that her accusations were probably without merit. "To be slandered and scorched by the love with which we operate such are the perils of our trade, which we are certainly not going to abandon on their account" (210). Jung followed with a letter written two months later, declaring he had to end his friendship with Spielrein because she was "systematically planning my seduction, which I considered inopportune. Now she is seeking revenge" (228). Jung then discussed the rumor he believed she was spreading about his decision to divorce his wife to marry a student, a rumor, he later ruefully admitted, that did not originate with her. Three days later Freud wrote a commiseration letter acknowledging that he himself had come "very close" a "number of times" to being in Jung's situation and had "*a narrow escape*," the last three words in English. Freud adds, in a comment that reflects the convention of blaming the female victim, symptomatic of the masculinist bias of the age, "The way these women manage to charm us with every conceivable psychic perfection until they have attained their purpose is one of nature's greatest spectacles" (230–231).

Gabbard and Lester observe that the affair nearly destroyed Jung's career and brought Spielrein to the edge of despair. Her reaction to Jung's efforts to end the relationship reveals what has been called "cessation trauma" (72), a common reaction to the end of therapy as a result of a sexual boundary violation. As Aldo Carotenuto, the editor of Spielrein's published diaries, remarks, "what we are witnessing is a sick young girl's struggle against Jung and Freud, and it is gratifying to acknowledge that it was the girl who, with shrewdness and perseverance, would win the battle, since both Freud and Jung later claimed her as a pupil!" (175).

Sabina Spielrein later became an analyst and made an important contribution to the early history of psychoanalysis. She was murdered (along with her two daughters) by the Nazis in the Soviet Union in 1942 at the age of 56. In an article published in the *Journal of the American Psychoanalytic Association* in 2015, Adrienne Harris raises a provocative question. "Do Spielrein's work and reputation continue to be filtered through the anxieties about her relationship with Jung, the hovering suspicions around boundary violations that so often impugn the reputation of the victim?" (732). By showing the significance of Spielrein's many noteworthy publications, Harris succeeds in "turning a ghost into an ancestor" (733).

Otto Rank, one of Freud's closest colleagues before their falling out in 1926, had a sexual affair with his patient Anaïs Nin in the early 1930s.

Nin later became an analyst (as well as a celebrated diarist) to whom Rank sent patients. In her 1995 biography, Deirdre Bair quotes a letter that Nin wrote to another paramour, Henry Miller, in which she described her relationship with Rank as "sometimes friends, other times lovers, and fellow professionals in still others" (188). Nin implied in one of her confessional diaries that her father, a notorious Don Juan and pedophile, sexually abused her when she was nine years old. He resexualized their relationship when they met again after an absence of 20 years, an experience that may have influenced her symbolic incest with Rank. E. James Lieberman remarks in his 1985 biography of Rank that as a sign of his esteem for her, Rank wrote two prefaces, one for her early *Diary*, the other for her *House of Incest*, which he encouraged her to complete (348). Both Rank and Nin authored books about incest, and their bond with each other recalls Hamlet's sullenly bitter opening words "a little more than kin, and less than kind" to describe his paradoxical relationship with Claudius.

Another prominent psychoanalyst involved in a sexual scandal was Ernest Jones, perhaps Sigmund Freud's most trusted "lieutenant." Jones eventually became President of the International Psychoanalytical Association and the author of a famous three-volume biography of Freud. Prior to his becoming one of the earliest practitioners of psychoanalysis in London, Jones, a physician, was charged in 1906 with two counts of sexually assaulting two young "mentally defective girls" at a special school in London and was jailed overnight as a result of those charges. Jones was later found innocent, but Philip Kuhn's 2002 investigation of the evidence raises new questions about his culpability. In 1903, Jones had been forced to resign another hospital post because of a similar accusation, and after the 1906 events, he concluded that his career in London was finished and moved to Canada.

In both London and in Canada, Jones lived for about seven years as the common-law spouse of his former patient Loe Kann, a fact that he casually disclosed to Freud in a letter dated June 28, 1910 (Paskauskas, 62–64). Kann was a wealthy heiress and a morphine addict. Jones and Kann claimed to have been legally married, but a scandal ensued when the truth came out during their period of residence in the hyper-Victorian Canada of that era. While in Canada, Jones was again accused of sexual misconduct, as Brenda Maddox observes (97), and eventually he returned to Europe where he entered analysis with Sandor Ferenczi at Freud's suggestion, while at the same time Freud undertook an analysis of Kann. Later, during the course of that analysis with Freud, about which he regularly corresponded with Jones, Kann fell in love with the son of another of Freud's patients, whom she eventually married and who also happened to be named "Jones." Ernest Jones, possibly with some bitterness, referred to his successor as "Jones II" (Maddox, 112).

A number of psychoanalytic scholars have pointed out—most recently, Andrea Celenza—that Freud wrote his papers on technique while he was corresponding with and implicitly criticizing Jones for his seductive behavior with patients. "There is an implication that Freud's development of abstinence, neutrality, and anonymity, as the hallmark components of a proper analytic stance, derived from his concern about Jones and the boundary transgressions of other analysts during this time" (193).

The legendary psychoanalyst Frieda Fromm-Reichmann at age 36 began an affair with her ten-year-younger patient, Erich Fromm, one year after her father's death and eight months after the marriage of her younger sister. At the time, according to her biographer, Gail A. Hornstein, she "was dangerously close to passing marriageable age and becoming a permanent embarrassment to her family" (58). Later Frieda said to friends, "I began to analyze him and then we fell in love. We stopped the analysis. That much sense we had!" (Hornstein, 60). Both had had Orthodox Jewish upbringings. Frieda, a physician, opened a treatment facility based on Orthodox Jewish principles for people with mental disorders, and she and Fromm worked there together. Unable to free themselves through psychoanalysis from the strictures of their religious upbringings, they finally decided to take direct action. As Hornstein relates it, "One Passover afternoon in 1928, Frieda and Erich went out alone leaving behind a house filled with Jews fervently enacting the ancient practices forbidding the consumption of leavened foods." They walked to a park, in a neighborhood where they wouldn't be recognized, sat down on a bench, and then "with great ceremony" unwrapped and slowly ate a loaf of bread they had secretly purchased. "Neither said a word. For all their sophistication, at some primitive level, they both expected to be struck by lightning or otherwise punished by God at that moment" (66). To their astonishment, nothing happened.

It's not entirely clear what this act of rebellion referred to, since Frieda Fromm-Reichmann and Erich Fromm had married two years earlier, on May 14, 1926. They separated in 1930, around the time Erich began an affair with Karen Horney, one of his teachers at the Berlin Institute. When Frieda and Erich immigrated to the United States, they came separately, but they continued to be friends thereafter. Both became well known personalities in the psychiatric and U.S. cultural world following their arrival. Frieda and Erich waited until 1942 before they formally divorced. Commenting on the marriage between Frieda, the analyst, and her patient, Hornstein points out, "Of course, things were a lot looser in the analytic world of the 1920s, where people were constantly having affairs with their patients or marrying them" (401).

Karen Horney's affairs with her supervisees and analysands at the psychoanalytic institutes with which she was associated were also well known at the time. According to the biographer Bernard J. Paris, Horney was described by a colleague, Roy Grinker, as a "very seductive woman" who had sexual relationships with younger analysts at the Chicago Psychoanalytic Institute; one of these analysts, Leon Saul, was "traumatized" by the experience (142). There were similar stories about Horney's disruptive behavior at the New York Psychoanalytic Institute, where she had the reputation of emotionally damaging the younger analysts-in-training with whom she slept. Horney's secretary at the New York Psychoanalytic Institute suggested that one of the reasons the sexually aggressive psychoanalyst had affairs with younger men was her need for disciples. Like Hornstein, Paris points out that the rules against analysts having sex with candidates in a training analysis or under their supervision are far stricter nowadays than in the past. Descriptions of these and other notable early examples can be found in Glen O. Gabbard's "The Early History Of Boundary Violations In Psychoanalysis."

Masud Khan

Of all the best-known psychoanalysts of the second half of the twentieth century, the one whose behavior was probably the most egregious was Masud Khan (1924–1989). He was born in the district of British India that later became Pakistan; his mother was a 17-year-old dancer when she became the fourth wife of his 76-year-old wealthy landowner father. A graduate of the British Psychoanalytic Association, he authored several highly regarded books. Anna Freud greatly admired the charismatic Khan, and his most recent biographer, Linda Hopkins, observes in *False Self: The Life of Masud Khan* (2006) that in 1976 Erik Erikson exclaimed, "The future of analysis belongs to Khan!" (xxii). But that was before Khan's career self-destructed. Hopkins documents how Khan slept with his patients, patients' wives, and daughters of friends and acquaintances. Hopkins shows how Khan's life spiraled out

OFF THE TRACKS VOLUME 1

of control as a result of alcoholism, grandiosity, and mental disease, which she speculates was bipolar disorder.

Can Sexual Relations Be a Form of "Therapy?"

Some of the most appalling examples of sexual boundary violations have taken place under the guise that erotic contact between the psychotherapist and the patient is a form of treatment. The idea of sex (acknowledged as that or not) as a form of treatment has its own history.

In her controversial *The Technology of Orgasm: "Hysteria," the Vibrator, and Women's Sexual Satisfaction* (2001*)*, Rachel P. Maines describes the use of "massage" and eventually the 19th century introduction of medical instruments (vibrators) by physicians to treat "hysteria," a condition that existed for possibly as long as thousands of years. According to Maines, physicians had been treating, with varying degrees of awareness of what they were doing, female hysterical patients by inducing orgasms in such patients through "massage" of the patients' genitals. The sexual nature of this "treatment" was seemingly unacknowledged or denied by both patients and doctors. Instead, this widely used procedure was said to produce an "hysterical paroxysm" (actually an orgasm) leading to temporary resolution of the symptoms. Although the origin of this practice in antiquity is uncertain, Maines' evidence for its having been used in more recent times is quite convincing.

In her book's opening chapter, "The Job Nobody Wanted," Maines describes the replacement by physicians of manual massage with medical vibrators and the mixed awareness among physicians as to what they were doing. A fictionalized story of the invention of the vibrator, based on Maines' book, was told in the play *In the Next Room (or The Vibrator Play)*, described by Charles Isherwood in his February 18, 2009 review in the *New York Times* as a "fanciful but compassionate consideration of the treatment, and the mistreatment, of women in the late 19th century." The invention of the vibrator also appears in the 2008 documentary film *Passion & Power*, written and directed by Emiko Omori and Wendy Blair Slick, and in the 2011 British film comedy *Hysteria*, directed by Tanya Wexler. Historians have been largely unaware of this practice in the early history of the psychoanalytic movement.

Yet Sigmund Freud was well aware of the role that therapeutic "massage" was playing in the treatment of hysterics in his day. Commenting on the treatment of "anxiety neurosis," he writes in his little-read 1895 essay "On the Grounds for Detaching A Particular Syndrome from Neurasthenia Under the Description 'Anxiety Neurosis'":

So long as an anxiety neurosis in young married women is not yet established, but only appears in bouts and disappears again spontaneously, it is possible to demonstrate that each such bout of the neurosis is traceable to a coitus which was deficient in satisfaction. Two days after this experience or, in the case of people with little resistance, the day after the attack of anxiety or vertigo regularly appears, bringing in its train other symptoms of the neurosis. All this vanishes once more, provided that marital intercourse is comparatively rare. A chance absence of the husband from home, or a holiday in the mountains, which necessitates a separation of the couple, has a good effect. *The gynaecological treatment which is usually resorted to in the first instance is beneficial because, while it lasts, marital intercourse is stopped. Curiously enough the success of local treatment is only transitory:* the neurosis sets in again in the mountains, as soon as the husband begins his holiday too; and so on. If, as a physician who understands this aetiology, one arranges, in a case in which the neurosis has not yet been established, for coitus interruptus to be replaced by normal intercourse, one obtains a *therapeutic* [emphasis in original] proof of the assertion I have made. The anxiety is removed, and unless there is fresh cause for it of the same sort it does not return. (*SE*, vol. 3, 103–104; emphases added; Fink 38–44)

Treatment of sexual dysfunction using actual sexual encounters became an established practice following the pioneering work of Masters and Johnson in the 1960s. The two world-famous sex researchers described in their book *Human Sexual Inadequacy* a therapeutic technique involving the employment of "sexual surrogates" whose assigned task was to work with the partnerless patients to resolve their sexual inhibitions or other problems by engaging in sexual relations. The "treatment" by the surrogate was prescribed by the patient's psychotherapist or "sex therapist" who made the referral and typically communicated on a regular basis with the surrogate. Cheryl T. Cohen-Greene became well known for her work as a sexual surrogate; she wrote about her experiences in her 2012 memoir *An Intimate Life: Sex, Love, and My Journey as a Surrogate Partner*. The film *The Sessions* depicts her work with a severely disabled client.

Although they popularized the use of sexual surrogates, Masters and Johnson eventually set forward the view in "Principles of the New Sex Therapy" (1976) that it was inappropriate for a therapist or surrogate to engage in sex as part of the treatment of a patient's sexual dysfunction. Using unusually strong language, Masters and Johnson went out of their way to condemn such behavior. "We feel that when sexual seduction of patients can be firmly established by due legal process, regardless of whether the seduction was initiated by the patient or the therapist, the therapist should initially be sued for rape rather than for malpractice, i.e., the legal process should be criminal rather than civil" (553). Masters and Johnson asserted that patients who are emotionally dependent on a therapist cannot make an "objective" decision to have sex in therapy. Nor did the two researchers believe that therapists would be willing to appear in court on behalf of colleagues who have had sex with their patients. Contrary to Masters and Johnson's recommendation, most patients who sue their therapists for sexualizing treatment do so in civil rather than in criminal court, mainly because the lack of corroborative proof generally associated with these cases requires only a "preponderance of evidence," a legal standard lower than that of "beyond a reasonable doubt."

The researchers' public statements, however, were duplicitous. According to Thomas Maier's account of their work in *Masters of Sex*, Masters and Johnson continued to employ sexual surrogates in their therapeutic practices but believed they needed to do so in secret after a lawsuit by a husband of a surrogate threatened to destroy their clinic (201). Masters "never wavered" in his belief that surrogates were essential in the treatment of certain disorders (309). In the operation of their clinic, however, they took steps to keep financial dealings with the surrogates off the books (314).

Although nearly all contemporary psychotherapists believe that sexual relations with patients are unhelpful and even dangerous, there were dissenting voices on this subject in past decades. In the midst of the "sexual revolution" during the 1960s and 1970s, at least two psychotherapists published their views along with anecdotal examples from their own practices that having sex with certain patients was an important contribution to their recovery. One of these therapists, Martin Shepard, we describe in a later chapter; the other, James L. McCartney, we describe below. Even those opposed to any such interaction, based on subsequent survey evidence that 90% of patients who have had sex in therapy have found the experience harmful, would have to admit that for the remaining 10% of patients, the experience might have been benign

21

or even helpful (Bouhoutsos et al.). Most health care experts would say, however, that a procedure with such a dismal risk/benefit ratio should not be considered except in major life threatening illnesses for which there is no alternative.

We will have much to say in a later chapter about Carolyn M. Bates and Annette M. Brodsky's *Sex in the Therapy Hour*, a book that was a catalyst behind the American Psychological Association's decision to reject sex between a therapist and patient, but for now we'll quote the authors' observation that several studies conducted in the 1970s and 1980s indicate a "persistent minority belief that there may be a positive value to sexual intimacy between patients and therapists" (130). Part of this minority belief may arise over the ambiguities of defining sexual intimacy: "kissing, hugging, affectionate touching, or stroking could easily have more than one meaning for either of the parties involved" (130–131). Bates and Brodsky cite a 1977 study conducted by Brodsky and Holroyd that asked mental health professionals who admitted having sex with patients to explain why they believed sex could help themselves or their patients. "Among the few respondents who reported believing that sexual intimacy could be beneficial, various contradictory circumstances were mentioned: The patient was particularly inexperienced and therefore needy of sex, or, conversely, the patient was very experienced and therefore needy of sex. Some believed sex might be appropriate only if it was related to the patient's problems or, conversely, only if it had nothing to do with the patient's problems. There was no consensus as to situations under which a patient might benefit" (151–152).

Andrea Celenza refers to a 1992 study by Gutheil and Gabbard indicating that slightly more than one-third of the patients who initiated sexual contact in therapy reported that they were "not adversely affected." Celenza rightly notes, however, that it's unclear if they would feel the same way over time. She then cites another study indicating that female victims who initially reported experiencing pleasurable feelings during sexualized therapy saw the experience as "hurtful or exploitative in retrospect" (132).

"Overt Transference"

During the "Sexual Revolution" of the 1960s, two articles appeared in a 1966 issue of the *Journal of Sex Research* devoted to "forbidden relationships" that either took an equivocal stance toward patient-therapist sex or a strongly positive attitude. In the first of these articles, Conrad Van Emde Boas suggests that gynecologists were involved most often in sexual relationships with patients, followed by dentists and family doctors, but psychotherapists lagged not far behind. Sex between a patient and doctor was often damaging for one or both, Boas concedes, but he was unwilling to endorse a "rigid medical ethics" that would "veto intimate relationships now and forever" (217).

In the second article, the psychiatrist James L. McCartney not only rejected rigid bans but also regarded sexual relationships as a psychotherapist's duty in some cases. "Every psychiatrist has seen the need of some patients to show affection physically, and in forty years of analytic practice I have found that 10 to 30 per cent require some overt expression," he opines at the beginning of his article. Sexuality is necessary during "overt transference," which he defines as a "visible, audible, or tangible muscular or glandular reaction to an inner feeling" (228). If a patient needs to be taken through overt transference, McCartney continues, the analyst must be of the opposite sex because a "homosexual response is immature, neurotic and adolescent" (230). Therefore, McCartney concludes that if both the analysand and the analyst are male, the patient should be referred to a female analyst. On the other hand, he points out that in the case of a female patient, with a male analyst, it might be difficult to find a "surrogate," and so the analyst may have to "remain objective and yet react appropriately in order to lead the immature person into full maturity."

Not surprisingly, McCartney's examples are between male psychiatrists and female patients. Provided that the patient is "beyond 'the age of consent," she may lie on the analyst's couch, sit in a chair, walk about his office, or even sit on his lap. He then describes for his patients and readers this therapeutic strategy:

> The process of psychosexual development is outlined and it is explained that in order to get well, the patient must emotionally grow up and accept full sexuality. If transference occurs, then the patient will have "fallen in love" with the analyst and will become completely dependent on him. I will at all times be appropriately responsive but objective, and the patient may be overt in any way that is desired in order to analyze the growing-up process. The analyst is first a father and a sexless god, then he becomes a man, and finally the love object and a sexually mature individual who will guide the patient to mature reaction. No limit is put on the patient's reactions but each overt reaction is fully analyzed and explained. (232)

McCartney admits that psychiatrists must overcome their moralistic upbringing and professional training, as he himself has done, to engage in this kind of therapy. "As a Methodist medical missionary's son, born in 1898, I was raised with a very narrow code of behavior, but in 1918 I began my metamorphosis when working in neurophysiology" (233). The metamorphosis, he concedes, is fraught with difficulty. Over the

24

years he discovered that the therapist's need for absolute freedom of expression created immense difficulties that must be overcome if therapy is to succeed. "The therapist must realize that Overt Transference is in conflict with most of the firmly defended positions of conservative society, and that for this reason he will be exposed to criticism, sarcasm, contempt and slander, because the theoretical and practical application of this treatment is rejected by the social order and vigorously condemned by most religions" (234).

McCartney's "Overt Transference" appears today to be so extreme and over-the-top that one wants to read it as unconscious self-parody, but there is nothing humorous about his language or tone. In retrospect, "Overt Transference" stands as one of the most outlandish defenses of sexualized psychotherapy. McCartney's publication of his account of decades-long liberated sexualized psychoanalysis may be a product of the Swinging Sixties, a decade when everything seemed permitted, but he comes across as distant and patriarchal. He asserts repeatedly his belief in the analyst's "complete objectivity," a view that no one today believes; implicit in his notion of objectivity is total non-emotionality, a chilling idea. He insists that therapists "should not mistake the erotic demands of his female patients for those of mature women" (235), though he never explains these differences. He implicitly denies that the therapist experiences sexual pleasure while helping his female patients experience theirs. In one curious passage he claims that the therapist takes on a different identity during treatment. "In working through the transference neurosis, the therapist should allow himself to be reacted to as though he were someone from the patient's past" (234).

McCartney never doubts that psychiatrists like himself can be totally objective when practicing sexualized psychotherapy, and he duly cites statistics from his own practice to support his scientific claims. He states that in his 40 years' experience, he has conducted over 1,500 psychoanalyses in his private practice, which represent, he says, 26% of all the psychiatric patients seen. Altering his therapeutic technique in the last 20 years to allow "full overt expression," he argues near the end of his article that of his adult female analysands, "30 per cent expressed some form of Overt Transference, such as sitting on the analyst's lap, holding his hand, hugging or kissing him. About 10 per cent found it necessary to act-out extremely, such as mutual undressing, genital manipulation or coitus."

McCartney represented a small number of analysts who believed that sex with a therapist could help a woman achieve, in his words, "full heterosexual maturity" (237). As we will illustrate, other therapists used different rationalizations but reached similar conclusions. As a result of "Overt Transference," McCartney was expelled from membership in the American Psychiatric Association. The expulsion might have been meaningless, however. The psychiatrist L. J. West pointed out in an article published in the *American Journal of Psychiatry* in 1969 that the grounds for an ethics violation against McCartney were shaky at best because no complaint had been filed against him:

A member of the APA was expelled because he publicly described and justified sexual intimacies with female patients as beneficial therapeutic procedures (1). But no complaint had been made by a patient in this case. What, therefore, was the written and published criterion for ethical behavior that this physician violated? Was it the Oath of Hippocrates? Other facets of that oath have recently fallen in the face of legal reforms, for example, concerning abortions. The former member in question could not really be accused of advertising, since his revelation was made in a professional journal. *Even a challenge that he was administering a valueless procedure in the name of therapy could be argued, since clinicians from Hippocrates to Freud have noted the beneficial effects of sexual intercourse in certain cases.*

Even if the Ethics Committee turned to the community for support in the form of laws forbidding extramarital sexual congress, it appears that such statutes may soon fall before the growing acceptance of the principle set forth in the Wolfenden Report that sexual acts between consenting adults in private are not a matter for concern under the criminal code. Nevertheless, I feel certain that the overwhelming majority of psychiatrists would agree that it is unethical to seduce patients and foolish (if not outrageous) to call it treatment. (West, 228–229; emphasis added)

West's ambivalence toward laws forbidding patient-therapist sex is palpable, particularly in his reference to the Wolfenden Report, the landmark recommendation issued in Great Britain in 1957 making homosexual behavior between consenting adults no longer a criminal offence, as it had been for the previous 400 years. Leonard L. Riskin infers from West's comments that the expulsion of McCartney from the APA was more likely intended to "protect the image of the profession than to punish a breach of ethics" (1008, n.42).

McCartney wrote a letter to the *American Journal of Psychiatry* in 1969 protesting his expulsion from the American Psychiatric Association. He pointed out that the Hippocratic Oath was "antiquated and has already been rejected by several medical schools and replaced by the *Declaration of Geneva* which makes no mention of sexual contact." He reiterated West's comment that no complaint against him, either from a patient or a colleague, had been filed since the publication of "Overt Transference." He went on to describe his 40 years of psychiatric practice and his 40 years of marriage during which "I have never had an affair and have never raped, seduced, or carnally abused any of my

27

patients. I married in 1924 and am still totally and exclusively in love with this same woman." McCartney declared, with self-satisfaction, that for the two years he was overseas during World War II he "at all times had remained celibate while away from home." With the apparent intention of distinguishing sexual acts per se (presumably intended for treatment purposes) from "emotional expressions of love," he added, "I can truthfully say that I was never in love with any of my patients." The letter, describing his longstanding involvement with the APA including election as a Life Fellow in 1959, took note that "until December 1968 my name was never besmirched," and ended with the hope that he would in the future "be given a vote of confidence and be reinstated in the American Psychiatric Association."

Charles Clay Dahlberg

Calling into question McCartney's "Overt Transference," the psychiatrist Charles Clay Dahlberg wrote a noteworthy 1970 article. He admits that he had difficulty finding a publisher for "Sexual Contact Between Patient and Therapist" because he was told it was "too controversial," meaning that professional organizations and journals did not want to acknowledge that some therapists were sleeping with their patients. Dahlberg walks a tightrope throughout the publication. On the one hand, he refers respectfully to McCartney's research, concluding that it is "conceivable" that his method and theory are valid. On the other hand, Dahlberg cites the work of Frieda Fromm-Reichmann, who agrees with Freud that intimacy between a patient and analyst is always harmful. Dahlberg doesn't mention the fact that her knowledge apparently came from painful experience as a result of her brief marriage to her own analysand, Erich Fromm. She later wryly advised other therapists, "Don't have sex with your patient. You'll always disappoint them" (quoted in Slovenko, 741).

Dahlberg discusses nine case studies of patient-therapist sex. In each case, the source of the information was either the patient or the therapist. The nine cases of sexual contact ranged from the "relatively harmless to the frankly destructive" (110; there is no evidence that Dahlberg had sex with any of these patients). Tellingly, the nine therapists were males over the age of 40 and from ten to 25 years older than the female patients. In most cases the therapists were separating from their wives or newly divorced.

The theme running through all nine case studies is that female patients at first feel triumph when sleeping with their therapists, then betrayal, and finally exploitation. Dahlberg is reluctant to argue categorically against sexual relations between patient and therapist. Instead, he proposes at the end of the article that researchers undertake a "Kinsey-type survey of therapists and patients to probe into the circumstances and results of sexual acting out and near acting out" (121). Despite his effort to maintain neutrality on the volatile issue, Dahlberg's disapproval of such relationships is evident throughout his article. In a memorable line, he argues that unlike other "therapeutic sins—laziness, pride, greed, and anger among them," all of which have consequences, and some of which can be reversed, a therapist's sexual acting out can never be undone. "We are specialists in dangerous illusions," Dahlberg asserts. "Everything in treatment happens in and about illusions. Most of its profit, all of its disasters, its high seriousness, its moral and spiritual riskiness, the bitterness and fatigue of both parties, the need for professional comradeship that draws us together for evenings like this all come from the fact that psychoanalysis is a procedure of encouraging illusory expectations. The role of analyst is simply not a good place for a person to be. It is not a healthy job. It is not what would ordinarily be called wholesome or honorable (as the general populace recognizes)" (quoted in Friedman, 824).

Current Professional Viewpoints and Legal Status

Writing in 1995, Glen O. Gabbard, an expert on the subject, pointed out in "The Early History of Boundary Violations in Psychoanalysis" that the problem of sexual violations is not only widespread but also a continuing abuse that must be faced by every practitioner:

> Every psychoanalytic institute and society has seen the ravages of severe boundary violations. It would be tempting for us to attribute these transgressions to a small handful of corrupt colleagues who suffer from severe character pathology and a propensity to act rather than reflect. This point of view allows all of us to projectively disavow our own vulnerability to boundary violations and see them as the province of a few who have nothing in common with the rest of us. The facts are otherwise. In my experience both of evaluating and treating individuals charged with sexual misconduct and consulting with psychoanalytic groups about problems in their midst, it has become increasingly clear that all of us are potentially vulnerable. (116)

By the year 2000, professional organizations, regulatory bodies, and the courts had come to view patient-therapist sexual contact as strictly forbidden, as Kenneth S. Pope wrote in 2001:

> The therapeutic relationship is a special one, characterized by exceptional vulnerability and trust. People may talk to their therapists about thoughts, feelings, events, and behaviors that they would

never disclose to anyone else. Every state in the United States has recognized the special nature of the therapeutic relationship and the special responsibilities that therapists have in relation to their clients by requiring special training and licensure for therapists, and by recognizing a therapist-patient privilege which safeguards the privacy of what patients talk about to their therapist.

A relatively small minority of therapists take[s] advantage of the client's trust and vulnerability and of the power inherent in the therapist's role by sexually exploiting the client. Each state has prohibited this abuse of trust, vulnerability, and power through licensing regulations. Therapist-patient sex is also subject to civil law as a tort (i.e., offenders may be sued for malpractice), and some states have criminalized the offense. The ethics codes of all major mental health professionals prohibit the offense. ("Sex Between Therapists and Clients" 955–956)

Sexual contact with patients is illegal in about half of the states. Beginning with Wisconsin's criminalization of sex between a therapist and a patient in 1984, a number of states began to consider how they could do more than rely on organizational codes of ethics and disciplinary proceedings to address the problem. As Colman M. Herman noted in 2012, although the laws vary widely, at least 23 states now make sexual abuse of patients by clinicians a criminal act. Herman adds that in in the early 1990s, "there was an effort to criminalize sexual misconduct by clinicians with patients in Massachusetts, but the legislation failed to pass."

Jay S. Kwawer, the Director of the William Alanson White Institute of Psychiatry, Psychoanalysis & Psychology, pointed out to us the important difference between the American Psychiatric Association and the American Psychological Association regarding the ethics

31

of romantic relationships with patients. The American Psychiatric Association insists that "once a patient, always a patient": the prohibition on therapist-patient sex exists for life. That's also true of the American Psychoanalytic Association. "Sexual relations between a psychoanalyst and patient or family member, current or former, are potentially harmful to both parties, and unethical." The American Psychological Association states that in rare cases it may be acceptable for a therapist to become romantically involved after two years. One of the reasons for this is that most of the 135,000 members of the American Psychological Association do not see patients in long-term, intensive psychotherapy or psychoanalysis. The combined memberships of Divisions 12 (Clinical), 29 (Psychotherapy), and 39 (Psychoanalysis) represent a minority of the membership of the American Psychological Association. Since most members of the American Psychological Association do little or no psychotherapy, a psychologist might meet with a patient only a few times. Consequently, there is no assumption in brief treatment, as there is in psychoanalysis, that an intense transference develops.

Arguing for an absolute and permanent ban on post-termination sexual relationships, Gabbard and Lester observe that termination is a "particularly high-risk time for the enactment of sexual longings between analyst and analysand. It is the bane of the analytic profession that practitioners must become extraordinarily close to their patients, only to lose them. Termination is a real loss for both participants. It represents the finiteness of the relationship and even the unbearable impermanence of life itself" (154).

According to Andrea Celenza, prevalence studies indicate that psychiatrists and psychologists have equivalent rates of erotic contacts with patients, with a lower incidence among psychodynamic therapists and those who provide long-term intensive psychotherapy. The explanation, Celenza speculates, is that there is a greater awareness among the latter of the "importance of clear, non-exploitative, and therapeutically oriented roles, boundaries, and responsibilities, such as maintaining the frame, the holding environment, and appreciation for transference" (*Sexual Boundary Violations*, 8). On the other hand, Margolis, admittedly using anecdotal evidence, estimated that the incidence of erotic contact with patients among psychoanalysts does not differ significantly from the incidence among other psychotherapists. Several of the following prominent therapists implicated in sexual boundary violations were psychoanalytically oriented:

1965: Victor Rosen

Victor Rosen, who had been elected as president of the American Psychoanalytic Association, and who was at that time married, met with a former patient at her request for a follow up consultation because of a disturbing nightmare. The ex-patient, Elise Snyder, was at the time an early career psychiatrist and psychoanalyst. She was married to a physician whom she met while in medical school prior to her graduation in 1958. Snyder stated to Evan Osnos, in his article "Meet Dr. Freud," published in *The New Yorker* on January 10, 2011, that during a consultation interview, Rosen, appearing not to be listening to her, suddenly blurted out, "I'm in love with you. I've been in love with you for the past two years" (54).

An earlier alternative version of the story of how the relationship changed from psychoanalyst and ex-patient to lovers appears in *Hollywood on the Couch*, based on an account from Rosen's daughter, Winifred Rosen. According to Farber and Green, Rosen hired Snyder after her analysis with him ended to edit a paper he had written; "within a few months their relationship had turned into a full fledged romance" (207). Believing that her father was "completely blind" to his own breach of ethics, Winifred Rosen reveals perhaps the strangest detail of the situation. When she told her father after she graduated college that she wanted to enter analysis to explore the issues raised by her parents' separation, he recommended that she seek treatment from Elise Snyder. "My dad didn't want me talking about the situation to an outsider," she stated to Farber and Green. "He didn't want any of this to be known. So he sent me to Elise, which was completely weird." Winifred Rosen said that her sessions with Snyder were "indescribable," adding, "My father was in love, so he was insane by definition" (Farber and Green 207). Finally, to illustrate the weird entanglements that can occur in the small world of psychoanalysis, Snyder's husband was, at the time she left him, a psychoanalytic patient of David Rubinfine (see below), who himself later married a high profile patient (Personal communication, Judith Schachter, September 25, 2014).

After leaving their respective spouses, Victor Rosen and Elise Snyder were married in 1965. The news of the marriage created a major scandal in the profession augmented by the high status Rosen held at the time. He consequently left his position at the New York Psychoanalytic Institute. The marriage turned out to be unhappy and ultimately tragic. Snyder discovered that Rosen was addicted to narcotics, and after seven years she decided to leave him. He was found dead in his car the next day from an overdose of narcotics and sedatives (Osnos, 54).

Snyder herself gained recognition in her career as a psychoanalyst and eventually was nationally elected to the board of directors of the American Psychoanalytic Association. When she ran for president of the Association, however, her political opponent's supporters attempted to cast aspersions on *her* character, claiming that she had committed a "boundary violation" by marrying her analyst, seemingly oblivious to the fact that it is the *analyst's* responsibility, not the patient's, to avoid such entanglements.

The Victor Rosen case occurred in the mid 1960s, two decades before Kenneth S. Pope and Jacqueline C. Bouhoutsos authored *Sexual Intimacy Between Therapists and Patients* (1986). The book's publication, Martin H. Williams remarked in his 2011 online article "Therapist-Patient Sex Twenty Years Later: A View from the Courtroom," marked the end of an era: "an era during which famous and respected psychotherapists married their patients, during which a surprisingly large number of psychotherapists became sexually involved with their patients, and an era during which this could be done without adverse repercussions to the therapists' careers." Williams, a forensic psychologist who has testified as an expert witness in many sexual boundary violation malpractice cases, believes that beginning in the 1980s, the decade which brought with it a new climate of zero tolerance for sex with patients, all psychotherapists have been exposed and re-exposed to educational messages that sex with a patient is "indefensible, inexcusable and is professional suicide." Perhaps, yet the following four high-profile cases occurred *after* the 1980s:

1992: Edward M. Daniels

Edward M. Daniels, a one-time president of the Boston Psychoanalytic Society and Institute, and a faculty member at Harvard Medical School, was accused in 1992 by four female patients of having engaged in sexual relations with them during their treatment in the 1960s and '70s. A hearing officer wrote in his decision that all four women were "believable, credible and truthful." The charges led to revocation of his medical license (Daniels vs. Board). Daniels seemed to be intent on putting his patient/victims in a subservient position. One testified: "Dr. Daniels used condoms. And he insisted that I buy those condoms . . . that was one of the most humiliating parts of the whole thing for me . . . because I was very embarrassed and very terrified to walk into drugstores to have to buy condoms." The same patient testified that Daniels would put the condoms into a Kleenex, wad them up, and then give them to her so that she would go into his bathroom and flush them down the toilet. "And he stood there to watch to make sure I did it, but he never walked out with them himself" (Wohlberg, 337, Pinsky, 360).

Alison Bass reported in the *Boston Globe* on May 15, 1992 that some Boston mental health professionals criticized the state's regulatory agencies for taking more than 20 months to discipline Daniels. "'I'm delighted the board is getting around to doing something about a situation that to us was pretty clear two years ago,' said Dr. Elizabeth Reid, past president of the [Boston] Psychoanalytic Society. 'What this shows is that the board needs better funding, so it can deal with these important situations in a timely manner.'" What makes the story so ironic and disturbing is that Edward Daniels had chaired the committee that wrote the ethics code for the American Psychoanalytic Association (Fall Meeting, 1972, 423). Judith Schachter, who was president of the American Psychoanalytic Association from 1994–1996, told us that Daniels had threatened to sue the organization if he was expelled. The threat did not prevent his expulsion (Personal communication, September 25, 2014). After the revocation of his medical license, Daniels continued to practice psychotherapy in Massachusetts, a state that did not require at the time a license to practice psychotherapy. Daniels died in 2004.

2001: William A. Kadish

William A. Kadish, a graduate of the University of Chicago and the Yale University School of Medicine, and the medical director of psychiatry at Marlborough Hospital in Massachusetts, had his medical license revoked in 2001 after being accused of having sex with a patient he had been treating for multiple personality disorder. According to the accuser, Kadish slept with two of her 20 different personalities on the theory that he could help her by recreating a childhood trauma (Lasalandra). In addition, Kadish "took nude photographs of a female patient and had her snap one of him as he lay sprawled beneath his framed degree from the Yale University School of Medicine wearing nothing but a black condom that read "lollipop," as Gretchen Voss reported in *Boston Magazine* in July 2005.

2005: Ralph Engle

Ralph Engle, a former chair of board on professional standards of the American Psychoanalytic Association, and at the time, chair of the Association's ethics committee, surrendered his medical license after admitting to an undisclosed "boundary violation" with a female patient. He was also a training and supervising analyst at the Boston Psychoanalytic Institute, a training facility approved by the American Psychoanalytic Association (Voss).

How do we explain the hypocrisy of those, such as Daniels and Engle, who serve on a professional ethics board while at the same time or at a later date engage in their profession's most abhorrent ethical violations? Are they, to begin with, aware of their hypocrisy? Do they decide to serve on ethics boards as a protection against later violations, a way to transgress with impunity? Are they so narcissistic that they believe they are entitled to break the rules? Are they masochistic, engaging in reckless, self-destructive behavior because of the unconscious wish to be punished? Celenza notes in *Sexual Boundary Violations* that the "one-time offender (usually narcissistically needy, lovesick, or from the masochistic-surrender category) is the most prevalent type of sexual boundary offender" (10). She also observes, however, that the "psychopathic predator probably accounts for the largest number of victim/patients" (135). Some psychopathic predators, as we shall see, were among the leaders in their fields, and their transgressions damaged not only their patients but also their professions. As Pope wrote in "Therapist-Patient Sex as Sex Abuse" in 1990,

> Sexually abusive psychotherapists cannot be dismissed as the most marginal members of the profession. They are well represented among the most prominent and respected mental health professionals. Cases involving therapists publicly reported to have engaged in sexual behaviors with their patients have included those who have served as faculty at the most prestigious universities (including those with APA-approved training programs), psychology licensing board chair, state psychological association ethics committee chair, psychoanalytic training institute director, state psychiatric association president, state association of marriage and family therapists president, prominent media psychologist, chief psychiatrist at a prominent psychiatric hospital, and chief psychiatrist at a state correctional facility. (233)

2012: Henry Smith

Henry Smith, another Boston psychoanalyst, was sued in 2010 by a patient he had seen from 2005 through 2009 and by her husband, both of whom claimed that starting in 2006, Smith had sexual relations with her multiple times. Smith surrendered his medical license in 2010 to avoid professional discipline. In his defense, he claimed that the sexual relationship, which he admitted had taken place, had done "no harm" to the patient. He also implied that his actions were acceptable because the patient was not "mentally ill" and that she was a "nationally respected psychologist" who was "well versed in the issues of transference," a rationalization that all the professional psychoanalytic, psychiatric and psychological associations, which categorically ban sex between a therapist and patient, would reject. At the time, Smith was the editor of the prestigious journal *Psychoanalytic Quarterly*, had served as associate editor of the *Journal of the American Psychoanalytic Association*, and had served on the editorial boards of at least three other publications in the field. He was a training and supervising psychoanalyst at the Psychoanalytic Institute of New England, East, another training facility approved by the American Psychoanalytic Association (C. Herman).

Sex with Celebrity Patients: David Rubinfine and Elaine May

David Rubinfine was a rising star in the New York Psychoanalytic establishment in the early 1960s. As a psychoanalyst he involved himself personally and professionally with a wide array of personalities from the arts. He was appointed as a training analyst at the conservative New York Psychoanalytic Institute at the unusually young age of 40. At the time that the famous comedienne Elaine May began analysis with him, Rubinfine was married with three children and was 11 years older than May. Losing her father at age 11, May dropped out of high school at age 14 and married for the first time at 16. Ironically, at the time Elise Snyder had left her husband to marry Victor Rosen, her husband, Art Snyder, was in analysis with Rubinfine. As Rubinfine's analysis of May went on, a mutual love relationship developed between them. After presumably informing his wife, Rosa, of the situation, he moved out of their home. Shortly thereafter, on April 30, 1963, Rosa committed suicide. Rubinfine married Elaine May on June 8, 1963. The marriage lasted for 17 years until Rubinfine's death due to a heart attack (Farber and Green, 201 ff.).

Janet Malcolm doesn't mention Victor Rosen or David Rubinfine by name in *Psychoanalysis: The Impossible Profession* (1981), but there's little doubt, as Farber and Green suggest, that she had them in mind when she referred to Analyst X and Analyst Y, the former a past president of the American Psychoanalytic Association who married a patient, the latter a man who became involved in a "messy triangle during the analysis." "The transgressions were instantly disciplined," notes Malcolm, summarizing the sharp disapproval of "Aaron Green," the New York analyst whose life and work she features in her book. "[T]hey were removed from the roster of training analysts, they were divested of their various functions in the ruling structure, they were dismissed from their teaching posts. Their careers in the higher reaches of establishment psychoanalysis [were] over" (92). In her next book, *In the Freud Archives*, Malcolm quotes Elise Snyder about the difference between the Western New England Institute in New Haven, of which she is a member, and the various New York institutes: "It is very gentle and sweet up here. It's incredibly different from the New York group, which suffers from paranoia of a high degree" (56).

Frederick J. Duhl and Anne Sexton

The psychiatrist Martin Orne treated the poet Anne Sexton from 1956–1964, but when he announced he was leaving Boston, she saw a new psychiatrist and began having sex with him almost immediately. "My therapy is degenerating to SEX," Sexton wrote to a friend in early 1964 (231). Under pressure from his wife, he ended therapy with Sexton in 1969, when she underwent the trauma of changing psychiatrists again. The Pulitzer Prize-winning poet committed suicide in 1974 at the age of 45, an event long foreshadowed in her poetry. Sexton's biographer, Diane Wood Middlebrook, refers to the psychiatrist in question as "Dr. Zweizung," a wry pseudonym that means "forked tongue" in German. Sexton saw the psychiatrist, who had completed his psychoanalytic training, twice a week. She called him her "doctor-daddy" (258), a possible recognition that her affair was forbidden and transgressive, symbolic incest, a repetition of her relationship with her father, who, according to Middlebrook and others, may have sexually abused his daughter when she was a child. Maxine Kumin, Sexton's close friend and fellow poet, was indignant over the affair with the therapist. "Imagine paying to get laid twice a week!" (259).

Alessandra Stanley's review of Middlebrook's biography in the *New York Times* on July 15, 1991, was the first to reveal the identity of Sexton's psychiatrist, Frederick J. Duhl. He refused to comment in a telephone interview with Stanley on the biography's revelations other than to say, "You are dealing with an explosive subject; basically any doctor who has an affair with a patient loses his license in Massachusetts." Barbara Schwartz, a psychiatric social worker who treated Sexton during the last months of her life, told Stanley that Sexton had asked her in 1973 to attend a conference with her at which Duhl was speaking. "She wanted to stand up there and say, 'J'accuse!'. . . . I felt I could not go to that meeting and let her expose herself that way." Sexton's on-and-off-again sexual relationship with Duhl continued for years. After spending an evening with him in Washington in 1969, Sexton wrote an anguished letter to Orne in which she contrasted her trust in her former psychiatrist, who had never sexualized therapy, with her mistrust in Duhl, who had. "He promised he'd never leave me but now he tells me it depends on how he works things out with his wife. I told him if we worked together we could keep it just therapy (after all we'd had our fling in Washington). . . . I pled with him. But he just said he'd see" (Middlebrook, 316).

"Anne Sexton was a very difficult person to treat," Orne told Samuel M. Hughes in an interview published in the *Pennsylvania Gazette* in December 1991. "She was very seductive. But you know, if you can't deal with that, you should not be a psychiatrist." Orne knew how to respond to her provocative behavior. Duhl didn't. He alone was responsible for her therapy degenerating to sex. He should have recognized her transference-love for him and his own countertransference-love for her, which ultimately destroyed their therapeutic relationship.

Alan A. Stone does not discuss Duhl in *Law, Psychiatry, and Morality,* but in his typology of therapists who have sex with their patients, Duhl falls into the category of those psychotherapists who exploit a patient's positive transference by telling her about their own problems. "Often there is talk of divorce and of marrying the patient. It is a scenario not confined to the psychotherapist's office" (211). The worst part of the sexual boundary violation for Sexton was that it was inevitably responsible for the end of therapy, which she experienced as another form of rejection and abandonment.

Frederick Duhl died in 2011 at the age of 81. An obituary published in the San Antonio *Express-News* on January 4, 2011 described him as a native New Yorker and a graduate of Columbia University College of Physicians and Surgeons. The obituary briefly mentions Duhl's sexual relationship with Sexton that "blemished" his career. "He never forgave himself," his second wife, Verne Lee Cooper admitted. "He said he betrayed his own honor."

Khristine Eroshevich and Anna Nicole Smith

Khristine Eroshevich, a California psychiatrist who was prescribing medication for Anna Nicole Smith, was accused of having been sexually involved with the well-known sex star. The *Los Angeles Times* reported that photographs found on Smith's computer after her suicide in 2007 showed her nude in a hot tub with the psychiatrist. The full nature of the relationship between Smith and Eroshevich is unclear because despite the prescriptions, written using several pseudonyms for the patient, Eroshevich kept no medical records regarding Smith. In October 2012, a California appellate court ruled that a judge erred when he overturned the convictions against Smith's lawyer and psychiatrist in a trial arising from the actress's death from prescription drugs.

There are relatively few examples of "celebrities" having been sexually abused by therapists, although there is no reason to assume such cases are rare. One legal scholar, Patricia M.L. Illingworth, argues against criminalizing therapist-patient sex, wondering whether the cost of using the criminal law as a way to support private remedies may be too high. "At some point, especially with respect to celebrities and other well-off members of society (like doctors), it will just be too costly for them to have their day in court and exercise their right to a trial. If the threat of criminal sanctions means more to those who have more to lose, then they—although innocent—may be forced to settle and forfeit their right to a trial" (414)

Society's response to these transgressions has been relatively weak. In many instances, although the perpetrator gave up his medical license to practice psychotherapy as a physician, he continued to practice as a "psychotherapist," as Edward Daniels did. Medical licensing bodies have no control over such practitioners in most states. Many of those accused, including practitioners who actually admit to their misconduct, are not forced to close their offices, as William F. Hammond, Jr., observes. One of the practitioners we describe in the following chapters lost his physician's license but continued to practice as a "hypnotist"; one lost his license but continued to practice as a therapist; one surrendered his license and retired; and another, a Canadian, was sentenced to a substantial jail term, but an appeals court overturned the guilty verdict, and in a second trial, the psychiatrist was acquitted of all charges. As an article published in the *Frederick News-Post* on April 7, 2013 suggests, only 23 states have criminalized patient-therapist sex. The practice of psychotherapy has been regulated in the State of New York only since 2001.

The Center for Feeling Therapy

Most sexual boundary violations occur among individual therapists, but sometimes transgressions are associated with a particular institute. Margaret Thaler Singer and Janja Lalich report in *"Crazy" Therapies* (1996) that the Center for Feeling Therapy, founded in 1971 in Los Angeles by two former members of Arthur Janov's Primal Institute, was "notorious for its scandalous behavior." The Center became cult-like and was closed in 1980 as a result of a variety of physical and psychological abuses. Some of the former patients sued the founding therapists, and the 1985 professional hearing that inquired into the alleged charges against the center became the "longest, costliest, and most complex psychotherapy malpractice case in California history." The hearing concluded that there were multiple abuses and ethical violations, many of which involved sexual transgressions. "Former patients testified during license revocation hearings that they were seduced by the therapists, given sex assignments, and publicly ridiculed and humiliated, sometimes being made to stand naked before the group.

Therapists slept with patients and ordered them to sleep with other patients. Female patients were put on extreme diets for years; at least one patient was commanded to masturbate in front of her therapist" (150–151).

Legal Issues

Legal scholars have raised constitutional questions about therapist sexual misconduct regulations, particularly prohibitions after the end of therapy. In a 2009 article published in the *UCLA Law Review*, S. Wesley Gorman remarks that many state constitutions recognize rights of sexual autonomy that are burdened by categorical bans on sexual relationships in therapy. Gorman, a Senior Editor at the *UCLA Law Review*, proposes a standard of sexual conduct that is based on the psychotherapist's fiduciary responsibility, which obligates the therapist to advance a patient's welfare on all matters related to professional treatment. Gorman admits that his proposed model has two shortcomings: "It's more ambiguous than a categorical ban, and it has a narrower scope" (1008).

Some mental health professionals have debated lawyers about sexual misconduct regulations. The psychologist S. Michael Plaut, a member of the University of Maryland School of Medicine, wrote a tongue-in-cheek "Statement of Informed Consent for a Sexual Relationship Between a Health Professional and a Client or Patient." Initially reluctant to share the document with victim/survivors, Plaut was persuaded to disseminate it to both therapists and patients. Anyone who reads the two-page document will recognize the harm of therapist-patient sex. "I understand that a sexual relationship with this Provider may ultimately have extremely damaging consequences for me including, but not necessarily limited to, feelings of betrayal, helplessness, anger, confusion, guilt, and depression, that these feelings could result in a need for psychiatric care beyond that which may have been necessary in the past, and that these feelings could possibly result in my suicide" (Plaut).

Svengali

Therapists who are psychopathic predators and have sex with many patients over a prolonged period of time have been called Don Juans, but they are also Svengalis. To appreciate the extent to which transgressive therapists are Svengali-like, one must be familiar with George du Maurier's *Trilby*, which became an immediate bestseller when it was published in the United States in 1894. The novel's heroine, Trilby O'Ferrell, is a poor young laundress in Paris who aspires to become a singer, a dream that the conductor Svengali promises to transform into a reality.

Svengali hypnotizes the tone-deaf Trilby, who is magically transformed into a diva with a golden voice, La Svengali. But her success depends upon hypnotic suggestion, akin to mesmerism, as a friend futilely attempts to warn her. "He mesmerized you; that's what it is, mesmerism! I've often heard of it, but never seen it done before. They get you into their power, and just make you do any blessed thing they please lie, murder, steal anything! and kill yourself into the bargain when they've done with you!" (52). The spell is broken when Trilby performs under a substitute conductor during her debut London concert. Losing her angelic voice, she is jeered by the audience, and Svengali unexpectedly dies of heart failure. Later, Trilby can hardly believe her behavior while under his evil spell, and she dies at the end of the novel, purified of guilt and shame.

Svengali's ability to exploit and dominate Trilby derives in part from her traumatic childhood. The daughter of alcoholic parents whose deaths have left her bereft, she was sexually abused by one of her mother's friends. Trilby is forced to model in the nude to support her illegitimate younger brother, whose death from scarlet fever shatters her. These losses heighten Trilby's vulnerability, enabling Svengali to take advantage of her. Svengali is himself self-abasing, hypersensitive, intensely jealous. Svengali is a musician, not a therapist, but he has the power to heal Trilby's psychic wounds both by convincing her she is "special," a word that is almost always used in sexual boundary violations stories, and by promising to marry her—though he was married to another woman with whom he had three children, all four of whom he deserted. Trilby becomes Svengali's imagined wife, slave, pupil and disciple. His sinister love for her represents a source of endless torment.

Elaine Showalter observes in her introduction to the 1998 Oxford edition of *Trilby* that Svengali, whom du Maurier describes as an "Oriental Israelite Hebrew Jew" (244), "stands alongside Shylock and Fagin in the annals of anti-Semitic literature" (ix). Writers who use the expression "Svengali-like" to characterize an analyst's hypnotic and seductive influence on a patient are not necessarily referring to a Jewish analyst, though as Edward Shorter notes in *A History of Psychiatry*, by the late 1950s, 80% of American psychoanalysts were Jewish (186). As we shall see later, several people used the expression to describe the Jewish analyst Gregory Zilboorg, who upon his entry to the United States became a Quaker and then later in life converted for a second and final time to Catholicism.

The term "Svengali-like" is particularly apt with respect to analysts who use hypnosis, suggestion and charisma as part of their treatment. Showalter reminds us that in the same year that *Trilby* was published, Freud was writing about his hypnotized patient Emmy von N., one of several case studies appearing in *Studies on Hysteria* (1895). Trilby is a fictional character, but she could easily exist within the pages of *Studies on Hysteria*. She mysteriously loses the will to live at the end of the novel, and her English physicians are baffled by her illness.

Du Maurier's novel has become a lightning rod for those who believe that psychotherapy is a cult and a hoax, and that Freud was a manipulative Svengali whose patients were in the position of a helpless Trilby. Without endorsing this caricature, Daniel Pick remarks in *Svengali's Web: The Alien Enchanter in Modern Culture* (2000) that the "predicament, real or imagined, of the gullible client influenced by the devious 'Svengalian' therapist persists as a stock talking point in much current media conversation of the 'healing arts.' Of course, manipulation, suggestion and interference may well operate in fact, rather than just in paranoid cultural fantasies" (218). The word "Svengali-like" appears in many sexual boundary violation stories to describe an analyst's seductive power over a patient. The reader's challenge in these stories is to determine whether the patient's predicament is real or imagined and whether the therapist is indeed a Svengali.

Seductive Patients

Elissa Benedek recommended, in her capacity as president of the American Psychiatric Association, that therapists who find themselves sexually attracted to a patient should seek help themselves or refer their patient to another therapist (Slovenko, *Psychiatry in Law/Law in Psychiatry*, 609). This sounds like good advice, but if psychotherapists followed that recommendation strictly, there would be a dire shortage of clinicians to treat their sexually aroused colleagues. How can one expect "purity" in a profession charged with erotic fantasies and desires?

Moreover, psychoanalysis has a long history of interpreting claims of seduction as originating from fantasies rather than reality. In the chapter on "Female Masochism" in her two-volume study *The Psychology of Women* (1944), Helene Deutsch asserts that both seduction and rape fantasies "often have such irresistible verisimilitude that even the most experienced judges are misled in trials of innocent men accused of rape by hysterical women" (vol. 1, 256). These fantasies, Deutsch adds, are often produced by women's "masochistic yearnings." In *The Assault on Truth*, Jeffrey Moussaieff Masson argued misleadingly that Freud abandoned the seduction theory because of his intellectual fear of acknowledging the truth of his patients' statements that they were sexually abused. Contrary to Masson's claim, psychoanalysis has always tried to be attentive to the often-ambiguous intersections of reality and fantasy. It remains true, however, that some analysts may be misled into believing that a patient's report of seduction by a relative, friend, or therapist is nothing more than a wishful fantasy.

Cautionary Notes

The psychotherapy community has generally remained silent about boundary violations, embarrassed by the negative publicity, particularly when the transgressive therapist is prominent. Phyllis Greenacre's comments in a 1954 article published in the *Journal of the American Psychoanalytic Association* are worth recalling. "I cannot in the least agree with the remark of a quite eminent analyst, repeated to me several times, that so many analysts overstep the boundaries of the transference even in grossly sexual ways that therefore the best thing to do is to say nothing about these incidents. It is only by discussing these possibilities (rather than by punishing the offenders) and by emphasizing their dangers to students and among ourselves that we can really develop our science to the research precision which must be aimed at in each clinical case" (681). Greenacre's recommendation that transgressive therapists should be free from professional discipline or the loss of their licenses may surprise us; yet we must remember that few if any mid-20th century psychiatrists or psychoanalysts were censured as a result of a sexual or nonsexual boundary violation. But if part of Greenacre's observation now seems dated, the essence of her remark about the extent to which transference-love reproduces the parent-child relationship remains as timely as ever. "For this very reason, the carrying through into a relationship in life of the incestuous fantasy of the patient may be more grave in its subsequent distortion of the patient's life than any actual incestuous seduction in childhood has been." Psychoanalysis is a "hard taskmaster," Greenacre continues. "The power of the unconscious is such that it 'gets back' at those who work with it and treat it too lightly" (684).

Before we examine in depth specific stories of sexual boundary violations, the following caution should be kept in mind. Although the authorities we have cited, from Freud onward, have been inclined to attribute the sexual peccadilloes of psychotherapists in general and psychoanalysts in particular to the complex and intense transferential relationship that the psychoanalytic situation engenders, there is another way of viewing this history and ongoing problem. As we mentioned, surveys of psychotherapists have placed the number of therapists who have admitted to sexual relations with patients in the 7–12% range, mostly due to male therapists becoming involved with female patients. However, a survey of attorneys using a similar technique found the number of attorneys who admitted to sexual involvement with clients at about the same percentage (Murrell). Most of these cases involved a male attorney with a female client who was going through a divorce (Livingston). Sexual involvement with clients, even with the client's consent, is an absolute violation of the ethics of the legal profession with the single exception of a sexual relationship that was in existence before the attorney-client relationship was initiated.

Greenacre's observation that transference, based on a primitive "mother-child relationship," promotes in the patient "an attitude of expectant dependent receptiveness toward the physician" (672), leads immediately to a consideration of the worldwide scandal among Roman Catholic clergy. Catholic priests' widespread sexual abuse of children reached a peak in the 1970s, an era in which many of the examples of sexual misconduct by psychotherapists also took place. Since the sexual abuse of children seems to trigger a higher degree of outrage than therapists' sexual interaction with (supposedly) consenting adults, it might seem odd to compare these two phenomena. However, when one considers that many adult patients slip into a dependent child-like state with their therapist, a development which therapy is structured to promote as a necessary element in the process, it becomes clear that the comparison is apt. The priest scandal grew so large that the Roman Catholic Church was eventually compelled to pay out about one half *billion* dollars in worldwide settlements, leading to the bankruptcy of several Church institutions.

As to the magnitude of these two phenomena, comparison is difficult because the data-gathering methods in the two instances are not comparable. As we have seen in the case of psychotherapists, estimates of the prevalence of sexual misconduct with patients have been based on anonymous surveys of psychotherapists. By contrast, estimates of sexual abuse of children among the priesthood are based on comprehensive surveys of the number of priests against whom complaints were made as the Church's intent to take this problem seriously crystallized in the early 2000s. The United States Conference of Catholic Bishops commissioned the John Jay College of Criminal Justice of the City University of New York to study the question. The college produced two reports, the first to document the *Nature and Scope* of the abuse problem (2004), the second to document the *Causes and Context* of the problem (2011). Findings from these studies

51

indicate that the percentage of priests involved in such misconduct appears to be about the same order of magnitude as analogous misconduct by male psychotherapists during the same era. Of the priests ordained in a given year, the statistics vary from a high of about 10% in 1970, to 8% in 1980, to a low of about 4% in 1990 (*Nature and Scope of Sexual Abuse,* 27). These results are reasonably consistent with the earlier results reached by A.W. Richard Sipe, a psychotherapist and retired (and married) ordained Roman Catholic Priest. Sipe concluded that the incidence of sexual abuse of minors was approximately 6% based on data available to him at that time (27).

Contrary to what many might believe, fewer than 5% of the accused priest-offenders were pedophiles. The priest-offenders were in their psychological characteristics not distinguishable from others in the priesthood. The majority of accused priests in treatment also reported sexual behavior with adult partners. "Sexual behavior in violation of the commitment to celibacy was reported by 80 percent" of such priests, "but most sexual behavior was with adults." It appears that the sexual abuse of children by priests was for the most part because the youngsters involved were "targets of opportunity" for a group of individuals inclined to engage in sexually deviant behavior in general and who encountered children in their roles as teachers, coaches, and counselors (*Causes and Context of Sexual Abuse,* 3).

It is therefore reasonable to wonder whether the particularities of psychotherapy are responsible for the number of boundary violations that are thought to occur, or whether the more important factor, present in the psychotherapy profession, the legal profession and the priesthood, should be mainly attributed to character deficits among the involved practitioners in combination with intense transferences that can exist in all these relationships.

Writing in 1997, M. Margolis wondered why the incidence of sexual boundary violations by psychoanalysts appeared similar to the incidence among other psychotherapists, despite the additional training and personal analysis required by psychoanalysts. (Celenza, we recall, believed that the incidence of sexual boundary violations by psychodynamic therapists is lower than that of other therapists, but she was writing a decade later, when the prevalence studies might have changed.) Margolis implied that the analyst's additional training and personal analysis are cancelled out, as it were, by the more intensive relationship:

> We pride ourselves on our stringent admission policies for training, longer periods of professional education and commitment to personal treatment as a safeguard against sexual exploitation of patients. Some of us therefore conclude that we are not so troubled by this phenomenon as other mental health professions. With all due respect to the importance of such selection and training standards, we should not overvalue the role of such factors. Perhaps our deeper involvement and immersion in the dark depths of patients' psychic lives expose us to greater temptation. We are therefore vulnerable in a special way, as well as sharing the vulnerabilities of therapists from other less intensive therapies. (Margolis, 352)

Additionally, such transgressions are thought to have a different meaning when they take place within the context of a psychotherapy in which the understanding and management of transference are core components of the therapist's work. In such a treatment, a sexual interaction between the therapist and the patient becomes more than unethical, as it would be considered in all forms of psychological treatment nowadays. It also constitutes a technical failure in management of the transference, a major requirement of the therapist and the therapy, and therefore is both more serious a violation and, arguably, an act of negligent malpractice (Bates and Brodsky, 133; Stone, *Law, Psychiatry and Morality*, 203).

Preventing Boundary Violations: An Optimistic or Pessimistic Outlook for the Future?

No one has written more incisively about boundary violations in psychoanalysis than Glen O. Gabbard, and it is instructive to compare his two editions of *Boundaries and Boundary Violations in Psychoanalysis*. In the first edition, co-authored with Eva P. Lester and published in 1995, Gabbard refers hopefully to the "sea change" (xii) that has occurred in recognizing the seriousness and prevalence of sexualized therapy. He remains cautiously optimistic throughout the book that the problem of sexual transgressions can be effectively addressed. In the second edition published in 2016, however, he has become more pessimistic. The problem of sexualized therapy remains despite greater institutional awareness and improved reporting. Sexual transgressions with patients continue to occur on a regular basis, Gabbard notes gloomily, "often among analysts and therapists who are well regarded and thoroughly familiar with the risks and dynamics of boundary issues. As a result, I have become increasingly pessimistic about our capacity to prevent the occurrences of sexual relations between individuals who practice psychoanalysis and their patients. I am even more pessimistic about preventing nonsexual boundary violations, which are nevertheless destructive and exploitative in light of their capacity for rationalization." The reason for Gabbard's pessimism? "The capacity for self-deception is extraordinary" (151).

To solve a problem, one must first acknowledge the magnitude of its seriousness, and Glen Gabbard and others continue to call attention to the sexually transgressive psychoanalyst. In "Rotten Apples and Ambivalence: Sexual Boundary Violations Through a Psychocultural Lens" (*Journal of the American Psychoanalytic Association*, 2016), Muriel Dimen captures the ways in which the problem threatens the entire institution of psychoanalysis. Writing as a trained psychoanalyst, anthropologist and self-admitted "whistle-blower," Dimen—who died as her paper was being prepared for publication—shows how sexual transgressions "generate a great and contagious anxiety prompted by how they pollute and stigmatize anyone and anything in their vicinity" (362). Sexual boundary violations are a social as well as a psychological problem, she suggests, and they result in the group's "muteness." In his commentary on Dimen's paper, Gabbard notes that sexual boundary violations are the "Achilles' heel of the psychoanalytic profession" ("The Group as Complicit in Boundary Violations," 379), a statement that applies to the entire mental health profession.

Behind the Couch

To return to the image of the lovesick analyst with which we began this chapter, few therapists have not been sexually or romantically attracted to a patient, "seductive" or not, during their careers. How should ethical therapists behave in this situation? Herbert S. Strean discusses this question in *Behind the Couch: Revelations of a Psychoanalyst*, co-authored with Lucy Freeman (1988). "Rarely does an analyst talk about his erotic fantasies when an attractive woman on the couch tells him he is the most desirable man in the world," Strean confesses early in the book (23). Strean is one of the few men—there are even fewer women—to write about an analyst's attraction to a seductive patient. In the chapter "Sometimes I Feel Like a Dirty Old Man: The Woman Who Tried to

Seduce Me," he discusses "Susan Brown," a woman who had sexual affairs with three different therapists. Her wish to turn her therapy sessions into a torrid if fleeting love affair, a "coup on the couch" (72), proves to be a challenge to Strean, who struggles with his own desire for her. "I felt I must be something of a Romeo if a woman as beautiful as Susan wanted me sexually. But as stimulated as I felt, I constantly reminded myself of how she used sexuality as a means of manipulation, a way of buttressing her shaky self-image and precarious self-esteem" (81).

Strean recounts, with self-lacerating humor, Susan Brown's rage when he refuses her various ploys to seduce him. At one point she threatens to leave him to find a "more potent" therapist. He describes his own retaliatory anger when she misses three sessions in a row, leaving a message on his answering machine, "You no-good son of a bitch. You have an icy personality. You sure are a cold potato" (75). By refusing to gratify her sexual wishes, Strean helps her to understand how she was projecting onto him her ambivalent feelings toward her father, whom she felt had stimulated her but then withdrew from her life. Sex on the analyst's couch, Strean concludes, leads inevitably to betrayal, a statement with which no 21st century psychotherapist would disagree. Not all of Strean's statements are factually accurate. He cites D.H. Lawrence's erotic novel *Lady Chatterley's Lover*, rather than Philip Roth's psychoanalytic monologue *Portnoy's Complaint*, as an example of a patient's outpouring of comments that has the effect of silencing an analyst. Despite this mistake, *Behind the Couch* reminds readers that ethical mental health professionals do not use sex as a guise of therapy. Herbert Strean's *Behind the Couch* could not be more different from "The Analyst's Couch," a monthly column appearing in *Cosmopolitan* magazine by the noted psychoanalyst Renatus Hartogs, to whom we now turn.

CHAPTER 2

The Analyst's Couches: The Story of Julie Roy and Renatus Hartogs

Dr. Renatus Hartogs was not a household name in the 1960s and '70s when he wrote a monthly column, "The Analyst's Couch," which appeared for several years in *Cosmopolitan* magazine. He was certainly not as famous as other celebrity psychotherapists such as Dr. Joyce Brothers, "Dr. Ruth," or more recently "Dr. Phil" McGraw. Nevertheless, he was widely respected, and his fame was growing.

Hartogs' European pedigree contributed to his psychoanalytic authenticity. His early life is enveloped in mystery. Some of his books list his birthplace as the Netherlands, stating that he came from an "old Dutch family." Other publications identify his birthplaces as Mainz, Germany. Born in 1909, he received a PhD in psychology from the University of Frankfurt in 1932 and a Master of Medical Science degree from the Brussels Medical School in 1939. His early interest in writing was apparent when he became the editor of a German-language professional journal devoted to psychological research. Recognizing that the Nazis would make few referrals to a Jewish physician, Hartogs immigrated to the United States in 1940, receiving a Master of Arts degree in clinical psychopathology in 1945 and a medical degree from the University of Montreal Medical School in 1948. He completed his psychiatric training in New York State, where his rise in the mental health establishment was steady if not meteoric.

Within a few years Hartogs became the Medical Director of Community Guidance Service of New York City and the Associate Director of the American Institute for Psychotherapy and Psychoanalysis. He taught at several universities, including Columbia University College of Physicians and Surgeons, where he treated patients at its outpatient clinic. In addition, he had a thriving private practice of psychoanalytically oriented psychotherapy in Manhattan. He generally saw 12 to 14 patients a day, six days a week, though on some days he saw many more.

Touched by History

In 1951, Hartogs became the chief psychiatrist at Youth House in New York City, a detention home for juvenile delinquents. There he encountered in 1953 a bright, disturbed 13-year-old who after attacking his mother had withdrawn ominously into a violent inner world. Hartogs diagnosed the adolescent as having a personality disturbance with "schizoid features and passive-aggressive tendencies." In less clinical language, the psychiatrist believed that the youth suffered from emotional isolation and deprivation, an absence of family life and rejection by a conflicted mother. Hartogs recommended that the troubled youth be treated at a child guidance clinic. A decade later, on November 22, 1963, Hartogs must have felt touched by history when he learned that the teenager he had examined and recommended for psychiatric treatment, Lee Harvey Oswald, assassinated President John F. Kennedy.

Hartogs seized the opportunity to offer his psychiatric insights into the Kennedy assassination in his 1965 co-authored book *The Two Assassins*, a study of Oswald and Jack Ruby, the man who, two days after the assassination, shot and killed Oswald in the crowded basement of the Dallas police station as the prisoner was being transferred from the station to a secure jail. Most of the book is based on the testimony of the Warren Commission and on the court record of Ruby's trial, but Hartogs offers his own recollection of interviewing Oswald and his speculations of the familial and communal factors that led to explosive violence. Hartogs returned to the subject in his 1970 co-edited book *Violence: Its Causes and Solutions*. Three essays by Hartogs appear in the volume, including "Who Will Act Violently: The Predictive Criteria," wherein he lists 48 signs, a taxonomy of violence never adopted by mental health or criminal justice professionals.

A Self-Help Writer

Hartogs' belief in the value of self-help books may be seen in *How to Grow Up Successfully* (1961), the first of four co-authored or co-edited books, all written with different professional writers who, with the exception of his only co-editor, were not themselves psychotherapists. He frequently uses the first person singular pronoun in these books, demonstrating that he is the lead author. He engages his readers in a strong, direct voice, as if he were addressing them individually. "This book speaks only to you, the teenage boy and girl, and it speaks in your language," Hartogs observes in the introduction to *How to Grow Up Successfully* (5). In a calm, reassuring tone, he promises his young readers that his book will provide solutions to the most intractable problems. "One of the main goals of this book is to show you why inner contradictions are entirely acceptable for a teenager and how they can be overcome and relinquished once the teenager is ready to make the transformation into an adult" (58). Much of his advice is commonsensical, as when he urges teenagers to see the positive value of criticism. "Even if a criticism is destructive, and, in your opinion, unwarranted, use it to learn something about the person who made the critical remark" (162).

Once he solved the age-old enigma of how to grow up successfully, Hartogs was prepared to unmask the psychological meaning of obscenity in *Four-Letter Games* (1967). He doesn't come close to rivaling the insights, originality, or wit of Freud's masterful *Jokes and Their Relation to the Unconscious* (1905). But then again, Freud had few equals as a writer. The creator of psychoanalysis discreetly allowed his followers to plumb the depths of profanity, and Hartogs proceeds to do this in his study of obscenity. "The person who habitually uses sexual obscenity fancies himself sexually masterful while, in fact, he is haunted by sexual fears. Though he may think that his obscenity is an instrument of sexual pursuit, it is often the camouflage for the sexual retreat of at least the subconscious part of his personality." Hartogs singles out the words "fuck" and "mother-fucker" for special attention, arguing that they reveal the fear, shared by nearly all men, of being "castrated as punishment for breaking the primal taboo against incest" (43).

An Expert on Women

Hartogs relished his role as a psychoanalytic guru, for in 1974 he published his only non-co-authored book, *Questions Women Ask*, based on a monthly column, "The Analyst's Couch," written for *Cosmopolitan* from 1967–1973. As he notes in the Preface, the book contains about 70 questions from among the thousands he received from female readers of that popular column. His answer to the first question, from the "new feminists"—Can a male psychiatrist help or understand women?—is a resounding "Yes!" He concedes that Freud was a product of his time, living in an age that was "definitely 'sexist,'" and he admits that there were still "diehard orthodox Freudians" practicing in 1974. Nevertheless, Hartogs cheerfully reassures his female readers that "both men and women tend to have the same problems in this threatening new world" (2), problems to which he vows to be sensitive and for which he has definitive answers.

Despite his determination not to sound overly Freudian, Hartogs protests too much, as in his answer to the question about a woman's pangs of envy. "Penis envy in some young females and vagina or breast envy in some young males are phenomena that can lead later on to intense envy in other areas of human endeavor—Women's Lib notwithstanding!" (9). One of his most revealing answers is to the question why a woman "always turns men off?"—a question symptomatic of her battle with men. "I wonder if you fully realize that you are at war with the male and his world, hiding behind the machine-gun fire of your conversation and the barbed wire of your hostile thoughts." Perhaps sensing that his militaristic metaphors may be too combative, he tones down his language, hinting that his female reader may be too attached to the males in her family. "If any man threatens to take the place of father or brother in her affections, she reacts with hostility. In some cases, this semi-incestuous source of hostility against the male can generate homosexual tendencies. (Please, I'm not *accusing* you of having a lesbian orientation, but I am mentioning it as a possibility)" (51–52).

There are other moments in *Questions Women Ask* when Hartogs comes across as accusatory. Witness his response to a woman who describes her life as a "mess" because of her tiny breasts, large thighs and stringy hair. "What seems to me to be wrong with your marriage is not your bodily imperfections, but the possible existence of horrendous boredom between you and your husband. This boredom may have led you to neglect yourself. I suspect that you overemphasize your defects and deficiencies in order to feel sorry for yourself and thus avoid feeling guilty about neglecting yourself and your marriage!" (6). His comment to a woman who admits she is a compulsive liar transfers responsibility from her to her parents. "'Why have I never found the courage to be truthful?' you may ask. The answer is simple: you are either the victim of emotional deprivation by your parents, or the victim of emotional *over*feeding by them. Both the frustrated child and the child who has been smothered by too much parental attention and indulgence are apt to have trouble adapting to reality" (24).

Pseudohomosexual Conduct

Hartogs has strong feelings about female homosexuality, and several of his statements imply that women who worry about being lesbians are heterosexual without knowing it. His advice to the "lesbian who would like to go straight" is to have the courage to return to her fantasies about the men in her life. "Try to understand your previous love for a woman as being merely a compensation love—a feeling-attitude designed to undo earlier disappointments with men and to offer some compensation for earlier pain and grief. It is simply not true that 'once a homosexual always a homosexual.' In quite a number of cases, seemingly homosexual behavior proves upon analytical inquiry to be merely the product of temporary necessity or opportunity and can be considered as pseudohomosexual conduct, behind which truly heterosexual trends and tendencies can be discovered" (*Questions Women Ask,* 116).

Addicted to Illicit Sex

The most interesting questions appear in the chapter "Problems of Sex and Love," where Hartogs counsels women who are unwilling to give up their extramarital affairs. "Rachel" is on the verge of a nervous breakdown because of excruciating guilt toward her faithful husband, Henry, a situation that represents, in the psychiatrist's judgment, a replaying of her parents' marriage. "Rachel's seemingly masochistic desire to be humiliated and dominated by crude partners was, she began to realize, an attempt to redeem her mother posthumously and also a means of expiating the guilt she felt toward him" (77). Hartogs speculates that Rachel's husband almost certainly knew about her affairs but was content to remain in the marriage. "When last I heard from her, she was on the best of terms with Henry while carrying on a discreet affair with a young man in her office" (78)—an enviable situation for which Hartogs implicitly takes credit because she has become "less compulsive in her philandering."

Another compulsively promiscuous woman was excited about the idea of being "naughty." Hartogs sees many women like this in his practice, and the motivation behind their illicit behavior is more problematic than they realize. Some promiscuous women feel trapped by marriage and long for independence and freedom. Other promiscuous wives seek extramarital affairs because they are frustrated by their sexually inhibited husbands. Others desire to destroy their marriages because of a "strong neurotic revulsion against happiness and lasting contentment." And others use infidelity as a way of "taking revenge for the real or fancied misdeeds of their husbands." Marital infidelity evokes Hartogs' sternest judgment. "Let me be frank. Whatever the reasons for your promiscuity, the chances are that sooner or later it will endanger your marriage, even if your husband never finds out what you've been up to. You will end up getting addicted to the strong excitement and varied satisfactions of illicit sex—which your husband naturally cannot offer to you, since your relationship is *not* illicit. Your feeling for him will inevitably undergo change and deteriorate. The same thing happens to men who are chronically unfaithful" (96).

Hartogs views promiscuous husbands, such as the "menopausal male," as frightened about getting older and turning against their wives in an "unconscious desperate search for a new life and new sexual powers" (112). These men realize the hopelessness of becoming a "rejuvenated, supervirile Don Juan" and turn their hopelessness and fears into aggression against their wives. Women who are married to such men, he adds, should be patient and understanding. "Give him lenient reassurance instead of meeting him with unmerciful hostility and vengefulness" (113). Hartogs ends "Problems of Sex and Love" with the question, "Is there such a thing as too many lovers?" After conceding that sexual experimentation may be helpful to younger people, or to women who do not intend to marry, he offers a judgment that he realizes may displease some *Cosmopolitan* readers. "At the risk of sounding hopelessly dated, however, I must tell you that in my experience promiscuity is nothing more than a crutch for the fearful, the disenchanted, and the discouraged—the amputees of love" (131–132).

Why would women in the 1970s read *Questions Women Ask*? Hartogs answers this question in the preface. "This book can be read simply as a document illustrating the sort of emotional, social, and sexual dilemmas encountered by today's woman, or it can be used as a self-help manual which may serve to give you at least some insight into your own problems together with suggestions for solving or alleviating them." Self-help books generally have a short shelf life, and *Questions Women Ask* is no exception. Few contemporary readers are likely to be interested in the psychiatrist's superficial, outdated and moralistic lectures. Nor do his case studies come alive as literary masterpieces, as we see with Freud.

There is, however, another reason to read *Questions Women Ask*, one that Hartogs never imagined. It turns out that the psychiatrist had a more intimate knowledge of pathological lying, compulsive promiscuity, misogyny and Don Juan behavior than he wanted his readers to know. His knowledge of the humiliation of women came from personal experience. Hartogs was himself an amputee of love, for while writing "The Analyst's Couch," he was using the same couch to have sex with his female patients, a betrayal of trust that led to a landmark court case.

Betrayal: The Case of Roy v. Hartogs

The story of the watershed psychiatric case appears in a 1976 book aptly entitled *Betrayal*, co-authored by Lucy Freeman and Julie Roy. Freeman was one of the most prolific writers of her age. She began her career as a reporter for the *New York Times* and came to be known as an authority on mental illness, psychotherapy and women's issues, all of which are evident in *Betrayal*. The other co-author of *Betrayal* was Julie Roy, Hartogs' patient who brought a lawsuit against him. A made-for-television film of the same title, directed by Paul Wendkos and starring Rip Torn as Hartogs and Leslie Ann Warren as Julie Roy, appeared in 1978. The film closely follows the nonfictional book. Shortly after Roy entered treatment with Hartogs, he began demanding to have sex with her as part of her therapy, a clinical "strategy" based on his self-serving claim that he could in this manner convert her from homosexual to heterosexual love. The case of *Roy v. Hartogs* is fascinating for reasons that extend well beyond those explored in *Betrayal*.

Born in Port Huron, Michigan in 1938, Julie Roy suffered from near debilitating depression for much of her life. Her mother, we learn, was isolated and withdrawn. "She was not a bad mother, not a mean person, but a victim of her life; she could not help what she did" (13). Julie's parents divorced when she was three, but even before that event, her relationship with her father was one of unceasing rejection. It appeared that her father never had wanted her. Her mother warned her to avoid entering the living room when her father was reading or listening to the radio. He never picked her up or showed any affection toward her. For the remainder of her childhood, she lacked any male affection whatsoever.

After her father's departure, Julie's family life became increasingly chaotic. She was constantly moving and attended at least 14 schools. She was unable to follow her teachers' instructions and did poorly in school. Julie was considered a candidate for a school for the mentally retarded, but when she was given psychological tests she turned out to have a high IQ. She had no close friends while growing up and was beset by multiple worries, including a fear of bugs, birds and toads. In her early 20s, Julie reconnected with her older brother Allan, but her mother had warned her never to live with him. Like Julie, he was depressed himself when she met him in 1968. His suicide in that year deepened her depression.

After graduating from high school, Julie moved first to Florida and then to Chicago, where she lived for four years. She met and married a man from Lebanon, Anton, but she never told her family because she knew that her mother would disapprove of her marrying a "foreigner." The married couple lived apart for eight months when Anton moved to New York City. She eventually joined him there, but their brief, unhappy marriage ended in divorce. She found work as a secretary at *Esquire* magazine, but aside from a friendly relationship with a warm supportive supervisor, she had no friends. She continued to be depressed, avoided other employees, and wore the same dress to work every day for two years. She thought of herself as ugly and couldn't stand to see her reflection in a mirror. After the end of her marriage, Julie began a sexual relationship with a woman who was in treatment with a clinical psychologist, Pauline Anderson. Growing increasingly suicidal, Julie reluctantly agreed to visit Anderson, who in turn referred her to Renatus Hartogs.

Julie began treatment with Hartogs in February 1969, when she was around 30 and he was close to 60. She saw him three times a week. In March he asked, "Why don't we have a bathtub party?" (41), a question that confused and repulsed her. He asked her to describe her feelings and fantasies about him, and it did not take him long to propose sex. "'It will cure you of being a lesbian,' he said. 'Your trouble is that you are afraid of men'" (43). We cannot be certain that Julie was the patient Hartogs wrote about in *Questions Women Ask*, but he implied that he could help her overcome her pseudohomosexual behavior.

Another incident in *Betrayal*, centering around the word "fuck," recalls Hartogs' discussion of that same word in *Four-Letter Games*. Julie discloses to Hartogs how upset she was, years earlier when she was living in Chicago, seeing "F-U-C-K" written on a cement tunnel, and when the psychiatrist repeats the word in a loud voice, she appears to be retraumatized. She declares abruptly that she doesn't want to see him anymore and flees his office. Later she wonders whether he used the word to help her overcome her inhibitions. The ambiguity is never resolved. This is perhaps the only moment in *Betrayal* when the reader is willing to give Hartogs the benefit of doubt. The suspension of disbelief disappears, however, if one reads what Hartogs has to say about a situation like this in *Four-Letter Games*: "To lead a patient toward obscenity during a therapeutic session in hopes of releasing his emotional blocks often nullifies the diagnostic advantage the therapist might hope to gain. If the therapist deliberately (even though indirectly) encourages the patient to say 'dirty things,' obscene words will come too easily and will be uttered without the therapeutically relieving emotional discharge. The patient must be allowed to locate and work through his emotional blocks by himself" (137).

Hartogs sexualized every aspect of Julie's therapy. She never knew how to respond to his increasingly insistent demands, and when she replied that she thought sex with him would destroy her, he responded confidently, "It would be good for you. . . . If you can love me, you can love another man" (*Betrayal*, 46).

Hartogs was relentless in his pursuit of Julie. In April 1969, he began touching her. The next month, he took off his clothes in his office and invited her to do the same, claiming that "Some psychiatrists will only treat their patients when they are nude" (53). Uncomfortable with the way treatment was going, Julie asked Hartogs in June whether she should see another therapist. He reassured her that she was making progress. Unconvinced, she was so distraught that in July she contemplated suicide. They had sex for the first time in August, after which she dutifully gave him a check for $10. "The lovemaking, she thought, if you could call it that, had consumed the same amount of time as her regular sessions—ten minutes" (67).

Julie continued to pay for each sexualized session. Hartogs had a ready answer to her question of why she must pay him: "'I spent a lot of time and money on my education and I work hard in this office to earn money,' he said. 'Besides, it's part of therapy that the patient has to pay'" (72). In November, he generously agreed that he wouldn't charge her for any more sessions.

Hartogs insisted that Julie was making progress in her therapy. On one occasion she told him that she didn't want to have sex, but he forced himself on her, stifling her screams so that she didn't disturb his patients who were sitting in the next room.

Acting Out or Working Through

Throughout his treatment of Julie, Hartogs invoked a central psychoanalytic concept to rationalize his predatory view of therapy. "It happens because of a process called 'transference.' If you love me, you can then transfer the feeling to other men who are more suitable" (47). His notion of transference is a cruel caricature of psychoanalytic theory. Significantly, nowhere in any of his publications does Hartogs refer to the vicissitudes of transference-love. He failed in each of the three battles psychoanalysts must wage with transference: he acted out his own sexual desires; he gave the general public additional reasons for mistrusting psychoanalytic psychotherapy; and he manipulated his patient by preying upon her trust and vulnerability. Indeed, Hartogs used every opportunity to exploit Julie's transference-love for him. Because he represented a father figure to her, having sex with him became symbolic incest. Just as her distant father abandoned her and her family years earlier, Hartogs' refusal to see her months later, when she was devastated over the end of their relationship, became a repetition of her father's earlier rejection and abandonment.

Julie's anger and indignation increased when she began to suspect that Hartogs was having sex with other patients. She developed a vaginal infection, trichomoniasis, which is usually transmitted by a man from woman to woman. A physician wrote her a prescription for Flagyl, telling her that both she and the "gentleman" with whom she was involved must take the medication. Hartogs agreed to take the pills, but four months later she still had the infection, suggesting that he was not taking the medication and still having sex with other women. Her suspicions were confirmed when she noticed a stained bed sheet in his apartment. There was never any verbal therapy throughout 1969 and 1970, yet Hartogs continued to reassure Julie she was making therapeutic progress. In late 1969, the psychiatrist began paying her for doing secretarial work for him, another boundary violation.

Leaving Hartogs

Julie announced she was leaving therapy in September 1969 and then changed her mind; but it was too late, for Hartogs was eager to get rid of her, though she was depressed and suicidal. When he refused her request to recommend another therapist, she returned to Pauline Anderson, confessing in tears about her sexual relationship with the man to whom Anderson had referred her 19 months earlier. Anderson was the first of many mental health professionals who was outraged by Hartogs' misconduct. The psychologist found herself in an ethical quandary when Julie informed her that she was planning to buy a gun to shoot Hartogs and then herself. "I'll have to go to the police and tell them of your threat," Anderson warned her, to which Julie responded, "I thought what went on in therapy was sacred" (96). It's never clear whether Julie posed an imminent danger to Hartogs or herself—he testified that she displayed 32 of his 48 criteria predicting violence. Anderson's threat to contact the police resulted in Julie's abrupt departure. As we point out in *Confidentiality and Its Discontents*, a psychotherapist's threat to breach confidentiality in a situation like this almost always results in a patient's termination of therapy, sometimes, as in the Tarasoff case, with dire consequences. Fortunately, Julie visited another psychiatrist, Walter Sencer, who, like Anderson, was appalled by Hartogs' behavior. She then contacted a lawyer, Robert Cohen, who set into motion what turned out to be a trailblazing legal case.

Lawsuit: Roy v. Hartogs

The lawsuit filed by Julie Roy and her lawyers in 1971 was for five causes of action totaling over $1 million. Two of the charges focused on malpractice, Hartogs' wrongful use of sexual intercourse as part of Julie's treatment, leading to "irreparable mental and emotional discomfort and harm to her" (104). The other three charges involved violations of the New York penal code. Her lawyers argued that because of the use of transference, which deprived her of the opportunity for informed consent, the psychiatrist's sexual intercourse with her was, from a legal standpoint, rape: rape of the body as well as rape of the mind.

Julie Roy's lawyers knew they confronted a formidable legal challenge, for without unambiguous proof of Hartogs' sexual misconduct, it was unlikely that a jury would believe a mental patient's allegations. All the mental health professionals who examined her agreed that she was seriously ill. She had been hospitalized twice for psychotic breakdowns after leaving Hartogs, spending much of her time in the hospital mute, unable to converse even with her lawyers. One of the psychiatrists who treated her, Paul Schneck, diagnosed her medical situation as "psychotic depression reaction, schizoid personality, catatonic schizophrenia, hysterical personality and transient situational disturbance" (118). Anderson's diagnosis was more tentative, though similar: "that of latent schizophrenia with paranoid ideation" (151). Paranoia is by definition an irrational and delusional fear of persecution. Why, then, would a jury trust the judgment of a severely ill mental patient over a widely respected psychiatrist?

At the beginning of the trial, Hartogs' lawyer filed a motion for dismissal on the grounds that a section of the New York State Civil Rights Act ruled out "seduction" in a malpractice suit against a physician. The defendant's lawyer cited a 1971 case that prevented a claimant from using seduction as grounds for a lawsuit against a physician who had intercourse with a patient being treated for gynecological problems. But Julie's lawyers contended that the two situations were different: Hartogs was a psychiatrist, not a gynecologist. Her lawyers also pointed out that in 1972, the American Psychiatric Association concluded it was unethical for a psychiatrist to have sex with a patient. Anyone who claimed otherwise was guilty of fraudulent misrepresentation.

Julie Roy's suit against Hartogs brought up a number of legal issues that had not been resolved up to that time. There was wide but not unanimous agreement that if sexual intercourse between Hartogs and Roy had taken place, such an act was "wrong." But what kind of wrong was it? Was it a criminal act, like a rape, or a civil wrong such as malpractice? Was it both—or neither? In his ruling on the question of whether a trial could or should take place, Judge Allan Murray Meyers decided that the wrong committed by Hartogs was a breach of a fiduciary responsibility that a psychotherapist owes to a patient, similar to the relationship between a guardian and a ward (*Roy v. Hartogs*, 81 Misc.2d 350). The judge allowed the civil case to continue.

Sexual Contact Between Patient and Therapist

Julie Roy's lawyers had to show that it was unethical for a psychotherapist to have sex with a patient, but such evidence was difficult to find and sometimes contradictory. (The American Psychiatric Association's ban on sex between psychiatrists and patients occurred after Roy left treatment.) The Hippocratic Oath, which Freeman cites at the beginning of *Betrayal*, specifically forbids sex between a doctor and patient: "Whatever houses I may visit, I will come for the benefit of the sick, remaining free of all intentional injustice, of all mischief and, in particular, of sexual relations with both female and male persons, be they free or slave." Freud reached the same conclusion, arguing in "Observations on Transference-Love" that analysis "must be carried out in abstinence." Lest readers fail to grasp the complexity of the last word, Freud then carefully expanded upon its meaning. "By this I do not mean physical abstinence alone, nor yet the deprivation of everything that the patient desires, for perhaps no sick person could tolerate this. Instead, I shall state it as a fundamental principle that the patient's need and longing should be allowed to persist in her, in order that they may serve as forces impelling her to do work and to make changes, and that we must beware of appeasing those forces by means of surrogates" (*SE*, vol. 12, 165).

Did Hartogs consider citing, as part of his legal defense for using sex as a part of psychotherapy, James L. McCartney's "Overt Transference," which was published in 1966? Hartogs and McCartney had a number of beliefs in common, including the view that an analyst can be a suitable love object for a female patient. Based on his behavior toward Julie in *Betrayal*, Hartogs would have endorsed McCartney's recommendation that patients need to touch, caress, fondle and sometimes have sexual intercourse with their therapist, behavior that should be reciprocated by the therapist. McCartney doesn't imply in "Overt Transference" that a female homosexual patient can learn to become heterosexual by having sex with her male psychiatrist, as Hartogs promised Roy, nor does he sanction the psychiatrist's expression of love for his patient, as Hartogs did. Despite these differences, Hartogs must have been tempted to cite "Overt Transference" as a rationalization for his behavior toward Julie Roy.

The psychiatrist we discussed in the preceding chapter, Charles Clay Dahlberg, who was affiliated with New York University Medical Center and Bellevue Hospital, examined Julie Roy and agreed to testify at her trial. The author of "Sexual Contact between Patient and Therapist," Dahlberg soon became her lawyers' "psychiatric keel" (150). Whatever uncertainty Dahlberg may have felt about sexual contact between patient and therapist when writing his 1970 article disappeared during his four sessions with Julie. He testified that her two hospitalizations were caused by her "brooding intensely over a long period of time about the sexual acts that she was engaged in with Dr. Hartogs" (175). He also testified unambiguously that "Sex with the patient is not any recognized form of therapy" (176).

Willard Gaylin, clinical professor of psychiatry at Columbia University Medical School, College of Physicians and Surgeons, also testified that sex between a patient and psychiatrist is never justified. "Having sex with a psychiatrist can cause the same kind of feeling as having sex with a parent. It is terribly destructive and dissociative, it can make your boundaries of right and wrong become terribly confused" (159–160). Employing a patient after treatment sessions is also wrong, Gaylin added, because it inevitably involves exploitation of the patient.

The Impotence Defense

During the trial, Hartogs denied any wrongdoing. He alleged that he not only did not have sex with Julie Roy but that he had been sexually impotent since 1965, at least four years before he began treating Julie, because of a "gross abnormality on the private parts of his body" (182). The abnormality, he added, was a large noncancerous tumor on one of his testicles, caused when he was kicked by a Nazi guard in a concentration camp in 1940. "It's a gross enlargement that anybody that has sex with me can see," he stated during the trial. Because Julie had testified under oath that she never noticed anything unusual about Hartogs' body when they were having sexual intercourse, his revelations during the trial seemed to undermine her credibility. No one asked Hartogs how he could have been in a Nazi concentration camp in 1940 if he came to the United States that same year.

Under the rigors of cross-examination, Hartogs' impotence defense failed him. The tumor, a hydrocele, did not render him impotent, he conceded, but rather made sex painful though still possible. A urologist told one of Julie's lawyers that he had never heard of a case of impotence arising from a hydrocele. Moreover, any urologist could have easily drained the hydrocele in a ten-minute office procedure; Hartogs could have even performed the procedure on himself. While it was true that Hartogs had visited a clinic several times for the hydrocele, his medical records indicated that the first time he mentioned he was impotent since 1965 was in 1974—on the eve of the trial.

"A Rotten Way to Be Wounded"

Hartogs spends a great deal of time in *Four-Letter Word Games* discussing impotent men, perhaps suggesting a long preoccupation with the subject. In the chapter "A Rotten Way to Be Wounded," Hartogs writes about Jake Barnes' war injury in *The Sun Also Rises*. "In picking impotence as a principal plot device, Hemingway had a sure thing. He was playing on one of the most fundamental and pervasive of all fears—the fear of losing one's manhood, which carries with it the corollary fear of never fully attaining it" (42). Hartogs implies inaccurately that Jake's testicles have been injured in the war when, in fact, Jake's situation is worse: his penis was severed. Jake's injury, Hemingway wrote in a 1951 letter, "came from a personal experience in that when I had been wounded at one time there had been an infection from pieces of wool cloth being driven into the scrotum. Because of this I got to know other kids who had genito urinary [*sic*] wounds and I wondered what a man's life would have been like after that if his penis had been lost and his testicles and spermatic cord remained intact. . . . [So I] tried to find out what his problems would be when he was in love with someone who was in love with him and there was nothing that they could do about it" (Meyers, 190). Jake's problem is not a lack of desire, which would occur if he were castrated, but an inability to act on his desire. Jake is filled with desire but cannot express it genitally.

Hartogs never discusses his identification with Jake's promiscuous girlfriend, Brett Ashley, who betrays him at every opportunity but to whom he remains strangely faithful. Like Brett, Hartogs maintained an equivocal attitude toward marriage in his writings. In some ways he resembled his patient Rachel, mentioned in *Questions Women Ask*, whose spouse almost certainly knew about her affairs but was content to remain in his marriage. By contrast, Hartogs' wife was *not* content to remain in her marriage. They divorced in 1970.

Hartogs returns to the subject of male impotence in his discussion of T.S. Eliot's play *The Cocktail Party*, which contains a psychiatrist who diagnoses the spiritual-sexual dysfunctions of men. Hartogs quotes one of the play's most suggestive lines: "To men of a certain type, the suspicion that they are incapable of loving is as disturbing to their self-esteem as, in cruder men, the fear of impotence" (*Four-Letter Word Games*, 58). Hartogs sometimes comes across as crude himself, particularly when he asks Julie, "Do you want a quickie?" (*Betrayal*, 68). Sometimes his language comes across as unintentionally crude, as when he declares during the trial that his sex life was once normal but then "it petered out" (227). Was he speaking about himself when he observed that educated men around the age of 50 discover the "lessening" of their "sexual capacity" or, what is an even more frightening situation, a "growing sexual indifference?" Such liaisons, Hartogs proclaims with prophetic insight, "rarely work out as rosily as they are imagined" (57–58).

Sex With Other Patients

The testimony of several female patients who had intimate relations with Hartogs as part of their treatment deflated his impotence defense. During a pretrial deposition, Julie's lawyer mentioned to Hartogs the names of nine female patients who said they had sex with him while they were his patients. Citing the confidentiality of the doctor-patient relationship, Hartogs refused to respond to the lawyer's statement. But the past came back to haunt him during the trial. "Pauline David," a New York City schoolteacher in her 40s, testified that she had sex with Hartogs from the beginning of her treatment in 1965 until she left him in 1972. Like Julie, she had sex with him and paid for each session. Again like Julie, she never noticed anything wrong with his testicles or penis. Pauline David testified that Hartogs implored her not to leave him when she decided she wanted to be treated by another doctor. "Trust me," Hartogs would say to her, "You need this love. You have been deprived" (241). The judge denied the defendant's attempt to have David's testimony stricken from the record because it was highly prejudicial. "This proof has been admitted for one purpose and one purpose only," Judge Myers pointed out. "The defendant testified that for the last ten years, because of a physical ailment, he had no sexual intercourse. This lady now says that during this ten-year period she had sexual intercourse with him" (241).

Other women came forward with similar stories. One person testified that she had sexual intercourse with Hartogs in 1949 when she lived in Montreal. Although the judge ruled to strike her testimony— as well as that of other female patients who had sex with Hartogs, on the grounds that their experiences were too remote from Julie Roy's case—the damage was done. The psychiatrist's defense was paradoxically rendered impotent.

A Matter of Proportions: The Analyst's Couch

An oddity of the trial was the size of Hartogs' analytic couch. One of the witnesses for the defense was a commercial photographer who had taken a photo of the analytic couch, upon Hartogs' request, to confirm the psychiatrist's testimony that the couch was too small for sexual intercourse. Another of Hartogs' defenses collapsed when Pauline David testified that she had sex with him on his analyst's couch.

A Landmark Case

After both sides rested their cases but before they gave their summations, the judge suggested that only one issue should go to the jury, that of malpractice. Despite some hesitation, Julie Roy's lawyers' agreed. The jury deliberated for about two hours before reaching its decision on March 10, 1975 that the defendant induced his patient to have sexual intercourse with him under the guise of therapy. The jury awarded Roy $250,000 (almost $1.2 million in current dollars) for compensatory damages (payment intended to compensate her for harm done to her by Hartogs' acts) and $100,000 for punitive damages (payment intended to punish Hartogs for his actions and to deter similar actions on the part of others in the future). Judge Myers allowed the punitive damages to stand but reduced compensatory damages to $50,000, largely because he inferred from Roy's demeanor during the trial that her sexual relationship with Hartogs was not as harmful to her as her lawyers claimed. *Roy v. Hartogs* became a landmark case, establishing for the first time that it is malpractice for a psychotherapist to have sex with a patient.

Hartogs' lawyers appealed the jury's decision and the amount of the awards to the Appellate Division of the New York Supreme Court. In a 2 to 1 decision, the court voted to uphold the finding against Hartogs but further reduced the compensatory damages from $50,000 to $25,000 (about $150,000 in today's dollars). The court's reduction of compensatory damages was based on the view that even if Roy had been hospitalized twice since her "treatment" by Hartogs, she had a history of mental problems that antedated their relationship; her subsequent bouts of illness could not be attributed solely to her mistreatment in therapy. The court also eliminated altogether the award of punitive damages against Hartogs based on the belief that Roy had consented to the sexual relationship. The court found no evidence that she would have been unable to withhold consent had she chosen to do so (*Roy v. Hartogs*, 85 Misc.2d 891, 1976).

The dissenting judge, Xavier Riccobono, however, saw the case differently. In his view, the lawsuit was brought against Hartogs not because of his sexual relationship with Roy but because Hartogs broke off the relationship. "[A]lthough the plaintiff was suffering from a number of emotional problems her competency was never placed in issue. Is it not fair to infer, therefore, that she was capable of giving a knowing and meaningful consent? For almost one and a half years while this 'meaningful' relationship continued, the plaintiff was not heard to complain. Upon the defendant terminating the relation, this lawsuit evolves." On the other hand, Judge Riccobono raised the possibility that Hartogs' behavior might have been criminal. "I neither condone the defendant's reprehensible conduct, nor maintain that it was not violative of his professional ethics and Hippocratic oath. If, however, the defendant has committed a crime, let him be brought before the criminal halls of justice. For violation of his Hippocratic oath, if there be any, let him suffer the sanctions of the Medical Ethics Board or other appropriate medical authority. But let him not be convicted of his acts of misfeasance and malfeasance by virtue of an action in malpractice" (*Roy v. Hartogs*, 897).

Prior to his trial, Hartogs attempted to get his medical malpractice company to defend him. The insurer, which ordinarily would have provided and paid for legal representation for the psychiatrist, believed that the act involved was not an act of malpractice and therefore "disclaimed" any responsibility for his coverage in the case. As a result, Hartogs declared bankruptcy and was forced to pay for his legal defense himself. Following the trial, the insurer— probably fearing that it might be on the hook for the $250,000 in compensatory damages awarded by the lower court, and unsure what could happen as a result of Hartogs' appeal— negotiated a settlement with Julie Roy of $50,000 to protect itself, which was the amount she finally received.

Hartogs was involved in a second lawsuit filed by Pauline David, whom the Troy *Times Record* identified in an article published on February 19, 1977 as Corinne Stern. Hartogs denied the accusation, but his insurance company settled that malpractice suit for $50,000.

Another Lawsuit: "Fornicatus Hartogus"

Hartogs continued to press the matter in court. The following year, he filed a lawsuit against his insurance company, claiming that they owed him a significant sum of money for both the cost of his legal expenses and compensation for the humiliation of having had to file for bankruptcy, along with punitive damages for their refusal to cover him in this matter in the first place. In what was clearly intended to be read as a humorous and sarcastic rebuke to Hartogs, Judge Harold Baer, who heard the case *Hartogs v. Employers Mutual Liability Insurance Company of Wisconsin* (89 Misc.2d, 468, 1977), coined a Latin phrase to describe the treatment that Hartogs had administered to Julie Roy: "*fornicatus Hartogus*." He used the term twice in his opinion, describing Hartogs' "treatment" of Roy this way: "at the trial it was established that Hartogs, under the guise of medical therapy to cure his patient's lesbianism, during a period of 13 months prescribed and personally administered multiple, repetitive doses of *fornicatus Hartogus.*"

In addition, Judge Baer described the outcome of the earlier trial as Hartogs' having "been adjudicated as having indulged his *concupiscentia medicus,*" medical lust, a term he apparently coined. Finally, taking account of the fact that malpractice insurance exists for a greater purpose than just the protection of the insured—it also is intended to provide a source of relief for the injured—Judge Baer made it clear that although the company had agreed to pay Julie Roy, he could not condone any claim that Hartogs might assert against the company because it is a principle that courts should not be used to "indemnify immorality and to pay the expenses of prurience." And with these words Judge Baer dismissed Hartogs' case.

Andrea Celenza reports in *Sexual Boundary Violations* that by the early 1980s, the American Psychiatric Association's Insurance Trust estimated that 18% of all malpractice cases and about 50% of the total costs of defense and payments were due to "sex cases" (xvi). *Roy v. Hartogs* had a far-reaching effect on the ways in which insurance companies covered—or did not cover—medical malpractice insurance.

The Ambiguities of Sexual Malpractice Cases

Ralph Slovenko, a professor of law and psychiatry at Wayne State University, has pointed out that *Roy v. Hartogs* illustrates many of the ambiguities inherent in sexual malpractice cases involving a patient and psychotherapist. Newspaper publicity of a lawsuit against a therapist may bring forth patients who have also been violated. Had other female patients of Hartogs not appeared and been willing to testify, it's unlikely that a jury would have convicted him of malpractice. Patients are often reluctant to come forth, however, because of the double stigmas of mental illness and sexual violation. Accounts of sex between a patient and therapist usually make newspaper headlines and are inevitably sensationalized. Unlike usual tort cases, in which a plaintiff must establish fault, causation and damage, juries often assume that a plaintiff in a sexual malpractice suit is always injured: "liability is established even in the absence of proof of actual injury" (742).

Sexual malpractice cases involving a patient and therapist have striking gender implications, Slovenko observes. "Surveys show that anywhere from 6 to 10 percent of male therapists and 3 to 8 percent of female therapists acknowledge being sexually involved with patients during treatment." And yet it is rare for a male patient to sue a female therapist. "To what psychological aberration can we ascribe this failure to file suit? Is it because a man who brings suit on this account would be treated with derision, or are men better able to handle such sexual episodes than women? Does transference turn women but not men into helpless waifs?" (746).

Troubled by an increasingly litigious society, Slovenko appears jaded at times in his comments about psychotherapy patients who are victims of sexual abuse. "Transference jargon has beclouded common sense and has gotten juries and judges to accept the existence of transference dementia" (741). Slovenko also laments the ways in which therapists must practice their craft defensively to stay out of trouble with the law. "One of the consequences of the current climate is that depersonalization has taken place between therapists and patients. Therapists sit defensively behind their desks, careful not to spontaneously smile, conduct themselves in a very prim and proper manner, and dispense their psychotherapeutic or medication products to consumers—no longer fellow human beings experiencing emotional pain" (746).

James Kelley is less cynical. A former lawyer and judge, his long-standing interest in psychiatric malpractice arose because several psychiatrists who treated him decades ago failed to diagnose him as suffering from manic depression. "Between 1967 and 1971, during my midthirties, I had three manic episodes, each followed by a long period of depression," he writes in the introduction to *Psychiatric Malpractice* (1996). "I was seeing a psychiatrist who prescribed Thorazine, an antipsychotic, but nothing was said about manic depression or lithium. My last severe depression in 1971 led to a month's stay in one of Washington, D.C.'s leading psychiatric hospitals. Although I was exhibiting the classic symptoms, manic depression was still not diagnosed. Based on what I've learned since, by that time it probably should have been" (5).

Kelley acknowledges in *Psychiatric Malpractice* Slovenko's help for his comments on the law, but he is more sensitive than Slovenko to the psychological suffering caused by psychiatric malpractice. "The most serious injuries caused by sex in therapy are psychic, not physical, and may involve long-term deterioration of the patient's mental condition. A patient's reactions may range from anger at being exploited to full-fledged post-traumatic stress disorder" (201).

Kelley limits his discussion of *Roy v. Hartogs* to a brief paragraph, pointing out that the "appellate court expressed the curious view that Dr. Hartogs' conduct had been 'inexcusable' but not 'so wanton or reckless as to permit an award for punitive damages'" (200). The result, Kelley declares, was a pyrrhic victory for the plaintiff. He concludes his book with the belief that the present legal system of psychiatric malpractice "works about as well as can be expected" (210). Sex between patients and psychotherapists is so common that insurance companies routinely refuse to cover this form of malpractice.

Therapist/The Rapist

How did Hartogs expect to have sex with several of his patients without eventually getting caught? What was he thinking? How would he have psychoanalyzed someone in his situation? We can only speculate what was going through Hartogs' mind, but we do have as clues—in his self-help books—his statements of advice to women married to promiscuous husbands. Tellingly, *Questions Women Ask* remains silent about a woman "falling in love" with her analyst, but Hartogs' defense of his profession now strikes us as cruelly ironic. On the opening page of *Questions Women Ask,* he asserts that analysts should never add to a woman's troubles, a pronouncement that must have sounded galling to the many female patients with whom he had sex on his analytic couch. His reply to the question, "How do I know when I ought to go to a psychiatrist?" is no less ironic. "Psychiatrists are much too busy to try to lure you into therapy if you don't need it" (26). Perhaps he should have added the caveat that some psychiatrists try to keep their female patients in therapy for as long as possible, mainly for the therapists' sexual pleasure. Vladimir Nabokov, one of the most outspoken foes of psychoanalysis, mordantly observes in *Lolita* that the difference between therapist and the rapist is a matter of spacing, a criticism that is not far from the truth with respect to Hartogs' treatment mode.

If Hartogs truly believed that he could therapeutically help his female patients by having sex with them, "transferring" their love for him to other men, then he would not have shamelessly lied during his trial. Nor would he have abandoned these women when they most needed his help. One suspects that what was most devastating to Julie Roy was her belief that she and Hartogs would remain together permanently; that she was "special." Slovenko points out that in the overwhelming majority of litigated cases, patients become sexually involved with therapists in the hope of developing a permanent relationship. "It is the termination of the relationship, not the sexual relations, that causes the outrage" (749). Hartogs' rejection of Roy proved unbearable to her.

Was Hartogs thinking about his own life when he responded to the queries from promiscuous wives in *Questions Women Ask*? Did he feel Rachel's "excruciating guilt" toward her spouse as a result of her constant and compulsive unfaithfulness to him? Did he experience Rachel's "seemingly masochistic desire to be humiliated and dominated" by her partners (77)? Was his own infidelity a way of taking revenge on his wife, as he suggested was true for a promiscuous woman who felt trapped in her marriage? Did he attempt to take to heart the advice he gave to his promiscuous patient to have a "torrid affair" with her spouse? (96). Was he thinking about himself when he told a woman who was going with a man "who is too friendly with other women" that he is likely a "deeply restless, chronically unsatisfied male, who must surround himself with hordes of appreciative women in order to avoid the frightening discovery of his own inner emptiness"—a man who in his "search for personal glory" chooses a "role of savior of all the 'helpless' women he encounters in his daily routine?" Such a man, Hartogs intimates, "may be quite frightened of women" (99). Was he looking into the mirror when he wrote about the "menopausal male" who struggled to become a "rejuvenated, supervirile Don Juan" (112)? In short, would he have included himself as one of the "amputees of love" (132)?

Writing the Story of Betrayal

There is never any doubt in *Betrayal* that Hartogs' exploitation of Julie Roy's transference-love for him renders *her* into an amputee of love. The

OFF THE TRACKS VOLUME 1

book is a cautionary tale of the differences between real and illusory love, between enabling and disabling love. Freeman allows us to enter Julie's consciousness, and we learn much about her damaged inner life. She is so fearful and suffused with self-loathing that she spray-painted the mirrors in her apartment to avoid looking at her reflection. Freeman's challenge as a writer is to erase the spray paint to show Julie's depth of character. She evokes Julie's zombie-like existence as a mute patient in a psychiatric ward, her searing jealousy when she realizes that her psychiatrist has sex with other patients, her embarrassment over her weight problem, her black depression that conceals massive rage, and her quiet dignity throughout the humiliating trial. Without Freeman's help, Julie would not be able to tell her own story. "There were no words to describe her fury at being exploited sexually, her even greater fury at being abandoned" (112). With Freeman's help, Julie finds the words.

Freeman functions as Julie's real analyst, a person who listens attentively to her story, helps her to express herself, and allows her to acknowledge and understand the shameful feelings and desires that make her human. Freeman's empathy for her biographical subject never wavers. Without judging her, Freeman conveys Julie's growing awareness that Hartogs was taking advantage of her. "She was astute enough to know the truth, but lacked the courage to act on it, as she had lacked courage so much of her life. She was still being the good little girl who did not make waves" (57). Without idealizing her, Freeman shows how Julie survived harsh public scrutiny during a trial, including frenzied media attention, that would have crushed a weaker woman. Sometimes Freeman offers insights into Julie's consciousness. of which the grief-stricken patient remains unaware, as when we learn that "she wondered at times as if her father's absence from home did not leave black holes in her personality, even though she was not conscious of them" (38). Freeman is particularly effective in conveying Hartogs' exploitation of

Julie's transference-love for him, using a metaphor that conjures up the image of an amputee of love. "And because she thought of him as the substitute for her mother and father, the sexual relationship was like an incestuous affair. No matter what her participation, he had taken the Hippocratic oath, which said that a doctor should not become sexually involved with a patient. Ever. Committed to healing, he had destroyed. It was as though a surgeon deliberately cut off a leg that could have been saved by a salve" (113).

In contrast to Julie Roy, Hartogs remains a flat, two-dimensional character throughout *Betrayal*. Freeman elicits his presence mainly through his dialogue, which Julie recalls, presumably accurately, as when he asks her during therapy, "Tell me your fantasies about me" (41). Readers are left to infer his destructive narcissism. In her review of *Betrayal* appearing in the *New York Times* on August 8, 1976, Susan Braudy describes the book as a "slick piece of confessional journalism" written in "spare uninspired language." The criticism may be harsh, but certainly the least effective part of the book lies in its weak depiction of Hartogs. We never see why female patients would be willing to have sex with him: there is nothing scintillating about his speech, nothing attractive about his physical presence. "He was short, slightly plumper than average, with a barrel-like chest" (32). The spell he appears to cast over his patients never extends to Freeman's readers. For this reason, Jeanne Smith's review of *Betrayal* published in a 1977 issue of the *American Journal of Psychoanalysis* is puzzling: "For psychiatric readers, the book achieves an undercurrent of ambiguous sympathy for both defendant and plaintiff." Few psychiatric readers feel any sympathy, ambiguous or otherwise, for Hartogs by the end of the book. Another statement by Smith is even more puzzling: "Not all sex in therapy can be rationalized as motivated by a desire to be 'helpful.'" One cannot read the sentence without irony, though none was intended.

Hartogs is more sinister and sadistic in the film *Betrayal* than in the book. The film is more successful in conveying Julie's powerlessness in Hartogs' office and her lack of will in opposing his sexual advances. The hospital scenes in the film, when the psychiatrists propose electroshock therapy and place her in "isolation," evoke the nightmarish horror of *The Snake Pit* and *One Flew Over the Cuckoo's Nest*.

A Betrayed Co-author

Three-quarters of the way into *Betrayal* we discover, almost as an aside, one of the most bizarre aspects of the story: "Dr. Hartogs' book *The Two Assassins* [was] written with Lucy Freeman" (190). The reader could not be more astonished by the revelation, which is buried in a sentence that Freeman may have hoped readers would neither closely read nor long remember. *Betrayal* is mainly about a patient's outrage over psychiatric malpractice, but Freeman must have felt similar shock, incredulity and horror when she discovered that the prominent psychiatrist with whom she co-authored her 1965 book could have been so unethical. Indeed, in light of Hartogs' history as a predatory therapist—which Freeman painstakingly researched and documented in *Betrayal*—she may have felt that the title of the book she wrote with him should have been called *The Three Assassins*, for he tried to assassinate the mental health profession that she did so much to popularize.

Freeman's Books Before and After Betrayal

There were few female reporters working for the *New York Times* when Lucy Freeman was hired in the 1940s, and she went on to write nearly 80 books, many of them focusing on mental health, an issue about which she cared deeply. Her first and perhaps most popular book, *Fight Against Fears*, was published in 1951, eventually selling over 1,000,000 copies worldwide. The bestseller, in print for nearly half a century, described her own long struggle with depression and her successful six-year psychoanalysis. Analysis helped her to understand her conflicted feelings toward her parents and freed her to develop her remarkable talent for writing. *Fight Against Fears* is the first book in English written by a patient about a long and involved psychoanalysis. Her experience was the complete opposite of Julie's.

"The public held two extreme viewpoints on psychoanalysis," Freeman writes early in *Fight Against Fears*. "One coterie believed it diabolical nonsense, indulged in by pseudo-scientific Satans who spoke strange jargon. The other, a smaller group, lauded psychoanalysts as supermen who freed the spirit with the magic wand of words—one wave of the wand and the sick would rise healed, the wretched grow joyous" (29). Freeman must have believed for years that Dr. Hartogs was, if not a superman, then certainly a healer devoted to the welfare of his patients, but she eventually realized as a result of writing Julie Roy's story that he was a diabolical, pseudo-scientific sexiatrist, a member of psychiatry's lunatic fringe.

Reading *Fight Against Fears*, we can see that Freeman identified with Julie Roy for many reasons. To begin with, Freeman was self-effacing to a fault. "It doesn't seem right to talk about myself," she tells her analyst, whom she refers to simply as "John." "We reporters look with scorn on the writer who puts everything in the first person. The 'I' doesn't belong" (36). She learns that there is nothing egotistical about writing in the first person—though she doesn't write about herself in *Betrayal*. She learns, again like Julie, that she had never confronted her wish to punish herself for her murderous feelings toward others. "I unconsciously hoped I might die and be relieved of the pain of living, but, not having the courage or desperation to take my life, I wished someone else might do it for me" (117). She learns, to use Thoreau's haunting expression, that she had been living a life of quiet desperation. She learns, using a literary allusion that Hartogs used more than two decades later in *Questions Women Ask*, that in her relationships with men, "it was less fearful to know many casually than to know one intimately (the Don Juans of both sexes fear to be close to one person). I could hide behind a hundred pairs of trousers, yet not be responsible for any one pair" (119). She learns, like Julie, that one reason she felt wicked and suicidal was because of her sexual desires. "I felt I must apologize to the world for the strange hunger that stirred me" (121). She learns that she was scared to death even mentioning the word "sex"—even more afraid than Julie. "The word 'fork' has always frightened me because I am afraid one day I am going to say, instead, a word that sounds like it" (133). And she learns, like Julie, that she was falling in love with her psychoanalyst, a desire that troubled and confused her.

Here is where the similarities between Julie Roy and Lucy Freeman end, for their psychoanalysts' responses to their patients' transference-love for them were strikingly different. Confessing that she desired John ardently, romantically, sexually, that she wanted to be his "slave, mistress, friend— anything to be with him" (145), she discovers that her desire for him reflects her desire for another man whose love she craved her entire life:

> "What you feel for me, you realize, is what you really feel for your father," he said quietly. "It's your father you have wanted all these years."
>
> "It's *you* I want," I said stubbornly. He could not tell me for whom I yearned. "What I feel for you *isn't* what I feel for my father."
>
> "You transfer to me the feelings you have for him," he went on, not heeding my opinion. "That is also what you have been doing with the other men in your life." (*Fight Against Fears*, 146)

It took years of further analysis for Freeman to realize the truth of John's statement, but the result is an expansion of her emotional intelligence. The opposite of Hartogs, John "derived satisfaction not from power or prestige but from watching sick persons grow healthier" (248). Near the end of the book she states that she no longer debates psychoanalysis with opponents. "Analysis is not witchcraft which destroys the spirit, neither does it clear up unhappiness like magic, saving lives in a twinkling of the psychic eye. It is a long, slow process involving guidance by a man who knows himself well and determined effort by the one who seeks help" (316).

Freeman was uniquely qualified to write *Betrayal*, for she knew from her own experience the vulnerability arising from a patient's transference-love for an analyst. It must have been difficult for her to focus on Julie's relationship with Hartogs without thinking about her relationships with her own analysts. Without elaborating in *Betrayal* on her collaboration with Hartogs in *The Two Assassins*. Freeman hoped that by helping to write Julie's story, she was helping to prevent other women from sexual exploitation during therapy.

In *Freud and Women*, co-authored with Herbert S. Strean, Freeman observes in the introduction that their goal in writing the book is "not to idealize Freud or repudiate him, but to show him as human—he above all others showed us that no man was a god—and to try to reveal faithfully and to evaluate objectively those attitudes toward women that affected Freud's theories about the emotional conflicts and psychosexual development of the female sex" (xiii). Published in 1981— five years after *Betrayal*—*Freud and Women* affirms that Freeman's belief in psychoanalysis was not destroyed by Hartogs.

The End of the Story

In retrospect, the title of Hartogs' 1961 book, *How to Grow Up Successfully*, reveals a central irony in his life. How can a man who was so eager to dispense with psychiatric advice to others fail to heed it himself? Did the analyst ever analyze himself? We know nothing about his relationship with his parents. Why is that important? Recall his comment to the female patient who lacked the courage to be truthful. "The answer is simple: you are either the victim of emotional deprivation by your parents, or the victim of emotional *over*feeding by them." We can only wonder whether Hartogs' parents would have agreed with their son's answer.

The author of "The Analyst's Couch" might have called his monthly column "Lying on the Couch," an expression even more fraught with irony and ambiguity. "Lying on the couch," which is the title of Irvin Yalom's celebrated 1997 novel, has three distinct meanings: the analysand reclining to engage in free association, as Freud suggested; the falsehoods, fabrications, and half-truths that an analysand must work through to reach the truth; and the transgressive sexuality that sometimes occurs in analysis, almost always ending in therapeutic failure. Hartogs' therapeutic strategy included all three meanings.

Little is known about Hartogs' life following *Roy v. Hartogs* apart from the fact that he lost his medical license but continued to practice as a psychotherapist. His reputation destroyed and his writing career over, he achieved celebrity status but not the kind he imagined. Jonathan Moreno remarks in a 2012 issue of *Psychology Today* that during Hartogs' much-publicized trial, when his photo was on the front pages of the major New York City tabloids, the psychiatrist appeared in disguise when he met his ex-wife (to whom Moreno was related) for lunch at a restaurant.

Was it anti-war sentiment or greed that explained the 945 letters Julie Roy typed for him in less than a year? These letters were "written in behalf of young men who did not want to serve in Vietnam" (*Betrayal*, 163). According to Julie's trial testimony, these letters were "all the same with the exception of a couple words," suggesting that Hartogs might have been mass producing and selling such letters (74). Hartogs paid her three dollars for each letter she typed; at the trial she produced checks written to her by Hartogs in payment for this astonishing number of letters that she typed in a period of ten months. It seems inconceivable that an ethical practitioner with an ongoing practice could actually have evaluated 945 potential draftees in a period of approximately ten months. Many psychiatrists, some of whom opposed the war themselves, struggled with the ethics of writing "draft letters" for young men to help them avoid the draft, as Ira M. Frank and Frederick S. Hoedemaker observed in 1970. We are unaware of any other practitioner, however, who produced such letters on an industrial scale as Hartogs seemed to have done.

Hartogs made another appearance in the legal system in 1985 as a comedic minor character in a lawsuit that was ultimately heard in the U.S. Court of Appeals for the Second District. The case is distinctive in that the opinion written by the court begins with these words: "In this weird, if not to say bizarre, case" (*Goldberg v. National Life Insurance Company of Vermont*). The lawsuit involved a New York garment manufacturer, Stephen Goldberg, who began to lose money in 1979 and ultimately went out of business after a bankruptcy in 1979. According to the court record, Goldberg took out two large disability policies in 1977. He claimed to have been mugged in 1980 and to have suffered injuries, although no such injuries were apparent when he was seen at a hospital that same day. Nonetheless, he submitted disability claims to both insurers in which he listed "Renatus Hartogs" as his "Attending Physician." Goldberg filed a claim form with one insurer that stated, "I will not be able to do any type of work again. I will not be returning to work again." He attached a statement from Dr. Hartogs who claimed that Goldberg "is incapable to do any type of work again" and that his sickness or injury was "post-traumatic stress disorder, chronic type."

A consulting doctor hired by one of the insurance companies evaluated Goldberg and concluded that the man was "currently totally disabled psychiatrically." The doctor added that Goldberg "consults Dr. Hartogs three times a week but refuses all treatments except psychotherapy," adding that prognosis was "impossible." However, it emerged in court that Goldberg was living an active life: "Outside the doctor's office, Goldberg's life was not quite as dismal as he made it out to be. In November 1980, for example, he wrote checks to Diners Club, Barney's, Columbia Tour and the Concord Hotel. In January 1981, he opened a Cash Management Account with Merrill Lynch, listing his occupation as 'retired,' and by Spring of 1981 was writing checks to four different securities brokers." Hartogs' status as an unlicensed physician emerged as well, further discrediting Goldberg's claims, none of which earned the court's sympathy.

Hartogs died in 1998 at the age of 87. Turning the Hippocratic Oath into the hypocrite's oath, he is now best remembered for betraying the solemn vow he took at the beginning of his career to do no harm. A paid death notice appeared in the *New York Times* on February 8, 1999:

HARTOGS—Renatus, M.D. Psychiatrist, PhD., Holocaust survivor, mentor, author, artist, father, grandfather and life partner; the only doctor to diagnose Lee Harvey Oswald will be beloved forever by friends, patients and life companion; will always be remembered for his courage, wit, wisdom, intelligence and generosity; helper of others, never of himself—a mensch. Beloved Forever, Charlotte.

We know nothing about Julie Roy's life following *Roy v. Hartogs*. She disappeared into the obscurity of history, no doubt relieved to be out of the public eye. Freeman continued writing books until her death in 2004 at the age of 88, her faith in psychotherapy strong to the end.

CHAPTER 3

The/Rapist: Four Survivors Tell Their Stories

The Boston psychoanalyst Elvin Semrad, known for his down-to-earth humor and homespun wisdom, once quipped to a female patient who was infatuated with him, "You feel this way for neurotic reasons and when you get better, I will be sad." The remark, quoted by Andrea Celenza in the beginning of her article "The Misuse of Countertransference Love in Sexual Intimacies Between Therapists and Patients" (501), is fraught with irony. Therapists who are aware of the potential countertransference problems of loving and being loved by their patients may be sad when transference-love diminishes, but they will be glad to know they have helped their patients live—and love—without them. Such restraint is not easy to practice, but therapy cannot succeed without it.

In this chapter, we present four book-length stories of therapists who may have been glad while they were having sex with their patients, but they were presumably sad when they lost the right to practice psychotherapy. The patients were also sad, though for different reasons. They knew from the beginning that sex in therapy was not in their best interest, despite their therapists' assurances that lovemaking was leading to "breakthroughs." The patients could not be blamed for becoming lovesick. They entered therapy because of conflicts that included feeling unloved and unwanted, and they needed the help, insight and empathy of a trained mental health professional. The patients could not know that their love was, in reality, transference-love, a phenomenon of therapy. They believed they were "special" if their therapists had sex with them and that their therapists' love would be curative, a common fantasy that seldom comes true. The patients' sadness gradually turned to dismay and confusion over time, then resentment and, finally, to outrage.

In describing the women patients in this chapter as "victims," we need to emphasize that the victimization involved is largely the product of the intense sexual impulses that can be unleashed within the psychotherapy patient. Pointing out the patient's role in sexualized boundary violations is not to "blame the victim" but rather to emphasize the therapist's burden of responsibility to avoid such transgressions.

The Literature of Sexual Boundary Violations

The four stories in this chapter were written by the patients themselves, though two of them had co-authors. We present the stories chronologically. *Therapist*, written by Ellen Plasil, appeared in 1985. *A Killing Cure*, co-authored by Evelyn Walker and Perry Deane Young, was published in 1986. *Sex in the Therapy Hour*, co-authored by Caroline M. Bates and Annette M. Brodsky, came out in 1989. *Sexual Abuse by Health Professionals*, written by P. Susan Penfold, appeared in 1998. Each of the four books describes a landmark case; each is often cited in the professional literature on sexual abuse in therapy.

Despite frequent clinical references to these sexual boundary violation cases, the human dimensions of these stories have been neglected. Most of what we learn about the therapists comes from the patients and accordingly, we focus on their stories: their problems upon entering therapy; their brief periods of lovesickness followed by heartbreak and crushing disillusionment; their feelings of prolonged powerlessness and humiliation; their efforts to terminate treatment and seek help elsewhere; their agonized decisions to file lawsuits against their therapist; and their lives following the end of a long ordeal.

I

LONNIE FRANKLIN LEONARD AND ELLEN PLASIL

Exploitation of transference-love characterizes Lonnie Franklin Leonard's treatment of Ellen Plasil. She describes in *Therapist* her five-and-a-half-year tumultuous relationship with the psychiatrist, who treated her as a sexual object for his own pleasure. She provides us with enough information about her childhood and adolescence to explain why she was a vulnerable target for prolonged exploitation. Growing up with a verbally abusive mother and a father who admitted he had once kissed her inappropriately when she was nine, Plasil made three suicide attempts before she turned 15. While still in high school, she spent two years in therapy with a female psychologist and found the experience valuable, but she began feeling anxious and depressed again years later when she was a wife and a new mother. Deciding to return to therapy, she chose Allan Blumenthal, a therapist in a distant city, whom she had read about in *Objectivism*, the monthly newsletter devoted to

97

Ayn Rand's philosophy. Blumenthal told her that he had a three-year waiting list and recommended his protégé Lonnie Franklin Leonard, whose waiting list was only six months. Plasil was so determined to begin therapy with an Objectivist psychologist that she, her husband, and young child moved from the Midwest to New York City, where Leonard practiced.

We learn only a few details about Leonard's background. A graduate of the University of Arkansas and the University of Arkansas College of Medicine, he interned at the U.S. Navy Hospital in San Diego and from there went to the U.S. Navy School of Aviation Medicine in Pensacola, Florida, where he trained to become a U.S. Flight Surgeon—an experience he apparently disliked and did not pursue further. Married and divorced twice, he had two sons who lived with their mother in Arkansas. He did a residency at Bellevue Hospital in New York City from 1966–1969, and after a brief experience serving as a consultant in psychiatry at IBM, he went into private practice. We never learn when, why, and how he became attracted to Objectivist psychology.

An Odd Psychiatrist

Plasil began treatment with Leonard in January 1972, when she was 21. Nearly everything about the psychiatrist surprised her. To begin with, he looked more like a patient than a doctor. His cropped Afro made his ears appear too large for his small face, and his eyes seemed to bulge from their sockets whenever he raised his eyebrows. During the first session, Plasil noticed a camera, tape machine, and television screens in his office, which was located in his apartment on the eighth floor of a building overlooking First Avenue in lower Manhattan. Each session would be videotaped, he told her. "I had never heard of videotaping therapy sessions before," she remarks to us (33). The psychiatrist charged $35 for each therapy session and an additional $10 for the viewing of each taped session.

Plasil's surprise turned to shock when, on April 5, 1972, three months after she entered therapy, she saw Leonard standing naked in the hall outside his office. Rushing to the door to leave, she heard him exclaim, "Stop!" in a tone that sounded like both an order and a plea. He offered her a drink and then requested her to undress so that he could check her vital signs. "I am a doctor. I was doing physical examinations long before I ever practiced psychiatry" (56). Confused by the situation, she proceeded to undress, received a sleeping pill, and was told that she should spend the night with him. She knew that psychiatrists do not offer patients a drink in bed, but she was too stunned to disobey him. The entire situation was bizarre and unnerving. "He remained naked. His incredible nonchalance told me that psychologically healthy people are not embarrassed by casual nudity. Only neurotics, like me I supposed, were. I must not show it, I told myself. Then I gave myself a standing order to fix that part of my psychology" (57). Plasil soon discovered that Leonard's nude jaunts were commonplace. Indeed, this was how he greeted all his female (but not male) patients in the early morning and after lunch. The female patients who experienced this spectacle, she adds, felt complimented when he greeted them in this manner.

As a sign of her therapeutic "progress," Leonard invited Plasil to his apartment in 1974 for a Christmas Party, where there were 15 other "select" patients. While under the influence of alcohol, he provoked a fight with a physically stronger patient, Tony, who could not bear to take arms against his beloved psychiatrist. Plasil was horrified, but when she asked Leonard's girlfriend and soon-to-be third wife

Patricia Street to stop the fight, Street replied, "He knows what he's doing. Don't worry about it" (108). The psychiatrist then took out a gun and ordered Tony, now covered with blood, to shoot him. The situation grew stranger when Leonard, finding himself disarmed, began shouting at Tony to leave. Leonard's explanation, as reported by Plasil, made no sense. "'You're violating my property rights!' Dr. Leonard accused. The Objectivist psychotherapist was accusing his patient of the equivalent of a mortal sin in Objectivism" (109). The next day, Leonard explained his behavior as his subconscious calling out for justice, and when Tony failed to grasp how the psychiatrist's cruel and hostile behavior could be considered justice, Leonard mystifyingly replied that it was Tony's own projection of his father onto Leonard, the therapist. It was a common occurrence, the psychiatrist assured Tony. "It's called *transference*" (111).

Sexual Humiliation

Therapy sessions with Leonard involved lectures on a variety of topics, including hostility, values and careers. His favorite lecture was on romantic love, where he stated that men are "polygamous by nature" and that they alone have the primary role in a romantic relationship. Leonard had no doubt that man is the *"primary actor"* in sex; a woman's sexual feelings, he declared unapologetically, "come from her response to a man" (51). In his view, a woman's sexual pleasure derives solely from responding to and admiring a man. It did not take Leonard long to sexualize his relationship with Plasil. To earn his therapeutic approval, she was forced to masturbate and fellate him. Because he did not regard her as sufficiently feminine to appreciate his sexuality, he did not yet deem her worthy enough to have intercourse with him.

Leonard introduced nudity into Plasil's therapy sessions. He was working on an "innovative" therapy technique that he learned as a result of having read Arthur Janov's 1970 bestseller, *The Primal Scream*. In the beginning, Leonard followed the techniques Janov described. Plasil would lie on the floor in a spread-eagle position in order to "derepress"—a technique to recall repressed memories. Leonard videotaped these sessions. He then developed his own technique to speed up the derepression process by ordering Plasil to take off her clothes and stand naked in front of him and his camera. "I felt powerless and humiliated, and ashamed for feeling so" (91).

In 1976, Leonard invited Plasil to his girlfriend's beach house in New Jersey, grabbed her from behind, thrust his penis into her vagina and ejaculated. The entire act, she recalls, lasted less than half a minute and left her feeling numb. "This was what I had become: a woman who could feel no fear, no outrage, no indignation, no anger at being used" (120). Perhaps as a result of this violation, Plasil became promiscuous for the next two years, compulsively seeking out new partners and sleeping with anyone except men with *honorable* intentions. She developed two personalities, *Big Me* and *Little Me*, the former, her 25-year-old self, able to function in the adult world, a product of what she bitterly calls the "paragon of *Sexual Psychology according to Leonard*," and the latter, a regressed stage of childhood, seldom exceeding the age of seven, the embodiment of all the feelings that had been "shunned, discouraged, and punished by my therapist whenever they had been expressed in my adult form" (125–126).

One of the rules of therapy was Leonard's insistence that Plasil always disclose everything on her mind, concealing nothing from him. "Your first responsibility is to report everything you can about what is occurring in your life and in your head. Everything" (31). Without making the connection, Leonard's demand for full disclosure recalls Freud's "fundamental rule" in psychoanalysis, as he states in "On

Beginning the Treatment: Further Recommendations on the Technique of Psycho-Analysis" (1913). "Act as though, for instance, you were a traveller sitting next to the window of a railway carriage and describing to someone inside the carriage the changing views which you see outside. Finally, never forget that you have promised to be absolutely honest, and never leave anything out because, for some reason or other, it is unpleasant to tell it" (*SE*, vol. 12, 135).

The irony was that unlike Freud's patients, who disclosed intimate details of their lives, Plasil could *never* disclose what was on her mind to Leonard, partly because he wanted to hear only that he was the healthiest and most attractive man in the world; partly because of his disbelief in the value of understanding the complexity of the affective world; and partly because of his ideological commitment to Objectivist psychotherapy, which posits the existence of "rationality, reason, and perfect mental health" (63). Plasil remained literally and metaphorically naked, exposed and defenseless before his gaze. Leonard's intrusive videotaping of therapy sessions is an example of Foucauldian surveillance. No wonder, then, that she became secretive about everything.

Plasil did not become aware until late 1972 that sexual relations between a patient and therapist are forbidden. The revelation was a turning point in her life, though it took her years to act on it. She telephoned Blumenthal and asked him whether she should remain in therapy with Leonard. Hinting that he was aware of Leonard's misconduct, Blumenthal maddeningly refused to speak with her as long as she remained Leonard's patient. Instead of terminating therapy immediately, as she would have done with Blumenthal's encouragement, she guiltily informed Leonard about her conversation with his former mentor. "You're scum," Leonard responded with cold fury, deepening her feeling of worthlessness.

Leonard demanded and received complete allegiance from his patients, tolerating no questioning of any kind with respect to their therapy. He had a cult following, and Plasil did everything possible to prove her loyalty to him. One of her fantasies was that he asked her to jump off the Empire State Building: she was willing to do so as an act of trust. "This fantasy did not alarm me. On the contrary, it showed me how far I had progressed in my therapy from the days of questioning his behavior in light of the APA's code of ethics" (102–103).

Seeking Justice

It took Plasil nearly five years to realize that Leonard was exploiting her transference-love for him. Her decision to take him to court alienated her from his other patients, who continued to idealize him and treat him as a cult figure. She had difficulty finding a lawyer who would take her malpractice suit, which dragged on for five years.

The lawsuit charged Leonard with negligence and malpractice from 1972–1977. The charges included inducing Plasil to engage in various forms of sexual relations with him, taking advantage of her weakened psychological condition, violating psychiatric technique, deviating from usual standards of conduct, failing to maintain professional detachment, causing her psychological condition to worsen, and failing to obtain proper and informed consent. Leonard admitted some boundary violations but denied most of the charges, claiming he could not recall the events alleged in other charges against him. Some of his former patients testified on Plasil's behalf, including a woman who was only 14 when Leonard had sex with her.

In a pattern that is common among patients who are sexually abused and want to have their day in court, bringing the accused to justice, Plasil reluctantly agreed to an out-of-court settlement in 1982, receiving $150,000. In a separate lawsuit, another former patient, Patricia Osborne, who was also told to lie naked and spread-eagled on Leonard's office floor while he suddenly penetrated her from behind, accepted a settlement of $100,000. A third case, *Breitbart v. Leonard*, went to a jury in 1982, which awarded the plaintiff $230,000, a figure that was reduced by the judge to $175,000.

Neither Plasil nor Osborne used the word *rape* in their malpractice suits, despite the fact that Leonard had sexual intercourse with them without their consent. Because of the lack of evidence and the fact that there were few statutory laws in the 1970s and '80s that would have applied to their cases, the two women did not bring criminal suits against him. But the legal situation during this time slowly began to change. In "Rape by Fraud and Rape by Coercion," published in *Brooklyn Law Review* in 1998, Patricia J. Falk discusses the cases in which psychiatrists and psychologists were prosecuted for having sex with their patients. In a 1991 New Mexico case, a male psychologist who pursued his male patient to have a sexual relationship with him was prosecuted under a relatively new statute that punished various forms of criminal sexual penetration through the use of force or coercion. Rejecting the prosecution's argument that transference rendered a patient incapable of giving informed consent, the Court suggested that, like Minnesota—which had recently enacted a criminal statute addressing sexual relations between a patient and therapist—New Mexico could also do so, provided the law was constitutional. New Mexico changed its statutes in 1993 by expanding force or coercion to include penetration or contact "by a psychotherapist on his patient, with or without the patient's consent, during the course of psychotherapy or within a period of one year following the termination of psychotherapy" (62).

"Grateful Entrapment"

Plasil's horror story implicates not only her psychiatrist but also Objectivist Psychology, with which Leonard had an ambiguous relationship. At times he seemed to be a faithful follower, while at other times he was a rebel. Plasil's feeling of "grateful entrapment" describes the attitude of many cult members who were obliged to give unquestioning obedience and loyalty to their masters and who were taught that "contradictions do not exist" (157). Because of her fear of abandonment, Plasil could not question or challenge *any* of Leonard's actions; to do so would have resulted in the termination of therapy and "excommunication." Near the end of the story, she notes the disquieting parallels between Leonard, who regarded himself as the "only perfectly healthy man" (51), and the hero of Ayn Rand's *The Fountainhead*, who rapes the novel's heroine in an act she experiences as the "kind of rapture she had wanted" (216). Objectivism was more than a psychology, philosophy, or political movement: it was a way of life. There were, Plasil informs us, right and wrong books to read, right and wrong plays to see, right and wrong people to be with. Her entire social circle consisted of Objectivist friends, many of whom were Leonard's patients. Her world became narrower and narrower. Everyone judged each other by the same prescribed and proscribed values. "It was," she notes wryly, a "perfect breeding ground for insecurity, fear, and paranoia" (45).

We have no way of knowing how many patients had intimate relationships with the sexually voracious Leonard, but Plasil implies at the end of the book that most remained fiercely loyal to him. Leonard announced a day after Plasil terminated therapy that he was taking an "indefinite sabbatical," claiming he needed a long rest to avoid "burning out." His followers, who had a subservient, worshiping relationship with him, viewed him as a martyr who had been persecuted by Plasil.

They were furious with her for filing a lawsuit against him. A Chicago friend, "Robert Berger," also Leonard's patient, responded with "stunned sympathy" to her revelations about the psychiatrist's sexualized therapy sessions, but Berger soon ended his friendship with her, declaring that Leonard was the "finest man" he had ever known and the "best psychiatrist in the world" (157). Other patients treated Plasil as a pariah. One telephone caller accused her of "destroying the closest thing Man has ever had to a god" (158).

Therapist shows how the immersion in a cult—in this case, Objectivism—predisposes one to weird, highly ideological forms of psychotherapy. Plasil's father, her first teacher of philosophy, ethics and morality, was blindly obedient to her mother's unreasonable demands, and as critical as Plasil was of her father, she behaved in the same way toward her psychiatrist. All of Leonard's patients, she implies, gave him unquestioning loyalty. Leonard's response to her questions about his treatment of her was always the same. "You'll understand that when you're healthier" (66), but she never did. The attitude of benevolent skepticism that Freud urged for students of psychoanalysis, and which regrettably he did not always put into practice, had no place in Objectivist psychology. Healthy patients, in Leonard's view, were those who surrendered their identity to him. The psychiatrist always reserved the right to change his mind, a freedom that did not extend to his patients. Much of the value of reading *Therapist*, as Richard E. Vatz and Lee S. Weinberg pointed out in their review in the journal *Psychotherapy*, is that it "educates readers as to how the process of mystification works to mold that [therapeutic] relationship; that is, the reader learns from her incredibly detailed accounting of her thoughts how patients can be persuaded to become unquestioning 'true believers'" (488).

Psychology, no less than philosophy, has been riddled with cult-like leaders and followers. In *The Sullivan Institute/Fourth Wall Community:*

The Relationship of Radical Individualism and Authoritarianism (2003), Amy B. Siskind chronicles the therapy-cult totalitarianism, emerging in the late 1950s, that characterized the more extreme followers of the American psychiatrist Harry Stack Sullivan (1892–1949). These followers, known as the Sullivanians, started as a breakaway group from the William Alanson White Psychoanalytic Institute and drew their inspiration from Sullivan and Erich Fromm, both of whom emphasized social and cultural factors in the development of neurosis. Members were encouraged to engage in sexual relations with as many of the other members as possible (Lewin). The ideology of the radical left-wing Sullivanian movement, which Jane Pearce and Saul Newton articulated in their 1963 manifesto *The Conditions of Human Growth*, was different from the radical right-wing Randian Objectivists. Both movements, nevertheless, demanded unquestioning obedience from their followers, over whom the leaders/therapists wielded enormous institutional and person power. Another example of cult-like ventures into "treatment" of mental disorders will be found in volume 2 of *Off the Tracks*, describing the fatal relationship between the Church of Scientology and Lisa McPherson, a church member.

Two Lifelines

Apart from her marriage to Tony's brother, Greg—another former patient of Leonard and the man who helped her begin her new life—Plasil had two lifelines: filing a lawsuit and writing *Therapist*. The lifelines were interconnected: the lawsuit helped channel her rage away from herself, where it had eroded her self-esteem and will to live, and onto the man who had exploited her for half a decade, while writing *Therapist* helped channel Plasil's dark emotions onto

107

paper, where she was able to understand what her life had become in therapy. Both *Plasil v. Leonard* and *Therapist* called attention to Leonard's crimes and succeeded in ending his career as a psychiatrist. Both the lawsuit and the book affirmed Plasil's agency, her ability to see herself not as a victim but as a survivor. Both allowed her to describe what had been indescribable. She writes with a testimonial fervor that is characteristic of authors of sexual abuse narratives. Nearly all her reasons for initiating a lawsuit against Leonard were the same reasons for penning her memoir. Writing became a strategy of resistance, a form of self-rescue. "To maintain the silence he had exacted from me for so many years meant that he still controlled me. To speak out in naming what he did and what he was, had less to do with the consequences that I hoped would befall Dr. Leonard than it had to do with reasserting the strength of my spirit, which I needed to believe had not been irreparably crippled" (201).

Plasil is never sure whether Leonard's actions were lunacy, evil, or both, but in writing the book, she documents his psychiatric practice—or malpractice. Writing the story, she admits, compelled her to relive the trauma. "It forced me back to times and places I would have preferred to avoid, but such travels back were necessary to find the answer to the question that had haunted me from the time of the trial's conclusion: How did it all happen? For until I understood that, I could never be certain that it would not happen again" (223). Writing the story was painful, but *not* writing it would have been more painful. As we shall see with some of the other stories in our book, the urge to write about psychiatric lunacy or evil became a lifeline for other former patients as well. Janet W. Wohlberg, herself a victim of sexual abuse by her psychotherapist, speaks from personal experience when she remarks on the therapeutic value of writing about sexual trauma. "Writing an extensive account of what took place often helps the victim gain necessary insight. While this is painful, victims who have been required to undertake such a writing process, usually in conjunction with pursuing a legal claim or proceeding before a board of registration, almost always cite it as an important step in healing" (338).

As a result of the lawsuits brought against him, Lonnie Franklin Leonard voluntarily surrendered his medical license in New York State, thereby avoiding an investigation and hearing. He now lives in Arizona, where he practices occupational medicine. Ellen Plasil is a lawyer in Connecticut specializing in divorce mediation.

II

ZANE PARZEN AND EVELYN WALKER

Zane Parzen was not the first psychoanalyst who was censured for unethical behavior by the American Psychoanalytic Association and regarded as an impaired physician, but he had the dubious distinction of being the first American analyst to have a formal ethics hearing and then be expelled from that organization. Evelyn Walker's medical malpractice suit against him resulted in a 1981 settlement of $4,631,666, which was up to that time the largest amount ever awarded against an American psychiatrist and the second-largest medical malpractice settlement of any kind up to that time. *A Killing Cure*, the story of Parzen's brutal mistreatment of Walker, describes in stunning detail the analyst's sexual exploitation of her and, perhaps even more disturbing, his chilling lack of guilt, remorse, or regret over his actions. Most of the book was written by the co-author, Perry Deane Young, an investigative journalist. *A Killing Cure* also shows how Parzen's colleagues analyze his startling misbehavior, giving us insight into his psychopathology.

109

Lucy Freeman characterizes *A Killing Cure* as a "new kind of savage killing—and soul murder." The description, which appears on the book jacket, is apt. Both a horror story and a double psychiatric case study of patient and analyst alike, *A Killing Cure* is based on official public documents, including court transcripts, psychiatric evaluations and the letters Walker wrote to Parzen, all of which Young quotes extensively. We read and juxtapose multiple and often clashing points of view: Evelyn Walker's poignant account; Parzen's rationalizations, as reflected in his therapy notes and court statements; and the reflections of Parzen's colleagues, who do not always agree in their interpretation of his behavior. Young interviewed as many of the characters in the book as possible. These interviews give us a wealth of information about the analyst, more information than we glean from other accounts of therapists having sex with their patients.

Most of *A Killing Cure* is narrated in third person, Young's authorial voice; but an essential part of the story is narrated in Walker's first person. We thus receive a largely objective third person account, written by an author who has meticulously researched the case, and a subjective first person account that evokes the trauma of a patient who was, by nearly all accounts, severely injured by her psychiatrist, a trauma that continues to the story's end.

Unlike Lonnie Franklin Leonard, about whom we know little, we learn much about Zane Parzen's life and character as a result of Young's investigative efforts and the court-ordered psychiatric evaluations Parzen was required to undergo. He was born in South Bend, Indiana in 1933 to Russian-born Jewish parents. His father died just before his eighth birthday, and the boy was raised by his mother and stepfather. Parzen went to Harvard and then transferred after a year to Indiana University, misleadingly implying that he was a Harvard graduate. He went to the University of Chicago Medical School and completed his psychoanalytic training at the Chicago Psychoanalytic Institute in 1971. The following year, he and his family moved to San Diego, where he became associated with the San Diego Psychoanalytic Institute. Less than a year after he and his family moved to California, his 15-year-old son died in a car accident. Parzen later indicated that the tragedy was the beginning of a downward spiral in his life, though Young suggests that the analyst's life was troubled for years before his son's death.

Parzen appeared to be a dedicated clinician, teacher, scholar, husband and father, a good analyst for someone with Evelyn Walker's history of headaches and depression. When she asked her neighbors Bettie Shepherd, a psychiatric nurse, and her husband, Gary, a psychoanalyst affiliated with the San Diego Psychoanalytic Institute, to recommend a therapist, the latter gave her a list of three names, one of which was Parzen's. Walker began seeing Zane Parzen in September 1974, when she was 34. "Treatment" lasted until January 1977.

"Gaslighting"

Parzen was attracted to the tall, slender Walker and, almost from the beginning of therapy, he tried to estrange her from her husband, Bruce, an engineer and computer consultant to whom she had been married for several years. Parzen's therapeutic strategy seemed to be based on the film *Gaslight*, the classic 1944 mystery-thriller (based on a 1938 play of the same name), directed by George Cukor, in which an evil husband, played by Charles Boyer, attempts to isolate his young, beautiful and psychologically fragile wife, played by Ingrid Bergman, and drive her insane. She is saved only through the intervention of a brilliant police inspector, played by Joseph Cotton, who discovers that her husband has been trying to ransack her house to find the jewels he had hidden years earlier when he murdered his wife's aunt.

In a strange example of therapy imitating life, Parzen's clinical notes indicate his belief that Evelyn Walker's husband was trying to destroy her, as the psychiatrist observed in his evaluation of her written on November 26, 1976: "When I expressed my concern about her husband's anger, and his tendency to act out towards her and to 'gaslight' her, she responded that she felt that that was not her problem, but only her fear that I would desert her" (114). There are multiple ironies here. Not only did Walker understandably reject the idea that her husband was trying to gaslight her, but it was her therapist who manipulated her through mind control for his own selfish reasons. Telling her she was not crazy made her wonder whether she was crazy, a possibility she had never considered. Similarly, suggesting to her that it was not uncommon for a patient to divorce while in therapy planted in her an idea that had never existed. Bruce Walker was not a perfect husband, as she thought when she entered treatment, but there was no history of marital strife before she entered therapy. In his clinical notes, Parzen recommended "martial therapy" for the couple, a Freudian slip that might reveal his hostility toward their marriage. In creating fears in Evelyn Walker that had never existed, Parzen ignored her greatest terror throughout therapy: the belief that her psychiatrist would desert her, a fear that prophetically came true.

Parzen succeeded in convincing both his patient and himself that her husband was trying to drive her mad. "In a matter of months, Gary Walker—in Parzen's notes—progressed from being merely a cold, unresponsive husband to being an impotent psychotic who was out to kill his wife" (99). Parzen was so certain about this that he began to use dialogue from *Gaslight* in his therapy sessions with Evelyn Walker. Like Boyer's maddening responses to his fraught wife, Parzen would respond to Walker's questions with a "similar brand of double-talk," or he would answer questions with questions. Parzen's rage toward Walker paralleled the fictional husband's rage toward his wife. Boyer's statement to Bergman, "Do you want me to get angry with you?", is the exact statement Parzen expressed to Walker in a therapy session. Young's conclusion about Parzen's use of *Gaslight* is psychologically acute. "On one level, Parzen seems to have been aware of the fact that he was to blame for Evelyn's disintegration, but, on another level, he could not cope with that fact. He had to blame somebody, so he blamed Bruce Walker. Word for word, line for line, he was accusing Bruce of doing to Evelyn what he, Parzen, was doing to her" (100).

Evelyn Walker came to realize relatively early in therapy that her psychiatrist was controlling every aspect of her life, but she was helpless to do anything about it. Indeed, she seemed to welcome his increasing influence over her life, which led her to believe he was her rescuer and savior. "I remember thinking that Zane had become like a puppeteer, with me as his puppet. I didn't see this as anything evil or sinister. He held all the strings; he had total control of my life—and I was so removed from reality that I liked it" (63).

Parzen succeeded in breaking up Evelyn Walker's marriage and becoming her lover. Their sexual relationship began with casual hugs and caresses and progressed to more intimate fondling and petting on the analyst's couch and finally, after two-and-a-half years, to sexual intercourse. He assured her that she was "special," that he knew and cared for her better than anyone else, that he loved her deeply, that her husband and two adolescent sons did not appreciate her, and that he would always be there for her. But the more she demanded concrete assurances that he was serious about forming a permanent romantic relationship, the more evasive he became.

At the same that time he was having sex with his patient, Parzen was also heavily medicating her, creating a drug dependency that had not previously existed. Nearly all the medical experts who were consulted agreed that this pharmacotherapy, quite apart from Parzen's sexual relationship with her, was evidence of malpractice. As therapist and patient became more and more emotionally and sexually involved, Walker requested more medication, and Parzen always obliged. "The prescriptions overlapped," she admits, "and then he would just tell me to help myself to all those he had in a cabinet in his office. I took the pills because Zane told me to, and then I simply needed them in order to get through the day" (40). Soon she was taking from 40–60 pills a day, many of which were powerful and potentially lethal. They included Emperin for headaches (an earlier version of what is now called "Excedrin") but ultimately went on to involve more potent medications given in ever-increasing doses: Seconal, Valium, Noludar, Elavil, Talwin and Placidyl. After Walker attempted suicide by overdose, Parzen would increase the medication that almost killed her. Astonishingly—upon realizing that she had gradually sunk into a drugged stupor—he ordered her to stop taking *all* the medication at once, instead of gradually weaning her from it, an act that produced a life-threatening withdrawal.

"Svengali-like"

Parzen's growing power over Evelyn Walker transformed her into a drugged zombie and produced a master/slave relationship, a result of what Walker's lawyer Marvin Lewis called the psychiatrist's "Svengali-like hold" over her (303). Just as Svengali used hypnosis to exert evil power over Trilby, resulting in a split personality, so did the puppet master-psychiatrist Parzen cast his spell over Walker by manipulating her transference-love for him. He promised never to abandon her, a vow he quickly broke. The parallels between Parzen and Svengali extend beyond mind control; du Maurier's character laughs and smiles at the wrong time and in the wrong place, suggestive of emotions gone awry. Similar malicious facial expressions also bedevil Parzen.

"Go Kill Yourself Then"

Evelyn Walker attempted suicide several times under Parzen's care. Apart from an incident when she impulsively swallowed several pills at the age of eight, she had no prior history of suicidal behavior before beginning treatment with him. Her first suicide attempt during the treatment occurred after having sex with Parzen in May 1975, when she became angry that he ignored her feelings. She went home, swallowed 50 Valium pills as well as other medication she had been hoarding, and woke up in the Scripps Hospital emergency room. Parzen was incensed with her. "What I probably needed," he later told her, was a "good screwing" (44).

Her second attempt occurred on February 2, 1976, when, again after having sex with Parzen in his office, she brought up the vexed subject of marriage. He became livid with anger. She went home and drank a pint of a poisonous substance. Visiting her in the hospital, Parzen was hardly comforting. "'Why should I waste my time over you?' he snarled at me. My worst fears were coming true." After threatening to "throw" her out of therapy, he made her feel even more of a failure. "You don't even know how to kill yourself—you used the wrong kind of poison" (93). Another time, when she told him that she would have no reason to live if he refused to leave his wife, he shoved her away and screamed tauntingly, "Go kill yourself then" (111).

Like the fictional wife in *Gaslight*, Evelyn Walker reached the point where she almost lost her mind. Her growing dependence on drugs; dissolution of her marriage; separation from her children, who lived with their father; loss of her job and assets; and permanent estrangement from her parents and siblings left her feeling lonely, isolated, abandoned and worthless.

A Timely Intervention: The Beginning of Help

Walker had often spoken about her involvement with Parzen to Gary Shepherd, Parzen's colleague. He accepted at first Parzen's statements that she was delusional, imagining a romantic affair that did not exist, but gradually Shepherd began to believe her. On December 30, 1976, Shepherd met with Sanford Izner, a founder and director of the San Diego Psychoanalytic Institute. Izner recommended that Parzen transfer Walker to another therapist. Parzen was furious with Walker during their last therapy session, not because he wouldn't see her anymore, but because she had revealed the truth of their relationship to his colleagues, thus damaging his reputation. Shepherd was sitting in his office when he overheard Walker's distraught words to Parzen, from Parzen's adjoining office, during their final therapy session. "Please don't do this to me. I love you. You can't let it end like this. You can't do this to me. Please don't. For God's sake, don't do this" (123).

Evelyn Walker suffered a breakdown after she was transferred to another psychiatrist, David Olenik, resulting in her being hospitalized for two weeks in January 1977. Parzen never acknowledged wrongdoing in his semifictional, self-serving therapy notes, which provide less insight into the patient's illness than into the psychiatrist's duplicity. Parzen told Olenik that Walker's erotic feelings for him were part of her "psychotic-like transference" (140), a term he would later use in an attempt to undercut the reality of her allegations. In the beginning, Olenik believed Parzen's version of reality, but he later realized that Walker's account was closer to the truth. Walker continued writing desperate love letters to her former psychiatrist after she was released from the hospital, expressing the hope that they would resume their relationship, which they never did. She became involved with another man whom she impulsively married; the marriage was disastrous and ended in divorce. She had a brief affair with her family physician but remained obsessed with Parzen.

"Pat Stern"

Evelyn Walker's belief that Parzen regarded her as "special" came to an abrupt end when she discovered he had another special patient with whom he was also conducting an affair, one that predated their own. Referred to as "Pat Stern," she had been Parzen's patient in Chicago and she followed him to San Diego, where she continued to see him. Walker had once heard Stern crying in Parzen's office and had glimpsed the tall, blonde woman running down the hall. There were striking physical similarities between the two women and their psychiatric situations: they looked alike—tall and thin. Both suffered from depression and anorexia (Stern was described as looking like a "concentration camp victim"). Each had threatened or attempted suicide multiple times, was taking toxic drugs without adequate medical supervision, and was similarly infatuated with and dependent on the psychiatrist.

In some ways, Pat Stern's story was more shocking than Evelyn Walker's. Stern became pregnant with Parzen's child and through his efforts, had an abortion. One infers from Stern's statements to friends that Parzen was a master not only of manipulation and mind control but also of rationalization. He once became so angry with Stern that he threw her against a wall, explaining that this was part of a therapeutic strategy advocated by the renowned psychoanalyst Bruno Bettelheim. Parzen took photographs of the naked Stern, stating he wanted her to see how emaciated she was. He also claimed that he was having sex with her to help her overcome her fear of men. Stern was in treatment with Parzen for five days a week and sometimes saw him more than once a day. She began working for a psychiatrist, Alvin Robbins, who was Parzen's student at the San Diego Psychoanalytic Institute. Horrified to learn that Stern was having a sexual affair with Parzen, Robbins, the chair (and only member) of the Impaired Physicians Committee of the San Diego Psychiatric Society, initiated the process of bringing ethical charges against Parzen.

Exploitation of Transference-Love

We see parallels not only between Parzen's two female patients, both of whom he exploited in identical ways over a period of several years, but also between Parzen and Lonnie Franklin Leonard. Both psychiatrists had sex with more than one patient and cynically exploited their transference-love. Both undermined their patients' self-esteem and efforts toward psychological health. Both encouraged their patients' abject dependency on them. Robbins used the word "fusion" to describe Stern's (and Walker's) relationship with Parzen: "an excessively intense attachment between people [that makes it] very difficult to perceive one from the other at that point" (174). Both psychiatrists were in some ways sicker than their patients. Both denied or minimized wrongdoing when they were brought up for malpractice. And both psychiatrists might have won the lawsuits against them were it not for the fact that other patients came forward with similar stories of exploitation.

There are also similarities between Evelyn Walker and Ellen Plasil. Both experienced unhappy childhoods and were narcissistically injured by rejecting mothers. Both were well aware that a psychotherapist's sexual relationship with a patient was inappropriate and wrong, but their fear of abandonment, along with their trust in their therapists' integrity, compelled them to gratify the therapists' sexual needs, often at the expense of their own pleasure. Both placed all of their hope in their psychiatrists, believing that they had their patients' best interests at heart. Both women felt hurt, angered, and betrayed when they discovered their therapists were having sex with other patients. And both women were victims of their psychiatrists' civil if not criminal actions.

The second half of *A Killing Cure* focuses on the ethical charges brought against Parzen, his limited admission that he had sex with Walker but not "voluntarily"; the various explanations and interpretations of his actions; and the two-part malpractice suit against him, the first to determine whether the lawsuit was brought within California's one-year statute of limitations for malpractice (it was), the second to determine whether he was guilty of the charges. Pat Stern refused to testify against Parzen, like some of Lonnie Franklin Leonard's patients who defended his behavior against overwhelming evidence pointing to civil if not criminal culpability. Stern was so enraged by the proceedings against Parzen that she made death threats against those participating in the trial; Evelyn Walker's lawyer told the judge that he feared Stern would storm into the courtroom shooting.

Analyzing the Analyst

The California licensing agency, the Board of Medical Quality Assurance, gave Parzen a choice near the end of 1979: either agree to relinquish his license for one year, with a ten-year probation, and undergo an administrative psychiatric evaluation, or face a hearing that could result in a permanent loss of his medical license. He bitterly chose the former, believing it was the lesser of two evils. The first evaluation was written by his friend and San Diego Psychoanalytic Institute colleague James Thickstun. After treating Parzen for a year, Thickstun observed in his October 1980 report that the most significant woman in Parzen's life, his mother, was "seen as a powerful, pre-Oedipal, phallic, controlling, needy, self-centered, spider woman." Thickstun maintained that Parzen's pathology focused on meeting his mother's needs and denying his own. Parzen's father's early death heightened the "tremendous burden of fear, grief, anger, guilt, helplessness" that he experienced as a child, contributing to the depression that characterized much of his life (78–79).

"Seeking Out the Woman in Himself"

Parzen's research and teaching interests focused on the treatment of male-to-female transgender individuals who, Young states, represented many patients in his clinical practice. "More than one of Parzen's psychiatric colleagues has suggested that he was drawn to these studies for personal rather than purely scientific motivations" (84). There is nothing unusual about personal motivation underlying scientific and artistic research: counterphobic motivation is a catalyst behind many forms of creativity. Indeed, it's doubtful whether "purely scientific motivations" exist. Nevertheless, it may be significant that Parzen often played the "traditional feminine role" when he and Evelyn Walker had sex. Young also cites the comment made by a psychiatrist who treated another female patient sexually abused by Parzen: "I can't discuss it because that is confidential and privileged, but I can tell you this: you cannot go too far in saying he was taking on the female role in his relations with these women" (84). Young takes this to mean that Parzen was "seeking out the woman in himself, or the woman he might have been—tall, needy, whiny—and, as his actions proved, that woman was someone he despised" (84).

There's too little biographical information to reach any definitive conclusions about Parzen's sexual identity, but we can raise questions about the motivation behind therapists who sexually exploit vulnerable patients. Most if not all psychotherapists realize that having sex with their patients is unethical, unprofessional and usually illegal. Is there, then, an element of unconscious misogyny behind a male therapist's transgressive sex with a female patient, especially since such actions almost always result in the end of therapy and the victimization of the patient? Do male therapists who sexually act out with their patients need to prove their masculinity and sexual prowess? Phyllis Chesler suggests in *Women and Madness* that male therapists, like male artists, "are seen, or fear themselves, as more 'feminine' than others in our society." If so, she muses, perhaps "it is more important to them to be able to 'have' as many women as their presumably more 'masculine' counterparts do" (141). Chesler makes this observation about James L. McCartney, who limits "overt transference" to heterosexual transference, but her comment may apply to other therapists, like Parzen, who sexually exploited vulnerable women only to abandon them.

Gabbard and Lester do not discuss Zane Parzen in *Boundaries and Boundary Violations in Psychoanalysis*, but they would probably consider him to fall into at least two of their categories of therapists who have sex with their patients: predatory psychopathology and masochistic surrender. There is also some evidence that his behavior was psychotic. Although he was not an example of a therapist who had risen to the top of his profession, he appears to have been highly narcissistic: "His grandiosity is fueled, and he begins to rationalize his boundaryless behavior as acceptable simply because of who he is. Ordinary standards of ethics do not apply to him" (Gabbard and Lester, 94).

121

Parzen admitted that he had problems with "grandiosity" (182), though he never elaborated on what he meant by the word. Thickstun found, not surprisingly, that Parzen was "depressed and distraught." Thickstun observed that "there are certain kinds of patients whose needs and psychopathology resonate with Dr. Parzen in such a way that difficulties may ensue" (208). He concluded, however, that Parzen should be allowed to practice psychoanalysis, a recommendation that failed to sway the members of the ethics committee, who urged the San Diego Psychoanalytic Society to dismiss him both as a teacher and a member.

Four other psychiatric evaluations, taken between December 1978 and September 1979, signify more serious psychopathology than Thickstun implied. Parzen's responses to these diagnostic tests are "quite damning," Young reports, a classic case in which the physician is sicker than his patients. Young quotes Parzen's true-false answers to the following questions:

Someone has it in for me. (True.)
I have no enemies who really wish to harm me. (False.)
There is something wrong with my mind. (True.)
Sometimes I feel as if I must injure myself or someone else. (True.)
I believe I am a condemned person. (True.)
Most of the time I wish I were dead. (True.)
Most times I think I am no good at all. (True.) (225)

One of the most significant findings of these tests is how negatively Parzen viewed his parents and childhood. "He describes his home life as unpleasant, with parents who were critical of him and unreasonable in their demands. His family was characterized by quarrels, isolation, and a lack of love" (225). The last report was the most negative of all, indicating that he is "an angry, suspicious person who has difficulty with impulse control";

is "evasive and defensive about acknowledging psychological problems"; "utilizes rationalization as a defense mechanism"; "and resents authority and is likely to be argumentative and irritable in social relations, especially with the opposite sex." One sentence is especially disturbing: "Although the patient may appear sociopathic, the possibility of a psychotic or pre-psychotic condition should be considered." The last report suggests that psychiatric patients with this pattern "are likely to show little response to psychotherapy, and the prognosis is poor" (226). Curiously, other parts of the same test, Young declares, reveal a more defiant Parzen, a "false image of himself" that helped him in his everyday life but was at the same time responsible for many of his problems.

His Own Most Damaging Witness

Parzen was at first conciliatory during the beginning of the proceedings against him, hoping for a dismissal of the charges, but he grew increasingly belligerent and confrontational, threatening to sue his colleagues who testified against him. One of his most striking oddities was his Svengali-like facial expressions during the ethics hearings and the two malpractice trials. These grotesque expressions mystified everyone present, though there was agreement that the gestures were inappropriate and disturbing, particularly coming from a psychoanalyst. "He would grin or appear to laugh at a most solemn accusation." The facial grimaces were so bizarre that the chair of the ethics committee had to stop a meeting to caution him that these expressions were distressing to Evelyn Walker, who was testifying.

Did Parzen have conscious control over these facial expressions, or were they nervous tics triggered by stress? What was the psychological significance of this unsettling behavior? Was it symptomatic of hostility, conscious or not? Young never raises these questions, but he points out that Parzen was his own most damaging witness during the ethics hearings and malpractice trials. "Everybody would remember that during the most sordid and horrifying testimony about his actions, he would respond by grinning, smiling, or making some other inappropriate gesture" (219). Parzen's lawyer, Mike Nell, tried unsuccessfully to tell him not to smile while testifying. "He would get up there on the witness stand and be describing the most horrendous thing in detail and he would smile. The jury, I'm sure, assumed he was enjoying it. It was a leering, lecherous type of look—which was not the way he felt" (240). Nell tried to portray his client in the most sympathetic way, but it's possible that the leering smile *was* an indication of how he felt.

Pathological Narcissism

Young remarks that Parzen's facial expressions and odd behavior were also characteristic of Jeffrey MacDonald, the Green Beret officer and physician who was convicted after a long and controversial trial of murdering his wife and two young daughters. In *Fatal Vision* (1983), Joe McGinniss characterizes MacDonald as suffering from "pathological narcissism," the diagnosis popularized by Otto Kernberg in his influential 1975 book *Borderline Conditions and Pathological Narcissism*. Young argues that Parzen also fits the description of a pathological narcissist, a person who functions well on the surface, is often highly successful, but whose main characteristics are, in Kernberg's words, "grandiosity, extreme self-centeredness, and a remarkable absence of interest and empathy for others in spite of the fact that they are so very eager to obtain admiration and approval. . . . It is as if they feel they have the right to control and possess others and to exploit them without guilt feelings, and, behind a surface which very often is charming and engaging, one senses coldness and ruthlessness. These patients not only lack emotional depth, but fail to understand complex emotion in other people" (220).

Young devotes only a paragraph to this suggestive diagnosis, but he might have quoted other sentences from Kernberg's book that appear to apply to Parzen's life. "These patients present an unusual degree of self-reference in their interactions with other people, a great need to be loved and admired by others, and a curious apparent contradiction between a very inflated concept of themselves and an inordinate need for tribute from others" (Kernberg, 227). One of the characteristics of pathological narcissism is that idealization of others turns into virulent devaluation, a pattern that seems to describe Parzen's attitude toward Evelyn Walker, to whom he professed love and loyalty one moment followed by hostility and rejection the next moment. The narcissist's haughtiness and grandiosity are defenses against paranoid traits related to the projection of inner rage, which Kernberg argues is central to the narcissist's pathology. A major problem of the narcissist, most psychoanalysts believe, is the inability to tolerate aggression. Parzen's gaslighting of Evelyn Walker, making her husband into a sinister alter ego or doppelganger, may be viewed as an example of projective identification, the process in which a person projects aggressive impulses onto another, with whom he or she then unconsciously identifies.

Kernberg believes that pathological narcissism arises in early childhood as a result of a chronically cold, self-absorbed parent who fails to give the child sufficient love. Kernberg's composite portrait of a narcissist's family background is a parent, usually the mother, who is characterized by callousness, indifference, or spiteful aggression—a description strikingly similar to Thickstun's image of Parzen's "spider woman" mother.

Ever since Freud's 1914 essay "On Narcissism: An Introduction," psychoanalytic and non-psychoanalytic writers alike have been fascinated by the vast implications of the subject, including pathological narcissism, as formulated by Kernberg, and healthy narcissism, as propounded by the other leading theorist, Heinz Kohut. Kernberg's theory continues to intrigue writers, as Elizabeth Lunbeck demonstrates in *The Americanization of Narcissism* (2014). "Kernberg's clinical writing chronicles the deformations of human relatedness, presenting readers with an astonishing range of ways we as humans have devised to mistreat, exploit, and destroy one another— and ourselves" (60). Nearly everything Lunbeck mentions about narcissists in general applies to Parzen in particular, including the trail of damaged and exploited female patients he left in his psychiatric wake.

In his testimony during the malpractice trial, Parzen denied that he had told Evelyn Walker to kill herself, insisting that none of her suicide attempts was "serious." But he admitted under questioning that three of his female patients in Chicago had committed suicide. He further admitted, again under tough questioning, that another female patient in Chicago had attempted suicide and that a California patient had killed herself after she was no longer under his care. Although the revelation about the unusually high number of his former patients who attempted or committed suicide was ruled inadmissible evidence in the lawsuit brought by Evelyn Walker, who herself had attempted suicide and come close to death while under Parzen's care, the information is sufficient to justify Young's otherwise sensationalistic characterization of the psychiatrist's notion of therapy as a killing cure.

Further Revelations—and Rationalizations

There were further revelations about Parzen, including the discovery of three other patients with whom he was having sex, one of whom was the wife of a fellow psychiatrist. This information did not come to light until years after the ethics hearings. "Possibly the full story of Parzen's involvement with his patients," Young observes, "will never fully be known" (208).

Parzen insisted repeatedly during the psychoanalytic institute's ethics hearing, the medical society's ethics hearing, and the malpractice trial that Evelyn Walker initiated sex every time it occurred. He also insisted that he had no choice but to acquiesce, implying absurdly that he was almost raped by her. According to Young, Parzen "swore that he had strongly resisted Evelyn's 'advances' from the beginning, first by saying, 'That's not what we're here for'" (108). Young does not accept this explanation, nor can we. But Parzen's next statement has the ring of truth. In his own words, his "problem manifested itself when I was seeing a particular type of female patient who was depressed, needy, whiny, who felt she needed to be given in to in order to feel decent. I could not say 'no' to her whether that was in terms of sex, drugs. I didn't set the limits" (108). Whether Parzen was motivated by a rescue fantasy, the belief that he could save a woman from depression only by having sex with her, or by his own grandiosity—both motives are interrelated—he seemed to believe, on one level, in a love, or rather, sex cure. But on another level, he was hurting these women, projecting his hostility onto them. Parzen apparently never worked through in his own personal analysis his profound ambivalence toward women, part of his self-destructive countertransference.

Evelyn Walker continued to believe that Parzen would rescue her years after she left therapy with him. Her despair over leaving Parzen—he literally shoved her out of his office—complicated her relationships with her next two therapists, David Olenik and his successor, Sydney Smith, who had been chief psychologist at the Menninger Foundation and editor of the well regarded *Bulletin of the Menninger Clinic* from 1964 until 1978, when he moved to San Diego. Smith kept detailed notes of "Mr. E.W." but regretted having done so when the therapy notes were subpoenaed as evidence for Walker's malpractice trial. The U.S. Supreme Court ruled in the landmark *Jaffee v. Redmond* decision in

1996 that psychotherapy notes are privileged information in the federal courts, but this was more than 15 years in the future.

While treating Evelyn Walker, Smith gave a talk at the American Psychological Association in August 1982 and, in the words of Bryce Nelson, whose article "Efforts Widen to Curb Sexual Abuse in Therapy" appeared in the *New York Times* on November 23, 1982, "denounced as sadistic therapists who have sex with patients." Bryce doesn't mention the Walker case, but he does refer to the malpractice suit against Lonnie Franklin Leonard. It's not clear whether Smith is the unnamed psychologist who refers in the *Times* article to "Don Juan therapists," but it is clear that both Parzen and Leonard fall into this category.

Smith's clinical notes in *A Killing Cure* reveal that Walker continued to be obsessed with Parzen. At times he was merged in her unconscious with a beloved uncle who had died years earlier; at other times she believed that Parzen would murder her, a fear that may have been connected with death threats she had actually received, some of which she thought came from him. Smith believed that Walker was deeply disturbed when she entered therapy with Parzen but that she could have been helped by a competent therapist.

Sydney Smith later wrote about the Walker–Parzen case in "The Sexually Abused Patient and the Abusing Therapist: A Study in Sadomasochistic Relationships," published in *Psychoanalytic Psychology* in 1984, two years before the appearance of *A Killing Cure*. Because the lawsuit was a matter of public record, Smith makes little effort to disguise the case apart from omitting the names of the abusive therapist and the sexually abused patient. He describes Parzen as a man who "mesmerized" his female patients and sadistically took advantage of them, behavior that was in stark contrast to his professional conduct outside his office, where he was "circumspect, knowledgeable, an effective teacher, and a man of impeccable credentials—in short, the perfect Dr. Jekyll" (90). Smith's most intriguing conjecture about sexually abused patients is that many engage in a splitting of the image of the therapist: the "supportive, 'loving,' aspects of the therapist are idealized, while the frightening sexual contact is psychologically isolated from the relationship. This process may involve a form of dissociation on the part of the sexually abused patient in which she presents herself as inadequate and damaged" (95).

The jury agreed with Smith and Walker's lawyers and awarded her a settlement of over $4.5 million. The award was cut in half and the amount she actually received was $1.25 million, a figure experts believed might not be enough to cover her future mental health expenses. The story of *Walker v. Parzen* ended with an ironic twist. Bruce Walker and Zane Parzen, long adversaries, each gave up his own career to enter the other's profession: Walker became a clinical psychologist, and Parzen became a computer consultant. The three remaining malpractice suits against Parzen were all settled out of court by his insurance company. Evelyn Walker's lawyer, who deposed Parzen for one of these cases, stated that he continued to grin and smile repeatedly when a former patient testified about his hideous treatment of her. By the end of the story, Walker was no longer the suicidal, out-of-control patient she was when she first began treatment with Sydney Smith, but she was still in therapy with him when the book was published. *A Killing Cure* concludes with Smith's guarded statement: "while she is much improved, she is not well and she never will be" (338).

III
DR. X AND CAROLYN M. BATES

An element of mystery surrounds the identity of "Dr. X" in *Sex in the Therapy Hour*, if only because the authors Carolyn M. Bates and

Annette M. Brodsky use a pseudonym throughout the book. Unlike *Therapist* and *A Killing Cure*, we never learn the name of the rogue therapist nor much about his background or training, though we learn the most intimate details of his patient's life. Nor do we learn the name of the state in which Dr. X practiced. The reasons for the pseudonym soon become apparent. "Our decision to refrain from identifying him was made only after great consideration. We have supplied him with the alias of Dr. X, because he could be any one of a number of people in any one of a number of places" (2). Another reason for using a pseudonym, we suspect, is that Dr. X repeatedly threatened lawsuits against those who took legal action against him. Bates and Brodsky do not use the word *evil* to describe him, but his maliciousness and vindictiveness are soon apparent. Even his own lawyers were forced to sue him for nonpayment of their fees. Bates and Brodsky never speculate on Dr. X's reasons for inducing his female patients to have sex with him and then discounting the destructive effect of his actions on their mental and physical health, but the authors present enough information to allow readers to reach their own conclusions about the psychologist's character.

Published in 1989, *Sex in the Therapy Hour* is noteworthy for several reasons. As Gary Richard Schoener remarks in the foreword, *Sex in the Therapy Hour* is the "first book to be coauthored by an expert in the field of psychology and a client who has been victimized by an unethical therapist" (xi). The first half of the book is written by Bates, who entered therapy in 1975 at the age of 20 and was sexually abused by Dr. X until she ended treatment 20 months later. The second half is written by Brodsky, a clinical psychologist who was chosen as an expert witness by Bates' lawyers, Suzanne Brown and Bill Whitehurst, to evaluate the ways in which the patient was harmed by Dr. X's treatment.

Most co-authored stories of a therapist's sexual abuse are written by a professional author who puts into words the patient's experiences. Writing is difficult for most people, patients and non-patients alike, and from all indications almost impossible for those who have been severely traumatized in therapy. Perry Deane Young recalls in the preface of *A Killing Cure* his amazement when, trying to push Evelyn Walker to relive in painful detail the horrors of her experience with Zane Parzen, she began to remember events she thought she had forgotten. "In one terrifying experience of what Freud had labeled 'transference,' I became in Evelyn's mind the psychiatrist whom she still loved with such confused intensity. She was crying to me as she had to him. 'Don't you see?' she asked. 'I had nobody else—no place to go but back to him. He had become my whole life'" (vii).

Unlike *Betrayal* and *A Killing Cure*, both of which were co-written by professional authors who were not psychotherapists, *Sex in the Therapy Hour* is genuinely collaborative, with two authors closely attuned to each other's point of view. Bates evokes her pre- and post-therapy selves; her portrait of Dr. X seems credible. Brodsky writes authoritatively about female patients who have been sexually abused by their therapists, and her insights into sexual boundary violations have withstood the test of time. We do not see in *Sex in the Therapy Hour*—as we do in *A Killing Cure*—confidential psychoanalytic evaluations of an analyst's misconduct, but we do see the first published detailed discussion of the psychological profile of a sexually abusive psychotherapist. We also see the therapist's rationalizations to justify cruelly exploitative behavior. *Sex in the Therapy Hour* is noteworthy as well for its painstaking account of the efforts undertaken to delicense Dr. X. Complaints of ethics violations against him were the first of their kind received by the state licensing board for psychologists.

131

The youngest of five children, Carolyn Bates was born in 1955 and grew up in a small town on the U.S.–Mexico border. Her parents were loving but strict and authoritarian. Her father was a lay preacher in a fundamentalist church, and she often felt humiliated when her parents meted out swift punishment for her angry outbursts. She learned at an early age to be obedient and not to question authority. The family moved to a college town in 1964 so that Carolyn's father could complete his undergraduate education and begin graduate school. His death from Lou Gehrig's disease in 1971 at age 59 was devastating to her, precipitating a depression that led her into psychotherapy with Dr. X four years later.

"Like a Handshake"

The first nine months of therapy were helpful. Unlike the odd looking Lonnie Franklin Leonard, Dr. X seemed to be the image of a therapist in the 1970s: middle-aged, graying, dressed conservatively, a heavy smoker. Bates viewed him as a version of her idealized father, the "incarnation of trustworthiness" (22). He helped her to express her anger toward her father for dying and her resentment toward her boyfriend, Steve, with whom she had a conflicted, co-dependent relationship. But slowly Bates' therapeutic relationship became sexualized. Dr. X's suggestion that she was sexually attracted to him was not only inaccurate but also upsetting. "This man was my surrogate father. A sexual attraction toward him was unthinkable, taboo, incestuous" (27). Dr. X began hugging her, then kissing her on the lips at the end of a session. In response to her statement that she wanted to remain faithful to her boyfriend, he told her that she needed to overcome clinging, dependent relationships; otherwise, she would never be psychologically healthy. He drew a parallel between her reluctance to be sexually adventurous with other men, which resulted, he said, in the creation of isolating walls, and her denial of her sexual attraction toward him. "Dr. X explained to me that sexual intercourse was like a handshake: a way men and women came to know one another" (29).

Dr. X also played upon Bates' homophobia by telling her that she must be a lesbian if she continued to deny her sexual attraction to him and other men. Raised in a strictly heterosexual, homophobic culture, she began to feel that she must have sex with Dr. X to prove her sexual orientation. Ellen Plasil's therapist used a similar argument, reassuring her that she would feel "totally feminine" (78) once she was able to enjoy having sex with him.

Praising Bates when she succumbed to the pressure of the various men in her life to have casual sex with them, Dr. X was oblivious to her plummeting self-esteem and loss of trust in him. In one of their sessions, he told her about a patient who came to therapy dressed in a skirt but wearing no underwear. She would sit in his office, Dr. X said, with her legs spread apart. Instead of helping his patient understand why she was seeking approval through provocative, manipulative behavior, Dr. X challenged her self-servingly to express her feelings more directly. The next session she came to his office, took off her clothes, and received his therapeutic approval. Hearing the story, Bates, desperate for Dr. X's approval, quietly took off her own clothes during her next session, earning his praise. She felt only numbness at the end of the hour. During the next session, Dr. X ordered her to lie on her back on his office floor while he stroked her stomach. She was so fearful that she covered her face. She went through the same ritual during the next session—and then, almost before she knew what was happening, he unzipped his pants and penetrated her. The act was so horrific that for the first time in her life she found herself dissociating, "floating in the upper reaches of the room, unable to abide what I saw on the floor" (34).

Unlike Ellen Plasil and Evelyn Walker, who deluded themselves into thinking, with their psychiatrists' encouragement, that their sexual relationships would lead to something more permanent, Carolyn Bates never believed she was in love with her therapist. Sometimes she felt she was "special" and attractive to Dr. X, but she mainly felt confusion, incredulity and distress. Dr. X's sex with her coincided with the breakup of his marriage, and therapy became more focused on his problems than on hers. She continued to pay him for the privilege of sex—and for listening to his marital problems.

It's not clear whether Dr. X was deliberately conning her when he praised their sexual relationship as a therapeutic "breakthrough—like I finally got through to you" (37). Dr. Leonard had made a similar statement to Plasil, reassuring her that as a result of their sexualized therapy, she was "getting better" (103). Were the two therapists so blind and self-absorbed that they couldn't see the destructive consequences of their actions? Or were they indifferent to the consequences? Bates terminated therapy in 1977, so humiliated by her sexual actions and lost in an unbearable depression that she was unable to reveal to Dr. X why she ended her "treatment" with him.

The Aftermath

Bates' sexual experience with her therapist recalls those reported by Plasil and Walker. All three women, largely or entirely monogamous before therapy, became promiscuous after therapy ended. Acting out sexually with multiple partners was not only unsatisfying but also psychologically numbing. All three women feared abandonment, a fear that intensified as a consequence of the loss of a supposedly trusted therapist. Bates did not develop two personalities, Big Me and Little Me, as Ellen Plasil did following her sexualized therapy, but she continued to use dissociation as a coping mechanism. She experienced certain other symptoms resembling those of what would later be called posttraumatic stress disorder, including recurrent nightmares in which Dr. X was chasing her with a knife. The dreams often ended when she woke up screaming. Shame overcame her as well as guilt for allowing herself to be victimized. She tortured herself for being a failure in therapy.

Within three months of leaving Dr. X, Bates reentered therapy, this time with a minister, to whom she confided her terrible secret. "The floodgates were opened," she writes, "and the sense of shame that I had for this incestuous-like relationship was overshadowed by a greater sense of relief that I could share it with someone" (42). To her surprise, the minister told her that Dr. X had a history of sexual exploitation. Sooner or later, he added, someone would "blow Dr. X's cover." The minister did not advise her, however, to be the one to do so. The second therapist validated her right to be angry and helped her through a suicidal time, but it was only when she discovered another victim of Dr. X that she was able to take decisive action and begin the process of recovery.

Another Victim

Bates learned in 1978, during her first year as a high school English teacher, that one of her students was seeing a psychiatrist whose office was across the hall from Dr. X's. "What would stop another child—or another adult, for that matter—from entering therapy with Dr. X?" (45). Bates' worry was not irrational, for she soon discovered that Suzanne Brown was representing a young woman who had been victimized by Dr. X. Unlike Plasil and Walker, Bates never believed that she was

135

OFF THE TRACKS VOLUME 1

the only patient with whom her therapist was having sex. She doesn't explain why she felt a "degree of relief in this realization" (45); it was not because of *schadenfreude* but because of the feeling she was not alone. Told by Brown that Dr. X would probably deny he had a sexual relationship with her, the other patient wore a microphone to a therapy session and recorded his admission that he had sexual intercourse with her during an earlier session. The psychologist's *modus operandi* during his treatment of Bates and the other patient was similar: "discussions of an alleged sexual attraction that we had for Dr. X, the gradually increasing physical contact, and his instructing us to relax on the floor. In addition, we sought treatment in order to resolve similar issues in our heterosexual relationships. Finally, we both perceived Dr. X as a father figure and subsequently grew dependent upon him and trusted his skills and intentions" (47–48).

A Master of Manipulation and Rationalization

Dr. X was masterful in his sexual manipulation of his patients. "He made no mistakes," Bates ruefully admitted. "He was very, very good at what he did" (6). Reading the two plaintiffs' accounts of their sexualized therapy, Dr. X offered a settlement through his lawyer that included the promise to enter therapy himself and avoid treating female patients for one year, but Bates and the other woman rejected the settlement as unsatisfactory. In the same year, 1978, a third patient, who read in the newspaper about the two lawsuits against Dr. X, approached Brown with a slightly different story of sexual abuse while she was his patient. Because she was a minor at the time sex occurred, Dr. X would be facing a felony crime—and it was for this reason that he denied having sexual relations with her.

Dr. X then created a series of rationalizations and initiated legal maneuvers that lasted for years. He admitted having sexual relations with Bates and the other adult patient but steadfastly denied any wrongdoing. He implied the existence of a "dual relationship" with both patients, maintaining that he had a personal friendship with each of them that existed apart from a professional therapeutic relationship. In his view, this dual relationship justified his behavior in two ways: sexual intercourse "was separate from, and in addition to, therapy"; and a personal relationship existed between himself and the other two women, both of whom were "psychologically free of a patient identity and thereby able to consent to the intercourse" (53). Both assertions were self-serving ones that the plaintiffs' lawyers and state licensing committees rejected. Dr. X also claimed that he was friends with the patients with whom he had intimate relations and that they experienced pleasure during sex. He used other rationalizations as a defense of his behavior as well. During the state licensing board meetings, his lawyer argued, first, that although the American Psychological Association had recently prohibited sexual relations between a therapist and patient, these 'intimacies" remained undefined, and second, that a "small minority" of psychiatrists and psychologists believed that sexual intimacy in therapy can be beneficial. Both of these rationalizations were also rejected.

Dr. X's legal maneuvers during the malpractice suits were no less insidious. Every aspect of Bates' private life was subjected to intrusive interrogations by Dr. X's lawyer, who portrayed the psychologist as a "victim of three vindictive seductresses" (65). Bates was asked about every kind of sexual interaction she had with all the men she had dated. No area of her life was off limits. A private investigator followed her, evidently in the hope of finding something that would besmirch her reputation. During the pretrial depositions, Dr. X admitted that Bates was not aggressively sexual toward him, but he insisted that she was "more softly, passively seductive in posture, mannerisms and particularly in her eyes" (98), which, he added, made him feel that she was yearning for a sexual relationship. In effect, Dr. X violated his patients in two different ways, by having sex with them in therapy, and then by characterizing them as promiscuous during the malpractice suits and ethics hearing. The adversarial nature of the legal system often results in plaintiffs in sexual malpractice suits feeling retraumatized. Dr. X demanded that he be given a photograph of one of the complainants to circulate at local bars. Such information, Dr. X's lawyer claimed, might provide evidence about her social life that could be relevant to the case.

"Macho-istic"—and Masochistic

In one of his most revealing comments about himself, Dr. X admitted that he was "Very macho-istic" (48) when he treated the third plaintiff, who was sixteen—and thus a minor—when he had sex with her. Explaining his history of infatuations with his patients and his faulty judgments while working in a psychiatric hospital, he averred that this behavior was in the past: "At the time I had an aura of machoism, and I don't really know how to explain that to you but chauvinistic machoism. Was real proud of myself. It manifested itself in the way I walked through the wards. I think I was cocky. I think I was flirtatious with the staff and manipulative of the staff in terms of getting things done" (93). Far from implying remorse or regret over his actions, his language here suggests continuation of his hypermasculine therapeutic style. At no point in the story does he make a good-faith effort to overcome his problems.

In the second half of *Sex in the Therapy Hour*, Brodsky quotes an observation by Sydney Smith, the psychologist who treated Evelyn

Walker in *A Killing Cure*, about therapists who sexually exploit their patients. These therapists, in Brodsky's words, "are unaware of their sexual behavior toward patients" and "exhibit a concurrent masochism that includes a need to experience danger—the danger of getting caught." Such behavior "may show less stupidity than a sense of excitement generated by daring to see whether one can get away with it" (153). One of the most conspicuous aspects of sexually exploitative therapists is that their self-destructiveness is apparent to everyone but themselves: Gabbard and Lester's observation is certainly true of Dr. X.

Throughout *Sex in the Therapy Hour* Dr. X comes across as highly self-centered, as can be seen during the hours of his pretrial testimony. "Once during Dr. X's deposition, his attorney, exceedingly frustrated by his client's refusal to answer my attorney's questions simply and then be quiet, threw his hands in the air and sank so far down in his chair that he nearly disappeared under the table. Dr. X would not stop talking about himself" (64). If his incessant self-chatter was an effort to prevent others from speaking, and thus a form of control, so were his repeated threats of lawsuits against other psychologists who might criticize him. His colleagues were so frightened by his reputation for threatening legal action that Bates received only one letter of support from a psychologist during the nearly five years of legal battles.

Macho-istic/masochistic behavior also seems to characterize Lonnie Franklin Leonard and Zane Parzen. Both psychiatrists had sex with multiple patients and must have known that sooner or later, their hypermasculine misconduct would get them into trouble and jeopardize if not ruin their careers. Both used rationalization as a defense of sexual misconduct; both believed they were being persecuted by the psychological community; both were evasive in acknowledging serious psychological problems; both had problems with grandiosity; and both demonstrated a glaring absence of empathy.

Other Women Come Forward

As a result of the media attention to the malpractice suits, Suzanne Brown was "flooded" with telephone calls from Dr. X's former patients who shared their own experiences of sexual exploitation in therapy. Their stories were too similar to be coincidental. Therapists implicated in sexual malpractice suits usually argue that former patients who come forward after extensive media accounts of medical malpractice litigation are cynically attempting to exploit psychiatrists and psychologists for financial gain. Some of Dr. X's former patients offered to appear as witnesses for the plaintiffs, but others were unable or unwilling to help, largely because of the fear of publicity or the reluctance to go through the ordeal of testifying about sexual violation. It soon became evident that Dr. X was a serial abuser. Contrary to the claims made by Dr. X's lawyer and those of other defendants in similar situations, most victims were not interested in monetary compensation.

Protracted Litigation

The lawsuits against Dr. X were unusually complicated and protracted. The litigation lasted nearly five years, from 1978 through 1982, and involved, in part, his refusal to answer certain questions that he claimed would violate the confidentiality of the therapist-patient relationship. He was twice held in contempt, twice jailed and twice released within a few hours. He won a partial victory when the state Supreme Court ruled in a five-to-four decision that he could withhold the names of other patients with whom he had sexual relations. Bates judiciously observes that the "far-reaching effects of this decision were positive for the state's community of professional psychologists as a whole; for us, however, it meant our first significant loss" (58). There were other losses, all of which proved minor, such as the judge's decision in favor of Dr. X's request for a change of venue, as well as another decision, again favoring Dr. X, for the consolidation of the three malpractice cases into a single class-action suit.

Brodsky's appearance in 1982 as an expert witness turned out to be the major turning point in the malpractice suits. She interviewed Bates and studied her responses to the battery of psychological tests she took when she first presented her case to Brown and Whitehurst. Brodsky gave Bates additional psychological tests, including the Rorschach Test, the Thematic Apperception Test, and the Minnesota Multiphasic Personality Inventory (MMPI), one of the most frequently used clinical assessments of mental health. Bates took the MMPI five different times, spanning a period of several years, to chart her psychological health. The tests indicated that she was indeed psychologically damaged by Dr. X's treatment. As a result of Brodsky's evaluations, Dr. X's insurance company offered a settlement of $110,000 (about $350,000 in current dollars) that was finally accepted by the plaintiffs. Bates' share was $26,000 ($80,000), part of which went to pay for her therapy with a new psychologist, Evelyn Hammond, and the rest to help her begin graduate training for a new career as a counseling psychologist.

Beyond Rehabilitation

The delicensing of Dr. X proved more difficult and frustrating than the civil litigation. His license had been suspended for one year in 1979. Nearly two years later, the licensing board presented him with five requirements necessary for recertification and "rehabilitation," one of which was to enter into psychotherapy for a period of one year with a therapist who was to provide quarterly reports for the board's consideration and approval. Dr. X saw at least three different psychologists, none of whom was able to work with him for more than a few months. "The psychological community apparently had grown wary of any voluntary professional interaction with this one-time colleague" (80). As an example of his refusal to take seriously his ethical responsibilities, he had sexual relations with a patient during therapy in 1984, while he was under the board-ordered supervision of a licensed psychologist. The patient later sued Dr. X and his supervisor and was awarded an out-of-court settlement $90,000.

Dr. X continued to wrestle with the state licensing boards throughout the mid-1980s. His tactic was always the same: threaten a lawsuit whenever he was faced with permanent delicensing. At one point he solicited funds from community business leaders to establish an organization, the Counseling Centers of America, of which he named himself Director. His career as a therapist came to an end only in 1988, when he pled guilty to a second degree felony charge for having sex with a teenage patient who was seeing him for marital counseling. He received a ten-year probated (suspended) sentence and was ordered not to practice "any type of counseling" during the ten-year probation period (216).

Writing the Book

Carolyn Bates notes in the epilogue to *Sex in the Therapy Hour* that it took her seven years to write the book. "The process has been at times both cathartic and grounding, and at times a great and unappreciated burden. But I would have had it no other way, for the process of telling this story has also provided me with a way to integrate into the realm of assimilated experience both Dr. X's betrayal and my role as victim. I have gained through writing, therapy, and simple reflection a greater understanding not only of the subtleties of my own experience but also the impact of Dr. X's mental illness on other women and on the entire profession of psychology" (115). As confirmation of the therapeutic value of writing, Brodsky points out that the fifth and final MMPI Bates took in October 1986, ten years after she ended therapy with Dr. X and four years after the malpractice suit was settled, was the best psychological profile of the series. Bates' remarkable progress, Brodsky suggests, was due to psychotherapy, a good marriage, a fulfilling career and writing the book.

Brodsky was not Bates' psychotherapist, but she helped Bates reconstruct her story and transform it into language. Judith Lewis Herman's observation in *Trauma and Recovery* (1992) that the goal of psychotherapy is not to exorcise trauma but integrate it into one's life applies to Bates and other victims of sexual boundary violations. "In the process of reconstruction," Herman notes, "the trauma story does undergo a transformation, but only in the sense of becoming more present and more real. The fundamental premise of the psychotherapeutic work is a belief in the restorative power of truth-telling" (181).

Coda

"I never want to see another therapist as long as I live!" (214) exclaims Ellen Plasil at the end of her story, leaving no doubt about her feelings toward psychotherapy. By contrast, Carolyn Bates not only returned to psychotherapy after her disastrous experience with Dr. X, benefiting from her experience with Evelyn Hammond, but she also became a psychotherapist herself. According to her website, she is a licensed clinical psychologist, with a PhD. from the University of Texas at Austin, and a Jungian psychoanalyst. She offers workshops on a wide range of topics, including "Moral Dilemmas for Psychotherapists: Sexual Impropriety," "The Self Care of the Therapist, or, Is 'Psychologists' Health' an Oxymoron?", and "Healing Through Literature."

Sex in the Therapy Hour never reveals the identity of Dr. X, but because Bates and Brodsky quote excerpts from the legal opinions in the case, we were able to discover his name and the city in which he practiced: John M. Abell of Austin, Texas. The information from the Texas State Board of Examiners of Psychologists confirms the details about his identity given in *Sex in the Therapy Hour* and provides new information as well. Abell was disciplined twice, first in January 1979, for "unprofessional conduct, sexual relations with patients," and then again in October 1984, for "violations of ethical principles and Board rules; unethical conduct, inappropriate billing practices [a detail not included in *Sex in the Therapy Hour*], dual relationship." We were not able to learn anything else about the ex-psychologist. There is no indication that he reapplied for his professional license after the ten-year-probation period ended. The only other information we have about his life following the loss of his professional license comes from Bates, who tells us at the end of her narrative that he attempted to build a new career as an actor in television commercials. "At 51 years of age," she adds, "he remains a person whose false sincerity can skillfully deceive" (114).

IV

DR. A AND P. SUSAN PENFOLD

Psychiatrist-authors rarely lament at the end of a textbook that they have not written more self-disclosingly. That's why P. Susan Penfold's confession in *Women and the Psychiatric Paradox*, co-authored with Gillian A. Walker in 1983, is so unusual. "Attempts

144

to conceptualize my own merging of feminism and psychiatry were very painful and difficult until I realized that I tended to devalue and consider suspect those understandings which arose from my own experiences as a woman, mother and wife." Because her medical and psychiatric training emphasized only "rational and scientific" approaches to clinical problems, she felt she could not disclose anything about her personal life.

Rereading the reports and case studies she had written in the past decade as a child and family therapist, Penfold now finds her language "bare and sterile" compared with the richness of her impressions of her actual work with children and their patients. "How I feel as people describe their problems and difficulties is absent." She regrets the absence of personal self-disclosure: her refusal to reveal her identification with patients' situations, her reaching out to talk about herself and her own children, her use of personal experiences to help clarify patients' problems. Writing *Women and the Psychiatric Paradox*, she acknowledges in the penultimate chapter, helped her to stop feeling apologetic about her "'unscientific' and intuitive approach to families" (234–235).

There are two ironies here, one that Penfold may have suspected, the other, almost certainly not. She seldom uses the first person in *Women and the Psychiatric Paradox*, and many readers will not be convinced that her voice throughout the book is anything other than rational and scientific. Yes, her commitment to feminist psychiatry is evident, as is her righteous indignation over the ways in which women, especially female patients, have been silenced and devalued, but there is little in the book to indicate how her self-disclosures helped reduce her patients' feelings of guilt and self-blame. *Women and the Psychiatric Paradox* is a thoughtful and well-written scholarly book, an important contribution to feminist psychiatry, but it is not personal or self-disclosing. Nor does it confront psychiatry's most taboo subjects. Penfold and Walker note in passing in the introduction that there is little in the institution of psychiatry to account for the prevalence of sexual abuse of female patients by male therapists, but the authors avoid this subject themselves, thus maintaining the shroud of silence, secrecy and stigma that envelopes this topic. Fifteen years later, however, Penfold *was* ready to write a personal book, searingly confessional. *Sexual Abuse by Health Professionals* is one of the most emotionally charged books about a patient's experience of being sexually abused by a therapist. What makes the book more singular is that Penfold was herself a psychiatrist when the boundary violation occurred, by her own psychiatry professor and supervisor who, following his suggestion, had become her therapist.

One of the unusual features of *Sexual Abuse by Health Professionals* is the use of two alternating voices. The "angry part," which emerged during the third year of therapy, conveys the dark, virulent emotions that are missing from academic discussions of sexual abuse. The literary and psychological power of the story resides in the "angry part." Penfold uses the first person pronoun throughout these sections, written with expressive power. The "other part," the scientific voice she uses in *Women and the Psychiatric Paradox,* allows Penfold to depict the larger picture of sexual boundary violations, comparing her story to others. She has read most of the research on sexual abuse by health professionals, and she includes a number of typologies of sexually transgressive physicians and psychotherapists.

Penfold's Dr. A is a psychiatrist, unlike Bates' Dr. X, who is a psychologist, but the two therapists have much in common, beginning with their anonymity to the reader. The authors state

146

that the reason they chose not to name their transgressive therapists is because they didn't want to appear vindictive. Another reason, we surmise, is the fear of a lawsuit. Both therapists were several years older than their patients and well established in their careers. Both sexually abused their patients by claiming the women were "special," a word that appears throughout the two stories. Both exerted an almost irresistible Svengali-like power over their patients' lives, creating a dependency, addiction, or spell that seemed impossible to break. Both exploited their patients' transference-love and rationalized their own behavior in several ways, asserting that sexual intimacy led to therapeutic breakthroughs when it fact it led only to humiliation and shame. Both claimed that their sexual relationships were consensual agreements separate from and in addition to psychotherapy. Both experienced marital problems around the time of the sexual abuse of their patients and struggled with depression. Both gave their patients advice on how to look and behave "more feminine." Both reversed the therapist-patient role by seeking advice and comfort from the female patients who continued to pay them for professional services. Both denied any wrongdoing when they were brought up on ethics charges and faced delicensing. Both appeared to help their patients at first but irreparably harmed them, creating many more problems than existed before treatment. And both therapists were forced to give up their careers, having demonstrated through their actions that they were beyond rehabilitation.

Penfold's story is different from Bates', however, in several ways. Unlike Bates, who was 20 when she began therapy, Penfold was older, in her 30s. Unlike Dr. X, who could not gain acceptance to an accredited doctoral program in psychology, Dr. A was a professor in a psychiatry training program in the United States. Penfold was nearing the end of her psychiatric training, married and pregnant with her second child, ready to return to Canada and begin a part-time faculty position, when Dr. A, her professor and supervisor, suggested that she go into therapy with him. The suggestion was itself a distinct sort of boundary violation, confusing the roles of teacher and therapist. Soon therapy became sexualized, creating a second and far more serious boundary violation.

Andrea Celenza makes two observations in *Sexual Boundary Violations* about the role of gender that apply to Penfold's story. Female students or supervisees are more likely to be involved with their educators or supervisors than are male students or supervisees: prevalence studies indicate 16.5% among the former and only 2% among the latter (67). Rates of sexual misconduct are higher for academic and supervisor situations than for therapist-patient sexual misconduct. Celenza's explanation is that the "imbalance and the transgression in the context of a therapy relationship is more extreme and more pointedly taboo" (86). Penfold's relationship with Dr. A was *both* academic and therapeutic.

Penfold remained in therapy with Dr. A for six-and-a-half tumultuous years. She was filled with self-loathing and self-doubt, but she felt powerless to end what she knew was an unprofessional and self-destructive relationship. Because she was herself a psychiatrist, supposedly aware of the phenomenon of transference-love and the incestuous nature of a patient's sexual relationship with a therapist, she felt doubly shamed. The worst part of her situation was the feeling of complicity in her own victimization.

Sexual Abuse by Health Professionals has a wider thematic focus than *Therapist*, *A Killing Cure*, and *Sex in the Therapy Hour*. After making the fateful decision to write about her story, Penfold interviewed dozens of people who were themselves sexually abused by health professionals. She tells two stories, her own and those of her interviewees. Penfold's ambivalence over self-disclosure is never entirely resolved. Her contradictory feelings may have been responsible for choosing a title that masks the personal, confessional voice of the "angry part." The title *Sexual Abuse by Health Professionals* conveys her scholarly, academic voice, not her angry, wounded voice. One could imagine the same book being called *"The Angry Part": A Psychiatrist-Patient's Sexual Victimization by Her Therapist*. One can understand Penfold's reluctance to sensationalize her story, her aversion to the language of tabloids. Nevertheless, she could have chosen a title that does justice to the courage and eloquence of her "angry part." Penfold's ambivalence over self-disclosure may explain a discovery we made while reading Christopher Hyde's *Abuse of Trust: The Career of Dr. James Tyhurst*, which we discuss in a later chapter in this volume. Penfold conceded under direct questioning by Tyhurst's lawyer that she abused alcohol, an admission that never appears in *Sexual Abuse by Health Professionals*. Curiously, she devotes only a sentence in her book to the notorious Tyhurst case, in which she served as an expert witness, while she devotes lengthy paragraphs to other cases of sexual abuse in therapy in which she never testified.

Penfold's account of the formidable legal challenges in filing complaints against a health professional is consistent with what we read in *Therapist, A Killing Cure*, and *Sex in the Therapy Hour*, but she goes into more depth about the defense lawyers' unseemly tactics intended to discredit, shame, and humiliate complainants. She also describes in more detail the daunting process of breaking the silence of sexual abuse. She was filled with anxiety and dread when she made the risky decision to go public. Readers can understand why she found herself procrastinating while writing the book. It is always professionally risky when therapists write about their own struggle with mental illness or self-destructive behavior. Penfold offers the most detailed discussion of the rationalizations used by the medical community to avoid acknowledging the problem of sexual abuse by health professionals. She reserves one of her biggest shocks for the epilogue, when she describes her dismay on learning something about Dr. A that she had not known earlier.

A Double Life

Born in England in 1936, Penfold experienced an unsettling childhood that she characterizes as a "double life." Her mother, who had recently recovered from tuberculosis and was still frail, was persuaded by her childless doctor and his wife, both of whom later became Susan's godparents, to move into their spacious house, called "Normans," to have her first child. For the next few years, Susan traveled between her parents' and godparents' homes. "After my birth, and for the next few years, a kind of tug of war went on, and I went back and forth between my parents and my godparents, who tried to convince my mother that they had more resources to care for me and that she needed to leave me with them while she regained her health and spent time with my father" (27). Her most devastating memory was when she was young, lying in her crib or bed, and her godfather, whom she called "Umpi," came into her room and licked her genitals. The memory was so frightening that she thought she was crazy. Umpi had a good side—nurturing and supportive—and a bad side, sexually abusive, unstable and maniacal. Penfold's brother was born when she was nine, and the family moved briefly to London near the end of World War II. Occasionally she returned to Normans, and though her godparents had divorced, her godfather still had his medical office there.

Penfold attributes many of the problems that developed later in life, and which drove her to Dr. A, to her confused and conflicted childhood and adolescence. These struggles included the repeated separation from her parents and her tendency to blame her mother for abandoning her. The clashes were intensified by her ambivalence toward her godmother, who demanded obedience by threatening to reject her and send her home. Central to Penfold's story was her mistrust of men, which arose from her godfather's early molestation of her, his drunken rages, when he would try to smash the door of his ex-wife's bedroom, and the actions of other adult males who tried to have sex with her between the ages of ten and 14.

Dr. A

We learn little about Penfold's life from her teenage years in England until her second year of a psychiatry fellowship in the United States, when Dr. A was assigned to her as a supervisor. She tells us that he was middle-aged, from a traditional family, with a stern, distant father and a controlling, infantilizing mother. As a younger son, he believed his parents favored his older brother. He admitted to her, in her own words, a "lifelong difficulty in addressing his feelings" (31). Younger colleagues in his department viewed him as "authoritarian," while older colleagues saw him as "rather ineffectual and unproductive." He felt disappointed with his career, believing that he had not lived up to his potential. Penfold describes his view of women as "very traditional," once telling her that she should use her "feminine wiles" with her husband and never get angry with him (31). Her use of "very traditional" is a euphemism; we would call him sexist if not misogynistic. As a lover he would "penetrate" her and "then rapidly ejaculate" (31), recalling Dr. X's perfunctory sex.

Her most humiliating sexual experience was when he ordered her to lie on the floor, motionless and silent, penetrated her, and then ordered her back to her chair when she began to cry.

Dr. A believed that their relationship was "mutual" even though after she moved back to Canada she would need to drive several hours to be with him. He never drove to visit her. His hypocrisy must have been infuriating to her. Once he self-righteously told her, "I couldn't deal with my feelings about having an affair" (66). Did he believe he was *not* having an affair with her? Another time he admitted, "I would never tell my private thoughts to a woman" (72). He convinced himself that she was learning something important about life, love, and womanhood by being with him. "You have found yourself through your love of me" (65). During the fifth year of therapy he told her, "The only reason you are coming here is because you love me" (69).

Like Umpi, Dr. A could be loving and supportive one moment, hateful and evil the next moment. He told her just before she left one session that "You feel like nothing without me," a statement that left her feeling when she was wandering on a beach that she was "less than nothing, less than a piece of sea scum" (31–32). Once she became so "hysterical" after he told her that their intercourse had been a "trivial incident" that she hit him, yelling that he was cruel and insensitive (69). She felt like a puppet during the six years she was with him; other times she felt he was playing a cat-and-mouse game with her.

Penfold presents us with several different typologies of therapists who are sexual abusers. She sees Dr. A as a combination of two different types as theorized by Alan Stone: the therapist who is "middle-aged, depressed, and has problems in his own marriage," and the therapist who is "introverted and withdrawn . . . and very uncomfortable with interpersonal intimacy" (30). Dr. A resembled the therapist who is "severely neurotic" in the typology developed by Gary Schoener and his associates at the Minnesota Walk-In Counseling Center: those who have "severe, long-standing emotional problems and focus on getting their personal needs met in the work setting" (39). The typology with which she most identifies is Peter Rudder's concept of "masculine woundedness": the man in power who perceives himself to be wounded by his mother, and who avenges himself on other women. Penfold believes that Dr. A's cruelty toward her was a reflection of his anger toward his mother. Encouraging Penfold to despise her mother was part of his own unanalyzed countertransference hatred of his own mother.

Dr. A's personality traits fall into several different typologies proposed by different clinicians (including Gabbard and Lester), suggesting that the search for a master typology to explain the therapist who has sex with a patient suffers from the same problem of overlapping categories that attempts to classify personality disorders in general is now acknowledged to have created. Many patients appear to meet the criteria for two or more personality disorders as presently defined. Similarly none of the therapists we consider fit neatly into one or another pigeonhole. Such typologies are therefore most likely abstractions while actual abusive therapists seem to share, in varying proportions, traits of each of the defined types.

Traumatic Transference

Like Bates, Penfold did not realize the transference/countertransference implications of a patient's sexualized relationship with a therapist, despite the fact that this issue was part of her psychiatric training. She never tells us whether she considered entering psychoanalytic training, which would have required a long personal analysis, where transference and countertransference dynamics are explored closely, but these concepts also presumably would have come up in her psychiatric training. (Even Brodsky, who seems to go out of her way to ignore psychoanalysis when she lists the various types of mental health professionals, emphasizes the centrality of transference and countertransference in psychotherapy.) Penfold realized at some point that Dr. A was a version of her godfather Umpi. Both were physicians, "wounded healers"; both inappropriately had sex with her, introducing her to the idea of "sex in the forbidden zone"; both alternated between loving and hating her; both were the recipients of her overidealization and devaluation; both made her feel angry, dirty and exploited; both were associated in her mind with dark secrets that could never be disclosed; both were members of the profession she herself had chosen; and both had ultimately destructive influences on her. Their similarities even extended to details that she did not realize at the time. In Dr. A's presence she was mesmerized by the way a lock of his hair fell over his brow. It was not until years later that she realized, when looking at a photograph of Umpi, that his hair was startlingly similar to Dr. A's.

Penfold invokes the psychoanalytic theory of "identification with the lost object" to explain her decision to become a physician, like her godfather, a way of taking on some of the characteristics of a person who has disappeared from one's life, either through death or separation. Would Dr. A have behaved so much like Umpi if Penfold did not have that experience with her godfather and then projected the object image into Dr. A? This is not to imply that Penfold was responsible for Dr. A's sexual abuse of her, but rather that her experience with her godfather created some of the conditions that Dr. A later exploited.

The diagnosis of posttraumatic stress disorder had not officially come into existence when Penfold was Dr. A's patient in the 1970s, but in retrospect, this is the diagnosis she now uses to describe her symptoms during and after treatment. She experienced three episodes of delayed onset posttraumatic stress disorder: the first when she began therapy with Dr. A, the second when she remembered being sexually abused by her godfather, and the third, years later, when she felt increased pressure from work and the demands of living in a blended family.

Penfold now believes that the reason it was so wrenching to extricate herself from Dr. A's baleful influence was because of "traumatic transference," a concept first named and described by Judith Lewis Herman in *Trauma and Recovery*. Patients who experience trauma, Herman suggests, form a characteristic type of transference in therapy. "Their emotional responses to any person in a position of authority have been deformed by the experience of terror." Traumatic transference reactions have an "intense life-or-death quality unparalleled in ordinary therapeutic relationships." Herman argues that traumatic transference often appears in the treatment of borderline personality disorders, where a "destructive force appears to intrude repeatedly into the relationship between therapist and patient." This destructive force, Herman believes, reveals the violence of the perpetrator. She adds that the "dynamics of dominance and submission are reenacted in all subsequent relationships, including the therapy" (136–138). Penfold's traumatic transference with Dr. A had the life-or-death quality of the reaction of a survivor of childhood trauma to a person in authority. Most of her metaphors of Dr. A's power over her imply her feelings of helplessness without him: she felt like his "toddler daughter" (48), as if she was "fused to him, perhaps like a tiny parasite" (104). The statement that she was "in thrall to" Dr. A (46) captures the feeling of being a slave held in bondage. What makes the spell so deadly is the feeling of rapt absorption that often accompanies it.

Trauma and Recovery was published after the appearance of *Therapist, A Killing Cure* and *Sex in the Therapy Hour*, but based on Herman's evocative descriptions of the aftermath of violence, Plasil and Walker and perhaps

Bates were similarly bonded to therapists who kept their female patients tightly under control, exerting a Svengali-like influence over them, reinforcing their helplessness and abject subjugation. Plasil, Walker, Bates, and Penfold all use the same images and metaphors of being held captive to their therapists, a captivity that lasted for several years.

Instilling Shame

The "angry part" of *Sexual Abuse by Health Professionals* is the voice of trauma, the dark, murderous, destructive voice that conveys the childhood and adult trauma inflicted upon Penfold by her godfather and therapist, respectively. She uses this expressive voice at the beginning of chapters 1 through 8. The "angry part" is italicized to distinguish it from the "other part," Penfold's academic, scholarly, intellectual voice—the voice that appears in *Women and the Psychiatric Paradox*.

The longest and most emotionally intense section of the "angry part" is in chapter 3, "Entrapment," which was the hardest chapter for Penfold to write because it raises the most onerous question: why it took her so long to break free of Dr. A's power. She begins the chapter with a dozen other questions that she knows incredulous readers will ask. She remains incredulous herself, still mortified that it took her so long to escape a situation that almost led to suicide. The questions dramatize the contrast between intellectual and emotional intelligence. She knew intellectually during the six years of her entrapment that she had to escape from Dr. A, but emotionally she lacked the intelligence—and the courage and strength—to flee. The "angry part" might have been called more accurately the "shameful part" because shame is usually a harder emotion to come to terms with than anger; indeed, it is the darkest and most destructive of all emotions. To understand its complex dynamics and the ways in which Dr. X came to be the instiller of shame in Penfold, we turn to the vivid definition offered by Leon Wurmser, perhaps the leading psychoanalytic theorist of shame:

> [T]he word shame really covers three concepts: Shame is first the *fear* of disgrace, it is the *anxiety* about the danger that we might be looked at with contempt for having dishonored ourselves. Second, it is the feeling when one is looked at with such scorn. It is, in other words, the *affect of contempt* directed against the self—by others or by one's own conscience. Contempt says: "You should disappear as such a being as you have shown yourself to be—failing, weak, flawed, and dirty. Get out of my sight: Disappear!" One feels ashamed for *being exposed.* . . . Third, shame is also almost the antithesis of the second one, as in: "Don't you know any shame?" It is an overall *character trait* preventing any such disgraceful exposure, an attitude of respect toward others and toward oneself, a stance of reverence—the highest form of such reverence being called by Goethe "die Ehrfurcht vor sich selbst," reverence for oneself. This third form of shame is discretion, is tact, is sexual modesty. It is respect and a sense of awe—a refusal "to touch, lick and finger everything, a nobility of taste and tact of reverence" as Nietzsche calls it in *Beyond Good and Evil.* (67–68)

Penfold would agree with Wurmser's evocative discussion of the three dimensions to shame, beginning with the first meaning, shame anxiety, which appears in her anxiety over self-disclosure, the fear that others will look at her with contempt for having dishonored herself. After filing a complaint in November 1991 with the Board of Medical Examiners, and then receiving a telephone call in September 1994 from a lawyer with the state attorney general's department, Penfold re-experienced the terror and shame she had felt years earlier in therapy. She points out that a patient's decision to file a complaint or a lawsuit results in a brutal cross-examinations that may last for days.

Public sympathy for victims of child sexual abuse is more easily evoked and sustained than for adult victims. Defense lawyers heighten the stigma of mental illness by attempting to discredit a victim's sanity, integrity, character and judgment. Penfold cites a 1991 study indicating that only about 4% of allegations of sexual abuse by health professionals are proven false (195). Moreover, the vast majority of sexual abuse is never reported: according to Celenza, studies indicate that only 8% of sexually abused patients come forward (96). Sexual abuse victims face formidable challenges, including insurance companies' high-powered lawyers; the adversarial nature of the legal system, which allows defense lawyers to interrogate nearly every aspect of a patient's sexual life; and the biases and stereotypes associated with mental illness.

But beyond these problems, writers of sexual boundary violations stories must overcome their resistance to self-disclosure, their shame anxiety. To a far greater extent than we see in *Therapist, A Killing Cure*, or *Sex in the Therapy Hour, Sexual Abuse by Health Professionals* reveals the intense ambivalence a victim must overcome to disclose a shameful secret. After collecting material for her book over a period of several years, including other survivor stories, Penfold considered avoiding any discussion of her own experience. In this way she could avoid disclosing her fears, shame, and embarrassment. But this would have meant not only disguising the most important insights that were connected to her own experience but also silencing or muting the powerful emotions that are the substance of the story.

Penfold found her determination to write her story fluctuating wildly, depending on the shifting external events of her life. Shame anxiety was ubiquitous. The fear of disgrace arising from the disclosure of a shameful secret became a painful reality. She was devastated when her husband, with whom she had three children, and who had been supportive of her when she first told him about her intimate relationship with Dr. A, suddenly left her for another woman, blaming the divorce on Penfold's sexual involvement with her therapist. His "group therapists and gurus," Drs. Y and Z, also blamed her for seducing Dr. A, which horrified her further. During this tense time, she was unable to write and retreated further into herself. "Consumed with shame, I longed to be able to vanish and imagined digging a hole in the garden, climbing in, and staying there" (109).

Instead of vanishing, Penfold spent four active years as a single mother; met another man, Keith, who eventually became her second husband; entered treatment with a new therapist, Dr. Naida Hyde; continued writing in her journal; and resolved to talk openly about her experiences. She became involved with an organization called the Therapist Abuse Action Group (TAAG), which consisted of women who had all been sexually abused by their physicians. Attending TAAG's monthly meetings emboldened her to come out of the closet. She describes how anger overwhelmed her during one meeting when she was reading aloud a paper on therapists' sexual abuse of patients. "Suddenly, I found myself consumed with rage, grabbed a carving knife, and, for just a moment, was ready to jump in my car and drive to Dr. A's city, locate him, and kill him!" (139).

Penfold admits that the reason *Women and the Psychiatric Paradox* did not include a chapter on the sexual exploitation of female patients was because she was still struggling with the guilt over her sexual involvement with Dr. A. In 1986, she wrote a paper for a Canadian journal but remained silent about her own experience, burdened by shame anxiety. In 1989, when a reporter from the Vancouver *Sun* called her for an article about a woman's recent disclosure of sexual abuse by a local psychiatrist, Penfold conceded, almost as an afterthought, that she too was a survivor. "Then, with mounting anxiety," Penfold confesses to the reader, "as I still had extremely mixed feelings about making my abuse public knowledge, I tried to backtrack and asked her not to mention my disclosure in the newspaper. She replied, 'Don't you want to back up [the victim]? It will give her much more credibility if you say you were abused too.' How could I refuse?" (156). A year later she was featured in an article that appeared on the front page of Canada's leading newspaper, the *Globe and Mail*. She worried once again about her colleagues' response to her disclosure, but only one male colleague made a prurient comment.

Writing did not magically purge Penfold's anger. She continued to write, revealing more of her story and re-experiencing more anger. Writing made her aware that she had been part of the conspiracy of silence surrounding health professionals' sexual abuse of patients. She began a different kind of writing, penning letters of complaint to the State Board of Examiners. She learned that, contrary to Dr. A's assurance to her that she was "special," the only patient with whom he had sex, another patient had filed a similar complaint during the same time Penfold was in treatment with him. Dr. A responded to the two complainants in the same way, contending, in the words of the Medical Examining Board's lawyer, that the allegations were "all fantasies" and implying, "How could they do something like that. I did so much for them." This was a "standard response" (159), the lawyer added.

Wurmser's second meaning of shame, the affect of contempt directed against the self by others or by one's own conscience, can be seen in Dr. A's many statements that awakened Penfold's stinging shame. She expresses these statements in the voice of the "angry part." She reveals, without giving us any details, that Dr. A once told her that he thought her husband ought to spank her (31). Dr. A judged her as her professor;

he continued to judge her as her therapist and lover, at times giving her failing grades. One of her worst fears was that she was a failure in therapy, which must have been doubly galling because she was a therapist herself. She remained dependent on his omnipotent judgment. He reminded her (not that she had forgotten) that she was nothing without him. He encouraged her to hate and reject her mother, thus depriving her of maternal support. His praise for her "new" femininity and attractiveness implied to her that she was not sufficiently feminine and attractive before she began treatment with him. She was pregnant with her third child when Dr. A abruptly penetrated her for the first time, an act that awakened passionate desire but also mind-numbing guilt. She felt special at the end of a sexualized therapy session but felt unwanted during the next session, when he was cold and distant. How could she not feel ashamed when, at the end of a session, he announced that he "wanted 'a little'" and then, without foreplay or tenderness, thrust his penis into her dry vagina? She was told, after she burst into tears when he ordered her to leave his office because another patient was waiting, that she was "hysterical." She began to bleed vaginally a few days after he informed her that he needed to reduce the frequency of his sessions with her because of a renewed commitment to his wife. Penfold was hospitalized for the bleeding, but no physical cause was found. She interpreted the bleeding as her body's "retribution" for her sexual involvement with Dr. A. "I felt like a whore, bad and seductive" (65). He seemed to regard her as a femme fatale, and, as if conforming to his image of her, she felt like a "witch, bitch, and a whore" (137).

Penfold rarely speculates on Dr. A's thoughts and feelings, preferring instead to remain more objective by limiting herself to reporting his statements to her, many of which convey his contempt for her and himself. What was he thinking during the years of transgressive sex? Did he believe his self-serving rationalizations?

Did he realize, when he accused her of a "masculine protest," implying that she was an angry woman who was threatening to men, that he was a source, perhaps the *major* source, of her fierce anger? Her letters to him expressed anguish and confusion as well as her efforts to cheer him up. In one letter she wrote, "You must have some fears of getting caught" (72). Was he macho-istic and masochistic, as we speculated about Lonnie Franklin Leonard, Zane Parzen and Dr. X? Part of the effectiveness of the "angry part" is that it awakens the reader's indignation over Dr. A's abuse of her. The reader identifies with Penfold's situation, experiences her pain and shame, and glimpses the aftermath of the years of entrapment. This identification is much deeper in the "angry part" than in the "other part."

Like Plasil, Walker and Bates, Penfold had affairs with several men after she ended therapy, becoming, in effect, the seductive, promiscuous woman Dr. A had accused her of being, and which she herself feared was true. The affairs only heightened her toxic shame, intensifying her belief that she was dirty, unworthy and out of control. Yet even while she had sex with other men, she remained obsessed with Dr. A. He was surprised when she told him, three years after her therapy had ended and two years after she had written him a letter expressing the depth of her outrage, the number of problems produced by their affair: "looking for sexualized, dependent relationships with men, putting men on a pedestal, not relating to women, not valuing women" (93). During this discussion Dr. A suggested that their therapeutic relationship had become a *folie à deux*, the phenomenon of one person's delusions infecting the other, resulting in shared madness. Penfold's experience with her godfather may itself have been a shared madness, setting her up for what later occurred in therapy. Dr. A then proposed at the end of their discussion that Penfold resume therapy with him, to which she incredulously responded, "No, no way!" and left.

Wurmser's third meaning of shame, an "attitude of respect toward others and toward oneself, a stance of reverence," appears in Penfold's growing commitment to feminism. She doesn't mention this positive meaning of shame, shame as a preventive attitude, but it had a transformative effect on her life. Nor does she mention Nietzsche, but she would agree with him that anything that doesn't kill you makes you stronger. She expresses gratitude for her recovery to several people, including her second therapist, whom she saw from 1984 to 1986.

Naida Hyde

Penfold's new therapist, Dr. Naida Hyde, was the opposite of Dr. X. Hyde studied at the Lawrence S. Bloomberg Faculty of Nursing, University of Toronto. A clinical instructor, then director of nursing education at the Queen Street Mental Health Center in Toronto, she was an instructor of psychiatric nursing in the graduate program at Boston College. In the mid-1980s she was Director of the University Counselling Center at Simon Fraser University in British Columbia, the same university where Penfold served for one year as chair of Women's Studies. Penfold attended a lecture given by Hyde about her experience treating adult survivors of child sexual abuse, liked what she heard, and telephoned her. Penfold was still conflicted over resuming therapy because of her experiences with Dr. A. Hyde made two promises: she would never sexualize therapy, and she would never relate to her socially as a friend. Both promises contributed to the success of therapy. Penfold was so apprehensive of becoming too attached to Hyde, as she had been to Dr. A, that she decided not to wear her glasses to therapy: she wanted to have "only a fuzzy image" of Hyde, to avoid an "indelible imprint" in her memory (136).

We learn little about Hyde's clinical orientation and even less about her personal life, but Penfold remarks that her "quiet confidence, warmth, and calmness" (133) were impressive. The turning point of therapy occurred during an early session when, in response to Penfold's assertion that she was complicit in the sexual relationship with Dr. A, the "mild-mannered" Hyde stood up and shouted, "Sue, you were a VICTIM! You must realize that. We can't get anywhere if you keep blaming yourself" (136). Hyde spoke plainly, directly, and warmly, and they quickly established a therapeutic alliance. Penfold avoids describing her transference relationship to Hyde apart from a fantasy that she and the therapist were putting together a huge jigsaw puzzle, a metaphor of Penfold's search for self-understanding. She left therapy after two years, immeasurably strengthened by what she had learned about her life.

Sexual Abuse in Health Professionals omits any references to Hyde's publications, but four of her articles cast light on her therapeutic relationship with Penfold. We can infer from "Psychotherapy as Mothering," published in *Perspectives in Psychiatric Care* in 1970, that empathy was at the center of Hyde's therapeutic model. Hyde took a psychodynamic approach to psychotherapy that emphasized a patient's strong transference relationship. Her assumption, shared by many psychotherapists during this time, that schizophrenic patients have been denied the experience of loving, trusting relationships with their mothers, is no longer tenable, but her emphasis on nurturing patients' strong transference relationships with their therapists remains useful. "Only as the therapist allows himself to experience and communicate the full intensity of his caring for the patient will the patient begin to have his needs met" (75).

Hyde's 1970 article focuses on her "therapeutic mothering" of Mr. B, a 37-year-old schizophrenic patient who had spent the last 15 years in a state mental hospital, but many of the therapist's statements also apply to her relationship with Penfold. Hyde experienced a conflict between her professional training, on the one hand, which required that she remain detached and "cerebral," lest she be overwhelmed by her patient's intense emotional demands and needs, and her intuitive understanding, on the other hand, which compelled her to assume the role of a "loving, mothering person" (74). Hyde's statement that "Mr. B's rage and anxiety were based on his helplessness and his need to be loved and cared for" (74) reminds us of Penfold's murderous rage based on her helplessness, need to be loved and, as the victim of sexual abuse, experience of betrayal. Mr. B's fear of the explosive and destructive quality of his rage reflected Penfold's own fear. Hyde encouraged both patients to integrate their anger and use it constructively. "To accept one's own rage," Hyde states, "and to understand that it is not of cataclysmic magnitude is a liberating experience" (77). Tellingly, Hyde wrote "Psychotherapy as Mothering" in the combined voices of her own "angry part," expressing Mr. B's raging storms and her fear of being swept away by violence, and the "other part," her scholarly, academic voice. She thus captures, as Penfold does in *Sexual Abuse by Health Professionals*, the therapist's integration of subjective, involved caring and objective, noninvolved caring.

Another Hyde article, "Play Therapy: The Troubled Child's Self-Encounter," published in 1971 in the *American Journal of Nursing*, would have special significance to Penfold, who also worked in a children's hospital. The child therapist "may say little," Hyde writes, "but she must communicate her acceptance of the child, her empathy with his pain, and her expectation that he has the necessary ability to work through his own difficulties" (1367). Two of the articles Hyde wrote in the 1980s, around the time Penfold was in therapy with her, relate directly to literal and symbolic incest. "Long-Term Effects of Childhood Sexual Abuse," published in 1984, warns of the dangers of sexualizing therapy. Health professionals who change roles and respond to a patient as a lover, Hyde writes, "repeat the incestuous events of the survivor's early life" and "orphan" the woman, "leaving her betrayed and bereft of healing and support" (449). Hyde cites the results of a 1973 study of first-year medical students in which 25% of the respondents believed intercourse with patients could be appropriate under the "right circumstances" if the doctor was "genuine" and "authentic" (449), a conclusion that Hyde found alarming.

It's surprising that Penfold doesn't refer to "Covert Incest in Women's Lives: Dynamics and Directions for Healing"; Hyde's 1986 article anticipates many of Penfold's own conclusions in *Sexual Abuse by Health Professionals*. "It has been shocking," Hyde writes in the opening paragraph, "for us as community mental health professionals and as members of this society to realize the pervasiveness of incest in our culture" (73). Hyde does not explicitly qualify her call for "therapeutic mothering" in her 1970 article, but she is now more cautious about a therapist's identification with a patient. Arguing that "boundary violations beget boundary violations" (80), Hyde makes a statement that foreshadows Penfold's trenchant criticisms of Dr. A. Male therapists "often function with women clients in covertly incestuous ways which tend to parallel father-daughter covertly incestuous behaviours. That is, male therapists may act in seductive ways with women clients, leading them to believe they are 'special,' offering compliments with sexual overtones, touching them inappropriately, discussing their own problems, and allowing the clients to take care of them" (81). One senses Hyde's impassioned commitment to feminism and her willingness to make bold statements, as when she declares that "There has never been a taboo against incest; the taboo has been against speaking about it" (81). Hyde's article casts light not only on Penfold's story but on Evelyn Walker's as well, as when Hyde quotes Adrienne Rich's observation that "Women have been driven mad, 'gaslighted' for centuries" (76).

Naida Hyde became a trusting and devoted figure who helped Penfold detoxify the poisonous shame deriving from childhood and adult sexual abuse. Hyde made possible Penfold's growing respect toward others and herself, the third meaning of Wurmser's discussion of shame. Hyde's name is ironic, for as Donald L. Nathanson suggests, "The very word shame is derived from an Indo-European root (*skam* or *skem*) which means 'to hide,' and from which also derive our words *skin* and *hide*, the latter in both of its meanings: the hide which covers us naturally, and that within which we seek cover" (8). Naida Hyde helped Penfold come out of the closet, break the silence of sexual abuse, and encourage others through her talks and writings to overcome the need to hide from the truth.

Only in the last chapter of *Sexual Abuse by Health Professionals*, "Towards Less Abuse and More Healing," do Penfold's two voices, the "angry part" and the "other part," merge, suggesting self-integration. The bitter anger of the first voice modulates to righteous indignation of the second voice. She ends with the hope that her book will contribute to a greater understanding of the subject and to survivors' healing, goals that she herself achieved through effective psychotherapy, her commitment to feminism and a support group, and writing the book.

The most recent information we have about Penfold's life following the publication of *Sexual Abuse by Health Professionals* comes from *Tell: Therapy Exploitation Link Line* (www.therapyabuse.org/papers.htm), which indicates that she is Professor Emeritus of the Division of Child Psychiatry, Department of Psychiatry at the University of British Columbia and BC Children's Hospital. She has not written additional books, but she remains involved at Children's Hospital as coordinator of the Child and Family Resource Manual Project for Children Who Have Witnessed or Experienced Abuse or Violence. She is also a psychiatric consultant to the Oak Tree Clinic for women and children with HIV/AIDS and to the Child Protection Service Unit.

Beyond Rehabilitation

Penfold learned from a lawyer with the state attorney general's department in late 1994 that Dr. A had agreed to the two demands issued by the State Medical Quality Assurance Commission. He was required to attend therapy for at least a year and to avoid treating women alone in his office. She was told that he admitted having sex with her but not with the other patient who had filed a complaint against him. Penfold was satisfied with this outcome but nevertheless disappointed that she would not have her day in court testifying against him. "Without this," she tells us, "the resolution did not seem quite real" (161). Unlike Plasil, Walker and Bates, she did not file a malpractice suit against her therapist: we never learn why she had ruled out this course of action. In the epilogue written in September 1997 shortly before her book's publication, Penfold reveals her recent discovery that several more complaints were filed against Dr. A. She never learned the names of the patients, when the charges of abuse took place, or whether any of the patients began as students of Dr. A, like herself. Penfold did learn, however, that as a result of these new complaints, Dr. A lost his license to practice.

Other Sexual Boundary Violation Stories: Undertow

The four books we have described in this chapter all involve landmark cases, but there are other book-length accounts of female patients sexually abused by male psychotherapists. Most of these memoirs are self-published and therefore do not attract national attention. These memoirs have much in common with the books we have discussed, including a male psychotherapist who exploits his female patient's transference-love for him and conducts therapy with few if any boundaries, resulting in the patient's confusion and heightened vulnerability. Trudy Seagraves' 2014 memoir *Undertow: Surviving the Predatory Psychiatrist* is noteworthy for offering an unusually detailed first-person account of her three-year therapy with Harry Brown, who seemed clueless about the ways in which his violation of professional boundaries drove his patient deeper into despair.

Seagraves began therapy with Brown in 1985, when she was 53. She hoped he would have the key to unlock the night terrors and flashbacks of incest from which she had long suffered. A New Age psychiatrist who practiced in the affluent community of Westport, Connecticut, Brown was known locally for pioneering esoteric spiritual systems, including past life regression therapy and channeling. He specialized in bioenergetics, a form of "body psychotherapy" based on the work of Wilhelm Reich.

A medical journal editor, Seagraves is articulate and smart. She knows that, transferentially, Harry Brown represented her father, whom she suspects sexually abused her when she was a child. But despite her knowledge that sex in therapy is transgressive, she became increasingly obsessed with her psychiatrist. She alternates between the belief that he is in love with her, as she is with him, and the fear that she is only one of many female patients toward whom he acts seductively.

Like Lonnie Franklin Leonard, Zane Parzen, Dr. X, and Dr. A, Harry Brown is a master of manipulation. He never acknowledged wrongdoing, though he admitted that he has a "slight tendency to rescue" (225)—meaning, acting out rescue fantasies. He conceded he might have been playing an "unconscious game" with her. Spreading his arms and legs wide, he says, "When you confront me, it arouses two parts in me: a deep, healthy part and a part that's not" (229). In addition to sexualizing therapy, he disclosed the intimate details of his other patients' lives to her, thus violating the confidentiality of therapy. Trudy Seagraves finally summoned the courage to leave therapy and file a complaint against Brown before the Fairfield County Medical Board. We learn at the end of the story that the complaint had "no effect," though we don't learn why it was rejected. Nor do we learn about the outcome of her malpractice suit against Brown.

In an effort to learn more about why the Fairfield County Medical Board did not rule in favor of Seagraves, we asked Thomas G. Gutheil, Professor of Psychiatry at Harvard Medical School who had written a back-cover blurb for *Undertow*, if he could cast further light on the case. He told us (Personal correspondence, May 23, 2016) that while he did not have additional information, "medical boards, though usually unduly punitive, are at best whimsical organizations. Furthermore, many malpractice insurers will not cover sexual misconduct as a claim, arguing that it is an intentional tort and they only cover negligent torts."

Undertow ends on a note of hope and release. Seagraves cites the last words of *The Sound and the Fury*: "They endured." Like Faulkner's characters, she too endured. As we have seen in other accounts of sexual boundary violations, the act of writing proves therapeutic. "Hoping for clarity," she began a journal after a year of therapy to understand what transpired during her sessions. "My habit of keeping journals and recording conversations verbatim has saved me in the past," she remarks midway through the book (120). Writing saves her in the present, allowing her to tell a disturbing story and move forward with her life.

We should mention one more account of a sexual boundary violation that did not result in any legal or medical sanction against a psychiatrist accused of drugging, raping and impregnating a patient: *Doctors Who Rape*, published in 1991. What's odd about the book is that the author's name is spelled three different ways: Pauline Trumpe on the spine of the book and the title page, and Pauline Trump as the holder of the book's copyright and in the Library of Congress Cataloguing-in-Publication data. A third spelling, Pauline Trumpi, is used for the revised and updated 1997 edition. Part of *Doctors Who Rape* focuses on the author's "personal holocaust" (1); the rest of the book offers generally accurate information about the moral, ethical and legal implications of sexual boundary violations.

CONCLUSIONS

Little was known about sexual boundary violations in the 1970s, when Lonnie Franklin Leonard, Zane Parzen, Dr. X, and Dr. A induced their patients to have sex with them. In 1973, the American Psychological Association appointed Annette Brodsky and seven other psychologists to a task force charged with studying the prevalence of the problem. The task force found that between 1970 and 1974, there were only four cases of therapist-patient sex investigated by the APA's ethics committee, three of which were dismissed. Brodsky's research helped her sketch a portrait of a psychologist "at risk" for having sex with a patient. Her portrait of the psychologist who sexualizes treatment characterizes Lonnie Franklin Leonard, Zane Parzen, Dr. A, and Dr. X:

> The therapist is male, middle-aged, involved in unsatisfactory love relationships in his own life, and perhaps going through a divorce. His caseload is primarily female. He becomes sexually involved with more than one patient, and his victims are, on average, 16 years younger than he. He confides his personal life to the patient, implying that he needs her, and he spends their therapy sessions soliciting her help with his personal problems. He is a lonely man, and even if he works in group practice, he is somewhat isolated

professionally, not in close contact with his peers. He may have a good reputation in the psychological or psychiatric community and have been in practice for many years. He tends to take cases only through referral. He is not necessarily physically attractive, but there is an aura of power or charisma about him. Although his lovemaking often leaves much to be desired, he convinces his patients that he, above all others, is the one with whom she needs to be making love. (Bates and Brodsky, 135)

Therapist, A Killing Cure, Sex in the Therapy Hour and *Sexual Abuse by Health Professionals* all involve psychotherapists who are off the tracks, derailed by personal and professional conflicts. The transgressive psychologists, psychiatrists and psychoanalysts in this chapter are all examples of Don Juan therapists. At least two of them exerted a Svengali-like influence over their patients. Stories about derailed psychotherapists are cautionary tales, awakening horror and indignation in readers. Most of these stories, however, also contain compassionate therapists who reveal the helping profession at its best.

A Literary Sub-Genre

Book-length accounts of sexual boundary violations represent a small but significant sub-genre of memoiristic writing. The most striking feature of this writing involves a female patient (mis)treated by a male therapist. But the word *mistreated* fails to do justice to what is in every case a traumatic story filled with pain and shame. Penfold's 1998 observation that all the published accounts of sex in therapy are written by women (164) appears still to be true, though *A Killing Cure* has a male co-author. This is not to imply that female therapists do not have sex with male patients—they do—but rather that male patients do not write books about their experience. Nearly all of the witnesses who testify against therapists in malpractice suits are female patients who were induced to have sex in therapy. These witnesses play a decisive role not only in determining the outcome of a malpractice suit, but also in shaping the reader's sympathy for and identification with the female patient. The protagonists and their witnesses in these stories are nearly always women. Gender thus plays a crucial role in the literature of sexual boundary violations.

There are many commonalities between victims of childhood sexual abuse and sexual boundary violations. Victims of both acts are more likely to be female, and they are nearly always filled with guilt and shame. They carry with them a dark secret they are afraid to reveal to anyone, fearful of losing the abuser's love and support. Victims of childhood sexual abuse and sexual boundary violations are invariably self-blaming, holding themselves responsible for what has happened. Self-blame complicates escape from a perilous situation.

The law plays a central role in sexual boundary violation stories. Patients who file malpractice suits against their therapists in sexual boundary violations cases often do not have corroborative evidence. It is the patient's word against the therapist's word. Given the stigma surrounding mental illness, female patients confront a daunting challenge in getting a jury or an insurance company to believe they have been victimized by a male therapist. Lawyers thus figure prominently in the literature of sexual boundary violations. The American legal system is inherently adversarial, and a plaintiff in a sexual malpractice suit— almost always a female—can expect her entire sexual history to be put on trial by a therapist's defense lawyer. There is always the possibility of a false complaint being filed, but this happens only in a small minority of cases. Usually, a transgressive therapist's former patients come forward as a result of media publicity and, without speaking with each other, report strikingly similar stories of sexual abuse, confirming the therapist's *modus operandi.*

Writing/Righting Wrong

The research on sexual boundary violations in psychotherapy largely ignores the value of patients writing about their experiences. The burgeoning interest in trauma theory offers us an insight into the importance of such writing. Authoring an account of one's sexual violation by a trusted therapist is an example of "writing wrong." The expression comes from the literary critic Sandra M. Gilbert, whose 1995 memoir *Wrongful Death* documents her malpractice suit against the University of California at Davis Medical Center, where her 60-old husband, Elliot, an English professor at U.C. Davis, died following routine prostate surgery on February 10, 1991. After completing her memoir, Sandra Gilbert then wrote the magisterial *Death's Door: Modern Dying and the Ways We Grieve* (2006), where she devotes a chapter to "Writing Wrong."

Many of Gilbert's observations about writing *Wrongful Death* also apply to memoirs like *Therapist, A Killing Cure, Sex in the Therapy Hour* and *Sexual Abuse by Health Professionals.* The "effort to write (record) and right (rectify) wrong involves both fear and ferocity" for both types of memoirists (*Death's Door,* 87). Writers like Gilbert, Ellen Plasil, Evelyn Walker, Carolyn Bates and Susan Penfold are compelled to "testify, bear witness," and in doing so they swear to the truth of their accounts (89). Such writing is therapeutic, "leading to moments of transformation when rage and grief yielded to visionary consolation" (91). Writing wrong may feel like a curse, but it is something one must do. "That which I feared the most, as I bleakly put it to myself, was what I had to confront, and I had to confront it precisely because in order to stand the pain of my loss, I had to stand *up* to the pain and loss, strive to *with*stand them by looking at them" (93). Plasil, Walker, Bates and Penfold would probably identify with Gilbert's admission that she might have embarrassed or distressed many of her listeners and readers. So, too, would patients who write about sexual abuse in therapy identify with Gilbert's fear that she has turned herself into a "loser," a "whiner," a "complainer" (94). Notwithstanding embarrassment or humiliation, these authors were compelled to tell their stories. Writing became a counter-shame technique, allowing them to expose and detoxify shame.

As wrenching as it is to write a story like *Wrongful Death*, it is more wrenching to write one like *Therapist, A Killing Cure, Sex in the Therapy Hour* or *Sexual Abuse by Health Professionals*. Sandra Gilbert was not responsible for her husband's death, and though she tortured herself for not insisting that the surgery be performed at another hospital—as some of their friends urged them to do—she was blameless for the tragic events that occurred. Her existential guilt pales in comparison to the guilt, blame and shame experienced by Plasil, Walker, Bates or Penfold for allowing themselves to be violated by a trusted therapist, an experience they and others liken to symbolic incest with a father figure. There is no calculus of shame, but that which arises from sexual trauma in psychotherapy may be overwhelming. The feelings associated with colluding in one's own exploitation are often beyond words. Few can write about such harrowing experiences, but Plasil, Walker, Bates and Penfold did, and we are the beneficiaries of their writings.

CHAPTER 4

The Not-So-Reluctant Exhibitionist: Martin Shepard

Sigmund Freud, no lover of "America" from afar, contemplated a possible first trip to the United States in 1909 to deliver what are now known as the Clark Lectures. The good doctor, however, was troubled by two issues. He feared, first, that he would lose money by having to take time away from his practice in Vienna and, second, that the heavy emphasis on sexuality in his theories—troubling enough to the reputation of psychoanalysis in Europe—would collide with America's prudish culture. Using unusually colorful language, he described his concern in a letter written on January 10, 1909, to his colleague Sandor Ferenczi:

> I was also sorry about declining to go to America, and if the trip does come about contrary to all expectation, I would also be in a position to ask you to accompany me. But I do find the

presumption to sacrifice so much money in order to give lectures there much too "American." America should bring money, not cost money. By the way, we could soon be "up shit creek" the minute they come upon the sexual underpinnings of our psychology. Brill writes, alternating between hopefulness and misgiving, that he thinks he will soon find this very hard. (*Correspondence of Sigmund Freud and Sandor Ferenczi*, vol. 1, 33–34)

Importing Psychoanalysis into the United States

Ultimately Freud and two colleagues did arrange to come to the United States, sailing on a North Lloyd liner named the George Washington, George Prochnik writes in his 2006 study of Freud's relationship with James Jackson Putnam. "As their ship entered New York harbor, Freud, Ferenczi, and Jung watched the approach of envy-green Lady Liberty, the ghost necklace of the Brooklyn Bridge, and the panoply of downtown scrapers circa 1909. Tired and ill after their ten-day passage, they floated through the East River mist. Suddenly, Freud turned to his companions and said, "Don't they know we're bringing them the plague?" (18).

Freud regarded his warm reception at Clark University with "benign ambivalence," the historian Nathan G. Gale, Jr. observes in *Freud and the Americans*, largely because American psychoanalysts "seemed to feel a stronger pressure to synthesize psychoanalysis with received medical and moral opinions" (331). American psychoanalysts "muted sexuality and aggression, making both more amiable" (332). Freud was so distressed by the growing popularity of psychoanalysis in the United States, particularly the New World's free and easy manners, which he felt lacked dignity, that he told Ernest Jones, "America is a mistake; a gigantic mistake, it is true, but none the less a mistake" (Jones, vol. 2, 60).

One consequence of importing psychoanalysis into the United States was the decision to maintain its medical stature. Only physicians would be able to deal with "delicate" topics. Another consequence was the young science's movement in a technical direction, away from its earthier European roots. American psychoanalysts have thus downplayed their European counterparts' emphasis on sexuality, and they become rattled when one of their own seems to go off the tracks.

One does not usually characterize American psychoanalysts as exhibitionists or "swingers." Analysts tend to be by temperament, training and selection a conservative group. Psychoanalysts have sometimes been described as leading monkish lives, largely because the profession attracts intellectual, introverted adherents who prefer relatively quiet and solitary existences. Whether by design or not, the long training analysis required of an analyst seems generally to encourage social conformity. Furthermore, anxious to avoid complicating the transference relationship, analysts try to avoid situations where a patient might be present, such as a dinner party or a social gathering. The idea of an exhibitionistic or swinging psychoanalyst—one who engages publicly in psychedelic drug use, wife or partner swapping, troilism (three-way sex) and other forms of "free love"—is antithetical to the culture of American psychoanalysis. That's why the story of Martin Shepard is fascinating.

Psychoanalytic Training

Much of our information about Shepard comes from his autobiography, which was published three different times under three different titles. It first appeared in 1972 as *A Psychiatrist's Head*. The first edition soon sold out, and when the publisher refused to reprint the book,

Shepard republished it in 1978 as *Memoirs of a Defrocked Psychoanalyst*, a misleading title because he had never actually received certification as a psychoanalyst. He republished the autobiography yet a third time in 1985 as *The Reluctant Exhibitionist*, a title fraught with irony. The three editions are identical except that the second edition, *Memoirs of a Defrocked Psychoanalyst*, contains a prologue and four appendices, with a document relating to his struggle with the William Alanson White Institute of Psychiatry, Psychoanalysis and Psychology and the New York State Education Department. The third edition, *The Reluctant Exhibitionist*, contains a brief author's note and an introduction by D.M. Thomas, author of the erotic novel *The White Hotel*. Thomas remarks that Shepard records his encounter group therapy sessions with a "dynamic gusto" reminiscent of Henry Miller. "The group leader is becoming healed along with the members. He is indeed a member himself; and the pun is intentional" (vi).

There was little in Shepard's early life or professional training that would have predicted his radical break with orthodoxy. Born in 1934, he describes a socially difficult and lonely childhood. He attended the High School of Music and Art in New York, with the dream of becoming an artist like his father. At the time of his high school graduation, he seems to have been socially isolated, unable to develop "anything even remotely resembling a satisfying affectional relationship with my peers" (*A Psychiatrist's Head*, 157). Realizing that as an artist he would probably not make a satisfactory income, and apparently fearful of entering the work world of adults with no social relationships, he applied to New York University as a pre-dental student. His academic record up to that point was mediocre at best because he had avoided reading assignments through much of high school. His father refused to fund Shepard's college education due to his demonstrated disinclination to study, and Shepard was required to take entry-level jobs while attending college.

He attributed a dramatic improvement in his academic performance to the fact that he was paying his own way. In addition, he began to take psychology courses, hoping to understand why he felt "shy, and bumbly, and foolish, and inept, and insecure and frightened." He decided to become a physician when he realized that his new academic success made it possible to gain acceptance to a medical school.

Shepard attended the New York University College of Medicine. His personal misery continued, however, and he eventually unburdened himself to an older male classmate to whom he had become emotionally attached ("loved"). This classmate had been significantly helped by psychoanalysis and advised Shepard to seek such treatment for himself.

While a medical student, Shepard applied to the White Institute's low-cost clinic and began a four session per week psychoanalysis with a student analyst at the cost of $1.00 per session. He seems to be at a loss—as many psychoanalytic patients are at the end of the process—to explain why and how the experience of analysis helped him. Yet, while in analysis at the clinic, he underwent a dramatic transformation which, he writes, "turned my life about completely" (161), changing him from a "shy, readily intimidated, fearful person, to someone who was capable of being clear about his feelings and needs and bold enough to act upon them" (146). He admits that he could not attribute his transformation to any standard analytic theory of "cure," but he speculates that a major factor was the unconditional acceptance he felt from the female analytic trainee, Helen Edey, his first psychoanalyst. This is a remarkable disclosure from a person who only a few years later became a strident critic of psychoanalysis.

Shepard interned for a year at the Bronx Hospital (probably Bronx State Hospital, later Bronx Psychiatric Center) and spent two years in a psychiatric residency at Hillside Hospital in New York. He then did a third year of psychiatric residency at Mount Sinai Hospital in New

York City, where he became Chief Resident. He was accepted at the White Institute for training as a psychoanalyst in 1964. For the next six years he took courses, treated patients under the supervision of senior analyst supervisors and underwent a second personal analysis. He was a recipient of a Harry Scherman Foundation grant from the White Institute in 1964 (Turkel, 83). During his psychoanalytic training, Shepard became involved in the "counterculture," at the time of its ascendance, a period generally dated from 1964 to 1972. He started an encounter group institute in New York said to have been patterned on the encounter groups at Esalen Institute in California, experimenting with mind-altering (and illicit) drugs and advocating sexual liberation.

"Some Major Drawbacks to Your Work"

By May 1966, Shepard was being advised that his work at the White Institute was problematic. "I was surprised to learn that his analysis has been 'completed,'" his first psychotherapy supervisor wrote about him. "He 'acts out' a great deal in treatment. He is frequently mocking and, at times, even supercilious with patients. He responds to very many statements with deprecating remarks" (Schechter, 3). Although the supervisor described him as "lively, intelligent, and sometimes helpful to his patients," the supervisor expressed the view that his behavior with patients was "defensive and characterological," concluding, "Shepard certainly needs a lot of work, whether psychotherapy or psychoanalysis." The supervisor's use of "sometimes," one suspects, might have been a way of damning with faint praise.

Shepard claims in *A Psychiatrist's Head* that his work at the White Institute was initially viewed as satisfactory. "From 1964, when I first entered the Institute training program, through 1966, I did quite well.

Evaluation of my work by supervisors and instructors was almost unanimously positive" (192). This claim is not true, however, for by July 1966, he had received a letter from the Director of Training that described the Institute's concerns. "Although you are seen as being a sensitive and alert therapist who is often quite helpful to patients there are also some major drawbacks to your work which need serious consideration" (Schecter, 3). Rather than taking the supervisor's advice to seek additional personal treatment, Shepard ended his work with that supervisor.

Another White Institute teacher filed a negative report on Shepard in May 1967. "I must say that I found this student *distressing*" (Schechter, 4). An additional report revealed the same judgment. "Dr. Shepard was the most *dismal presence* in the class. He was *disruptive, hostile*, pointlessly quarrelsome, sadistic to a number of others [i.e., students]" (5). Faculty reports continued to show increasing concern about Shepard's work. He received another letter from the Director of Training at the end of 1967 reiterating these concerns along with a warning that his political activities might be taking time away from his psychoanalytic work. "We feel it would be useless for you to continue psychoanalytic training until you are able to make a much more significant commitment to it" (6).

Initial Attention from the Press for an Anti-War Activist

Shepard had strong feelings of opposition to the Vietnam War. He became involved in organizing a grassroots movement to draft Robert Kennedy as a presidential candidate to oppose Lyndon Johnson. According to an article appearing in the *New York Times* on September 11, 1966, the formation of a New York chapter of a group supporting Kennedy had taken place in Shepard's office on the prior day, although he was quoted as saying that the group had no backing from Kennedy. In another article in the *Times* published on March 5, 1967, Shepard was described, or perhaps described himself, as "leader of Citizens for Kennedy-Fulbright." He later referred to himself in *A Psychiatrist's Head* as the national co-leader of a "movement" to draft Kennedy (195). According to K. Dun Gifford, the national Presidential campaign advisor to Kennedy, when the senator actually did announce his candidacy, Shepard assumed he would become Kennedy's national campaign manager. In an oral history interview with Larry J. Hackman, Gifford's response to a question about Shepard's role in the Kennedy movement is revealing:

HACKMAN: Was there any serious consideration to using them in any kind of useful way? Was there a potentially useful way they could be used?

GIFFORD: Well, you know the history of them. They started out as the genuine "draft Kennedy" movement. Kennedy had nothing to do with it, nor any of his people, and no encouragement was given to him, Martin Shepard. He had a group of people in all the states theoretically, mailing lists, people who sent in money to buy bumper stickers. When Senator Kennedy did announce, I think Martin Shepard expected, quite honestly, to be campaign manager, and it took.... I don't know as we ever did dissuade him that he wasn't going to be campaign manager. You were right that I was left to handle that particular situation. I liked the guy. You know, he's a little bit.... No, I like him; you know, he's not a little bit anything. I like him. He's enthusiastic and aggressive and politically naive, but what the hell, you wouldn't expect anything else. He'd never been in a campaign before of any size. (K. Gifford)

Shepard's naive aggressiveness manifested itself in both his political and psychoanalytic activities, twin commitments that seemed to be competing for his time. A seminar supervisor described Shepard's presentation of a case as showing the use of a "rather peculiar technique of teasing the patient, as well as being ironic and sarcastic toward her." Although the supervisor noted that Shepard's technique seemed to improve, she also pointed out that his political activities were taking a great deal of his time and that he "talked at length over the phone while the patient was there, both to other patients and about political involvements." On an audiotape he brought to her, the supervisor could hear the telephone ringing frequently during the session. "Each time Dr. Shepard had long telephone calls at the expense of the patient's time. When the supervisor pointed this out as an unconscionable neglect of the patent, Dr. Shepard indicated he could see nothing wrong with this behavior." The supervisor interpreted Shepard's conduct as revealing an "almost psychopathic lack of concern for his patients' rights and feelings" (8).

In *A Psychiatrist's Head*, Shepard defends himself against his supervisor's criticism that a public persona would be harmful to his patients' transference relationship with him. "Top that for myopia," he indignantly mutters, and then contrasts himself with the emperor Nero. "I should fiddle while the world burns. Here is a supervising analyst at the White Institute telling me that it is more important for me to be publicly silent about the war (so that I could be the good blank screen that my patient could 'transfer' his childhood feelings on to) than to work openly to end the slaughter. And she kept up this nagging advice for the several sessions I saw her" (196). Commenting on another supervisor's criticism about his extended political phone conversations during analytic sessions, Shepard writes: "Most analyst's phones didn't ring so frequently. Or if they did, the analyst could afford to let an answering service pick up for him. I couldn't do that, for I was committed to stopping the war by promoting this revolution within the Democratic Party" (197). Shepard realized that these interruptions might upset a patient's train of thought, but he also felt that his public commitment to nonviolence could serve a useful therapeutic purpose. One wonders whether this flirtation with national politics and the newspaper headlines it brought him might have contributed to or simply presaged what at times appears to be a grandiose self-regard in the next phase of Shepard's career.

New Age Therapy and the Human Potential Movement

After Robert Kennedy's assassination in June 1968, Shepard began work with two supervisors who generally thought his work was improving. The progress was short-lived. During the summer and fall of that year, he broke off his work with them even though they each felt he needed additional supervision. He became involved in the pursuit of other non-psychoanalytic forms of psychotherapy and in the "human potential movement," both of which were distinctly "1960s" in character. He was particularly attracted to encounter groups in which participants were on occasion nude and engaged in various forms of sexual contact. He studied with a leading therapist associated with the Esalen Institute of California when that leader came East in the winter of 1968. His interest in Fritz Perls began at that same time. "Sex, drugs, Gestalt, and encounter groups made Esalen a magnet for affluent educated seekers in their twenties and thirties who would soon be joined by the first wave of baby boomers" (Goldman, 55). Started in 1962, "Esalen's many paths to self-discovery and personal transformation quickly became more intense and included marathon encounter groups where people displayed extreme emotions and sometimes attacked one another physically, as well as nude massage, group sex, and psychedelic trips" (13). Infatuated by the new wave "therapy" being practiced at Esalen, Shepard and two nonprofessional associates in the fall of 1969 established Anthos, "a New York version of the openness that was Esalen" (*A Psychiatrist's Head*, 201).

Shepard's involvement in politics, the anti-war effort and the human potential movement did little to improve his relationship with the White Institute. Finally, he received a terse letter, dated January 13, 1970, from the Institute's Director of Training. "I regret to inform you that at a recent meeting of the Training Committee it was decided to drop you from further training at the White Institute since you have failed to meet the criteria for graduation. We will be pleased to meet with you to discuss any questions this may raise in your mind" (*Shepard v. White Institute*, Exhibit A12).

Games Analysts Play

In the same year that he was expelled from the White Institute, 1970, Shepard published two books, *Games Analysts Play* and *Marathon 16*, both co-authored with Marjorie Lee. The books reflect his growing antipathy to psychoanalysis. Inspired by Eric Berne's bestselling *Games People Play* (1964), *Games Analysts Play* begins and ends with an earnest plea for greater honesty and authenticity in the patient-therapist relationship, a goal with which few could disagree. Nor could anyone disagree with the challenge of humanizing therapy—and urging both patients and therapists to be more human. The book opens with the famous statement of Harry Stack Sullivan, one of the founders of the White Institute: "We are all more simply human than otherwise." In light of Shepard's battle with the White Institute, quoting a statement by one of its founders was surely ironic.

Games Analysts Play offers an insider's look at psychoanalysis, satirizing every aspect of the patient-analyst relationship. The best jokes and anecdotes in *Games Analysts Play* are witty and irreverent, good enough to appear in *The New Yorker*. Shepard's humor turns darker and edgier when he describes the games analysts play to deny their sexual attraction to patients. These games, he suggests, are symptomatic of the analysts' countertransference, "the most dreaded of all therapeutic pitfalls" (82).

It's possible that some of the more authoritarian analysts of the White Institute might have taken offense at *Games Analysts Play*, particularly if they were honest enough to recognize the painful grains of truth in Shepard's cutting humor. It's doubtful, however, that the publication of the book alone would have gotten the young Shepard in serious trouble with his teachers. The White Institute prided itself on its toleration of a wide variety of theoretical points of view—it was founded, in fact, in 1946 as a protest against psychoanalytic rigidity. *Games Analysts Play* is provocative but not subversive. Shepard's next book, however, was a different story.

Marathon 16

Shepard's interest in Albert Ellis' encounter groups led to his second book, *Marathon 16*. Held at Shepard's office on 12 West 96th Street in

Manhattan, the session involved ten participants, all of whom selected their own pseudonyms, along with the two co-authors: "Marjorie," the 48-year old woman who was the observer and "preordained nonparticipant," and "M," Marty, the 34-year-old psychiatrist who was the leader of the marathon. The session, which took place from 10 a.m., June 21, 1969, through 2 a.m., June 22, 1969, chronicles 16 hours that are often tense, grueling, and sometimes violent. The publication of *Marathon 16* must have further horrified the White Institute analysts who had earlier in 1970 sent him a letter of dismissal.

The theory behind *Marathon 16* is avowedly antipsychoanalytic. "Often fantasy is an expression of what we would like to do, but don't have the courage to do, because we're embarrassed or ashamed," Shepard avers. "But if you want to live your life more adventuresomely, you can try doing more things" (75). The psychiatrist thus contrasts Freudian psychoanalysis, where "you're not supposed to *do* anything—just *understand* everything" (75), with acting out fantasies, especially sexual fantasies. This "Acting-Out Technique," Shepard effuses at the end of the book, "attempts to create a climate in which accelerated learning is possible" (251).

No one could accuse Shepard of being a *reluctant* exhibitionist in *Marathon 16*. To illustrate how people are "hung up," he invites the participants to undress, as he does, and then he "sprawls in an attitude of ease" (176–177). He invites the group members to touch each other and makes the rounds, obviously enjoying himself. When asked if he feel awkward without clothes, he responds, "No. I feel exhilarated," to which a participant responds, "M is not uncomfortable. This is what he's been waiting for all night!" (177). In a gesture of friendship, he shakes hands with Bernard's penis. Shepard embraces Little Prince, who has apparently recovered from her breakdown, her "freak-out," and lifts her off the floor. "Marty," Bernard exclaims enviously, "you're the only guy I know who is more lecherous than I am" (178).

Was the writing of *Marathon 16* an act of provocation, defiance, naiveté, idealism, or self-destruction? At what point does the acting out of fantasies become dangerous and countertherapeutic? When does an analyst's unanalyzed countertransference sabotage therapy? Shepard doesn't concern himself with any of these questions. There's little doubt that he regarded the marathon as a transformative experience, but it did nothing to help his ongoing struggle with the White Institute.

Suing the White Institute—and Dismissal

Following receipt of the dismissal letter in January 1970, Shepard filed a lawsuit against the White Institute in a New York Court, claiming that he had been expelled because of the publication of *Games Analysts Play*. He insisted that he had met all the requirements for graduation and moreover, that the Institute had violated its own rules by not allowing a dismissed student a formal hearing, thus denying him due process. The Court sided with Shepard, and the Institute was compelled to grant him a formal hearing that took place in November 1970.

At the hearing, the Institute presented a formal statement of its professed reasons for Shepard's dismissal, concluding that he had not met the requirements for graduation based on his "overall record." The Institute did not offer specific examples of his unsatisfactory work. In reply, Shepard stated that he believed he had met the requirements and again asserted that the dismissal was due to the publication of *Games Analysts Play*. He was provided a full transcript of the hearing, which is reproduced in the 1974 court record. In April of the following year, the Training Committee reaffirmed its view that he should be dropped.

The next day the Committee informed Shepard by letter that "he had not achieved the degree of competence which meets the standards of the Institute and that it could not conscientiously certify such competence by issuing a certificate." Shepard tried to appeal this decision in the courts again, but in the 1974 decision the court held that he had not filed this new petition in a timely way; and the case was dismissed (*Shepard v White*, 1974).

A dismissal from the Institute was no small matter. As Shepard states in *A Psychiatrist's Head*, "I managed to weather the storms and eventually completed all of the courses, supervision, and analysis necessary to secure my certification as a psychoanalyst. However, one week after this expensive training ended (I would estimate that the Institute cost me well over $20,000) [about $125,000 in today's dollars], my first book, *Games Analysts Play*, was published. Some days later, instead of receiving my certification, I received a letter dismissing me from the Institute for not 'completing the training requirements'" (145). Explaining the discrepancy between his idealized first analysis with a White student analyst and his bitter experience at the Institute, he elaborates on his shattered idealizations. "The biggest secret I learned in the course of that training was that the analysts were made of the same clay as other mortals—that they were as presumptuous, arrogant, blind, competitive, uptight, and as capable as being tin gods as all of the nonanalytic therapists I had seen in the course of my training" (146).

Did the White Institute dismiss Shepard because of his highly exhibitionistic and sexual interactions with patients appearing in his second book, *Marathon 16*, or because of public knowledge of the Anthos encounter groups? The latter possibility cannot be ruled out. While the Institute never directly raised this issue in any public document, there is the unanswered question as to why, in its submission to the Court, the Institute included, without comment, several clippings from the national press describing Anthos and the sexual activities in its groups, including two articles published in separate issues of *Newsweek*: "The Sensuous Therapist" (September 20, 1971) and "All About the New Sex Therapy" (November 27, 1972). Both clippings refer to events that took place after the 1970 dismissal. What could the Institute have been trying to accomplish by submitting these articles to the court in 1974?

Shepard raises these questions in the form of a self-interview in *A Psychiatrist's Head*. This allows him to dramatize two sides of his personality: the accusatory self, identified with his conscience, and the rebellious, transgressive side, struggling to break free from convention. "*You claim that the William Alanson White Institute dismissed you for rather petty, parochial reasons. Has it not occurred to you that they might well have dropped you for conduct unbecoming a member of their Institute? For sleeping around so readily, for example?*" Shepard's evasive answer shows his unwillingness to consider this possibility in any depth. "The only 'unbecoming conduct' I was guilty of, so far as I know, was the conduct of honestly saying what I felt, what I thought, and what I did" (148). After spending a couple pages describing his conduct in Institute classes, he realized he had not answered the question. "*But my earlier question to you was whether or not you thought the Institute might have dismissed you for your sexual adventures?*" His answer? "If they did, they never raised that question with me. Also, I never had these so-called 'sexual adventures' prior to my being dismissed from the Institute" (152). He returns to the question one more time. "*How do you reconcile sleeping with people who attended your encounter groups last summer with your claims of not sleeping with patients?*" His answer is the same that he later gave when the state revoked his medical license. "People who register for these weekend workshops don't consider themselves 'patients,' nor do I. The programs at Anthos were open to the general public—to 'normal people' who might wish to explore certain themes in living or want to learn more about human interactions" (153).

How did Shepard finally feel about his expulsion from the White Institute? His comments about Fritz Perls in the biography *Fritz*, first published in 1975, almost certainly reflect his feelings about his own situation. "The White Institute's unwillingness to grant him full membership proved to be one of the factors that liberated him from slavery to orthodox hours and a conventional practice" (56). The feeling of liberation, however, did not diminish Shepard's bitterness.

The Love Treatment: Raising Hell

Published in 1971, *The Love Treatment* is Shepard's most cited book. As an indication of its subversive content, *The Love Treatment* is dedicated to three controversial people: Albert Hoffman, the Swiss chemist who first synthesized and experienced the mental effects of the powerful hallucinogenic drug, LSD, which had become illegal in most jurisdictions in the mid-60s; John Lennon, a member of the Beatles and counterculture hero who was said to be almost constantly under the influence of LSD starting in 1967; and Alan Watts, a philosopher and New Age guru who wrote about the spiritual/religious effects of psychedelic drugs. Shepard admits in the preface to *The Love Treatment* that "conventional therapists" warned him not to embark on the research that culminated in the publication of his book, an admonition he regards as "specious." The caution is a clever opening: his book is *bound* to be incendiary. Why? "Sleeping with your patient—indeed, even daring to discuss the question—represents the last taboo in a field that otherwise prides itself on bringing light into dark places" (2).

Shepard supports Charles Clay Dahlberg's call for a large-scale Kinsey-type survey of patient-analyst sex. *The Love Treatment* may be seen as a small-scale survey, based on two-hour interviews with 11 patients who had sex with their therapists. Shepard notes correctly that Dahlberg had difficulty finding a professional journal that would publish his article and quotes several passages from "Sexual Contact Between a Patient and Therapist," but he fails to mention Dahlberg's extreme skepticism over the ethics of such transgressive relationships. One can agree with Shepard's observation that sex between a patient and therapist is more common than most people realize without agreeing with his conclusion that patients should not be "'protected' from the harsh realities of life" (ix).

Shepard's call in *The Love Treatment* for research on the benefits and risks of sexualized therapy was echoed in a 1979 law review article, *"Sexual Relations Between Psychotherapists and Their Patients: Toward Research or Restraint,"* by Leonard Riskin, a law professor at the University of Houston. Riskin acknowledges that despite the prohibition on therapist-patient sex, such conduct appeared to be continuing and was frequently not reported. Even when such behavior was reported, professional organizations were often hesitant to take action. By contrast, the actions of licensing bodies were often stern. Taking note of the lack of scientific data on the question of whether such "treatment" could be beneficial to some patients, Riskin urged the adoption of a policy allowing for sexual relations between therapists and patients. Such relations would be justified, he added, only if performed under research conditions. This research would supply the missing evidence of whether therapist-patient sex was helpful or harmful. In his discussion of the actual implementation of such a policy, however, Riskin admits the myriad obstacles that, to his apparent regret, would prevent such research from taking place.

Rationalizing Patient-Therapist Sex

Shepard's reasons for rationalizing patient-therapist sex in *The Love Treatment* are not those that James L. McCartney uses in his theory of overt transference. Rather, Shepard argues that sexual intimacy should be permitted as long as patients are not hurt. Who determines whether patients are helped or harmed by sleeping with their therapists? The patients themselves, Shepard insists, not the therapists. He concedes that some of the patients he interviewed were injured by sexual intimacy with their therapists, as were some of the therapists themselves, though he did not interview the latter. He asserts, with little convincing evidence, that some of the patients and therapists were helped. Shepard's conclusion is that rather than place himself in the "sterile bind of being either a proponent or abolitionist" of sexual intimacy between a patient and therapist, he prefers simply to say, "It's there. It exists. What can we learn from it so as to minimize its hazards and maximize its assets?" (201).

The Love Treatment reflects the Swinging Sixties, a decade of free love, hippies, psychedelic drugs, communitarianism and defiance of social conformity. The age emphasized Nietzsche's belief that "Everything is permitted"—or, in Freudian terms, a championing of the id over the superego. The book was criticized as soon as it appeared. Phyllis Chesler refers to it in her article "The Sensuous Psychiatrists," appearing in *New York Magazine* the same year. She disagrees sharply with Shepard's assertion that sexual involvement between patients and therapists is positive. Her own interviews of women who slept with their doctors indicated that the situation was not only harmful but a "new variation on a very old routine: exploitative sex."

There are several flaws in Shepard's argument in *The Love Treatment*, beginning with his own admission that patients cannot know in advance whether they will be helped or harmed by sexual intimacy with therapists. A number of the patients who believed they were helped by sex were interviewed shortly after therapy ended, suggesting they did not have sufficient time to evaluate their experiences. Having sex with a therapist invariably ended therapy, something on which Shepard doesn't comment. He promises to present his patients' points of view objectively, without adding his own subjective bias, but his three-page chapter "Confession" contradicts this claim.

Shepard's confession, it turns out, is that he did *not* have sex with an "attractive lesbian" at the beginning of his career. He saw her for the first time as a psychiatric resident, when she was hospitalized after having made several suicide attempts, and then he saw her years later when he was in private practice. She was "one of those painful shy and fearful souls who slipped into active homosexuality accidentally"—seduced when she was drunk at a party in her early teens by an older lesbian friend. Had she been seduced by a boy at the same impressionable age, Shepard asserts with absolute certainty, but with no concrete evidence, she would not have become a lesbian. Her overwhelming fear, she revealed to him in therapy, was being "penetrated." Shepard now believes that she needed a gentle heterosexual man to teach her the pleasures of sex—a man not only like himself but, more specifically, Shepard himself! He didn't act on the belief at the time, he ruefully admits, because of his professional training. "I *knew* I was wrong to withhold this offer, even if other professionals told me that such an involvement would have been a manifestation of my own neurosis, my own 'counter-transference,' my own *transferring* onto her my secret agendas, misperceptions, and inappropriate responses that arose out of my own needs and hangups" (19–20). We recall Shepard's mocking reference in *Games Analysts Play* to countertransference, the "most dreaded of all therapeutic pitfalls." Now it's clear that in this case he regards the analyst's, i.e. his, countertransference as nothing more than sexual cowardice.

Some of Shepard's statements have a distinct ring of truth about them, as when he states near the end of *The Love Treatment* that "Aside from their general personality quirks, some of the therapists mentioned by those I interviewed obviously had sexual problems of a far greater magnitude than the people whom they were treating" (201). The ring of truth also surrounds the statements made by those patients who admitted that having sex with their therapists was destructive. Less credible are the statements from patients who found sex with a therapist beneficial. These patients' endorsements appear, despite Shepard's claims to the contrary, as defensive rationalizations. Few readers will share Shepard's dismay when he states at the end of *The Love Treatment* that there are "no reputable therapeutic training centers that deal with the subject except in a completely prohibitive way" (202).

The American Journal of Psychiatry refused to publish an advertisement for *The Love Treatment*, prompting Shepard to pen a letter of complaint to the presidents of the American Psychiatric Association and the American Psychological Association. In his letter he described the ban as "arbitrary and outrageous." In addition, Shepard called for a large-scale investigation of "the incidence of sexual relations between patients and therapists in the hope of establishing 'guidelines' for circumstances under which such relations would be helpful or harmful." Shepard's letter was noteworthy enough to be mentioned in an article, "Psychiatry Journal Accused of Ban on Ad for Sex-Expose Book," published in the *New York Times* on September 7, 1971.

A Psychiatrist's Head / Memoirs of a Defrocked Psychoanalyst / The Reluctant Exhibitionist

Writers generally publish autobiographies near the end of their careers, when they attempt to sum up their lives and offer a retrospective analysis of their work, but Shepard first published his autobiography near the *beginning* of his writing career, when he was 38. *A Psychoanalyst's Head* created a firestorm of controversy as soon as it was published. Much of the book is based on a "somewhat fictionalized" journal entitled *Summer On the Tantric Road: An Erotic Autobiography*. Shepard's first literary agent advised him *not* to publish the book. "It's boring, second-rate pornography without redeeming social value or literary interest. And it's also extremely self-destructive. Not only will you ruin a promising career as a serious writer, but you will likely be censured by the medical authorities" (14–15). The agent's literary evaluation of the book is questionable but not the accuracy of his prediction.

In *A Psychiatrist's Head*, Shepard offers several graphic accounts of his sexual experiences with "members" (not "patients," he insists) of his encounter groups at Anthos. "During the twelve hours of talking, touching, and risk-taking, interesting things happened: the lesbian turned on to men for the first time, the homosexual went through some exotic masturbatory acts with one of the women, the straight girl suckled from a bisexual girl's nipple, and the superstraight guy gave me a bath, washing and touching every nook and cranny of my body. The participants left with a richer appreciation of their own sexuality, and I left with material for another book" (77–78). Shepard quotes an old Yiddish expression, "when the prick is up the brains go out the window" (132), and wonders whether that phenomenon was happening to him. It's a good question, one that he never resolves. There may be a double entendre in the original title of his autobiography, *A Psychiatrist's Head*, for given the amount of time he spends chronicling his phallic exploits, he seems to be thinking with his other head.

In a scathing review published in the *New York Times* on October 8, 1972, the counterculture-sympathizing psychoanalyst Joel Kovel (Douglas Kirsner, personal communication, July 9, 2015) faulted *A*

Psychoanalyst's Head for working to "debase any exploration of the very issues it raises." In his review, Kovel characterizes the self-admittedly counterphobic Shepard in these words: "Look at me, he demands of us, how can a man who pulls down his pants so often in the presence of relative strangers be afraid, or ashamed, or guilty of anything? And such is his narcissism that the whole world should change its ways to meet his needs." Stung by this and other criticisms, including Kovel's charge of narcissism, Shepard wrote a letter to the *Times* published three weeks later in which he made the tactical error of repeating all of the reviewer's excoriating statements, which allowed Kovel to offer a devastating rejoinder: "If Dr. Shepard doesn't want his reputation damaged, he should try to write better books."

Shepard's campaign to attract attention, however, appeared to be succeeding. Through this exchange, the publicity he received in the New York press and national magazines for his work on behalf of Robert Kennedy and his sexualized encounter groups; his appearances on television; and his books, he became well known. Indeed, in a 1973 book review in the *New York Times* of *"My Secret Garden,"* in which he had written a "perfunctory expert's 'defense' at the end," the reviewer, Caroline Seebohm, described him as "Martin Shepard, M.D, ubiquitous psychiatrist."

Losing and Regaining His Medical License

Shepard begins the prologue to *Memoirs of a Defrocked Psychoanalyst* with the statement that as a result of the prior first edition of his autobiography, the New York State Board of Regents revoked his license to practice medicine. "It was a *Catch 22* situation," he protests. "'If,' the State contended, 'the book were fiction, Shepard should lose his license for having held the profession up to ridicule.' On the other hand, if the

OFF THE TRACKS VOLUME 1

work were fact, 'he ought to have his license revoked for having been sexually intimate with patients.'" To which Shepard responds, "Heads we win, tails you lose" (vii).

A Psychiatrist's Head was published in 1972 and on October 18 of that same year, a letter of complaint of professional misconduct was filed with the New York State Education Department, at that time the administrative agency responsible for licensing physicians in New York State. The letter came not from a patient but rather from "a member of the Board of Directors of the William Alanson White Psychoanalytic Institute" (*Defrocked* 258). An investigation by the Committee on Professional Conduct took place, and a report was filed by the state investigator almost four years after the complaint (245).

In May 1976, the investigator Daniel O'Leary reported that "sometime in the years 1970 to April 29, 1971 [Shepard] while purportedly engaged in the practice of medicine as a psychiatrist, engaged in sexual intercourse with one or more of his patients, as set forth in a book entitled *A Psychiatrist's Head.*" The book, O'Leary wrote, claimed that the sexual encounters were part of the "treatment." The investigator also noted that even if Shepard's autobiography were a work of fiction, its publication brought medicine and psychiatry into disrespect, another form of professional misconduct. Apart from publication of the autobiography, no other evidence against Shepard was provided. No patient had complained about Shepard's conduct. The investigator recommended the revocation of Shepard's medical license. A hearing on the charges against Shepard began in December 1976, and it did not conclude until June of the following year. Shepard includes in the appendix to *Memoirs of a Defrocked Psychoanalyst* the entire report issued by the Department of Education of the State of New York Board for Medicine Committee on Professional Conduct that resulted in the revocation of his medical license. Unwisely, and perhaps as an indication of disrespect for the process in which he was now embroiled, Shepard served as his own attorney "using the attorneys who accompanied him only as advisors" (Abbott, 2).

Laurie Johnston reported on the hearing to revoke Shepard's medical license in the *New York Times* on December 23, 1976. According to Johnston, Shepard asserted in an interview, "I was sleeping with a lot of people . . . but I didn't consider them patients." While the press was denied admission to the hearing, Johnson noted that the "tall, slim, dark-haired psychiatrist wore blue jeans with a green cotton kurta shirt from India and a neck pendant he identified as the Tibetan character for the syllable 'OM,' use[d] in meditation." Shepard's unprofessional appearance at such a momentous hearing could well have been viewed by the Committee as an act of defiance or disrespect. Johnston also reported that Shepard "said his swansong to psychiatric practice had been *The Do-It-Yourself Psychotherapy Book*, published in 1973, and that he now considered himself a writer." It's as if Shepard were saying, "You can't fire me, I quit!" In fact, however, this was a turning point in Shepard's life, ultimately leading to a new and evidently more suitable career as a book publisher.

The Committee found Shepard guilty of unprofessional conduct because he claimed in *A Psychiatrist's Head* that he "engaged in sexual intercourse with patients as part of his psychiatric treatment of those patients" (*Memoirs of a Defrocked Psychoanalyst*, 249). The Committee went on to list several incidents in Shepard's book that it deemed unethical. Shepard published in *Memoirs of a Defrocked Psychoanalyst* his own lengthy counter-report in which he argues that not a single patient or former patient charged him with sexual involvement, that alleged "patient" intimacies occurred when he was leading encounter groups that were "human potential" workshops rather than therapy sessions, and that the Committee's investigation of and charges against him were "without precedent."

After receipt of the investigator's report and the hearing, the Committee recommended to the State Board of Regents, the final authority on professional licensing matters, the revocation of Shepard's medical license. The Committee also recommended, however, that the revocation be suspended and that he be placed on probation for five years—a significantly milder sanction than recommended by the investigator. Under such an arrangement, Shepard would have been allowed to continue to practice but would not be allowed to continue his transgressive activities. Shepard regarded the Committee's recommendation as a "slap on the wrist," as reported by Laurie Johnston in the *New York Times* on November 6, 1977. "If they find a doctor is sexually exploiting a patient, they should have the courage to take away his license," he added. Shepard's punishment-seeking taunt, thrown at the licensing system through the press, might be seen as an example of "twisting the lion's tail," a provocative piece of behavior that seemed to recur throughout this phase of his life. Predictably, the lion bit back. The Committee's report was taken up by the Board of Regents' own Review Committee in December 1977, but the Review Committee took a "more serious view" of Shepard's "misconduct" *and unanimously recommended that Shepard's license to practice medicine be revoked.* In Shepard's words, he was thus "defrocked." On December 17, 1977, the *New York Times* reported Shepard's reaction. "Reached at his Long Island home Shepard called the revocation of his license 'absolutely outrageous.' 'I never had sex with my patients,' he said, adding that the people described in his book were 'friends, associates, and neighbors.'"

At that time, and until 2001, the practice of psychotherapy in New York State was not regulated. Thus, a physician whose license had been revoked could continue to practice as a "psychotherapist" and could retain the designation of M.D., since the state has no power to rescind an academic degree. However, playing the event for maximum impact, the jacket of

Memoirs of a Defrocked Psychoanalyst shows Shepard's name with the "M.D." prominently X-ed out in red. Contrary to the disavowal of his identity as a physician displayed in his earlier published interviews, Shepard chose instead to fight the authorities to get his license restored—but he proceeded at first in his typical anti-authority style.

Shepard's first maneuver was to file an appeal for reconsideration of the previously rejected Regents' decision. The appeal was denied. Shepard then filed a lawsuit against the New York Commissioner of Education. Among the claims in this lawsuit was the assertion that the sexual interactions, while correctly described in his autobiographical book, were not with patients. The Court rejected all his arguments and he appealed the decision. He once again lost. In March 1979, the Appellate Court upheld each of the findings of the lower court (*Shephard* [sic] *v Ambach)*, including supporting the lower court's proper procedure in finding that the people with whom Shepard had described having sexual relations *were patients*. Apparently, at that point Shepard sought legal advice and seems to have learned, or at least been advised, that his confrontational manner was not likely to gain sympathy from the courts or the licensing authorities. He then tried a different maneuver, contrition, with the aid of an attorney, Richard Cummings.

In December 1979, the attorney filed a petition with the Committee to have Shepard's license restored, and a hearing was held on that petition on October 21, 1980 (Abbott "Report"). Attributing Shepard's earlier behavior to "stress" related to the breakup of his marriage, the attorney stated that despite "his marital troubles" and the revocation of his license, Shepard "had been able to remain a stable member of the community." Shepard testified at the hearing:

> He now realizes that he "trod a thin line" in the writing of his book, and while he does not believe that his writing of it justified

the loss of his license, he does understand how it could have been misinterpreted to mean that he was intimate with patients. He assures the Board of Regents that he would not venture into this territory again or do anything that would cause the medical community aggravation.

He maintained that that he had never engaged in sexual relations with a patient or former patient and that no physician-patient relationship existed between him and any person with whom he had been intimate. . . . He claimed that he would never have written the book if he knew it would be misinterpreted and cause a scandal.

Petitioner referred to his anti-authoritarian behavior in defending himself against the charges in the earlier hearings and said at the time he had an egotistical need to challenge existing law and authority. He said that this attitude resulted in his being convicted, in December of 1977, of a charge relative to having marijuana plants in his house, because he refused to accept an adjournment in the case which would have resulted in dismissal of the charge. He now feels it is better to effectuate change by working within the system rather than by using confrontational tactics. (Abbott 3–4)

The Committee report concluded unanimously that Shepard is "rehabilitated and felt that he is more thoughtful, mature, and less self-centered than he was at the time his book was written and even in 1977 when the [earlier] hearings were held, and therefore recommended unanimously that his license be restored." The Committee accepted his conciliatory admissions. "He further stated that he could see how [*A Psychiatrist's Head*] could give the impression that he was consorting with patients, he referred to his behavior 'when called to account five years after publication . . . I made such a stupid stink'. [He] further stated that he has done a disservice to himself and to the profession. He said that since then he has experienced difficult times, has had time to rethink his behavior and has given considerable thought to what he would do if his license was restored" (Abbott, 4).

Shepard then claimed that, with the return of his license, he could enter general medical practice and could become a "house call doctor" in an area with a shortage of physicians. "The Committee felt that he presented an impressive self-analysis but were concerned about his ability to practice medicine." They therefore ordered that he submit a plan for a one-year residency in general medicine as a condition for restoration of his license.

Beginning three months later, in January 1981, Shepard's attorney submitted a series of proposed plans for the additional training the Committee required, all of which were, in turn, rejected by the Committee as inadequate. In July 1981, his lawyer submitted evidence that he had not been granted acceptance to a residency program of the kind the Committee would accept, and at that point the committee evidently threw up its hands, relented, and recommended that his license should be restored and that "he be permitted to return to the practice of psychiatry."

A mere two years after the restoration of his license and the contrition he had expressed for having published the first edition of *A Psychiatrist's Head*, Shepard published yet a third edition of his autobiography, *The Reluctant Exhibitionist*, which contains the same material that caused the outcry leading to the license revocation in the first place. This could easily compel a reader to question the depth of the contrition and the maturation upon which the restoration of his license had been based. In a tone that cannot entirely conceal an attempt to convey a triumph, but with no mention of his contrite *mea culpa*, Shepard two years later wrote in the preface to *The Reluctant Exhibitionist* that in "late 1981, upon petition to the State of New York, a probationary license to practice medicine was restored to me and, on the 31st day of December, 1983, I was once more restored to full good standing within the medical fraternity" (iii).

We have provided this account of a downward spiral of Shepard's relationship with the White Institute and the New York State Board of Regents to offer a perspective on the books he was writing during and after this troubled time in his life. We need to point out that his account of the same events in *A Psychiatrist's Head*—as well as in its subsequent editions, *Memoirs of a Defrocked Psychoanalyst* and *The Reluctant Exhibitionist*—paints a strikingly different picture from those offered by the White Institute and by the Board of Regents, both of which he depicts as rigid, doctrinaire and unfair.

Beyond Sex Therapy

Shepard admits at the beginning of *Beyond Sex Therapy* (1975) that his book "is as much a product of the times we live in as it is a product of mine" (11). Nevertheless, he maintains that, despite accusations to the contrary, he has never had sex with a patient. In the six months he has been with his present wife, Judy, he exclaims, "I haven't felt like sleeping with anyone else. It isn't worth the hassle. For one thing, I'm phenomenally well taken care of. And for another, I wouldn't want to jeopardize what I have. Or cause Judy pain. Because I love her" (166). Tellingly, his reasons for not having sex with a patient include nothing to do with the *patient's* welfare. Indeed, despite his extensive psychoanalytic training, he never thinks like a psychoanalyst, ignoring the unconscious forces that shape thought and behavior. In his 1972 letter published in the *New York Times Book Review* complaining about Kovel's review of his earlier book, Shepard had characterized himself as "an anti-analytic psychiatrist," a description that not only might explain his refusal to think as an analyst but also causes one to wonder why just two years earlier he had taken the White Institute to court for failing to give him a certificate as a psychoanalyst.

The Incest Taboo

No one can disagree with Shepard's assertion in *Beyond Sex Therapy* that in "these sexually liberated times there is a place and a forum for almost every sexual point of view" (134). In *The Love Treatment*, he rationalizes breaking the *symbolic* incest taboo in psychotherapy, sex between a patient and therapist. In *Beyond Sex Therapy*, he considers shattering the *real* incest taboo in the nuclear family.

What's probably most striking to 21st century readers of *Beyond Sex Therapy* is not Shepard's graphic descriptions of having sex with supposed nonpatients, which he dutifully records in his "erotic journal," but his long and sympathetic discussion of incest. Nearly all of his comments focus on the actual or potential benefits of incest, including parent-child incest. Startlingly, he never seems disturbed by the traumatic implications of incest for many of those who have such experiences. Can incest be nonabusive? A few studies, such as those by Yorukoglu and Kemph in 1966, Narcyz Lukianowicz in 1972 and James Henderson in 1983, conclude that incestuous experiences appear to have caused little harm. Most studies, however, have shown that incest during childhood usually results in harm to the child.

The only time childhood incest is nonabusive, Diana E.H. Russell suggests in *The Secret Trauma*, a 1986 study of the impact of incest in the lives of girls and women, is when "brothers and sisters or cousins who are peers engage in mutually desired sex play" (39). Russell's research, which involved in-depth interviews with 930 randomly selected women from a variety of backgrounds, revealed that most incidents of childhood incest are unwanted and traumatic. "After careful evaluation by the research staff of the degree to which each experience was wanted or unwanted," Russell writes, "85 percent were judged completely unwanted and 7 percent, mostly unwanted; ambivalence was apparent in 7 percent of the cases, and 2 percent were judged mostly or completely unwanted." Some of Russell's findings were counterintuitive. For example, 54% of the experiences that were deemed unwanted were judged to be considerably or extremely traumatic, whereas 83% of the experiences considered ambivalent were judged to be considerably or extremely traumatic. Russell's explanation? "Perhaps victims who experience some positive feelings are more apt to blame themselves for what happened. This in turn might mute their anger and make them feel at least partially responsible for their own pain" (48).

By emphasizing the possible benefits of incest, Shepard adopts a stance seemingly calculated to call attention to himself by provocatively thumbing his nose at strongly held cultural beliefs. Shepard's omission of any comment on the traumatic aftermath of parent-child incest is most apparent when he describes a 14-year-old girl whom he saw while he was a consulting psychiatrist for the New York City Board of Education. She had spent an entire year of high school without talking with anyone, claiming to be "deaf and dumb." Later she told a counselor that she heard voices and was sexually intimate with her father. The counselor doubted her story, diagnosed her as schizophrenic, and referred her to Shepard, who concluded that she was probably telling the truth about the incestuous relationship with her father:

According to her account, her parents had ceased sleeping together when she was eight. For lack of an extra bed, father crawled into hers one night and soon afterwards began fondling her. She felt funny about it and told her mother. Mother reacted with a "Don't bother me" retort, and apparently felt that giving her daughter to her husband was one way of keeping him sexually fulfilled and out of her bed. When father suggested fellatio, she felt queasy, but later came to enjoy turning him on. Her one funny feeling about it all was not being able to share it with anyone else. As with her school counselor, she had tried to tell several people but nobody believed her. (*Beyond Sex Therapy*, 133–134)

To his credit, Shepard believes her story; to his discredit, he never imagines the psychological harm to the girl. Why would he include the detail about how she learned to enjoy arousing her father without suggesting the implicit horror, violence and trauma of incest? Nowhere in his discussion of the girl does he convey dismay, indignation, or outrage. Indeed, nowhere in the 17-page chapter does he consider any of the traumatic implications of incest that nearly all contemporary psychotherapists would inevitably raise. He tells us that her parents refused to speak with him—"Their reasons, I suppose, were fear, shame, and/or a desire for privacy"—but he never suggests that her recovery and well-being are unlikely without a therapeutic intervention. Nor does he suggest that she might require protection from her parents.

Instead, Shepard offers what can only be described as a pro-incest point of view. Reports of the harmful consequences of incest "must be taken with several grains of salt," he claims, because psychiatrists see only traumatized individuals. "Someone whose incestuous relationship has not impaired his or her stability is unlikely to offer lamentations to a therapist." Another criticism of these reports, Shepard opines, is that "it is usually impossible to establish a one to one relationship between incest and neurosis" (*Beyond Sex Therapy*, 135). He talks about the royal families throughout history who have depended upon incestuous unions and suggests that, biologically speaking, "incest may be no more damaging than masturbation" (136), meaning, not at all. He refers to a "research-oriented" psychologist, Jan, who described her uneasiness when her four-year-old daughter wanted on one occasion to kiss her father's penis and on another occasion to have her vagina manipulated by her mother. "It's the typical liberal dilemma" (144), Jan confesses to Shepard, a dilemma, he implies, that need not exist in a sexually enlightened society where everything is permissible. He refers to another psychologist who told him that she is now in favor of incest as a result of visiting a Canadian family where everyone had intimate sexual relations with each other. "I only wish my family," the psychologist effuses, "were capable of the same warmth and intimacy" (140).

Near the end of *Beyond Sex Therapy*, Shepard discusses the "child users/abusers," telling us that an adult who can have satisfying sex only with a child often suffers from a "performance complex." He then makes an astonishing statement about these child users/abusers and their victims, a word that is not part of his vocabulary. "He cannot allow himself to be sexually free except with people (children) who are, by virtue of their inexperience, unlikely to find him wanting as a sex partner" (181). One must read this sentence several times to understand what Shepard means. Yes, it's true, we want to tell Shepard, children may not have the experience to judge an adult's sexual performance, but shouldn't children be protected from adult predators? Aren't there compelling reasons—psychological, biological, sociological, moral, legal—to avoid parent-child incest? Doesn't a therapist have an obligation to protect children when they are being psychologically harmed? Shepard raises none of these questions.

Few of Shepard's colleagues in the 1970s knew of the incidence of incest and child sexual abuse. In her 1982 book *Sexual Abuse*, Jean Goodwin cites in stunned disbelief the author of a prominent 1975 psychiatry textbook that estimates the incidence of incest as only one per million (160). In the second edition to *Sexual Abuse*, published in 1989, Goodwin, a Professor of Psychiatry and Mental Health Sciences at the Medical College of Wisconsin, states that surveys indicate "16 percent of women in the general population have experienced sexual conduct with a relative and 1% to 4% have experienced father-daughter incest" (1). These figures are close to those presented by Blair Justice and Rita Justice, who report in *The Broken Taboo* that between 5% and 15% of the population is involved in incest (16). The incidence of incest is much higher in psychiatric populations; according to Goodwin, 35% of female psychiatric inpatients report incest experiences (1). Shepard cannot be faulted for not knowing the incidence of incest and child sexual abuse, but he can be faulted for his indifference to the suffering arising from these sexual crimes. Nowhere in any of his extensive writings does he discuss the legacy—or illegacy—of sexual abuse, including feelings of isolation, alienation, stigmatization, helplessness, fear, rage and guilt.

A Question of Values

None of Martin Shepard's patients filed a sexual malpractice suit against him, but he imagines this unsettling scenario in *A Question of Values*, his 1976 novel. Published one year later in a paper edition under the more provocative title *Couch* and subsequently under the still more provocative title *The Seducers*, the novel centers on a psychoanalyst who has sex with a "seductive" patient and pays the consequences. Part autobiography, part fiction, part veiled confession, and part cautionary tale, *A Question of Values* is intriguing for what it reveals and conceals about the myth and reality of therapist-patient sex.

Shepard's self-portrait in his autobiography as a "maverick, an iconoclast, a demystifier of the holy grails of psychiatry" also applies to the protagonist of *A Question of Values*. Tanned from weekends at his East Hampton summer home, Dr. Jonas Lippman has an enviable life. A graduate of the "Analytic Institute," the hipster psychoanalyst defies the stereotype of his monkish colleagues. Dressed with studied casualness, he wears sandals, tailored blue jeans and a gold-fisted *figa* necklace. In his early 40s, he seems to be in the prime of life, but all is not well. He has been married for 20 years to a cold, distant woman, Phoebe, who has fallen out of love with him. His patients respect him, but he is slowly becoming disillusioned with psychoanalysis, which he now believes is little more than "lamentation therapy." And so when Arlene Lewis, the attractive 27-year-old patient whom he has been seeing for five months, twice a week, exclaims, "I still want to go to bed with you" (5), Lippman finds himself offering little resistance.

Tellingly, Lippman resembles the portrait of the transgressive therapist that Annette Brodsky sketches in *Sex in the Therapy Hour*. Lippman is middle-aged, several years older than his patient, unhappily married and soon to be divorced. In other ways, however, he is different from the typical at-risk therapist. He has never before slept with a patient, and he doesn't appear manipulative or exploitative. He seems to have the best interests of his patients at heart—though his heart will soon lead him into trouble. He *tries* to act professionally and ethically. We are never sure whether macho-ism or masochism inclines him to have sex with Lewis.

Difficulty Suspending Disbelief

The description of Lippman and Lewis passionately making love in his office could not be more different from the sexualized therapy portrayed in *Betrayal, Therapist, A Killing Cure, Sex in the Therapy Hour* and *Sexual Abuse by Health Professionals*. Renatus Hartogs, Lonnie Franklin Leonard, Zane Parzen, Dr. X and Dr. A coldly, crudely and selfishly penetrate their startled and reluctant female patients, exploiting them for their own selfish pleasure. Readers of these real-life accounts of sexual boundary violations will have difficulty suspending their disbelief in viewing Lippman as a gentle, attentive lover and his lovemaking with Lewis as a therapeutic breakthrough. Indeed, those familiar with sexual boundary violation memoirs will find themselves resistant readers, reading against the grain.

Problems between Lippman and Lewis develop the third time they have sex, shortly before "Analytic August," when therapists typically go on summer vacations, leaving patients to fend for themselves. Lovemaking unleashes Lewis's violent feelings, including a frightening sense of power that may signify the novel's misogyny. "She was a black widow spider toying with her doomed mate, an Amazon besting some puny male, a whore plying her trade, a patient back on her analyst's couch" (35).

Lippman begins to regret their lovemaking, not because he believes it has harmed his patient's therapy, but because love has always been associated with tenderness for him. He also feels guilty over his marital infidelity: he is no philanderer. Ironically, unbeknownst to the analyst, his wife has been unfaithful to him. He rushes from their summer home and, returning to the city, calls Lewis, who invites him to her apartment and, in a role reversal, tries to comfort him. They spend the night together, and when Lewis asks him the next morning why he called her rather than someone else, he replies that she is "special," a word that always foreshadows heartbreak and betrayal, as we have seen in real-life stories of sexual boundary violations. Sure enough, Lewis begins feeling anger and resentment. Lippman has never promised her anything but friendship, but she wants a more permanent relationship.

She thinks about Elaine May's marriage to her analyst, though not about the fact that David Rubinfine's ex-wife, Rosa, committed suicide after her husband left her and their three children. Immediately after receiving Lippman's rejection letter, Lewis attempts suicide through an overdose of the barbiturate Seconal.

A Sexual Malpractice Suit

Events quickly spiral out of control for the besieged psychoanalyst. Arlene Lewis is hospitalized for several weeks, catatonic and depressed, She is later persuaded to file a sexual malpractice suit against Lippman. Some of the events that follow in the novel replay in disguised form Shepard's own legal and ethical troubles with the State licensing authorities, such as his belief that unorthodox therapists like himself are caught in the worst straits imaginable, between the "Scylla of psychiatry and the Charybdis of law" (210), and his guarded confession that he may have slept with his patients.

A Narrow Couch

The second half of *A Question of Values* focuses on Lippman's defense. Two details eerily foreshadow the legal issues that occur in the actual trials described in *A Killing Cure* and *Betrayal*. Lippman's lawyer, Norman Rosenkrantz, warns him that unless he becomes more concerned with survival than with truth, he will be portrayed by Lewis' lawyer, Al Newfield, as a "medical Svengali, exploiting a host of helpless Trilbys" (123). It is the exact image that Evelyn Walker's lawyer uses to characterize Zane Parzen's "Svengali-like hold" over his patient in *A*

Killing Cure, published in 1986, ten years after Shepard's novel appeared. During the malpractice trial, Rosenkrantz asks Lewis to describe the width of Lippman's analytic couch on which they had sex. Four feet wide, she replies. Upon further questioning, she insists she is certain about this detail. The lawyer then undercuts both her answer and credibility by introducing into evidence a photograph of the couch and a yardstick showing its width to be only two-and-a-half feet wide, presumably too narrow for sex. The same issue arose in reality in Julie Roy's malpractice suit against her psychiatrist, Renatus Hartogs, as we saw in chapter two. One of the witnesses for the defense was a commercial photographer who, on Hartogs' request, took a photograph of the psychiatrist's couch and testified that it was too small for sexual intercourse. The claim was later contradicted by another of Hartogs' former patients, who testified that she also had sex with him on the couch. The story of Julie Roy's successful malpractice case against Hartogs appears in *Betrayal*, published one year after *A Question of Values*. It's easy to imagine that Shepard learned about this curious detail from the extensive media accounts of the sensationalized *Roy v. Hartogs* trial.

Three psychiatrists testify for the plaintiff in *Lewis v. Lippman*, including a corpulent associate professor of psychiatry named Charles Clayburg, the author of a book called *Sexual Intimacy Between Therapists and Patients: Twelve Case Studies*. Shepard's model for Clayburg was Charles Clay Dahlberg, an actual witness in the *Roy v. Hartogs* case, whose 1970 article "Sexual Contact Between Patient and Therapist" takes a disapproving stance toward therapists sleeping with patients. When cross-examined, Clayburg answers Rosenkrantz's questions "smugly," reflecting Shepard's negative judgment of him. Clayburg's sanctimonious testimony in *Lewis v. Lippman* could not be more different from Dahlberg's modest but effective testimony in *Roy v. Hartogs*. Described by Julie Roy's lawyer as our "psychiatric keel" (150),

Dahlberg comes across as authoritative without being authoritarian, and when asked whether he believes Roy was telling the truth, the psychiatrist replies without hesitation, "Absolutely" (176). By contrast, Clayburg allows himself to be trapped by Rosenkrantz into stating that a correct diagnosis of a psychiatric patient often takes several weeks, admitting that he interviewed Arlene Lewis for less than a day. Dahlberg was a training and supervising analyst at the White Institute; Shepard's spiteful portrait of Charles Clayburg thus may be seen as the novelist's revenge against those associated with his former institute.

Rosenkrantz's strategy of denial proves effective, and Lippman wins the malpractice suit but simultaneously loses his integrity. Whatever sympathy Shepard conveys earlier in the story for Arlene Lewis, whose reputation has been destroyed by the tawdry trial, disappears at the end, when she announces her plan to marry her opportunistic lawyer. "So who is to say that it was all a catastrophe?" Lippman muses on the last page of the book. "In fact, she might have even benefited from the entire experience. Now wouldn't that be something? What a way to ultimately help your patient" (218).

Novelists have the freedom to imagine characters and events in whatever way they wish, disregarding "reality" whenever they wish. We feel compelled to observe, however, that one of the most striking ways in which *A Question of Values* differs from memoirs describing a patient's sexual abuse by a therapist is the use of other victims' testimony. Real-life stories almost always involve other witnesses who come forth, as a result of media attention during a criminal or civil trial, with similar experiences of abuse by a therapist. Some of these witnesses may seek to file their own malpractice suits. Nearly all of the witnesses in *Betrayal*, *Therapist*, *A Killing Cure*, *Sex in the Therapy Hour* and *Sexual Abuse by Health Professionals* have credibility. The witness who is eager to testify against Lippman, a former patient who has a grudge against him, does not.

Not surprisingly, Shepard became increasingly critical of psychotherapy and psychotherapists, concluding that his long and expensive training analysis was largely a waste of time, money, and effort. He believed as early as 1973 that he knew how to help people dispense entirely with psychotherapy and become their own therapists. "It is my contention, after more than ten years of clinical practice," he writes at the beginning of *The Do-It-Yourself Psychotherapy Book*, "that most troubled individuals can make this transition without spending—or, in many cases, *wasting*—their money on a therapist" (2).

Fritz

Shepard's belief in quick, radically unorthodox psychotherapy can be seen throughout his biography of Fritz Perls. Enamored of Perls, the "black sheep" of psychoanalysis, who eventually founded his own influential psychological movement, Shepard identified with many aspects of Perls' stormy and controversial life, especially the freedom to become involved with patients, "challenging and overcoming all his preexisting limits, including the taboo against sexual intimacy" (*Fritz*, 58). There was nothing reluctant about Perls' exhibitionism, narcissism or machoism, qualities that come across as strengths, not weaknesses in Shepard's biography, which approaches hagiography. Shepard admires Perls' phrase-making abilities and quotes several of his iconoclastic and sometimes scatological statements: "Meditation is neither shit nor get off the pot," and "Intellect is the whore of intelligence." Oddly enough, Shepard gives credit to Perls for originating the quip, "Psychoanalysis is an illness that pretends to be a cure" (161), the same line for which the ex-psychoanalyst Paul Cook, a fictional representation of Perls, takes credit in *A Question of Values*. But the actual originator of the witticism was Karl Kraus, an early 20th century Viennese satirist and critic of psychoanalysis ("Psychoanalysis is the illness which it pretends to cure"). Shepard's characterization of Perls on the penultimate page of *Fritz* reveals how Shepard himself would like to be remembered: "All of us, if we could write the script for our own lives, would invariably create ourselves as perfect beings. Failing to achieve this ideal state we are left with three choices. We can berate ourselves for falling short of our goal, we can pretend to be better than we are, or we can honestly be ourselves. It is to Fritz's credit that he stood for the last alternative" (221). This idealized view of Perls echoes Shepard's similarly idealizing view of his first psychoanalyst, and perhaps of his own father.

Ecstasy

Shepard took a different strategy in profiting from his avant-garde views on sexuality when he allowed the use of his name as the author of *Ecstasy: The Moneysworth Marriage Manual,* published by *Moneysworth* in 1977. *Moneysworth* was a monthly newsletter published by a notorious publicity-seeking entrepreneur, Ralph Ginzburg, who had become well known in the 1960s as a result of his involvement as a defendant in two high profile legal cases, both of which he lost. These cases centered around Ginzburg's unsuccessful strategy of trying to sell his publications using eye-wink hints promising buyers or subscribers that the material was "erotic" in nature.

In the first case, in 1963, Ginzburg, at that time the publisher of *Eros* Magazine, was convicted in federal court of obscenity because of his publication and distribution of non-pornographic but suggestive advertisements for *Eros*. Ginzburg's conviction was based on assertions that the magazine contained sexually explicit material and that the magazine itself was obscene. Ginzburg's company "sought mailing privileges from the postmasters of Intercourse and Blue Ball, Pennsylvania, before settling upon Middlesex, New Jersey, as a mailing point" (*Wikipedia*). The *New York Times* described Ginzburg as "an entrepreneur in a disreputable business who took chances on the borderline of the law." In 1966, Ginzburg served seven months of a five-year sentence in federal prison. Current accounts of this case are much more sympathetic to Ginzburg than was the public's view at the time. To use Shepard's word about his own writings, as viewed from the perspective of the 21st century, the entire issue seems "quaint" in the present day when the most graphic and explicit video of every conceivable sexual act is available for free viewing on the Internet by any adult, or for that matter, any child in the country (Ogas and Gaddam). Such material was considered anything but quaint in the 1960s, however, and for many publishers, erotica in print, or the promise or even any hint of erotic material, could be lucrative (*Ginzburg v. United States*).

In the second case, Ginzburg, at that time the publisher of *Fact* Magazine, carried out a poll of American psychiatrists, purportedly to seek opinions as to whether Barry Goldwater was mentally fit to be elected President of the U.S. Ginzburg published the results in the magazine's September/October 1964 issue. The story was titled "The Unconscious of a Conservative" (a play on the title of Goldwater's book, *The Conscience of a Conservative*) and carried the cover headline: "Fact: 1,189 Psychiatrists Say Goldwater Unfit To Be President." The poll had been sent to over 12,000 psychiatrists, but the magazine article was based only on the 2,417 responses. Of these, 1,189 saw Goldwater as "unfit"; 657 judged him as "fit"; and 571 offered no opinion since they did not "know enough." The article became a cause célèbre in the psychiatric profession. Outrage over the article led to an important addition to the American Psychiatric Association's Code of Ethics, an ethical precept colloquially known as "The Goldwater Rule," which prohibits psychiatrists from commenting on public figures without their permission and without having personally examined them. In a high profile court battle, Goldwater sued Ginzburg for libel and the jury found for Goldwater. Ginzburg appealed all the way to the Supreme Court, which declined to reverse the decision (*Ginzburg v. Goldwater*).

It is inconceivable that Shepard was unaware of Ginzburg's involvement with both psychiatry and the publication of exploitive racy material. And so it is an indication of Shepard's attempt to regain the spotlight that he authored a book, *Ecstasy*, published by Ginzburg. Readers received a free copy of *Ecstasy* if they subscribed to Ginzburg's latest publishing venture, the personal finance newsletter *Moneysworth*. In typical fashion, Ginzburg announced *Ecstasy* in a full page advertisement for *Moneysworth* in the *New York Times*. Under a huge white headline on a black background, "FREE MARRIAGE MANUAL ILLUSTRATED" (January 22, 1977), the ad described the book freebie as "the most generous magazine subscription offer in history," adding, "we have commissioned as author of *Ecstasy* one of the nation's most renowned figures in the field of sex education, Martin Shepard, M.D." Similar ads for *Moneysworth* featuring Shepard's book as a free premium for subscribing continued over the next year, each featuring a titillating headline. An example: "AMERICA'S HOTTEST-SELLING, MOST CONTROVERSIAL SEX MANUAL FREE!" (September 3, 1977). Ginzburg's pandering ads peaked, as their depiction of Shepard nosedived, with a new full page version on August 27, 1977. The ad featured in the upper half of the page the words "WOULD YOU TRUST THIS MAN WITH YOUR SEX LIFE?" in inch-high, white block letters dramatically emblazoned on a black background. On the upper portion of the page was a goofy-looking photograph of Shepard occupying one-sixth of the page.

A diminutive 140-page book, *Ecstasy* seems to have been cobbled together from disparate pieces. A relatively small portion of *Ecstasy* appears to have been written by Shepard, although his name alone appears on the book's front or back covers. Of the text's three sections, only the first section, "The Sexual Relationship: An Overview" (pages 11–40), looks to be Shepard's work and of these pages, fully eight are taken up with full-page illustrations of couples engaged in sexual acts, drawn in the style of Matisse's erotic sketches. Similar images, which have no numbers or captions, appear throughout the book but with no discernible relation to the text. In other words, Shepard wrote just 22 pages of the book, which, according to the front matter, are the only pages to which his copyright applies. The bulk of the book, pages 45–115, appears to be reprinted material obtained from Planned Parenthood, a source credited in the front matter of the book and again at the top of that chapter's first page. The reprinted text consists of a sober, straightforward, factual account of human sexuality titled "Basic Sex Facts," punctuated by the same kind of line drawings appearing in the first chapter. The final chapter, "Questions and Answers," consists of a series of seemingly random questions and answers about sex, attributed to the "editors of *Moneysworth*" at the start of that chapter. Shepard's small section of the book contains some seemingly original material written in an informal and helpful style, meant to reassure readers about their sexual wishes and "problems" no matter how varied. Some of his stated statistics about sexual behavior appear exaggerated, however. His discussion of homosexual impulses and acts includes a reference to his own first homosexual act at age 35 that he first described in "*A Psychiatrist's Head.*"

In the section about male erectile dysfunction, Shepard describes the onset at age 24 of his own erectile issues, which started, he notes, "shortly after analysis began." With the reassurance of his analyst, he concluded that his failure had been due to a fear of deeper involvement with his partner. The "problem" appeared resolved. Two years later, however, the same symptoms reappeared whenever he "shared a bed with a new woman," requiring him to return to the analyst's couch. In this second attempt to address the issue, he came up with a new explanation, but it didn't solve the problem until he decided that his penis "has a mind of its own," that is, he wasn't in control of his body, and there was no use worrying about or apologizing for recurrences. At that point, the "problem" disappeared almost entirely. Nevertheless, one wonders in what way, if any, his difficulties in the analytic institute, discussed earlier, might be connected with the onset and failure to resolve completely this problem during his own analysis. *Ecstasy: The Moneysworth Marriage Manual* was published around the time that Shepard began to drop out of the public eye and begin his new, seemingly more successful life as a builder, designer and eventually, a small book publisher.

It would be an exaggeration to claim that Shepard became a cultural hero, but he does make a cameo appearance in Richard Raznikov's *Notes from a Parallel World*, a 2012 self-published historical novel in which a time traveler revisits the early 1960s to discover the people responsible for President Kennedy's assassination. The novel's hero is a friend of Shepard, who at the time of the story is writing *Games Analysts Play*, the "beginning of his difficulties with the poobahs of the psychiatric community." Noting ambiguously that Shepard "may or may not" have had sex with women who "may or may not" have been his patients, depending on your definition, the narrator states that the real reason Shepard was expelled from the mental health community was because he challenged a central myth of psychoanalytic practice, "the one that says you've got to pay somebody a hundred bucks an hour, probably for life, in order to get some help" (252–253). Raznikov pays tribute to Shepard at the beginning of the novel, characterizing him as a "class act and old friend who once tried to save the world and nearly succeeded."

Giving Up Medicine and Psychotherapy

After losing but eventually regaining his medical license, Shepard led encounter groups for several years; became a political activist; designed and built homes in the fashionable Hamptons on the eastern tip of Long Island; and with his wife Judith co-founded the Permanent Press, a small independent publisher of fiction. In 1980, he was found guilty of possession of a controlled substance: he had been growing marijuana plants in his home. Joan Baum observes in a 2012 interview that Shepard lost his youngest son, Yan, to a heroin overdose. This terrible loss, ironically, was presaged by a passage in *A Psychiatrist's Head* in which he discusses the impending death of his idealized father to cancer. "Until I had sons of my own, no one's passing would have saddened me more than my father's. The loss of a child would grieve me far more. When I told my father this he said, 'Of course. That's the way it should be.' There is no one I love more than my father" (45). Baum notes that though his medical license was restored, Shepard has given up the practice of psychotherapy. Nor does he read therapy books. "I'm beyond this."

On the Record

Unsurprisingly for a man who has published three editions of his autobiography, in 2005, at the age of 71, Shepard wrote yet another book about himself, *On the Record*, published by his own press. His title has a double meaning. The book is a set of reflections on life and the state of the world as Shepard sees it, built around a series of his own song lyrics. Accompanying the book is a music CD in which Shepard and others perform his songs. In this new memoir he offers some reflections on the earlier part of his life, some regretful, and others self justifying, and comments on the publication of *A Psychiatrist's Head* 33 years earlier:

> In my earlier memoir, and in my former practice of psychiatry, I made a big issue of honesty, elevating it to the top of the list of things to strive for. While still believing in the cliché that 'honesty is the best policy,' I think it's fair to say that as the years have passed, I've had further thoughts about it, one being that my zealotry was simple-minded, as zealotry usually is, for the issues of truth-telling and lying are a lot more complex and nuanced than the arguments I put forth in my *Do-It-Yourself Psychotherapy Book*, and which formed the premise of my autobiographical memoir, *The Reluctant Exhibitionist*. (39)

Shepard points to the "negativity" with which *A Psychiatrist's Head* was received by some at that time, along with the championing of the book by others. "Despite this negativity, on a personal level the writing of that book was a valuable experience, for it made me realize I could tell anyone exactly what was on my mind. I also came to realize that this freedom might cause unnecessary hurts, and that selective honesty might be a kinder policy. One learns only through mistakes. My first marriage fell apart, in part, because of this openness" (45). Freud expressed a similar thought in "Remembering, Repeating and Working-Through" (1914). Cautioning analysts not to interfere in most patients' actions outside the analysis, even if these actions are foolish, Freud reminded his readers that "one does not forget that it is in fact only through his own experience and mishaps that a person learns sense" (*SE*, vol. 12, 153). Shepard expresses his regret about having been too "honest" in his autobiography in disclosing what he had done, but he never expresses regret about the acts themselves: his involvement in what others, firmly convinced that his group members were patients, would view as sexual boundary violations by a therapist.

What shall we say, finally, about Martin Shepard? The psychiatrist who concluded in *The Love Treatment* that the "hazards" in therapist-patient sex could be minimized and the "assets" maximized never modified his position. He never acknowledged that the overwhelming majority of psychotherapy patients are hurt by sexual boundary violations, which usually end treatment and destroy the possibility of therapeutic progress. He states in *On the Record* that shaming is a "tool regularly employed by the self-appointed Morality Authorities (hardly a 'Moral Majority' in my opinion)," and there's little doubt that he viewed himself as a victim of this shaming. To judge from *On the Record*, Shepard has mellowed over the years, but his bitterness toward the William Alanson White Institute is still palpable. He apparently has no regrets about ending his career as a psychiatrist and psychoanalyst, though he never rules out psychiatric treatment for patients in need of help. Yet despite his awareness that "a lot of the work in any psychiatric practice has to do with overcoming this mechanism [of shaming] that goes against one's nature, for it stifles the life force, pinching self-expression and self-acceptance" (46), nowhere does he acknowledge a patient's pain and shame arising over sex in therapy.

CHAPTER 5

The Marquis De Sade of Psychiatry: The Story of James Stewart Tyhurst

The photograph of the 69-year-old psychiatrist appearing in the prestigious *Canadian Medical Association Journal* could not look more distinguished: a trim, bespectacled man in a corduroy suit, wool vest and tie with a quietly self-confident gaze and dignified smile. With his arms crossed, he exudes a relaxed, almost serene appearance. He could be anyone's psychiatrist—or grandfather. His credentials were no less impressive, those of a wunderkind: a professor of psychiatry at Cornell University, chair of the Canadian Mental Health Association's Committee on Psychiatric Services and the first head of the Department of Psychiatry at the University of British Columbia Faculty of Medicine. He held these positions when he was still in his 20s and 30s, an age when most professionals are just beginning their careers. Now he was nearing the end of his professional life, doubtlessly looking forward to a well-deserved retirement during his golden years. Anyone looking at the photograph would expect the psychiatrist to be receiving a lifetime achievement award from grateful colleagues. That's why the title of Eleanor LeBourdais's 1991 article that contains his photograph is so jarring: "Case Involving Prominent BC Psychiatrist Puts Medical Profession on Trial."

Material republished with the express permission of: Vancouver Sun, a division of Postmedia Network Inc.

Most stories about transgressive therapists involve a mental health professional convincing a female patient she is "special" and, therefore, worthy of being "loved" by an appreciative middle-aged man. These therapists succeed in manipulating a patient's transference-love and, in some cases, may convince themselves that they too are in love. As Kenneth S. Pope and Jacqueline C. Bouhoutsos pointed out in *Sexual Intimacy Between Therapists and Patients* (1986), the "power differential between therapist and patient, the deep trust necessary to an effective therapeutic relationship, and similar factors significantly diminish a patient's ability to resist sexual advances" (14). But James Stewart Tyhurst widened this power differential to a level perhaps never seen previously in psychotherapy. He enacted elaborate master-and-slave erotic rituals with his patients, ordering them to dress like Roman slaves, as if they were in the film *Ben Hur*. His patients, as part of the "therapy," endured cruel whippings that often raised painful welts on their bodies while he commanded them, contemptuously, "Pleasure me, slave!" One could hardly imagine a more sadistic form of "psychotherapy" than that which he practiced with several patients over a period of more than 20 years. When the story became public, in the early 1990s, it quickly became one of the worst medical scandals in Canadian history.

Much of our information about Tyhurst and the details of his criminal trial come from Christopher Hyde's 1991 book *Abuse of Trust: The Career of Dr. James Tyhurst*. A freelance broadcaster for the Canadian Broadcasting Corporation and the author of several popular novels, Hyde researched the psychiatrist's life and four-week sensationalistic trial in which Tyhurst was charged with four counts of indecent assault and one count of sexual assault over a 22-year period beginning in 1966. *Abuse of Trust* was written quickly and sometimes carelessly, from June 1991— the time the disgraced psychiatrist was found guilty of sexual abuse and sentenced to four years in prison—to October of the same year, when he was free on bail pending appeal. Despite its limitations, *Abuse of Trust* tells a story that should not be forgotten. The Tyhurst scandal became a cause célèbre throughout Canada, demonstrating not only the pathology of a prominent psychiatrist who traumatized several patients but also the inertia of a medical establishment that unconscionably delayed taking meaningful action when it first received a credible report of abuse in therapy.

As Hyde acknowledges in the preface, some of the information he used to describe Tyhurst's family came from his acquaintance with Tyhurst's older son Robert, whom the author knew from boyhood. Hyde is generally accurate in his facts and sympathetic to Tyhurst's victims: *Abuse of Trust* is dedicated to the "four women who came forward." Hyde is less reliable in his psychological pronouncements. He also misses, through no fault of his own, the ironies of the case that occurred after the publication of his book.

Another source of our information is Ric Dolphin's "Borderline Case," an article published in the Canadian magazine *Saturday Night* in February 1992. Dolphin is scrupulously fair in presenting both sides of the Tyhurst trial, and he is alert to the story's many ambiguities and oddities. The Tyhurst case becomes for Dolphin a version of *Rashomon* or, better yet, Henry James's 1898 gothic ghost story, *The Turn of the Screw*, in which the nature of evil remains mysterious. Is Miles' death at the end of James' novella caused by a sinister ghost whom no one sees or by an hysterical governess who literally frightens the boy to death? "The story won't tell," a character tantalizingly observes, "not in any literal, obvious way." Similarly, Dolphin implies throughout his article that it is impossible to tell whether Tyhurst's former patients are suffering from hysteria or borderline personality disorder and, if so, whether psychiatric illness undercuts their credibility. Everything about the Tyhurst story for

Dolphin remains a borderline case, doubtful and unsettled, including the question of the psychiatrist's guilt and the correctness of the jury verdict.

Tyhurst was born in 1922 in Prince George, the largest city in Northern British Columbia. The most unusual detail of his early life, which appears to be related to one of the most curious details of his professional career, is that Tyhurst's father was murdered under mysterious circumstances while working in Quebec. Hyde incorrectly dates the murder as occurring on August 23, 1926, and offers no details about the event. According to the newspaper accounts we examined, Robert Tyhurst was sitting at his desk the night of December 4, 1925, when he was killed by a bullet fired through his office window. Tyhurst, acting manager for a pulp and paper business, was completing an investigation of the cause of missing logs at the company. Calling the shooting an "assassination," the *Prince George Citizen* described the event, as reported by a witness, in graphic detail. "Tyhurst had his back to the window, and his figure, silhouetted against the lighted interior of the office, made a perfect target. The motor car was driven a short distance past the office, turned and moved slowly past again. When immediately in front of the window one of the occupants of the car took aim at Tyhurst with a high-powered rifle and sent a bullet crashing through his brain, killing him instantly." Two brothers were arrested. Following a two-week trial in which 120 people testified, the defendants were acquitted. Tyhurst was 36 at the time of his death and left behind his wife and only child, James.

Surprisingly, Hyde remains silent about the impact of Robert Tyhurst's murder on the family except to note that his son became an expert witness for the defense in dozens of homicide trials. He also served as an expert witness at seventeen rape trials, always testifying on the side of the accused rapist, never the victim.

A Psychiatrist Without Being a Physician

The metaphor "off the tracks" describes a therapist's career that has potentially been derailed as a result of transgressive behavior, but oddly enough, according to Hyde, Tyhurst was never on the tracks. That is, despite the prominent positions he held in the Canadian medical establishment, he had little psychiatric training and never received a medical degree, a glaring misrepresentation that did not arise during his 1991 trial. As Hyde notes, the prerequisites for a medical license in Canada in 1939, when Tyhurst began college, were rigorous: "an undergraduate degree, preferably in science, two years of pre-med, four years in medical school and at least one year as a hospital resident" (13). Psychiatric training involved a further year of study and then an additional year as a psychiatric resident. The total training was 11 years, but Tyhurst somehow short-circuited the process. After four years of college and only one more year in formal training, he received a Diploma in Psychiatry in 1944, his only academic certificate. He began referring to himself as a psychiatrist after only 90 days of formal training. In an article he wrote for the college newspaper in 1944, Tyhurst described himself as a fourth-year medical student when he had only an undergraduate degree. No one challenged his lack of a medical degree.

MKULTRA

Tyhurst's early professional career was spent under the shadow of MKULTRA, a top-secret CIA project that experimented with the use of hallucinogenic drugs, mind control, prolonged sleep therapy, massive electroshock treatments, sensory deprivation and psychological torture. In volume 2 we discuss MKULTRA, but for now it is sufficient to note that it was housed at the Allan Memorial Institute, which was loosely associated with McGill University but a separate entity accountable to no one. Tyhurst admitted that he was an "assistant resident" at Allan Memorial, an ambiguous title that conceals the nature of his involvement with Canadian patients who were used as unwitting guinea pigs in experiments secretly funded by the CIA. Anne Collins extensively documented the crimes against these patients in her 1988 exposé *In the Sleep Room*. Some of the victims' comments appearing in Collins's book "bear a terrible similarity," Hyde observes, "to testimony given by Tyhurst's victims at his trial" (40). Hyde doesn't elaborate on this terrible similarity, however, and a careful reading of *In the Sleep Room* fails to reveal that any of the patients at Allan Memorial were sexually abused, though they were certainly abused in other ways.

Tyhurst later denied that he was aware of the tortures sanctioned by MKULTRA, but Hyde finds the denial unconvincing, largely because Tyhurst attended a June 1, 1951 MKULTRA planning meeting at the Ritz-Carleton Hotel in Montreal, where he met D. Ewen Cameron, the director of the Allan Memorial Institute. Tyhurst knew Cameron and published a paper, "Therapeutic Uses of LSD," indicating his experimentation with the drug Cameron ordered in large quantities from its Swiss manufacturer. Colin A. Ross reports that Tyhurst received funding from Canada's Defence Research Board for studies of individual reactions to community disasters, one of the subjects of investigation of MKULTRA (130).

Shortly after his arrival in Vancouver in 1957 to begin his tenure as the first full time head of the University of British Columbia Department of Psychiatry, Tyhurst was charged with failure to file a tax return. The case was dropped by the Vancouver Police Court but reopened by a higher court. The resolution of the case was never made public.

Tyhurst amassed considerable power during the early years in Vancouver, pursuing several political and psychiatric enterprises. He was the driving force behind the creation of a new psychiatric wing for University Hospital. He lectured widely, seeking to create in Vancouver his own version of the Allan Memorial Institute in Montreal. He portrayed himself as a medical liberator, freeing the mentally ill from outdated, oppressive psychiatric institutions. Enlarged psychiatric power eventually matched the grandiosity of his ambitions. He also made many enemies who succeeded in extinguishing the rising star. In 1970, he was forced to resign as head of the psychiatry department, though he was allowed to continue as a tenured professor. Recognizing the end of his career as an administrator, he expanded his private practice.

Tyhurst chose his victims carefully. They were women who struggled with depression, anxiety disorders, weight problems, suicidal thoughts and low self-esteem. He ordered them to diet and exercise, punishing them if they failed to lose weight. He abused many of them over a period of years, requiring them to sign master-slave contracts and treating them as if they were subhuman. Some of the women came forward only when they learned from the extensive media coverage that Tyhurst was charged with sexual crimes. The patients told remarkably similar stories despite the fact that prosecutors had prevented them from speaking to each other to avoid contaminating their testimony. Some former patients were willing to give evidence against Tyhurst but refused to testify or file charges, because they feared losing their jobs if it became public knowledge that they suffered from mental illness.

A Gothic Horror Story: The Four Victims

Hyde makes no attempt to describe Tyhurst's point of view, which perhaps only a novelist can imagine. He does attempt, with varying degrees of success, to describe the viewpoints of Tyhurst's victims. The psychiatrist's treatment of his female patients resembles the plot and characterization of a gothic horror story. "Annie White" (Hyde uses pseudonyms to protect the victims' privacy), perhaps the "most normal" of Tyhurst's patients, was trapped for more than five years. Severely depressed while working as a nurse at Children's Hospital in British Columbia, she was referred to Tyhurst by her physician. Tyhurst told her she needed discipline and structure in her life; he required her to keep a budget book, monitor her weight and to exercise. After three months he told her to sign a contract agreeing that he would be her master and she his slave. He began seeing her for "therapy" in her apartment where he initiated the master-and-slave rituals. He beat her with a half-dozen different whips. Insisting that she have sex with him, he promised to teach her how to experience love with a man. She refused his demands at first, which only heightened his anger, and she felt only nausea and self-disgust when she finally relented.

Like many of Tyhurst's other victims, Annie White was terrified he would abandon her. She did everything he ordered, including looking at pornographic pictures of women bound and chained, reading words from a script and then making him breakfast while he verbally abused her. "While he ate she would stay at his side, on her knees, head bent. From time to time, if he was in the mood, he would drop scraps of food on the floor and tell her to eat them 'like a good slave,' and she would" (9). She was forced to sign a letter in 1984 acknowledging her servile relationship to Tyhurst. "I am willing to commit myself to being a slave which includes total obedience, accountability, a submissive attitude and taking punishment quietly. I realize that I must be made to submit to orders so that I don't avoid or procrastinate commitments. Until I learn self-discipline, I need to have external discipline." She also promised to learn "more productive habits" (72).

OFF THE TRACKS VOLUME 1

"Voluntary Cooperation"

In selecting verbs like "forced," "ordered," "required," and "commanded" to describe Tyhurst's abuse of his patients, we realize that he may not have used physical violence to control them. They were outpatients when they were abused, not inpatients in an institution, and therefore there was a voluntary aspect to their acceding to his verbal demands. This ambiguity is what makes the Tyhurst story so interesting. As in accounts of S&M non-physical bondage, an element of voluntary cooperation exists on the part of both parties who are able to enact their conscious or unconscious sadomasochistic erotic fantasies. We do not imply, of course, that Tyhurst's patients were responsible for his abusive treatment of them. They trusted their psychiatrist, who portrayed his abuse of them as part of their therapy. He betrayed that trust. In just the same way that people today with sadistic and/or masochistic erotic preferences meet in so-called "BDSM" (bondage, dominance, sadism, masochism) online groups, BDSM parties and BDSM clubs, Tyhurst was able to sniff out masochistic women among those who came to him as patients. He exploited their inclinations to indulge erotic masochistic inclinations complementary to his own sadism. The patients' willingness to go along with him illustrates the latent power of the transference that can develop in psychotherapy and its availability for misuse in the hands of an evil psychotherapist. This is different, as we shall see, from the case of Jules Masserman, who did use "force" on his patients while they were under the influence of sodium Amytal.

Tyhurst's second victim, Barbara Henry, had the misfortune of choosing him at random for treatment in 1979, when she was about 20. The psychiatrist rolled his eyes in exasperation when she told him during her second therapy session about her alcoholic and physically abusive parents. She knew then he was not the right person to speak to and left, trying to live on her own, but within a few weeks she had become more depressed and suicidal. Her parents locked her in the bedroom basement of their home and called Tyhurst. He became furious when he couldn't hypnotize her, and she learned to be compliant.

Barbara Henry was a "bad patient," even when she allowed him to touch her. Unable to lose weight, be hypnotized, or appreciate his sadistic treatment of her, she threatened to commit suicide and suddenly found herself admitted to the Psychiatric Unit of University Hospital, where she spent three months, drugged most of the time. Grateful when she was finally released into a daycare program, she entered a new stage of "treatment," submitting to his master-and-slave routine. "Your body is mine," he intoned, and then the whippings began. She testified that Tyhurst ordered her to break all social contacts. "I wasn't supposed to go on dates, and then he said I wasn't supposed to have sex. Over the years it got to the point where I wasn't supposed to talk to anyone between appointments" (115). She thought about breaking away from him only when she heard him talking to another "slave" in his office. Nevertheless, it took her another five years to flee. In escaping from Tyhurst, she was also escaping from an unconscious desire to remain enslaved or in some way to be cared for by him at any price.

Tyhurst's third victim, Caroline Benson, began seeing him in 1977 when, caught shoplifting in a drugstore, she agreed as part of her probation to have court-ordered psychiatric counseling to avoid imprisonment. Like Annie White, Benson had to sign a slave contract; she also had to wear a slave ankle bracelet. Using a Polaroid camera, Tyhurst photographed her bare breasts. She told her probation officer about the mistreatment, but Tyhurst denied any wrongdoing.

The fourth and final victim, final only in the sense that she was the last woman to file formal charges against him—many other victims were too frightened to bring charges—was Debbie Vreeland. Her physician-husband had diagnosed her as a "hypomanic-depressive" and put her on an antidepressant, but her depression only deepened when he divorced her after she gave birth to their third child. She began seeing a psychiatrist with whom she became infatuated, but when he maintained appropriate boundaries and sought to help her understand her transference-love, she left him for another psychiatrist, Tyhurst, in 1966. He promptly exploited her vulnerability, informing her that she had been "enslaved" by her physician-husband and the other psychiatrist, and promised to assist her. Help consisted of ordering her to wear a pseudo-Roman slave costume, ritualized whippings and forced oral sex. "I could never say 'no' to Dr. Tyhurst," she told the court (89). Tyhurst often took her to his 120-acre family estate on Gabriola Island, where she served as his cook and sexual slave. Vreeland was the most fragile of the four patients, the one whose psychiatric testimony was the most confused—a confusion Hyde sometimes shares: on one occasion in his book, he mistakenly identifies Vreeland, not Benson, as the woman who had been caught shoplifting and sent to Tyhurst by a court order (85).

Why did Tyhurst's patients often spend years with him? The question can be asked about any protracted abusive relationship. The answer, predictably, is complex. Many people remain in destructive relationships for a variety of reasons, including the fear of loneliness and isolation; the belief that cruelty is "normal;" the presence of low self-esteem; the hope that one can change an abuser's behavior; the stigma of a failed relationship; and the worry that one cannot live on one's own ("Why Do People Stay in Abusive Relationships").

Tyhurst's patients, particularly Annie White and Debbie Vreeland, feared abandonment, probably believing that a known evil, Tyhurst, was better than the alternative: loneliness, isolation and helplessness. Though they must have known on some level that their relationships with him were improper, inappropriate and self-destructive, they tried to convince themselves otherwise. Many people in destructive relationships believe that abuse is deserved. Tyhurst was, after all, a psychiatrist; indeed, a professor of psychiatry. His patients may have felt that they were to blame for their "enslavement"; Tyhurst's degrading treatment confirmed their low self-worth. The more time they invested in the relationship, the more they believed they would be a failure if they ended it. They probably felt that one day they would be worthy of his love, a period of time that eventually turned into months and then years.

Patients who remain in protracted sexually abusive relationships with therapists almost certainly feel ambivalence, an emotional state that Kenneth S. Pope regards as perhaps the major characteristic of what he calls the therapist-patient sex syndrome. "The phenomenon is similar to the experience of many survivors of child or spouse abuse: At times the individual fears, despises, and wishes to escape at all costs from the abusing authority figure; at other times, the individual feels close to and wishes to cling to, take care of, and even protect the abuser. Occasionally, the individual may experience both sets of feelings simultaneously" ("Therapist-Patient Sex Syndrome," 40).

Sydney Smith, the clinical psychologist who treated Evelyn Walker, contends that sexually abusive therapists arouse a patient's regressive self-image. "It is as if the woman patient loses control over her own will as well as the dimensions of a powerful, controlling, parental figure who cannot be crossed or disobeyed. This return to an infantile state weakens the patient's resolve and leaves her with the conviction that she is a helpless figure, unable to overcome the strength of the treater or to escape his psychological hold on her" ("The Seduction of the Female Patient," 63). Research on sadomasochism, Smith adds, suggests that if one person assumes the role of the sadist, the other person is forced into the role of the masochist, a role that many sexually abused women have played earlier in their lives when they were abused by a relative.

An Expert Witness Testifies: "Kill Men"

One of the stranger ironies of the Tyhurst story, one that no one has commented on, is that Caroline Benson was told by her probation officer to see a female psychiatrist who later testified as an expert witness: Patricia Penfold. She was the same psychiatrist, P. Susan Penfold, who later wrote *Sexual Abuse by Health Professionals*, published eight years after Hyde's book. Noting that Penfold was trained first at St. Mary's Hospital Medical School in London and then received further training in Ontario, information omitted from *Sexual Abuse by Health Professionals*, Hyde remarks that Tyhurst's lawyer, David Gibbons, appeared curiously uninterested in her testimony about Benson. Instead, the defense lawyer questioned Penfold about her participation at a recent conference organized by the Canadian Health Mental Association. Attempting to call into question Penfold's credibility as an expert witness by implying she was a man-hating feminist, Gibbons asked her if she had made a speech that condoned "killing men." When she said that another person had used the expression, he tried to suggest that Penfold had agreed with the incendiary language. Penfold's testimony is the oddest moment during the tense trial; indeed, the only moment that evoked laughter from the witness, lawyers and judge:

"But when she said 'kill men,' there was resounding applause," persisted Gibbons.

"Um-hum."
"What did you think 'kill men' meant?"
"It was a metaphor."
"It was a metaphor?"
"Um-hum."
"That's why you applauded that aspect of her speech along with the other feminists who were there?"

Penfold, unable to hold back a derisive smile, answered, "Do I take it that you had spies there who noticed when I applauded?"

"You are darn right, ma'am," said Gibbons. "We're following you everywhere."

"I'm horrified," said Penfold, raising a single, expressive eyebrow.

"Paranoid as well," offered [Supreme Court Justice Douglas] Wetmore.

"You've been a slave to alcohol," continued Gibbons. "That's a metaphor for saying you abuse alcohol."

"Um-hum."

"'Yes' is your answer?"

"Yes." (123–124)

A Profession's Refusal to Discipline an Offender

Perhaps the most infuriating aspect of the Tyhurst story is that his victims failed to receive justice when they came forward with their tales of humiliation and sexual abuse. When one of the patients complained to the British Columbia College of Physicians and Surgeons in 1981 that Tyhurst had ordered her to disrobe, kneel and call him master, an inquiry was followed by a meeting of the college ethics and discipline committee. The meeting resulted in a resolution passed by the college that his "management of the case and therapy was unacceptable, the degree of subjugation was unwarranted and its effectiveness questionable" (65). The college demanded that Tyhurst stop using slave contracts in his therapy treatments. Hyde points out that not only were the inquiry and its results never made public, but Tyhurst was never disciplined. He continued to abuse his patients with impunity. It was not until 1991 that he was stopped, not by a college ethics committee or the provincial professional licensing department, but by the Royal Canadian Mounted Police.

Sexual Sadism

Tyhurst exemplifies in a dramatic and disturbing way a sexually abusive psychotherapist who was in many ways sicker than his patients. Gabbard and Lester do not refer to Tyhurst by name in *Boundaries and Boundary Violations in Psychoanalysis*, but he would fit into their category of "predatory psychopathy," which includes "not only true antisocial personality disorders but also severe narcissistic personality disorders with prominent antisocial features" (93).

Hyde observes that Tyhurst used the theory of "episodic discontrol" when testifying on behalf of accused rapists. Offenders committed acts in a state of "sleep drunkenness," the psychiatrist claimed, for which they were not legally responsible. Tyhurst's testimony helped free one man who was charged with being a dangerous sex offender; years later the man was found guilty of sex crimes and manslaughter. There is evidence to suggest that Tyhurst's efforts as an expert witness to acquit defendants charged with sexual crimes revealed his attempts to explain and rationalize his own sexual deviances. Referring during his own trial to a notorious rapist, Tyhurst testified that "some people find bondage useful because the struggle against constraints increases excitement and because there is evidence that sexual ardour is increased by aggressive behaviour" (49). Hyde plausibly infers that Tyhurst was revealing his own pathology in this statement. Tyhurst elaborated on the dilemmas encountered by the sadomasochist in his pursuit of pleasure. "One of the problems is to find a woman who will indulge him, so he must resort to prostitutes." Or to female patients, we might add. Tyhurst later agreed with his defense lawyer that a "good sadist is hard to find" (49). The psychologist chosen as a witness for the defense, Murray Jason Jackson, concluded from a series of personality tests that Tyhurst exhibited no major psychological dysfunction. Jackson admitted, however, that he never tested the defendant for sexual sadism.

Dolphin points out that Tyhurst had first proposed the theory of episodic discontrol in 1977, when he appeared as the star expert witness for the defense in a bondage and rape case that resulted in a tightening of Canadian sexual assault laws. "Tyhurst, testifying in a losing cause, had suggested that for males the role of aggressor during sex was a turn-on, perhaps even an instinct" (46). Tyhurst's testimony infuriated feminists, whose organization Women Against Violence Against Women (WAVAW) turned out in full force throughout the trial.

We don't have enough biographical information to explain the origins of Tyhurst's sexual sadism toward his female patients. The mystery deepens in light of his father's murder and the fact that the three-year-old child was raised by his mother and grandmother. Tyhurst's defense of accused rapists and murderers suggests his identification with the aggressor, a psychological defense mechanism that was only strengthened by his work at Allan Memorial, where he learned to exert brutal control over patients. His master-slave relationships with his patients reveal his need for power—along with the need to humiliate the powerless. Did he despise the part of himself that was powerless, helpless, defenseless and seek to overcome weakness by dominating others?

Without referring to Tyhurst, Michael B. Sussman calls attention in *A Curious Calling: Unconscious Motivations for Practicing Psychotherapy* to the destructive motivations behind sexualized therapy. Judd Marmor, for example, refers to an "unconscious hostility toward women with a sadistic need to exploit, humiliate and ultimately reject them" (quoted in Sussman, 48). Jean Holroyd and Annette Brodsky contend that, in Sussman's words, "deep-seated attitudes regarding power, status, and sex roles influence the abusive therapist's behavior" (48). These observations are shared, Sussman adds, by Gabbard and Twemlow, who argue that the "sadistic wish to destroy is the perverse core of the lovesick therapist's relationship with his patient" (48–49). But the extent of Tyhurst's sadism seems qualitatively different from that of the prototypical lovesick therapist. In questioning why therapists dominate and control their patients, Sussman cites Max Hammer's speculation that such therapists were themselves dominated and controlled by their parents (112), which once again returns us precisely to the part of Tyhurst's life about which we know the least.

What does seem clear, notwithstanding these irresolvable biographical speculations, is that the sadomasochistic master-slave rituals Tyhurst imposed on his female patients betrayed his own dark compulsions. Here Freud's bold theorizing in *Beyond the Pleasure Principle* (1920) may be helpful, the belief that "masochism, the component instinct which is complementary to sadism, must be regarded as sadism that has been turned round upon the subject's own ego" (*SE*, vol. 18, 54). Freud was never sure about the existence of "primary masochism," but he conjectured that the main difference between sadism and masochism was whether the instinct was directed against another person or oneself.

Tyhurst's sexualizing of "therapy" demonstrates Charles Clay Dahlberg's belief that therapists make poor lovers. Barbara Henry reported that Tyhurst appeared to be masturbating while he lashed her against a wall, an experience reported by Tyhurst's other patients. Debbie Vreeland testified that he was impotent during the early stages of their relationship. His whippings of her would regularly end in forced oral sex. Without using quotation marks around the word, Hyde tells us that at a certain point Tyhurst's impotence had been cured and he would insist that she fellate him to ejaculation (88).

Much has been written of the "wounded healer," a term we cannot apply to Tyhurst because he never seemed to be much of a healer. But he was certainly wounded—and wounding. He may have become a psychiatrist to understand himself and master his own conflicts, a motive that is shared by many who become mental health professionals, but it is hard to find evidence that he was a successful healer of either others or himself.

How could Tyhurst have been be so sadistic and still maintain an apparently normal family life? How was he able to mask his bizarre alternate self for so long from his relatives, friends and colleagues? To add another ironic twist to the story, his wife, Libuse Jukickova Tyhurst, was also a psychiatrist. Didn't she see his sexual sadism? The Czech-born psychiatrist defended her husband, insinuating, in Dolphin's words, that the four accusers "had obviously invented their stories as a means of converting their unrequited love for her husband into something that reflected more favourably on themselves" (60). According to Hyde, husband and wife lived together but had entirely different lives. Their son Robert told a group of high school friends that he and his two siblings had minor speech impediments as a direct result of, in Hyde's words, "having parents who were both psychiatrists, who hated each other's guts and who were completely out of their minds" (50). The only reason his parents never divorced, Robert Tyhurst told Hyde, was because it would hurt their careers. Apart from both being psychiatrists, Robert Tyhurst's parents had nothing in common. "They went on separate vacations, rarely spent any time together on the Gabriola estate and had entirely different groups of friends, other than people they both worked with at UBC" (51).

Children of Psychiatrists

Robert Tyhurst and his siblings were not the first adults to complain about the burden of having psychotherapist-parents. Having one parent who is a therapist is bad enough, Thomas Maeder contends, but having

245

two psychotherapist-parents is a double whammy. Maeder, whose father was a psychoanalyst and mother a clinical social worker, explores this phenomenon in *Children of Psychiatrists and Other Psychotherapists* (1989). His conclusion is that although children of mental health professionals are not always harmed, as a group they feel different from other people. In some cases, psychotherapists' children believe they suffer from a common syndrome of personality problems that they attribute to their parents. Maeder admits candidly that his book, based on interviews of over two hundred children of psychotherapists, emphasizes the unfavorable effects of this relationship. Yet he comes across as being judicious in his observations and conclusions, acknowledging that it is harder to be a good parent than a good therapist. Maeder shows how and why children may feel burdened by having parents who seem to read their minds, overanalyze their innocent statements, invade their privacy, and heighten their self-consciousness. The children may grow up to be smart and articulate but nevertheless believe that they were deprived of spontaneity, freedom, and a sense of self. Therapists who are narcissistically impaired, Maeder adds, do the most damage to their children.

Robert Tyhurst's complaints go far beyond the typical ones experienced by children of therapists. He blamed his parents not only for despising and having nothing to do with each other but also for showing no affection for their children. "Robert Tyhurst seemed to accept this as a fact of life," Hyde suggests, "putting it down to the fact that his father hated to be touched by anyone and was an extremely private man" (50). Robert Tyhurst's only explanation for why his parents never divorced was his father's need to maintain a facade of health and stability.

No one has commented on the significance of Tyhurst's three children all becoming lawyers, a phenomenon that Maeder implies is unusual for children of psychiatrists. Maeder's research indicates that relatively few children of psychiatrists become lawyers, yet he concedes that Ralph

Slovenko, a professor of law and psychiatry at Wayne State University, reached the opposite conclusion. In an 1987 article published in the *Journal of Psychiatry and Law*, Slovenko, who did a residency in psychiatry at Tulane University where he was at the time a professor of law, points out that children of psychiatrists often have an affinity for the law, especially children of forensic psychiatrists. (Recall that Tyhurst was often an expert witness for the defense.) Slovenko offers many reasons why children of psychiatrists go into the law. "Psychiatry is so formless and arbitrary, and its ability to define things and tell people what they ought to do is so purposefully limited, that these children, having grown up in a world full of gelatinous values, might flee to a field where everything is more precisely defined. In their eyes, lawyers have taken the high moral ground, with psychiatrists being placed on the defensive" (342).

Without agreeing with Slovenko's belief that children of psychiatrists find the law an attractive profession, Maeder understands why they might find the "law's rigidity a welcome relief" from the "arbitrary rule of behavior with which they have grown up" (241). Was this the reason Tyhurst's children went into law? Was there a relationship, we wonder, between a psychiatrist-father who denied his female patients their dignity—"He would frequently say that I had no rights," Annie White testified. "He would say, 'You have no rights, I am the master, you are the slave'" (101)—and his children's decisions to enter a profession based on justice and the rule of law?

"Cool and Collected"

Shortly before the jury reached its decision, Tyhurst was asked, as recounted in an article that appeared in the June 11, 1991 edition of the *Vancouver Sun*, how a psychiatrist like himself handled stress under difficult circumstances. The article, which contained a photo of the smiling Tyhurst taken in the forecourt of the BC Law Courts building, the same photo that was later reprinted in the *Canadian Medical Association Journal*, offers the psychiatrist's seemingly relaxed reply: he planned to "accept the situation, review the options and do the right thing. . . . I'm retired from teaching, all I really plan to do is writing" (Hyde, 189).

As far as we know, Tyhurst never did any writing after the verdict. For a man who spent several years as a professor of psychiatry, a position in which scholarly publications are generally expected, particularly for someone who wishes to rise on the academic ladder, he wrote remarkably little. Tyhurst claimed to have published 30 journal articles and book chapters, along with his "major book" on mental health services, *Patterns of Care*. Hyde, however, notes that no such book was listed under Tyhurst's name in the Vancouver Public Library, the UBC Medical Library, or the UBC Main Library, another example of the psychiatrist's self-misrepresentation. We were able to locate one article, "Individual Reactions to Community Disaster: The Natural History of Psychiatric Phenomena," published in 1951 in the *American Journal of Psychiatry*. Based on Tyhurst's collaboration with D. Ewen Cameron, who had received a grant from the Canadian government to study community responses to disaster (Turner, 98), the article began as a talk Tyhurst gave at the American Psychiatric Association in 1950, when he was a rising star. The publication, about stress, reveals nothing of a ground-breaking nature, but it does offer us an insight into Tyhurst's own response to stress decades later. In a comment buried in a footnote, he observes that when it comes to "psychodynamics," there is a "close relationship between author and theory" (764, n. 2). What can we infer about Tyhurst, then, from his theory?

Tyhurst argues in the article that there are three overlapping phases to acute disaster: a period of impact, a period of recoil, and a posttraumatic period, the latter of which "lasts, hypothetically, at least, for the remainder of a person's life, and includes the period of rehabilitation." During the initial period of impact in an acute situation, only about 12–15% of the population remain "cool and collected." About three-quarters of survivors are "stunned and bewildered"; the remaining survivors show states of "confusion, paralysing anxiety, inability to move out of bed, 'hysterical' crying or screaming" (766).

Tyhurst draws his data from four disasters: two large fires involving apartment-houses, a marine fire and a flash flood, but if we apply his taxonomy to personal crises, there is little doubt that his reaction to his legal problems fitted perfectly into his category of "cool and collected." He steadfastly denied all the charges of his patients, never showing guilt, remorse, regret, or sadness. Describing the category of "cool and collected," he wrote, "They are able to retain their awareness, make an 'appreciation' of the situation, formulate some plan of action, and carry it through" (766). He never displayed the characteristics of the overwhelming majority of those who confronted a disaster: a "need to ventilate," which he associates with a "childlike attitude of *dependency*"; a "need to be with others"; and a "disinclination to be left alone" (767). Nor is there evidence that he exhibited publicly any of the posttraumatic symptoms he mentions in his article: "temporary anxiety and fatigue states, psychotic episodes, recurrent catastrophic dreaming, depressive reactions" (767). By contrast, to judge from their testimonies, Tyhurst's victims experienced *all* of these problems, including "severe and prolonged reactions that are included in the general terms 'traumatic syndrome.'" He ends his description of traumatic syndrome with the ironically-charged words, "Full presentation of these data must await completion of follow-up investigation" (767).

Tyhurst's story raises several irresolvable questions. Why did he serve as an expert witness for the defense rather than for the prosecution, as one might expect of a son who lost his father to an act of inexplicable violence? Hyde declines to speculate. On the last pages of his story, however, he cannot resist observing that "in some ways, it is hardly surprising that Tyhurst, deprived of his father by an act of murder before he was five years old, then given access to enormous personal and professional power, turned out the way he did. With hindsight it seems clear that Tyhurst should have never embarked on a career that by definition requires a nurturing, supportive personality" (186–187). Such hindsight does nothing to explain why Tyhurst chose to become a psychiatrist, why he identified with victimizers rather than their victims, why he had no empathy, why he became misogynistic, or why he turned out to be autocratic and cruel.

Hyde discusses the many similarities between Tyhurst and other transgressive therapists, using Phyllis Chesler's expression "the problem with no name" to describe female patients sexually assaulted during treatment. Occasionally Hyde gets his facts wrong. He observes that Henry A. Cotton, the superintendent of the New Jersey State Mental Health Hospital in Trenton, New Jersey, believed that mental illness was related "to the fact that the human body simply had too many organs"; as we shall see in the next volume, Cotton believed that mental illness was caused by chronic infection, usually caused by infected teeth, but also possibly present in other organs. Hyde states that Julie Roy spent almost three years in therapy with Renatus Hartogs (184), when in fact her treatment lasted only six months. Hyde might have been more sympathetic to Penfold had he read her 1983 co-authored book, *Women and the Psychiatric Paradox*, where she comes across as being authoritative without being strident or ideological. He refers to a 1989 book, *Sexual Exploitation by Health Professionals*, written by three San Francisco female psychiatrists whom he doesn't name, telling us that the American Psychiatric Association refused to fund the project or allow the women to invoke the authority of the professional organization due to "fear of adverse publicity" (182). He fails to list the book in his brief bibliography, however, and there is no listing of it in the Library of Congress. And he misleadingly implies that Freud "became involved" with one of his patients, "Anna Von. R.," who "almost destroyed his sanity" (180). Freud never reported having treated a patient of this name, though in *Studies on Hysteria* he refers to the case of "Fräulein Elisabeth von R.," for whom he felt considerable sympathy. It was in this case that Freud used for the first time the word "resistance" (*SE*, vol. 2, 154), a cornerstone of psychoanalytic theory.

A Unique Criminal Case: The Marquis de Sade of Psychiatry

As Ric Dolphin reported, during the trial the prosecution referred to Tyhurst as the "Marquis de Sade of psychiatry" (44). Dolphin criticized the Crown prosecutor, Gregory Weber, for his failure to depict Tyhurst as cruel and despotic. "When my researches led me beyond the courtroom, I found no shortage of people from his school days onwards who would call Tyhurst abrasive, arrogant, aggressive, autocratic—'prick' was a word I often heard. Psychiatrists who knew him from residency described him as 'narcissistic' and 'paranoid'" (60). The prosecution also inexplicably failed to mention Tyhurst's failures as chair of psychiatry at the University of British Columbia and the fact that the college ethics and discipline committee reprimanded him for the mistreatment of a patient. "The Crown case was almost entirely circumstantial," Dolphin states. "There had been no strong corroboration, no photos of the supposed whipping welts, little documentation of the master-slave contracts, and none of the supposed Polaroids. No-one else testified to

Tyhurst's perversity. The case rested on the testimony of four witnesses, and however sympathetic they might have been, they were also to varying extents disturbed women" (61).

Dolphin describes Tyhurst's criminal lawyer, David Gibbons, as the best in British Columbia. Gibbons suggested that all four women were suffering from the same psychiatric illness and that they had somehow communicated with each other before the trial. In Gibbons' view, all four women had heard about the master-slave metaphor and were then deluded into thinking that it was literally true. A patient's use of a slave metaphor or slave contract, Tyhurst explained, occurred because he might occasionally accuse her of being a "slave" to her compulsion.

During the closing arguments of the trial, the prosecutor observed that the Tyhurst case was unique in Canadian criminal history because "only a psychiatrist could be subjected to the accusations made by the Crown or could offer the defence that he has made" (177). During its early deliberations, the jurors asked Justice Wetmore to clarify the term "reasonable doubt." The judge gave a lengthy and convoluted answer to that and other questions, causing both the prosecuting and defense lawyers to raise repeated objections. Dolphin reports how two Canadian newspapers described the judge's "clarification" as well as his own impressions. According to the *The Vancouver Sun*, Wetmore "repeatedly stammered and made three or four attempts at enunciating some words, such as 'Dr. Tyhurst.'" The Vancouver *Province* reported that "sheriffs covered their eyes, jurors exchanged glances and the dozens or so onlookers seated in the public gallery variously giggled, rolled their eyes and shifted uncomfortably in their seats." Dolphin's perceptions were similar. "Wetmore, as I watched him, dropped papers, slurred words, misread portions of transcripts, and confused rather than clarified the issue of 'reasonable doubt'" (43). Justice Wetmore later denied he was drunk while giving instructions to the jury, as the newspapers covering the trial suggested. Instead, he stated that he was suffering from exhaustion over the protracted trial.

Quite apart from Justice Wetmore's difficulties, defining "a reasonable doubt for a criminal court jury," as E. Denisoff, K. E. Whittemore, and E. M. Coles pointed out immediately following the Tyhurst decision, is one of the most daunting challenges for a judge. They cite the findings of empirical research suggesting that "jurors generally exhibit a very low level of comprehension of legal instructions" (57). In an observation that proved prophetic about the Tyhurst case, Denisoff, Whittemore, and Coles noted that verdicts "are often reversed on the basis of improperly worded instructions to the jury" (60).

"It is very difficult to believe someone you find charming is a monster," Dolphin admits near the end of his article. "In two and a half days of talking to Tyhurst while we waited for the jury to return, I grew to like him." Yet Dolphin is quick to add, "where is it written that we must be plausible in our atrocities? Wasn't I perhaps just succumbing to the favourable image Tyhurst had projected, to his brilliant past, and to that something in all of us that seizes on the strong and tries to dismiss the weak and infirm?" (64). In the end, Dolphin adds, he could not make up his mind whether Tyhurst was innocent or guilty. "Both newspaper reporters covering the case were betting on an acquittal but the phrase that kept echoing in the courtroom was, 'I'm glad I'm not on that jury'" (64). Dolphin then notes that Tyhurst was convicted of all five counts and sentenced to four years in prison.

The Nightmare of Therapy

As it turned out, Tyhurst's story was far from over. Tyhurst's lawyers appealed the 1991 conviction, and in 1992 the BC Court of Appeal ruled that Justice Wetmore had indeed erred when he instructed the jury about the issue of reasonable doubt. Therefore, a second trial was held in 1992, but only two of the original four patients testified against Tyhurst. Doctors stated that the stories of the other two complainants were similar to those of the two who testified at the second trial. As Ellen Saenger noted in the *Alberta Report*, Tyhurst's lawyers tried to undercut his former patients' credibility by suggesting they were "lunatics," deluded by sexual fantasies and motivated by financial gain. Additionally, the psychiatrist's lawyers portrayed his accusers as part of a "feminist conspiracy," brainwashed by the WAVAW, the same argument they had put forward unsuccessfully during his first trial the preceding year. This time, however, the trial's outcome was different. A 12-person jury equally divided between men and women deliberated for six days before acquitting Tyhurst of all charges. On hearing the verdict, one of the complainants, "Jill Gorman," jumped to her feet and began hurling obscenities at the jury. "She was dragged screaming out of court by a sheriff's deputy. 'I kind of went blind,' Ms. Gorman says." Three days later, women's groups protested against the decision and Crown prosecutors branded the verdict as "bizarre." In 1996, the Supreme Court of Canada refused to hear the Crown appeal, ending Tyhurst's criminal problems.

How do we explain Tyhurst's acquittal during the second trial and the Supreme Court of Canada's refusal to hear the Crown's appeal? We can't! We can suggest, however, that there seemed to be a backlash against the WAVAW collective, along with what Dolphin calls "politically correct thinking [that] is strongly allied with the accusers" (61). It was apparently easier to believe that four mad women had conspired together to plot against a well-respected psychiatrist, despite a lack of evidence to support a conspiracy theory, than to accept the possibility that the esteemed Dr. Tyhurst could be so sadistic.

There were several conspicuous omissions in the prosecutor's presentation of the case, which become more glaring in light of our discussion of "the/rapist" in chapter 3. There was no discussion of Tyhurst's Svengali-like power over his patients, creating a hypnotic dependency that was nearly impossible for them to break. There was no discussion of Tyhurst's exploitation of his patients' transference-love. There was no discussion of other psychotherapists in Canada or the United States who were found guilty of sexualizing therapy. There was no discussion of Tyhurst's nonsexual boundary violations, such as visiting his patients at their homes or "inviting" them to his family estate on Gabriola Island. There was no discussion of the "incestuous" nature of a patient's sexualized relationship with a therapist. And there was no discussion of the extent to which the stigma of mental illness, along with the intense ambivalence over disclosing painful and shameful secrets, prevents many sexually abused patients from coming forward to file complaints against transgressive therapists.

There's an irony about the murder of Robert Tyhurst, James Tyhurst's father, on which no one seems to have commented. The people indicted for the crime were later acquitted, resulting in a transgression that went unpunished. Decades later, Robert Tyhurst's son was indicted for a crime, or series of crimes, for which he was later acquitted, once again resulting in misdeeds that went unpunished.

Tyhurst's civil problems, however, were not over. As reported by Jon Kelly in the online publication *the province*, on March 14, 2001, Jill Gorman successfully sued Tyhurst for damages resulting from his abuse of her from 1979 to 1988. During this time, Gorman was forced to strip to the waist and was lashed with a leather-braided whip. Justice David Vickers stated that he doubted Tyhurst's repeated denials of the significance of the master-slave contracts she signed. "Tyhurst should have been alarmed at their contents, he said. Instead, the psychiatrist testified that patients 'write all sorts of things' and dismissed them as trash" (Kelly). An article published in the November 21, 2000 issue of the Vancouver *National Post* indicates how Gorman eventually escaped Tyhurst's baleful influence. "Gorman said the event that triggered her breaking away from Tyhurst was his suggestion that she begin doing housework for a friend who could keep tabs on her progression as a slave while Tyhurst was at work. 'He wanted someone he knew to watch his slave so he would know how I was doing during the day.'" A court awarded Gorman damages of $556,790. Justice Vickers found that Tyhurst mistreated Gorman so badly, Jon Kelly observed, that she lost the ability to trust others, including therapists and men in general. "The nightmare of his 'therapy' will live with her for the rest of her life," the judge said, adding, "No similar case has been cited to me where the abuse of a care-provider in a position of trust has been so appalling." The award was sustained on appeal. "Dr. Tyhurst's treatment of Ms. Gorman," the appeals court concluded, "as established by the record, constituted a very grave breach of his fiduciary duty to a very troubled person with a serious mental disorder" (Mickleburgh).

According to an obituary published in *The Vancouver Sun*, Robert Tyhurst died suddenly on September 16, 2014 at age 63. At the time of his death, his father was still alive. We have no further information about James Tyhurst. The psychiatrist who craved fame and recognition early in his professional career succeeded in making headlines throughout his country and then vanished completely from public sight. Libuse Tyhurst died in 1997 at age 79. An associate professor of psychiatry at the University of British Columbia, she wrote a number of articles on the plight of refugees. Libuse Tyhurst stated during her husband's first trial that their backgrounds were entirely different. "I'm a Slav, I wear my heart on my sleeve; he's a Scot, very principled" (Hyde, 176). Like her husband, she served as an expert witness, not on behalf of men accused of sexual crimes, as he did, but in support of female complainants. Martin van den Hemel reported in the now-defunct Canadian newspaper *The Richmond Review* that a Richmond school vice-principal found guilty in 1994 of raping two female elementary school students had his conviction overturned by the BC Court of Appeal and won the right for a new trial. The two chief witnesses were both 29 years old when they testified the vice-principal had molested them in the mid-1970s. "The defense had argued that therapy sessions involving a complainant and psychiatrist Dr. Libuse Tyhurst improperly influenced the retrieval of memory." One can only imagine how two psychiatrists committed to such antithetical points of view could remain married to each other. Similarly, one can only imagine how Libuse Tyhurst felt when her husband used the theory of episodic discontrol to rationalize the actions of accused rapists.

History or Hysteria?

In researching the Tyhurst story, we used the vast resources of the world wide web, and we were struck by an anonymous review of a book, *J'accuse!*, by Giardana Bjornsen, published in 1995 by Bonfire Books. We were unable to locate the book, which is not listed in the Library of Congress. Nor could we find any information about the author. But the review itself is worth commenting on; partly because it reveals unexpected sides of every story, or at least implausible interpretations of a particular story, and partly because of its startling resemblance to the next chapter in our book.

The unnamed reviewer relies on only Bjornsen's account of the Tyhurst story; all other versions are suspect, including the extensive newspaper coverage. About the only accurate fact in the review is the observation that Bjornsen's title refers to Emile Zola's 1898 *J'accuse!*, a celebrated study of the notorious Dreyfus Affair, in which virulent anti-Semitic hatred sent an innocent Jewish army officer to prison. Bjornsen presents the Tyhurst story as a contemporary reenactment of the Dreyfus Affair, with the wrongly accused Tyhurst victimized by trumped-up charges. The reviewer invokes the hysteria generated in the 17th-century Salem witchcraft trials to explain the Tyhurst trial. In Bjornsen's version of the story, Tyhurst is victimized by his loony patients, feminist crusaders (both female and male), over-jealous Crown prosecutors, and a climate of fear and hysteria. The reviewer fully accepts all of Bjornsen's judgments. "Guilty of suborning false evidence, guilty of malicious prosecution, guilty of premeditated defamation, guilty of gross negligence and maleficence in high office, guilty of false imprisonment, and guilty of suborning the courts to carry out a witch hunt for ideological purposes." Bjornsen and the reviewer also condemn the reporters and editors involved in publicly disseminating the "crazed and venomous charges." The reviewer laments the fact that the judges, prosecutors and members of the original convicting jury cannot be tried for their misdeeds; these people will be found guilty before the "bar of history." Everyone involved with the prosecution, the reviewer opines, including those who discussed the story, deserves prosecution.

The reviewer concludes by noting sadly that Bjornsen is not a Zola, and that the "lessons of the Tyhurst trial have already been dissipated by the usual social amnesia." One can only wonder how the reviewer would respond to a story about an even more well-respected psychiatrist, indeed, perhaps the world's most famous psychiatrist, Jules Masserman, who, as we shall see in the next chapter, one year before Bjornsen's *J'accuse!*, published a book in which he invoked the same Salem witchcraft trials to defend himself against accusations of sexual crimes that were even more repugnant than those committed by Tyhurst.

CHAPTER 6

The Most Prominent Psychiatrist in the World: Jules H. Masserman and Barbara Noël

Everything about the story of Barbara Noël's accusations of sexual abuse by her psychiatrist, Jules H. Masserman, strains belief. Most stories about a patient having sex with a therapist fall into a familiar pattern. The patient is usually a young woman in her 20s or 30s who has sex with an older, middle-aged man. Masserman was nearly an octogenarian when his patient brought charges against him in 1984— and nearly a nonagenarian when he publicly responded to the allegations. Sexual boundary violations often begin with a patient more or less giving "consent," though all professional medical and psychotherapy organizations deem such permission as improper and unethical. Far from giving consent or even being aware of what was happening during her sessions with him, Noël instead alleged that she was drugged and raped by Masserman, an

259

act, she implied, that occurred *throughout* her 18-year therapy. Few stories of sexual boundary violations involve therapists using drugs considered unacceptable for general psychotherapy, but Masserman routinely used sodium Amytal in her treatment, despite the widespread recognition that the repeated use of this so-called "truth serum" is dangerous and addictive. Stories of sexual boundary violations sometimes involve prominent therapists, but Masserman was a superstar, the president of several national and international mental health organizations. How could a therapist of Masserman's stature have repeatedly done such a vile deed over such a long period of time?

What makes the story even stranger is that after he voluntarily surrendered his medical license, Masserman, protesting his innocence, wrote a book that further calls into question his own character, integrity and judgment. The Noël-Masserman story is so bizarre that the mental health community has not known how to respond to it, for the most part remaining silent about one of its biggest scandals in recent history.

The story begins with *You Must Be Dreaming*, written by Noël and Kathryn Watterson, an award-winning journalist who has taught writing at Princeton and the University of Pennsylvania. Published in 1992, the book received a great deal of media attention. Based on the Noël-Watterson book, *Betrayal of Trust* appeared two years later, a made-for-television movie directed by George Kaczendor and starring Judd Hirsch as Masserman and Judith Light as Noël. Wasting little time in penning a rebuttal, Masserman published his own version of reality in *Sexual Accusations and Social Turmoil: What Can Be Done?*, written with the help of his wife, Christine McGuire Masserman. As the title of his 1994 book implies, Masserman claims that his patient's false and malicious accusations are part of a larger and growing menace against "innocent victims" (including psychiatrists), a McCarthyesque witch hunt that soon will victimize others.

The Reader's Dilemma

Shock and horror were our first responses to the Noël story. Masserman must have been sick to have committed the deeds of which Barbara Noël accuses him. Next we felt doubt: maybe the patient actually had been dreaming or inventing these experiences. Then we felt doubt about our doubt: Masserman's actions were too incredible to have been fabricated. By the end of the story, we were convinced of the truth of her charges. Those who read *You Must Be Dreaming* and *Sexual Accusations and Social Turmoil* will probably conclude that the Noël-Masserman story is not a modern retelling of *Rashomon*, where colliding points of view and subjectivities cannot be reconciled, but a cautionary tale where a female psychotherapy patient faces an uphill fight to win a lawsuit against a renowned but unscrupulous physician.

You Must Be Dreaming is more persuasive than *Sexual Accusations and Social Turmoil* not only because Watterson is a better writer than Masserman. The irony implicit in the title of the Noël-Watterson book is apparent early in the story. *You Must Be Dreaming* abounds in irony, all deliberate. The title of Masserman's book is also ironic, but it is unintentional irony. As it turns out, Masserman is blind to the many ironies that recur throughout his story. His unreliability as a narrator undermines his credibility as a psychiatrist.

Beginning Treatment with the "Most Prominent Psychiatrist in the World"

Barbara Noël began treatment with Masserman in 1966, when she was in her early 30s and he was 61. Her family internist had recommended Masserman and when she went to the library to look him up, she was dazzled by his credentials, as anyone would have been. In 1952 he was appointed professor of neurology and psychiatry at Northwestern University Medical School, serving as co-chair of the department from 1964 through 1969. He was named director of education for the Illinois Psychiatric Institute in 1955, overseeing 33 physicians. He was the past president of several leading professional organizations, some of which he helped to create, including the Society of Biological Psychiatry, the American Society for Group Therapy, the Society for Biological Psychiatry and the American Academy for Psychoanalysis.

Masserman's national and international prominence only increased during the years Barbara Noël was in therapy with him. He was president of the International Association for Social Psychiatry from 1969–1971. Not content to be a world-famous researcher, teacher, administrator and clinician, Masserman was described by Harold M. Visotsky, professor and former chair of the Department of Psychiatry and Behavioral Studies at Northwestern University Medical School, as "psychiatry's ambassador to the world—having visited, lectured, or chaired conferences in almost every western European country and in South America, Africa, the Near and Far East" (1023). The American Friends of the Jerusalem Mental Health Center honored Masserman in 1974 for his "pioneer work in community health." In 1978, he led a tour of the Middle East in which he presented documents signed by influential Israeli psychiatrists to the Secretary General of the Egyptian Psychiatric Association. In 1971, he published a six-hundred page autobiography, *A Psychiatric Odyssey*, and announced his retirement from all his duties for the American Psychiatric Association. That retirement was only temporary. In 1978–1979, he was elected the 107th president of the APA, a position of great power and prominence. In 1974, he received the Sigmund Freud Award from the American Society for Psychoanalytic Physicians. In 1981, he was named "Honorary Life President" of the World Association for Social Psychiatry.

Masserman's fame was visible in the many framed and autographed letters in his office from such luminaries as Albert Einstein, Adlai Stevenson and President Lyndon B. Johnson. There was also a photo of Masserman standing beside former President Dwight D. Eisenhower. Masserman was the author of nearly a score of books and over 400 articles. How could any patient fail to be impressed by the man who was called by John Carlton, past president of the World Association of Social Psychiatry, the "most prominent psychiatrist in the world?"

Barbara Noël began seeing Masserman partly because of marital problems—she had recently married her second husband, Richard, shortly after divorcing her first—and partly because she felt she was losing her voice, a potentially career-ending problem for a professional singer. "Losing my voice makes me feel crazy" (31), she tells Masserman, who responds sympathetically. She also reveals conflicts with her mother, who recently admitted that she and her husband had made "serious mistakes" with their daughter when she was little, mistakes, the mother adds cryptically, which Barbara might wish to disclose to a psychiatrist. Masserman assures her she is a "relatively well-adjusted young woman" and that within a year or two she will become a "different woman, a calmer woman," one with a "healthier way of looking at life, a woman in a happy marriage" (34). None of these predictions came true during her treatment with him.

The first six months of therapy seemed to go well for Barbara. She saw Masserman three days a week in his downtown Chicago office. He kept her "spellbound," she reports, and he looked exactly as a psychiatrist should: "quaint, slightly ugly, small, and very wise" (36), much like, in her view, Gandhi. One annoying peculiarity was that he called her "Miz Nole," rhyming Nole with mole, instead of pronouncing her name as she asked him to do—"No-elle." He pronounced her name correctly only when her husband occasionally attended therapy with her. She was surprised to learn years later that President Lyndon Johnson purposely mispronounced names to keep people in their place, which might be true of Masserman too—"an experiment in depersonalizing the patient" (37).

Masserman could be gentle, kind and solicitous, but he could also be unempathic and abrasive. Admitting she was heartbroken that she had an abortion when she was dating Richard but not yet divorced from her first husband, she is shocked by Masserman's callous response: "This discussion is a waste of time." To her confession that she cannot think about the abortion without crying, he replies, "Don't you think you're being a bit self-indulgent about all of this?" (40). He makes other harsh, even cruel statements throughout treatment. Many of his angriest comments arise when she announces that she intends to leave therapy. He reacts like a hurt child, and he gleefully reminds her when she returns that he was right about her need for further treatment with him. His vindictiveness resurfaces when she leaves therapy a second time and then returns months later, chastened. Throughout the long treatment he is patriarchal and controlling, telling her after she is divorced from her second husband whom she can and cannot date.

Near the beginning of her therapy Barbara's mother died. Several weeks later she told Masserman, "Sometimes, thinking about my mother, I get this ugly feeling and I can't say anything. I don't know why. I stare at the red and gold feathers in the birds' wings on your screen, and I get this bitter feeling in my throat. I feel as if someone is sitting on my chest and holding me down, but I can't cry and I can't speak" (41). Masserman takes copious notes, appears troubled by her words, informs her that she is no longer making therapeutic progress because she is "blocking," and requests that she bring Richard to the next session for a three-way conference. During the next session Masserman declares that they have reached an "impasse" and recommends a different kind of treatment.

The Sodium Amytal Interview

At their joint meeting, Masserman gives Barbara and her husband a brief lecture on the history and use of sodium Amytal. He offers to give them a copy of his 1955 textbook *The Practice of Dynamic Psychiatry*, which contains a chapter on the drug. He emphasizes its positive role on psychiatric casualties in past wars. A barbiturate, sodium Amytal was discovered in 1923 and used extensively during the Second World War to give shell-shocked soldiers enough symptomatic relief to return to battle. The drug was also used during the Korean War to help soldiers recover from traumatic injuries. Masserman claims that he has used Amytal successfully with many patients and that it will aid Barbara too. "I believe it will help you overcome your resistances and open up so that you can get to what is troubling you. I believe it will give you relief from your anxiety and depression over your mother's death and open up new areas of memory for exploration" (44). The Amytal will be given, he explains, by slow infusion through one of her veins, and though the treatment takes only about an hour, she will be sleepy for much of the day. He downplays Richard's worry about the addictive nature of Amytal. "I understand your concern, but this drug has been in use now for more than forty years and is completely harmless when properly used" (45).

It's true that the sodium Amytal interview was used as an occasional adjunct to psychotherapy in the 1950s. Two psychiatrists, Paul H. Hoch and Phillip Polatin, published a chapter on "Narcodiagnosis and Narcotherapy" in *Specialized Techniques in Psychotherapy* (1952) describing that use of sodium Amytal and sodium pentothal. The authors indicate that the drugs may sometimes be useful for patients who are not sufficiently helped by "standard" psychotherapeutic techniques. "In these cases when sodium Amytal interviews were used, the patients became more cooperative, more verbally productive, the transference relationship became more intense, and the repressive forces were loosened with a resultant upsurge of associative material" (14). In general, however, Hoch and Polatin acknowledge that many patients do not do well with the sodium Amytal interview, and they conclude that, "with the exception of some rare instances," the narcotherapeutic method should not be used in the "framework of a prolonged psychoanalytic treatment" (15).

In retrospect, it's likely that Masserman did not expect that Barbara or her husband would read or understand his own published comments on sodium Amytal, for if they had, she never would have agreed to his use of the drug. Passages from Masserman's *The Practice of Dynamic Psychiatry* indicate that the drug was *not* recommended for people like Barbara who, in her own words, have "deep longings for passivity and protective domination," or who, in Masserman's words in his 1955 textbook, have "latent paranoid tendencies" and may become "suspicious, hostile, and recriminative" (47). In his use of the Amytal interview with her, Masserman followed none of the therapeutic protocols he outlines in his textbook. Nor did he disclose to her anything she said while she was under the drug's influence, thus depriving her of the potential benefits of the "truth serum." Instead of learning more about her repressed memories, many of which might be related to her mother's mysterious remark to her, she could remember nothing.

Masserman never warned Barbara or her husband that it was highly unusual, if not improper, for Amytal to be used in prolonged psychotherapy. If a physician does use the drug, it's most usually given once, not regularly, as a diagnostic adjunct to assist catatonic patients recall a traumatic incident or help physicians distinguish between clinical depression and dementia. She estimates that Masserman administered the drug to her by intravenous injection at least 180 times (during a total of least 1250 therapy sessions), something that is unheard of in psychotherapy. Because sodium Amytal depresses the central nervous system, patients must be closely monitored, preferably in a hospital or outpatient setting equipped with emergency equipment. Despite Masserman's promise that his nurse-secretary, Billie Laird, would be close by to monitor Barbara when she was under the influence of the drug, this *never* occurred.

The most unsettling detail surrounding Masserman's use of the Amytal interview with Barbara Noël was his request that she remove all tight-fitting clothing before each treatment so that nothing would be "binding." She found the request to remove all her clothes strange at first but then came to accept it as a part of the therapy. "Treatment" regularly began at 7:30 a.m. in his small examining room immediately adjacent to his psychotherapy office, and she would regain consciousness slowly, remaining on the daybed until mid or late afternoon.

Initially Barbara experienced a sense of euphoria following each Amytal interview, but after a few treatments she began to feel jumpy and uncomfortable, as if her "senses were turned up to full volume" (59). She experienced other common side effects of the drug, such as wild mood swings, headaches, itchy skin and irritability. These adverse effects gradually disappeared, leaving only a pleasant high. Sometimes she had unexplained physical bruises on her body following the Amytal sessions, including marks on her arms and, once, a bruised and sore pelvis. Masserman seemed to become indignant when she brought these bruises to his attention. "*Obviously*, you were flailing around on the springs of your daybed and you got a bruise!" (62–63). She was mortified by his anger, particularly when he threatened to end the use of the drug on which she had become dependent. She noticed during the next session that he had turned the examining bed around. She never had any more bruises after that.

There were, however, Masserman's puzzling statements to Barbara that seemed to indicate his close contact with her body, such as his response to her announcement to him that she was considering breast reduction surgery. "Your breasts look just fine," he exclaims. "In fact, some people would call you beautiful. So why would you do such a thing like that? Men like their women attractive, not scarred" (95). She realized only later how he came to acquire such intimate knowledge of her body.

Playing Dead

The moment of horrified revelation occurs on September 21, 1984 when, regaining consciousness earlier than expected from a lighter dose of Amytal than usual, she hears a man groaning while he is on top of her. Terrified that he might kill her if he knew she is awake, she pretends to be asleep. Moments later she hears water running, opens her eyes, sees Masserman at the sink, totally naked with his back toward her, washing his genitals, and then closes her eyes again to "play dead" before he leaves the examining room.

You Must Be Dreaming captures Barbara's nightmarish reality. She fears not only that Masserman might kill her but also that he had murdered Billie Laird, who was said to have died unexpectedly in her sleep three months earlier, at the age of 63, and who seemed to have a premonition of her impending death. Shortly before her death, Laird had advised Barbara that she should end therapy with Masserman, a suggestion that in retrospect seems a warning. Barbara realizes that the possibility Masserman was responsible for Laird's death is an "irrational unjustifiable thought" (20). She never seriously pursues this idea, but Masserman returns to it several times in his book as a way to discredit her sexual charges. Another reason Barbara fears her therapist might kill her, an explanation that does not appear in her book, is that it is common for patients to experience fear or anxiety after they have charged their therapists with wrong-doing. As Pope and Bouhoutsos observe in *Sexual Intimacy Between Therapist and Patients*, "Those who had filed against their therapists began to have fantasies about being chased, harassed, and even murdered by the previous therapist (such fantasies are particularly understandable in light of the violent threats made by many sexually exploitive therapists)" (79).

"I Suppose I Could Have Been, But I Wasn't"

What next happens feels almost as surreal as her premature awakening from Amytal. Barbara races to her internist, a Masserman "protégé," who advises her to see her gynecologist immediately after she recounts her ordeal. The gynecologist informs her that this is a "police matter" and urges her to rush to the emergency room of a nearby hospital. While waiting for the police to arrive, she momentarily wonders whether she has been "dreaming," but she never seriously doubts the reality of her perception. At the police station she tells her story to incredulous officers who ask her repeatedly whether she has been dreaming. "Yes, I suppose *I could have been*, but I wasn't," she replies (126), only later regretting the qualification, which Masserman's lawyers try to use to impeach her credibility.

The first third of *You Must Be Dreaming* chronicles a psychological nightmare, the second two-thirds a legal nightmare. A lawsuit against Masserman seems unwinnable because of his reputation and the lack of corroborating forensic evidence of a sexual crime. Why would a jury believe a crazy mental patient rather than a world-famous doctor?

This is the same issue that Tyhurst's victims confronted when they filed charges against him. Indeed, the psychiatrists Barbara Noël consults assume she must have been hallucinating; one man urges her to return to treatment with Masserman! Lawyers also doubt her story. One attorney, "John Michael Flynn," believes her but refers to "dead man's laws": she could spend a great deal of money in pursuing the elderly Masserman, but if he should die before a jury reaches a decision, certainly a possibility given his advanced age, the case would end with neither a decision nor a settlement. Flynn agrees to file a civil complaint on October 9, 1984 charging Masserman with two counts of intentional assault and battery and medical negligence, but then Flynn, citing his lack of experience with psychiatric medical malpractice cases and Masserman's reputation, reluctantly withdraws from the case—a withdrawal that the psychiatrist's lawyer will try to exploit. Barbara doggedly pursues her search for a different lawyer and finally locates a man who agrees to help, William K. Carroll, a professor of law at John Marshall Law School and, serendipitously, a clinical psychologist. Another law professor, Kenneth Cunniff, a former state's attorney, joins the case.

Other Former Patients Come Forward

There are no sudden breakthroughs in the case, no discovery of a smoking gun, eyewitnesses, or admission of guilt by Masserman. Based on the lack of forensic evidence, it's unlikely that a jury would have believed Barbara Noël's story.

There is a startling development, however, or rather several related developments, that influence the outcome of the case. Two of Dr. Masserman's former patients learn about the lawsuit, declare that they too were victims of malpractice, and begin their own lawsuits against him. Their stories strikingly parallel Barbara Noël's. Unlike Barbara, who bravely decided to use her own name in her lawsuit, they chose to remain anonymous. "Daniella Biagi" began seeing Masserman in 1980, when she was 31 and completing law school. Masserman was recommended by her friend "Annie Morrison," a businesswoman who was in treatment with him. Both women had been sexually abused by relatives when they were children and thus were a "perfect target for a sex offender" (157). In therapy Masserman dismissed Biagi's efforts to talk about her childhood sexual molestation with the words, "Oh, it's nothing you have to deal with" (157). He often referred to her as a "spoiled brat," the same epithet he used to characterize Barbara.

Biagi had no memory of an explicit sexual encounter with Masserman, but he took her flying in his small airplane and sailing on his boat; two obvious, if less serious, boundary violations. He also required her to undress for each Amytal session. Beginning in 1982, when she wasn't working, he administered two Amytal sessions a week. She became pregnant and decided to have the child, but Masserman urged her to have an abortion and continue with the Amytal treatments. Unsure whether the drug would harm the fetus, she called the Northwestern Department of Obstetrics and was told that under no circumstances should she have Amytal. "And that's when I started wondering about him," Biagi confides to Barbara (161). Despite her misgivings about Masserman, she invited him to her wedding, during which she toasted him for the help he had provided her, a detail Masserman later mentions to his advantage in *Sexual Accusations and Social Turmoil*. Biagi ended therapy with him in 1984 when she relocated to Denver.

Like Barbara Noël and Daniella Biagi, Annie Morrison hated the idea that the godlike Masserman could do any wrong. Yet nearly everything about her therapy with him seemed inappropriate and bizarre. She began seeing him in 1980, and about eight months into treatment he suggested Amytal. "The Amytal would kill my day. I'd lie there sleeping for a few hours and then go home and sleep some more. I'd go in very early—I'd have to cancel a day at work. There was this feeling of 'I don't really want to do this,' but he would make me feel like there was some neurotic reason I didn't want it when it was really so helpful" (163). As he did with Barbara, he offered to lower his fee whenever Morrison told him that she wanted to end therapy because it was not helpful and too expensive. He suggested an unusual form of bartering. Morrison managed a jewelry store, and he was willing to trade therapy time for an expensive necklace. "So he bought this three-hundred-dollar necklace—it was garnets—and he made a big deal over it: it was quite beautiful. But then he changed his mind about the arrangement; he didn't want to trade time or pay for it" (163). She was left with the bill.

Unlike Barbara Noël, who played dead when she realized Masserman had sex with her, Morrison confronted him with her recollection of his having been kissing her when she was naked during her previous Amytal session. "I know this can't be true, but I think I remember something happening under Amytal. I know it can't be, but I remember I was on my knees, and I remember you kissing me, and it was really upsetting" (164). Masserman remained "very composed and very Freudian." Rather than denying what she saw, he asked her why she found the experience "upsetting," implying it was only a fantasy. Like Biagi, Morrison went flying in Masserman's airplane and found the experience uncomfortable. She speculates that the 79-year-old Masserman enjoyed being seen with attractive women. Once, when he couldn't find a vein in which to inject the Amytal, he injected it into her ankles and hand, and when her arms began bleeding, before she lost consciousness, he began pacing in the examining room, masturbated himself with his clothes on, and wiped the blood off her arm and onto her breasts. He became furious when she demanded to know what he was doing, and she thought to herself, "Am I crazy, or is this man sitting here stroking my breasts?" (165). Another time, when she was on his boat, he began fondling her breasts and kissing her. "It was so horrible, this old, disgusting creature. Then— this is unbelievable—he took his teeth out and put them on this little shelf above us, and he kissed me some more" (166–167). Masserman's behavior horrified her, and she concluded that he was a "megalomaniac" and never went back to him.

Because they lacked physical evidence or eyewitnesses, Daniella Biagi and Annie Morrison filed civil, not criminal, lawsuits against Masserman, using the pseudonym "Doe." To avoid the possibility of collusion, Cunniff advised Barbara not to speak to the two women until after the lawsuits were resolved. Their lawsuits and testimony left Barbara feeling vindicated.

Pre-Trial Depositions

Masserman's lawyer, Debra Davy, tried to impeach Barbara Noël's credibility by insinuating she was sexually promiscuous, alcoholic, vindictive and greedy, a line of attack Masserman would later pursue in *Sexual Accusations and Social Turmoil*. Barbara anticipated that Davy would interrogate her about the events occurring on September 21, 1984, and she had little difficulty answering most of the questions. Sometimes her answers were wry. To the question whether she assumed the man who raped her in the examining room was Masserman, Barbara replied: "Whoever was in the room, nude, with a suntan and white buttocks and with a bald head—yes, ma'am" (174). Some of the lawyer's questions offended her, such as whether she had a "climax" during the rape. "'No,' I answered sharply" (175). In a later videotaped deposition, Masserman did everything he could to undermine her character, talking about her two failed marriages (he, himself, had been married three times), her alcohol addiction (a diagnosis he had never told her about while she was in therapy), and her disappointments in her career (which was remarkably successful both artistically and financially).

During Masserman's pre-trial deposition, Carroll presented compelling information acquired from experts in psychopharmacology about the potential lethality of Amytal and its inappropriateness for use in a private psychotherapist's office. Using Amytal on a repeated basis, Carroll pointed out, is not only highly unusual but also bad medical practice. Raising the specter of sexual abuse, he added that the "factors of having patients come into a private office so early in the morning, asking them to undress, and keeping them asleep or groggy all day indicates that something clearly unusual and extremely odd is going on" (182).

Medical and legal experts have long known about the problem of sexual ideation of dreams in sedated or anesthetized patients, along with the difficulty and sometimes impossibility of distinguishing between real and imagined claims of sexual abuse under anesthesia. In an article published in *Anesthesiology* in 2007, two physicians, Robert A. Strickland and John F. Butterworth, IV, provide an historical review of a problem that had been well known as early as the mid-19 century. The two anesthesiologists do not cite in their extensive bibliography the Masserman controversy, but the title of their article seems to allude to Barbara Noël's story: "Sexual Dreaming during Anesthesia." After documenting the many medical and legal ambiguities of the phenomenon, the authors quote a statement made by a member of the Royal College of Surgeons of England more than a century ago: "no administrator of an anesthetic is safe from having such a charge preferred against him, and if he and his supposed victim are alone, it is simply a case of word against word." Agreeing with the admonition, Strickland and Butterworth conclude that for those who administer anesthetics or intravenous sedatives, including all postanesthesia care unit personnel, it is "mandatory to have a third party in the immediate vicinity" (1235)—a warning that Masserman ignored, perhaps intentionally, at his own peril.

Carroll never imagined that during the deposition Masserman would respond specifically to his questions about the Amytal interview, but to his amazement, Masserman admitted that he administered the drug as a routine, common practice. Proud that he had written about Amytal in his textbook 30 years earlier, Masserman appeared to be frighteningly out of touch with the research that had been published since 1955, indicating that the drug was no longer viewed as acceptable for psychotherapy. Nor did he admit knowing that the drug could be addictive when used in the way in which he administered it. Some of his answers appeared nonsensical, such as his assertion that barbiturates are not addictive if given intravenously. In a later cross-examination, Masserman acknowledged the discrepancies between the number of times he claimed Barbara had visited him for therapy and Billie Laird's records, which indicated a much higher number. He admitted that he used his boat for his patients' therapeutic help and conceded that there was no one else in his examination room on September 21, 1984 when he administered Amytal to Barbara.

Accepting a Settlement

On October 8, 1986, a judge determined that there was sufficient evidence for a trial and set the date for 1990, four years later, when Masserman would be 85. Rather than risk a trial and a huge settlement if he was found guilty of malpractice, Masserman's insurance company offered a settlement of $125,000 (about $275,000 in current dollars), a figure they later increased to $200,000. Barbara's lawyers urged her to accept the offer despite her bitter disappointment that she would not have her day in court. She reluctantly agreed to the offer. Her share of the settlement was $118,000, about $18,000 more than she had paid, lacking insurance, to Masserman during her long treatment with him. She did not know at the time that Masserman's insurance company also offered to settle with Daniella Biagi and Annie Morrison: each woman received settlements of $25,000. The case thus came to an end— but it was not the end of the story.

The last third of *You Must Be Dreaming* describes Barbara Noël's agonized discovery, with the help of a compassionate female psychologist, that she had been sexually abused as a child by both her parents, thus explaining her mother's enigmatic reference to the "mistakes" she and her husband made while raising her. She acknowledges to herself that she is a drug addict and describes her involvement in an outpatient program for chemical dependency.

More Victims

A brief article appearing in the *Chicago Tribune* on January 6, 1987 reported the three successful lawsuits against Masserman, emboldening ten other women to come forward with their own horror stories. One person told Barbara that after her son committed suicide, she sent her 16-year-old daughter, Vanessa, to Masserman, and while she was talking about the death, he asked her, "What would you do if I unzipped my pants and took out my penis right now?" (237). Vanessa burst into tears and fled. Another woman, "Lillian," thought she was in love with

Masserman for six of the ten years she was in therapy with him. He confessed that he had an unhappy marriage and offered to marry her. "He said he was getting a divorce, but then, when I got a job offer in New York, he told me to go ahead and take it. I was sure there was another woman, so I left" (238). The experience of "Jennifer" may have been the most heartbreaking. She and her husband desperately wanted a child, and when she finally became pregnant, Masserman assured her that Amytal, which he said would help her understand how she felt about the child, would not harm the fetus. He may have been wrong. She hemorrhaged soon after a treatment and lost the baby, an event she was still grieving. Another former long-term patient told Barbara that she had practically written one of his major books and that they were deeply in love with each other from the beginning of their affair in 1960.

Still another former patient, "Laura Davis," read the *Chicago Tribune* article and began crying uncontrollably, realizing that she wasn't "crazy." She saw Masserman in 1979 and felt like a zombie after an Amytal treatment. During another session, Masserman was on top of her, repeating over and over again, "Oh, you have beautiful breasts" (244). The experience was so bewildering that she could hardly believe it was real. "Sure, you have some kind of a shadow of a doubt that it could all be in your head, because there is a dreamlike sensation to the thing." It was the same experience Barbara had in 1984. But the experience was real, Laura Davis concluded, and after she read the newspaper article she realized how stupid she had been to pay all his bills and not go to a lawyer.

All of these stories followed the same depressing pattern, a psychiatrist having sex with a vulnerable woman who was either under the influence of a drug or believed that he was willing to marry her. The women later felt foolish, exploited, manipulated and betrayed. They were too scared or embarrassed to give their full names to Barbara or help her get Masserman's medical license revoked. Nor were they willing to file charges against him because they felt the ordeal would be traumatic. They had never met each other, but their stories were too similar to have been coincidental or fabricated. All were all outraged over what had happened to them. Not motivated by monetary compensation, they spoke with Barbara Noël to share their stories with a sympathetic listener who had gone through a similar experience. Perhaps most shocking of all was that Masserman's behavior was not recent, nor a result of illness, injury or senescence: "the pattern stretched back thirty years; perhaps it had been going on all his life" (239).

In his 1984 book *Law, Psychiatry, and Morality*, Alan Stone offers a typology of psychotherapists who have sex with their patients, including those therapists who render their patients unconscious through drugs. The book was published before the Masserman story became public, but the typology applies to Masserman's situation. "In these cases," writes Stone, a professor of law and psychiatry at Harvard, "there is no exploitation of the transference; it is an exploitation of the therapeutic situation" (212).

"Research on Women"

In the process of studying Masserman's work, Watterson perceived a possible link between Masserman's research on women under the influence of Amytal and the experiments he conducted on cats and monkeys in the 1930s and 1940s, research that earned him the coveted Lasker Award in 1946. Watterson quotes from a 1953 *Chicago Tribune* article, "They're Making People Out of Monkeys," which reported how Masserman and his research assistant, Curtis Pechtel, drove monkeys insane and then attempted to cure them through experimental brain surgery. One monkey, Lucretia, proved that neurosis can be cured by such surgery, but she was left "oversexed and slightly stupid." In an astonishing sentence, Pechtel is quoted as wondering, "Since most women don't use all their brains anyway, why wouldn't it be practical to sacrifice part of them on the operating table to cure their neuroses?" (248–249). In a letter to the editor titled "Professor Squares Self with Housewives" published in the *Chicago Tribune* on June 21, 1953, Pechtel apologized for his misogynistic remark which, he claimed, represented the "opinion of others," not that of Masserman and himself. "We feel that all humans—which [he was forced to concede] include housewives and all other women—need all the adaptive capacity they have."

Surrendering His Medical License

After the publication of the *Chicago Tribune* article detailing the successful lawsuits against Masserman, the Illinois Department of Registration and Education launched an investigation. Demanding that he be censured, Barbara Noël contacted the Illinois Psychiatric Society (IPS) and the Chicago Psychoanalytic Society to register a complaint. The IPS refused to act on the complaint while he was being investigated by the Illinois Department of Registration and Education. Around this time Barbara learned from Shari Dam, a lawyer for the Illinois Department of Registration and Education, that another lawsuit against Masserman, brought by a female patient who charged him with medical negligence for permanent scars caused by Amytal injections, had been settled in 1985 for $50,000. The case, *Cheryl Russell v. Dr. Jules Masserman*, was settled out of court. (The appendix of *You Must Be Dreaming* lists the many lawsuits filed against Masserman in Cook County Circuit Court.)

Like Barbara, Shari Dam was incensed over Masserman's behavior toward her and looked forward to a hearing. Faced with the evidence against him and backed into a corner, Masserman voluntarily surrendered his medical license on October 7, 1987. He thus gave up his right to prescribe drugs or practice medicine or any form of psychotherapy, psychoanalysis, or counseling (255–256). By voluntarily surrendering his medical license, Masserman sought to avoid the publicity arising from a prolonged investigation.

Suspension

One of the most dismaying aspects of the Noël-Masserman story was the length of time it took the major psychiatric and psychoanalytic organizations to censure Masserman. Two physicians from the Illinois Psychiatric Society Ethics Committee promised to contact Noël shortly after its meeting in 1989 but had not done so a year later. She telephoned the Chicago Psychoanalytic Society but received no response. What was perhaps most infuriating was that Masserman's name was still listed on the roster of the American Psychoanalytic Association. His co-authored book *Adolescent Sexuality* was published in 1989 with a glowing foreword written by his colleague Harold M. Visotsky.

Dismayed by his continued fame and unwilling to do nothing, Barbara Noël wrote a letter in 1990 to Donald G. Langsley, the co-chair of the Illinois Psychiatric Society and, like Masserman, a former president of the American Psychiatric Association. Langsley, who figures conspicuously in *Sexual Accusations and Social Turmoil*, promised to hold a hearing. Of all the women who were victimized by Masserman, only Laura Davis agreed to testify with Noël at the hearing, which was held in the summer of 1990. Masserman and his wife attended the hearing, which was co-chaired by Langsley and Brenda C. Solomon, also from the Illinois Psychiatric Society. Several other psychiatrists attended the meeting, including Langsley. Under cross-examination by Masserman's lawyer, Barbara Stackler, Davis acknowledged that she had lost her lawsuit against him, but only because the statute of limitations had run out. Raising questions about privileged clinical information, Stackler rhetorically asked Davis how a mother like herself could desert a son, information with which Masserman had obviously provided her. Davis screamed, "I don't have a son!" and ran crying out of the conference room. After the hearing, Langsley sent Barbara a letter in October 1991, informing her of the American Psychiatric Association's decision to suspend Masserman from both the APA and the Illinois Psychiatric Society for five years due to violations of medical ethics. The decision came seven years after Noël first became aware that Masserman had raped her.

Barbara Noël's feeling of vindication was short-lived, however, for she soon learned from Watterson that by suspending rather than expelling Masserman, the APA did not have to report its decision in the APA's national newsletter, *Psychiatric News*. Consequently, the public never learned of his suspension. "Their decision did not receive even one word of publicity" (282). Widespread public recognition came only with the publication of *You Must Be Dreaming* and its dramatization in the film *Betrayal of Trust*.

A Compelling Book

You Must Be Dreaming received critical and popular acclaim. Believing that the book could win the Pulitzer Prize for reporting, Shana Alexander praised Noël's "Boswell," Kathryn Watterson, for "extracting the whole

terrible tale from Miss Noël and writing it so vividly and cleanly." Francine
Prose described the book in *Newsday* as "a frightening account of the evil
that can be done when cruelty and power interface all too perfectly with
vulnerability, female passivity, and simple unquestioning human need." The
New York Times listed *You Must Be Dreaming* as a Notable Book of 1992.

Unlike *Betrayal*, the story of Julie Roy's sexualized therapy with Renatus
Hartogs, *You Must Be Dreaming* is narrated in the first person. Barbara
Noël's voice sounds strong and authoritative throughout the book, fully
in command, with her co-author's help, of recounting and understanding
her story. It is, as it says in the prologue, "a story about knowing and not
knowing, telling and not telling, living and not living" (13).

You Must Be Dreaming captures Masserman's alluring and threatening
sides. He comes across as erudite and sophisticated, capable of great
charm and charisma. He seems to know everyone in his profession,
including many of the most famous people in the world. A lover of
the arts, Masserman was also a musical prodigy. He concluded his
presidential address at the American Psychiatric Association's annual
meeting by playing the violin—he owned two prized instruments, a
1709 Albani violin and a 1712 Albani viola—to demonstrate music's
healing power. But he also comes across as a rogue psychiatrist who
preys upon helpless women.

Kathryn Watterson speaks in her own voice, equally strong and
authoritative, in the "Notes and Sources" of the book. She interviewed
scores of people, including Masserman's former patients ("Laura Davis,"
"Daniella Biagi," "Annie Morrison"), experts on incest and other forms of
sexual abuse, representatives of the American Psychoanalytic Association
and the New York Psychoanalytic Institute, and lawyers specializing
in the treatment and disposition of sex offenders. Watterson also read
Masserman's many publications. An extensive bibliography appears at
the end of *You Must Be Dreaming*. A meticulous researcher who is always

balanced in her judgments, Watterson cites a 1987 study concluding that 7.1% of male and 3% of female psychiatrists admitted having sexual contact with a patient during or after treatment. She investigated every aspect of the story, including the use and misuse of sodium Amytal. Some of the psychopharmacologists whom she interviewed suggested that because Amytal is a short-acting barbiturate, unlikely to keep a patient unconscious for seven hours, Masserman may have used an IV of Amytal administered continuously or other medications to keep a person unconscious for five to eight hours. Other experts speculated that Masserman may have used another drug, such as morphine or Valium, to deepen amnesia.

The Afterword contains an account of Watterson's interview of Masserman prior to the publication of *You Must Be Dreaming*, in which she invited him to tell his side of the story. He declined her request to tape-record the interview. His wife, who was present during the interview in the couple's apartment, stated that *they* were tape-recording the interview and would provide Watterson with a copy, something which they in fact failed to do. Watterson's interview captures Masserman's old-world charm; his fierce pride in his many publications, honors, and awards; his almost child-like defenselessness; and his mystifying logic. Throughout the interview he seemed to be living mainly in the past and out-of-touch with the present. "I had the sensation that I was in a time warp," Watterson admits at the end, "and after I left, I felt an amazing sadness" (321).

Sexual Accusations and Social Turmoil

Masserman was 87 when *You Must Be Dreaming* was published, an age at which few people are able or willing to defend themselves by writing an entire book. Yet he did not wait long to counterattack. Remaining silent was not an option for a man who believed the pen was his sword. Swords, literal and metaphorical, were capable of wielding magical power for Masserman, as he reveals on the penultimate page of *A Psychiatric Odyssey*, where he writes about a series of university lectures he had given in Australia and New Zealand shortly after his 60th birthday. An internationally respected psychiatrist and ethnologist who was a firm believer in native Maori lore showed Masserman, in great confidence, an ancient jade sword sacred to the supreme gods. Masserman's host told him that the sword was so charged with *tapu*, mystic power for good and evil, that it could be possessed only by the greatest chiefs. Lesser men who owned it mysteriously—and prematurely—died. The host showed him how to wield the sword in a secret ritual, "a procedure he now considered safe because he had concluded from observing me that I possessed sufficient *mana* (thaumaturgic knowledge, prestige, and potency) to withstand its evil *tapu* and instead increase my own longevity and power" (565).

Wielding his own metaphorical sword, Masserman penned *Sexual Accusations and Social Turmoil*, but the book did not increase his own longevity and power—he died shortly after its publication. Everything about the book that he rushed into print is strange and haphazard. It's carelessly written and filled with misspellings, including the names "Kathleen" Watterson and the conductor Bruno "Walther." He dedicates the work to his wife, Christine McGuire Masserman, who, "with characteristic grace, declined to be duly credited as co-author of this book, yet her wisdom imbues every page." Two of the seven chapters of Part One, Sexual Accusations, are, in fact, written by her, chapters that contain little grace and less wisdom. Part Two, Social Turmoil, is an awkward and unsuccessful attempt to connect Masserman's story with the events occurring during the Salem witchcraft trials of late seventeenth-century colonial America and the McCarthy Communist

284

witch hunts of the 1950s. The material in Part Three, Youth and Age, repeats information copied from Masserman's earlier *A Psychiatric Odyssey*. The appendix contains various documents showing the lack of forensic evidence surrounding Barbara Noël's sexual charges and other information related to the case. The appendix ends with a bibliography of Masserman's extensive publications, suggesting that a person of unusual professional achievement cannot be guilty of sexual misconduct.

Rage, not sadness, animates Masserman's counterstory, a protracted smear campaign that masquerades as social commentary. The rage is combined with studied contempt. It might be too much to expect a therapist to empathize with a patient who is suing him, but Masserman goes out of his way to attack not only Barbara Noël's credibility as a witness but also her dignity as a human being. He pours contempt on her "extramarital sexual liaisons (one with a homosexual physician also my patient)"—note how Masserman gratuitously insults *two* of his patients—and her "disappointments in her operatic aspirations (she now sings only occasionally with a dance band)" (6). He presents intimate personal information only to humiliate her, as when he describes her "ill-fitting dentures" (7).

Ann Landers

Masserman sees betrayal everywhere. Former acquaintances and friends are now his enemies. His strategy is not to take the high road and respectfully disagree with those who have criticized him but to take the low road and eviscerate his critics. This is best seen in chapter 4, "Book of Job," where he portrays himself as the long-suffering righteous man who has been pushed to the limit. It is not God or Satan who tests or torments Masserman but the nationally syndicated columnist Ann Landers

(Eppie Lederer), whose endorsement of Barbara Noël's story appears on the cover of *You Must Be Dreaming*: "This shocking documentary, beautifully written, is guaranteed to keep you riveted." Masserman begins by recounting his happy experiences with Landers, who had once invited him and his wife to her "posh" Lake Shore apartment overlooking Lake Michigan. He quotes the columnist's grateful letters to him and then, hardly disguising his *schadenfreude*, confesses that he was "saddened to hear" the "disconcerting developments" in her life, which he enumerates in inquisitorial detail, including the fact that "she and her first husband had been divorced and that she was having difficulties with their daughter Margo" (34). Masserman then cites an article published in the *New York Times* on September 16, 1992 tracing the evolution of the Noël-Watterson book from, to use his own words, an "illiterate manuscript submitted by Miss Noël to Ann Landers, who passed it on to her daughter Margo, whose literary agent recruited Ms. Watterson to write the book and arranged its publication. The *Times* article implied that all are profiting handsomely with Ms. Landers as broker for the enterprise" (35).

It's unlikely that Masserman expected or desired his readers to examine the *Times* article, Esther B. Fein's "Book Notes," but if they did, they would see his distortions and omissions. He insinuates that everyone involved with *You Must Be Dreaming*, including Ann Landers, is "profiting" from the book, when in fact Fein implies that neither the columnist nor her daughter had a financial stake in its success. Fein declared that Ann Landers believed the first draft of the book was "poorly written," not "illiterate." Masserman omits crucial information from the article, including Ann Landers's statement that the book "will send shivers down the spine of the psychiatric community." He also conveniently forgets to mention the most startling detail in the article. Ann Patty, the head of Poseidon Books, which published *You Must*

Be Dreaming, was reported as saying that she had not expected Ann Landers publicly to endorse the book, but "what truly shocked" Patty "was a phone call she received recently, after the book came out and was serialized in McCall's magazine. The caller was Dr. Masserman, wondering if Ms. Patty might be interested in publishing his memoirs."

Masserman refers to Ann Landers one more time in *Sexual Accusations and Social Turmoil*, when he tries to convince his readers that somehow she has had a change of heart toward him. In the appendix he quotes what he calls her "three words of heartfelt sympathy for the falsely accused" in her column of September 10, 1993, when she printed a letter from a man who was arrested, indicted and imprisoned on a malicious charge of rape, and experienced months of anguish before he was able to clear his name and obtain compensation. Masserman prints part of Ann Landers's letter—even though she ends it by declaring that although there are many innocent men in prison on rape convictions, she bets that there are "an equal number . . . who are guilty . . . [and] . . . are . . . free as the breeze" (165). Why Masserman believes that Ann Landers suddenly sympathizes with *his* situation remains a mystery.

"Et tu Brute?"

Masserman feels no less betrayed by Alan Stone, his successor as president of the American Psychiatric Association. Stone's credentials were impeccable. A graduate of Harvard University, Yale Medical School, and the Boston Psychoanalytic Institute, Stone was Professor of Law and Psychiatry in the Faculty of Law and the Faculty of Medicine at Harvard and had written a positive review of *You Must Be Dreaming*, published in the *Psychiatric Times* in 1993, that Masserman found galling. Stone observed in the review that he found the charges against

Masserman credible based on the available evidence and suggested that the American Psychiatric Association's "damage control experts must have been hoping and praying that the Masserman scandal was going to fade away." Stone was critical of his profession, in general, and of the Illinois Psychiatric Society, in particular, for having suspended Masserman instead of expelling him. Stone also wondered what the American Psychiatric Association would be prepared to do in 1996 when Masserman's five-year suspension ended. Stone ended his review by describing his moral revulsion over Masserman's "depraved sexual abuse" of Noël during the Amytal sessions:

> Although I have served as a consultant for numerous women who have been sexually exploited by their therapists, none has recounted a more sickening story than is described on these pages. The multiple complainants make the allegations difficult to ignore and, if true, *as I have been convinced they are*, disgrace Masserman and cast a pall over our profession as well. For Masserman's former patients and for psychiatry, *You Must Be Dreaming* describes a nightmare. Noël could have tried to forget this nightmare. Instead, she has attempted to work it through. The psychiatric profession should respect and support her efforts as we try to work through our own feelings of betrayal and disgrace. [emphasis added]

Stone's review of *You Must Be Dreaming* is noteworthy in light of his comments in *Law, Psychiatry, and Morality* when he addressed the legal and ethical problems of male therapists sexually exploiting female patients. "I wrote about this problem and the possible avenues of redress in 1975 and have since been consulted by a number of female patients seeking advice about how to proceed in such situations, as well as by psychiatrists trying to deal with ethical complaints and the conflicts

CHAPTER 6: THE MOST PROMINENT PSYCHIATRIST IN THE WORLD: JULES H. MASSERMAN AND BARBARA NOËL

and difficulties involved in passing judgment on a colleague." Admitting that the results of the questionnaire surveys on which he relies is not large, he concludes that what he discovered is chastening. "[N]one of the women who have consulted me were fabricating. If once on the basis of my professional training I presumed that such complaints were false, I now presume that they are true" (192).

Stung by Stone's sympathy for Barbara Noël's situation, Masserman wrote a bitter letter to the editor of *Psychiatric Times*, expressing regret that Stone "did not follow his juristic training to ascertain the truth about the Noël book before writing his grossly misleading review." Masserman reprints his letter in *Sexual Accusations and Social Turmoil*. The most telling sentence in the letter is Masserman's Shakespearean allusion. "When Dr. Stone's review of the nine-year-old episode was brought to my attention by indignant colleagues, I sent my erstwhile friend a letter with the salutation 'Et tu Brute?' and a summary of legally attested data confirming all the statements in this letter. I have received no reply, but I suppose I should be grateful for his decision to render his final verdict when my 'suspension' terminates five years hence. Since I am now in my eighty-ninth year, this presumably expresses his kind wish for my longevity" (60).

Christine McGuire Masserman

Rage also dominates the two chapters in *Sexual Accusations and Social Turmoil* written by Christine McGuire Masserman, combined with perhaps the darkest emotion of all, contempt. Her rhetoric in chapter 5, "Familial Travails" (which contains her husband's letter about Stone's review) and chapter 6, "Perspectives and Proposals," is even more incendiary than her husband's. Witness this description of the motives and ethics of Jules Masserman's accusers: "Smelling blood drawn by the carnage of the initial charge, scavenging accusers, greedy attorneys and salacious media gather for the kill and, most disgustingly of all, ambitious prosecutors and pandering colleagues join in. Like a pack of wild dogs nipping at the heels of an injured creature, they try—with all too frequent success—to bring down with a thousand wounds, even the most majestic prey" (39).

Throughout *Sexual Accusations and Social Turmoil* Christine McGuire Masserman portrays her husband as majestic prey—and herself as equally majestic in her ferocious protectiveness of her mate. There's no evidence to suggest that she doubted her husband's innocence or his accusers' ill will. It's precisely the stark contrast she presents between the forces of good and evil that calls into question her reliability and judgment. She cannot imagine that those who impugn her husband's professional behavior might be as principled and fair-minded as those who defend it.

"The Hypocrisy of Our 'Old Friend'"

The most striking example of her demonization of her husband's critics appears in her comments about Donald Langsley. In the first of two letters written to him that appear in chapter 5, she asked Langsley to correct the committee's "defalcations"—implying that the ethics committee misappropriated or wasted its funds because it reached the wrong conclusion about her husband. She asked Langsley not to blame her husband for anything that she might have said in her letter to Langsley. She then hinted darkly at her husband's and her own state of health and what might occur if the committee reached the wrong judgment. "But Don, I do know that everyone, no matter how strong, has a breaking point; what I do not know is how close we are to ours" (56).

Christine McGuire Masserman's "sincerely friendly and heartfelt letter to Langsley did no good," she admits ruefully, and she was now "antagonized by the hypocrisy of our 'old friend.'" Antagonized is a euphemism; *enraged* is more accurate. She sent Langsley a second letter in which she "more candidly appraised his character as witnessed by his recent arrogance, insensitivity and disregard for the rights of others, especially evident in his recent misdirection of the IPS Ethics Committee." What's astounding is not her charge that the IPS proceedings were "unethically and illegally persecutorial" but her aside to the reader: "Though I realize that such a letter will hardly transform a man of Langsley's character, I doubt that I, at least, will ever again have to endure his particularly odious form of 'sexual harassment,' which for years consisted, every time he saw me, of waddling across a room with arms outstretched, yelling 'Hello Dear Heart'—and then planting a wet, slobbery kiss on my reluctant cheek" (58).

The Wrong Side of History

Christine McGuire Masserman cites Joseph Cardinal Bernardin as an example of the growing pandemic of false allegations of sexual misconduct. "At a recent luncheon of the Chicago Bar Association held to honor him, Joseph Cardinal Bernadin expressed great concern that the rights and reputations of accused people be respected and protected, and that the presumption of innocence be maintained, lest blameless victims lose their good name, their liberty and their future." "Regrettably," she adds, "some months later the revered Cardinal was himself victimized" (70).

There may have been doubts about Cardinal Bernardin's complicity in protecting pedophiles in 1994, when *Sexual Accusations and Social*

Turmoil was published, but these doubts have disappeared. Internal archdiocese documents released on January 21, 2014 reveal his widespread efforts to contain the growing priest scandal at the end of the 20th century. The internal memo (Archdiocese of Chicago Documents) and the whitewash confirm that Cardinal Bernardin not only refused to pursue a canonical trial to remove a convicted child molester from the priesthood but also increased the priest's salary to help him in prison for his criminal defense. Cardinal Bernardin also protected other priests guilty of sexual crimes. One wonders how Masserman would have responded to Pope Francis, who has begged forgiveness from victims of sexual abuse and promised not to tolerate bishops who fail to protect children from predatory priests.

Jules Masserman's defense of then President Bill Clinton is no less ironic. "To those who wish to doubt and condemn, President Clinton, himself, can never *dis*prove that he had been unfaithful to his wife, Hillary" (98). One can only speculate how Masserman would have responded to the Monica Lewinsky scandal, which became public in 1998, four years after his death.

Masserman's most disturbing statements in *Sexual Accusations and Social Turmoil* involve his refusal to acknowledge the prevalence and long-lasting harm of child sexual abuse. He cites one study by a former president of the American Psychiatric Association concluding that children or adolescents "may be," in Masserman's own words, "less deeply and enduringly disturbed by the sexual experience" than by the trauma of prolonged police investigations and media publicity (124). This may sometimes be true, but Masserman implies here and elsewhere that it is better not to pursue child sexual traumas. This is exactly the advice he gave to Barbara Noël and his other female patients who were sexually abused in childhood: "It's nothing you have to deal with."

Stonewalling

Sexual Accusations and Social Turmoil fails to address many of the issues raised in *You Must Be Dreaming*. In attempting to discredit the motives of the women who filed malpractice lawsuits against him, Masserman remains silent about the other women who came forward with similar stories of sexual abuse but who were unwilling to endure the humiliation of a public trial, women who were not interested in financial compensation. He remains silent about the many instances of sexual and nonsexual boundary violations: inviting his female patients to visit his apartment, sail on his boat, fly in his airplane, and, in Barbara Noël's case, serve as his unofficial hostess and interpreter when he presided at the World Congress of Social Psychiatry at the University of Paris. He remains silent about the inappropriate and dangerous use of sodium Amytal as part of routine psychotherapy. He invokes the false memory movement to discredit the incestuous abuse of children, but he neglects to point out, as Diana E.H. Russell and others document, that 16% of girls are sexually victimized by relatives before the age of 18—and that the trauma of abuse continues to haunt their lives throughout adulthood. Masserman suggests in *Adolescent Sexuality* that the best approach to incest is sometimes to remain silent about the crime, applying the dubious precept that the "unnecessary induction of familial, social, and legal turmoil may be more traumatic to all concerned than the incest *per se*" (49). Masserman's recommendation for victims to ignore incest and other forms of sexual abuse is contradicted by clinicians like Judith Lewis Herman, who argues in *Trauma and Recovery* that psychotherapy facilitates the healing process. Finally, Masserman ignores the increasing number of studies, written by those inside and outside the mental health profession, which confirm the alarming number of psychotherapists who have sex with their patients.

293

Communicating with Fellow Odyssiasts

Masserman ends *Sexual Accusations and Social Turmoil* by paraphrasing the opening paragraph of the prologue to *A Psychiatric Odyssey*, when he was at the height of his fame, untroubled by litigious patients:

> Here in my Center sanctum high above San Francisco Bay I sit listening to Mozart's deeply introspective String Quintet Opus 516 in perfect counterpoint to my own reflections. Can this *Odyssey* ever empathetically convey my own troubled and ever-partial transitions from reader to understander, from experimenter to researcher, from schoolman to scholar, from physiologist to physician? Yet should I not try to emulate the autobiographic accounts of the many historic and current mentors—from Aristotle through Maimonides and Spinoza to Freud, Schweitzer and Adolf Meyer—who have inspired me? Here, then, my own efforts to communicate with fellow Odyssiasts. (*Sexual Accusations and Social Turmoil*, 140)

To compare one's "own reflections" to the profundity of Mozart's string quintet boggles the imagination. No less grandiose is Masserman's identification with his "fellow Odyssiasts," some of whom are among the greatest geniuses in history. Curiously, the opening paragraph to the prologue of *A Psychiatric Odyssey* contains no mention of Masserman's identification with the above luminaries or the assertion of the perfect counterpoint between Mozart's music and his own thoughts. How do we account for the differences between the original paragraph of *A Psychiatric Odyssey* and Masserman's revision decades later? The autobiography does not suffer from a lack of self-esteem that requires silent emendation. Nearly every page of *A Psychiatric Odyssey* reveals

Masserman's grandiloquence. He quotes hundreds of letters extolling his momentous contributions to psychiatry, and he ends the book with a 36-page curriculum vitae. But as the above paragraph demonstrates, in the 23 years that passed between *A Psychiatric Odyssey* and *Sexual Accusations and Social Turmoil,* his grandiosity became even more pronounced.

Did Masserman believe that he could get away with his outrageous conduct with his patients? Was he so delusional as to believe that he would never be caught? He never comments in his writings on out-of-control psychotherapists or sexual (or nonsexual) boundary transgressions, but he offers a hint in *A Psychiatric Odyssey* of "three of man's essential beliefs, precepts, categorical imperatives, or ultimate (Ur-) defenses," one of which applies to himself with a vengeance: "a *presumption of personal invulnerability, power, and vicarious immortality,* rooted in primary narcissism and never completely surrendered" (404). Masserman was fond enough of this Ur-defense to repeat it in *Theory and Therapy in Dynamic Psychiatry* (1973), where he suggests that the quest to extend power and control over the forces that menace us sometimes results in our creations turning into Frankensteins (135).

Masserman was far from being the only psychiatrist who demonstrated outrageous behavior toward patients. John Rosen (1902–1993), famous for his claim that he discovered the cure for schizophrenia through what he called "direct analysis," was physically violent toward his patients, beating them, humiliating them, and in some cases forcing them to have sex. Rosen surrendered his medical license in 1983 rather than stand trial for incompetence. But Rosen, who worked with patients from wealthy families, never had Masserman's prestige and political power. Masserman stood at the pinnacle of his profession, which made his actions more shocking. Rosen's "direct analysis" was shown to be completely ineffective as a treatment for schizophrenia in at least two follow-up studies of patients Rosen had treated. When compared with matched control groups of untreated patients, Rosen's patients remained just as ill as those who were untreated (Horwitz, et al.; Bookhammer, et al.).

The Cloak of Silence

No psychoanalyst has offered a psychodynamic interpretation of Masserman's sexual misconduct. According to *Psychoanalytic Electronic Publishing* (*PEP*), a full text database that covers 51 major journals in psychoanalysis published during the past 100 years, there are *no* reviews of *Sexual Accusations and Social Turmoil* and only two articles that briefly mention the Noël-Masserman case. In one of these articles, "Boundary Violations and the Abuse of Power: Commentary on a Paper by Philip Kuhn," Glen O. Gabbard makes a passing but noteworthy reference to the Noël-Masserman case, remarking that multiple complainants "are almost always evidence of a pattern of sexual misconduct by a practitioner, and the assumption of a conspiracy is usually the least likely explanation" (384–385). In the other article, "Psychoanalysis and Feminism: A Personal Journey," Brenda C. Solomon recounts her experience, as an early career psychiatrist, serving on the Illinois Psychiatric Society Ethics Committee that investigated Masserman. "Intimidated by the presence of seven psychiatrists, three lawyers, a court reporter, Dr. Masserman, his wife, and the complainant, I persevered and learned about power, abuse, and the law" (154). Seeking to learn more about how sex in therapy damages patients, Solomon created, with her colleague Bernard Rubin, one of the first required courses on ethics and psychoanalysis at the Chicago Psychoanalytic Institute. Her experience chairing the Masserman ethics case influenced her later decision to study the relationship between narcissistic personality disorders and domestic violence.

Apart from these references, we have not been able to locate any discussions in the psychoanalytic literature of Masserman's outrageous behavior. From this we conclude that a "cloak of silence" surrounds the case, an expression that is less judgmental than a "conspiracy of silence." P. Susan Penfold's interpretation of the health profession's tendency to remain silent about the sexual abuse of patients is particularly relevant here. "Health professionals as a group often respond like the parents and other relatives in a family in which incest is disclosed. Although there may be an initial response of outrage, it is all too often lost in attempts to deny, distort, minimize, trivialize, and obscure the victim's complaints, protect the offender, and ostracize the victim" (114).

Speaking and Not Speaking the Unspeakable

Some of the most highly respected and influential psychoanalysts who have written about sexual boundary violations have remained conspicuously silent about the Masserman scandal. Glen O. Gabbard's edited volume *Sexual Explorations in Professional Relationships* was published in 1989, around the time the Noël-Masserman case started to receive attention. There's nothing about the case in the first edition of *Boundaries and Boundary Violations in Psychoanalysis*, co-authored by Gabbard and Eva P. Lester, published in 1995, three years after the publication of *You Must Be Dreaming*. Nor is there any mention of the case in the 2001 article "Speaking the Unspeakable: Institutional Reactions to Boundary Violations by Training Analysts," written by Gabbard and Morris L. Peltz. The omission of any information about Masserman becomes more surprising in light of the fact that the Gabbard and Peltz article was based on a study group in which Brenda Solomon took part. Most surprising of all is the continued absence of information about Masserman in the second edition of *Boundaries and Boundary Violations in Psychoanalysis*, published in 2016. The only reason Gabbard didn't write about Masserman, he told us (Personal communication, May 11, 2016), was because he felt that Masserman's major contribution was in psychiatry, not psychoanalysis. Gabbard has added much new information in the second edition. He notes in passing that the "complexities involved in sexual boundary violations grow more challenging with greater study," adding, the "capacity for self-deception is extraordinary" (x). Nowhere is the truth of the observation better seen than in the Masserman case.

A few publications reviewed either *You Must Be Dreaming* or *Sexual Accusations and Social Turmoil* and came to strikingly different conclusions. Psychiatrist Judith Lewis Herman's positive review of the Noël-Watterson book was published in the *New York Times Book Review* on January 10, 1993. "Rape survivors," Herman observed, "who recover best are those who discover a larger meaning in their personal ordeal and who join with others to seek justice. Like many survivors, Barbara Noël has discovered the healing power of truth-telling." Herman asserted in her review that no peer could be found to testify as an expert witness against Masserman, a statement that was challenged by William K. Carroll in a letter to the *Times* published one month later. Carroll pointed out that Lawrence Z. Freedman, formerly on the faculties of both law and psychiatry at Yale, Cambridge and Stanford, was willing to testify on behalf of Barbara Noël.

In a brief review published in *Library Journal*, Bonnie Hoffman refers to Masserman's "convincing reply" to Noël's charges. A brief review in the journal *Adolescence* states, contrary to the truth, that "thorough medical, laboratory, and police investigations proved the allegations false." The same misrepresentation of the outcome of the Noël-Masserman story appears in Yolanda Lucire's "Sex and the

Practitioner: The Victim," published in the *Australian Journal of Forensic Sciences* in 2002. Defending the right of doctors and patients to have consensual "social friendships," Lucire, a medical anthropologist and a forensic psychiatrist in private practice in Australia, asserts that Barbara Noël had indeed been dreaming. She concludes, "When her allegations and those of the copycats were subjected to proper investigation and forensic procedures, Masserman was acquitted."

Lying on the Couch

One therapist unafraid to comment on Masserman's behavior is Irvin Yalom, the distinguished existential psychiatrist. Yalom's 1996 novel *Lying on the Couch* remains probably the best fictional study of sexual and nonsexual boundary violations. Near the beginning of the story Marshal Streider, a training analyst at a San Francisco psychoanalytic institute, speaks with his supervisee, Ernest Lash, about the many psychiatrists in the Boston area who had recently been charged with sexual abuse. Suddenly Masserman's name comes up:

"And then, of course, there is the case of Jules Masserman—who . . . was a past president of the American Psychiatric Association. Can you believe what he did—giving patients sodium pentothal [sic] and then having sex with them while they were unconscious? It's unthinkable."

"Yes, that was the one that shook me up the most," said Ernest. "My internship roommates often kid me about spending that year soaking my feet—I had terrible ingrown toenails—and reading Masserman: his *Principles of Dynamic Psychiatry* was the best textbook I ever read!"

"I know, I know," said Marshall, "all the fallen idols. And it's getting worse! I don't understand what's happening." (81)

Lying on the Couch is essential reading for anyone interested in learning about both the seductive allure and self-destructive consequences of boundary violations. Yalom offers every possible rationalization that either a patient or therapist can make in support of erotic contact. He then shows how and why each rationalization breaks down under the crushing complexity of reality. An ironist, as can be seen in the clever title of his novel, Yalom unambiguously concludes that "sexual contact between patient and therapist is invariably destructive to the patient—and ultimately to the therapist as well" (116).

"Unfortunately," admits Jeffrey A. Lieberman in *Shrinks: The Untold Story of Psychiatry* (2015), "unsound methods have never been far from the main currents of psychiatry, and leading psychiatric institutions have often credited techniques that were questionable, if not wholly inept" (21). Lieberman has in mind Wilhelm Reich's bizarre theory of orgone therapy, but he never mentions Jules Masserman's exploitation of sodium Amytal. Lieberman, the chair of psychiatry at the Columbia University College of Physicians and Surgeons, director of the New York State Psychiatric Institute, and, like Masserman, past president of the American Psychiatric Association, misses few opportunities to lambast those whose unsound methods and moral turpitude have blackened psychiatry, but he utters not a word about Masserman. Lieberman refers to his own use of Amytal as a "truth serum" for one of his patients, but there is no indication that he uses this "old procedure" (47) as a regular therapeutic technique.

Predatory Psychopath"

In a study of over 100 cases of analysts who have been charged with sexual misconduct, Gabbard has identified four broad categories, one of which, "predatory psychopathy," characterized by a "ruthless exploitation of multiple victims, with no remorse or shame," seems to apply to Masserman, a training analyst at the famed Chicago Psychoanalytic Institute:

> While we like to think that such unscrupulous individuals are screened out of analytic training, the distressing fact is that some analysts with this type of pathology have risen to positions of leadership in psychoanalytic organizations. They often have a form of grandiosity whereby they feel the "rules" no longer apply to them. They seem to have a severe form of narcissistic pathology that is an example of what Goldberg [in *The Problem of Perversion: The View of Self Psychology*] (1955) and others have called a *vertical split*. Separate from the "real me" is a disavowed sector of the personality that initiates and promulgates perverse acts. While one aspect of the self is predatory and corrupt, other dimensions may be generous, funny, warm, charming, wise, and generative of younger colleagues. (Gabbard and Peltz, 699)

Two Parallel Stories

Striking parallels exist between the Noël-Masserman and Roy-Hartogs stories. Both psychiatrists were influential physicians who were also prolific authors, enjoying large audiences and taking pleasure in publicly dispensing advice. Both men sexually exploited several female patients over a long period of time and exhibited a pattern of sexual abuse that was frighteningly consistent. Despite a few vague statements about being in love and empty promises about marrying their patients, neither psychiatrist seemed to suffer from countertransference-love. Both psychiatrists' sexual misconduct seemed to be symptomatic of arrogance and misogyny. Each of them steadfastly denied any wrongdoing. Both of their female patients Barbara Noël and Julie Roy, stigmatized as being "crazy," "hysterical,"

301

delusional, vindictive or greedy, faced daunting battles in pursuing lawsuits in a legal system that disadvantages psychotherapy patients. With the help of professional authors, both Noël and Roy wrote books about their psychiatric ordeals; their stories were later developed into made-for-TV movies. The Noël-Masserman story is the more shocking of the two partly because Masserman was at the pinnacle of his profession, the "most prominent psychiatrist in the world," and partly because he had sex with drugged women who did not know they were being violated.

There are also parallels between Jules Masserman and James Tyhurst. Masserman did not enact elaborate master-and-slave erotic rituals with his patients as Tyhurst did—ordering them to sign master-slave contracts and subjecting them to cruel whippings—but he exerted omnipotent control over them, using them for his own pleasure. Just as Tyhurst's patients "could never say 'no'" to him, as Debbie Vreeland testified, Masserman's patients could never say no, mainly because they were blinded by transference-love. Tyhurst manipulated his patients by exploiting their low self-esteem and unconscious wish for punishment; Masserman manipulated his patients by drugging them. Like Tyhurst's patients, Barbara Noël remained in a long therapeutic relationship that was fundamentally abusive. Both psychiatrists were defended by wives who were either unable or unwilling to acknowledge their husbands' sexual sadism. Ric Dolphin's statement about Tyhurst—"It is very difficult to believe someone you find charming is a monster"—echoes statements of those who later learned about Masserman's behavior.

Somnophilia

In retrospect, Masserman's actions might be considered a form of "somnophilia," a term the sexologist John Money coined in 1986 to characterize a sexual perversion or paraphilia in which there is an intense erotic attraction to a sleeping person. In Money's description of the phenomenon, the sexual object is awakened by the sexual stimulation, which may involve non-genital erotic stimulation, oral-genital stimulation, or actual intercourse. Somnophilia is also called the "Sleeping Beauty Syndrome." In an article published in a 1972 issue of the *International Journal of Psychoanalysis*, Victor Calef and Edward Weinshel view the Sleeping Beauty Syndrome as the neurotic equivalent to the presumably psychotic syndrome necrophilia, erotic attraction to or sexual behavior with a corpse. Danielle Knafo suggests in a 2015 article that examples of both somnophilia and necrophilia appearing in the same person or of any progression of one to the other are either rare or nonexistent.

Although "somnophilia" is now coming into more common use, no longer applying strictly to interactions in which the object awakens during the act, the word does not appear in any general English language dictionary, including the *OED*. Following John Money, *The McGraw-Hill Medical Dictionary* defines somnophilia as a "predatory paraphilia in which sexuoeroticism hinges on intruding and awakening a sleeping stranger with erotic caresses—e.g. oral sex, without force or violence." Somnophilic acts may be forced or coercive, as in the use of "date rape" drugs, but there are also descriptions of such acts that are consensual (Griffiths). Interestingly, the first case in the Calef and Weinshel article discussed a female patient, although most case descriptions of somnophilia appear to be of male patients or perpetrators (Lauerma).

Mark Griffiths points out that, while researching somnophilia, he came across a 2006 article by Mark Knowles that explored a somnophilic fantasy in one of James Joyce's letters to his wife, Nora Barnacle. Somnophilia also appears in popular culture. The 2003 French film *Qui a tué Bambi?* (*Who Killed Bambi?*) tells the story of the fraught relationship between a somnophilic physician and a nursing student. Somnophilia also appears in the Spanish film *Hable con ella (Talk to Her)*, written and directed by Pedro Almodóvar. The film was awarded the 2002 Academy Award for best screenplay and is now considered a classic. The villain of Robert B. Parker's 2002 novel *Shrink Rap*, Dr. John Melvin, is a psychiatrist and possible member of the Boston Psychoanalytic Society and Institute who sedates his female patients and then rapes them (Parker 57–58). *Shrink Rap* was a New York Times bestseller for several weeks in 2002. As Jeffrey L. Geller observed in a review, the plot device "could easily have been taken right from the pages of *You Must Be Dreaming*" (1653).

What was Masserman thinking when he had sex with his comatose patients? More specifically, what were his somnophilic fantasies? We cannot answer this question, but we can consider what others have theorized about somnophilia. Calef and Weinshel emphasize the "pivotal role of the wish to return into the maternal body and to explore its interior" (75). Money views somnophilia as a form of sexual fetish. (One of Masserman's victims, a law student who was first his patient and then the recipient of several anonymous telephone calls that she suspected were from Masserman, referred to his foot fetishism [Watterson, 241].) Knafo argues that the underlying dynamics of somnophilia and necrophilia "commonly involve reunion with the mother, an inability to mourn, fear of the female, and an attempt at mastering and transcending the fear of death" (857). All of these writers believe there is a link between somnophilia and incest. Sex in therapy is often considered symbolic incest. Tellingly, some of Masserman's comments about incest imply that it is generally not problematic. Long critical of psychoanalytic orthodoxy, Masserman made a number of pronouncements that in retrospect may have been rationalizations of his behavior.

Our Interview with Kathryn Watterson

To learn more about Barbara Noël's story, we sent an early version of this chapter to Kathryn Watterson. She generously offered to read our chapter and agreed to a telephone interview, which occurred on June 20, 2016. As we did with the people we interviewed as part of our research for *Confidentiality and Its Discontents*, we promised Kathryn Watterson that we would show her how we were using her comments to make sure we accurately quoted and contextualized her words. We learned many details of the story that were not in *You Must Be Dreaming*. Some of these details came from our telephone interview; others came from the responses she emailed to us nearly a year later.

Watterson found out about the project through her literary agent, who was a friend of Ann Landers's daughter, Margo Howard, a writer in Boston. Landers had sent her daughter Noël's original manuscript, a rough account of her experience with Masserman that the singer had written with the assistance of another person, along with a handwritten note: "This is an important story that needs a writer. Any ideas?" Watterson, who began her career as a newspaper reporter, had already written five books—including *Women in Prison* (1973), *Growing into Love* (1981) and *The Safe Medicine Book* (1988)—and was looking for a new project that would focus on one person or one event as a way to examine a meaningful issue. "It was perfect timing." Watterson took on the project and was soon immersed in conversations and interviews with Noël, psychopharmacologists, therapists, lawyers, doctors, ex-patients and others who corroborated or illuminated aspects of Noël's story. Watterson read depositions and testimony from Masserman, and began to reconstruct carefully the story from Noël's vantage point. *You Must Be Dreaming* is Barbara Noël's story, and authorship is listed as "Barbara Noël with Kathryn Watterson," but we inferred from our interview that the preposition "with" should be changed to the conjunction "and."

Watterson remarked that once she began to realize the enormity of the research involved, she told Barbara she would have preferred to write this book in the third person. But Noël insisted on the first person. Watterson found it a challenge to write in Noël's voice; nevertheless, she could see the value of first person, which allows the writer to achieve greater closeness and intimacy with the reader. She reconstructed dialogues from Noël's verbal recollections during their interviews, listened closely to Noël's rhythms of speech, heard her sing at a nightclub, and checked transcriptions of their interviews for accuracy. One of Watterson's biggest difficulties, however, was how to include information, background, context or insights that she, not Noël, had discovered during interviews and research that went beyond Noël's personal experiences. Watterson solved this problem by using phrases such as, "what I would later learn was . . ," or "what I would be surprised to find was that . . ." throughout the book. When Noël finally read the manuscript, it would be true that Barbara had "later learned" whatever it was. In this way, Watterson felt she could narrate important information and still remain faithful to Barbara's experiences.

You Must Be Dreaming (Watterson chose the title) was drawn from Watterson's lengthy interviews with Noël and others, court transcripts, medical and pharmaceutical journals, and extensive research. As a professional writer, Watterson knew the importance of observing boundaries; while researching the book in Chicago, for example, she stayed at a hotel, and the two women did not socialize. Only after completing three drafts of the book did she show the final draft to Noël. They sat side by side, each with a copy of the manuscript, as Noël read and responded to it for the first time. Watterson took notes on her copy when Noël had questions or corrections. Noël wept while reading several parts of it; it was a deeply moving experience to see her life through the eyes of another. ("You mean the Amytal could have killed me?") Noël hadn't known the details about Masserman's own writing about the unnecessary use of Amytal, his research on cats and monkeys decades earlier, or the intimate details of Masserman's sexual abuse of his other patients. It was heartbreaking for her to learn more about their stories. Throughout the writing of the book Watterson enjoyed a good working relationship with Noël, who confirmed that the book was true to her own experience. Both women felt that Watterson had honored Noël's words and experience.

Did Watterson ever doubt Masserman's guilt? This was one of our first questions. Once she began interviewing Noël, Watterson told us, she believed her story, mainly because of Noël's vivid description of waking up in Masserman's examining room and feeling a man on top of her. At first Noël was disoriented when she woke up from the Amytal, but she could see the ceiling lights of Masserman's examining room, which helped orient her. Moments later she saw Masserman washing his genitals at his sink. "She knew at this time it was Masserman"—and Watterson felt as she listened that the story was real. The more Watterson researched the story, the more convinced she became of its truth.

Watterson became "totally convinced" of Masserman's guilt when she began reading the journal articles he had published in the late 1930s and 1940s describing his early use of Amytal on cats. Watterson read these articles in the university library at Princeton, where she was teaching at the time. Masserman collected female alley cats and, by inserting a pipette filled with Amytal into their vaginas, sought to discover whether they found the experience sexually stimulating. Watterson was struck not only by the sadistic nature of these experiments but also by the fact that Masserman later deleted the sexual references when he cited the journal articles in his books. We had not known this detail of Masserman's research. While researching our own chapter, we had read Masserman's many books but had examined none of his 400 journal articles. "Masserman was a damaged person," Watterson observed, "and it would make sense that he might justify his sexual "experiments" on unconscious women as a continuation of his early "research" on cats.

What was it like interviewing Jules Masserman and Christine McGuire Masserman? Watterson had telephoned the psychiatrist at his residence, and each time Mrs. Masserman answered, "as nasty as could be," unwilling to convey the message to her husband. During the third or fourth telephone call, Watterson began to suspect that Masserman was on another phone, silently listening as his wife spoke. When Watterson appealed to her silent listener by mentioning that she had read Masserman's writings and thought that he should have the opportunity to defend himself, Masserman chimed right in and agreed to an interview. Watterson wanted the interview to take place at the office of Masserman's lawyer, Debra Davy, but Davy disapproved of the idea of an interview, so instead it took place at the Massermans' residence.

Kathryn Watterson's most surprising statement to us was that others were concerned about her safety when she interviewed the Massermans. She didn't sensationalize the issue of safety; it was only when we pressed her for details that she spoke about this aspect of the story. She believed, as did Barbara Noël, that Masserman might have been responsible for Billie Laird's unexpected death. While she was writing the book, Watterson wondered whether the police should exhume Laird's body to investigate whether there was foul play. Before the meeting, Watterson's young son warned her not to accept any drinks or food that the Massermans might offer during the interview. She hired a private detective to accompany her to their apartment. The Massermans expressed surprise and anger that Watterson brought "a friend" along and refused to permit him to remain in the room where the interview took place; nevertheless, they knew that Watterson was not alone.

Watterson had never seen Jules Masserman, and she was shocked when she saw him in person. "He looked like a shrimpy old guy, so different from his immense reputation." Mrs. Masserman "towered over him, like a big bulldog or behemoth." Mrs. Masserman struck Watterson as "ferociously protective" of her husband. Of the two, Mrs. Masserman was the more "openly hostile" to Watterson. During the interview Masserman "droned on," protesting his innocence. He tried to be charming, while Mrs. Masserman glared at her. During the interview Mrs. Masserman held up to her husband large note cards, which served as a crude equivalent of a teleprompter.

Did Mrs. Masserman know that her husband had committed unspeakable crimes as a therapist? Unless she was in total denial, Watterson told us, Mrs. Masserman had to know on some level about his behavior. It was not just one patient making an accusation, but several patients. How could they all be wrong? Moreover, Masserman brought patients to his residence, an obvious boundary violation. Watterson compared Mrs. Masserman's situation to that of Bill Cosby's wife, who steadfastly defended her husband's reputation at a time when the evidence of wrongdoing—drugging women and then raping them— appeared overwhelming.

Watterson was frustrated during the beginning of her research that psychotherapists wouldn't speak to her about Masserman. "I called people and they wouldn't comment." Only after *You Must Be Dreaming* was published and received extensive media coverage were therapists willing to talk to her. "I always thought he was a little odd," many therapists admitted. The eminent British anthropologist Ashley Montagu (1905–1999), author of over 60 books, telephoned Watterson early one morning, exclaiming, "I think I must be dreaming." He then proceeded to speak about his relationship with Masserman, whom he knew personally. Like many of the people who spoke to her after the book's publication, Montagu conceded that he had long heard rumors about Masserman. These rumors appeared corroborated by the accusations in the book.

How does one understand the mental health community's silence over the Masserman scandal? "You protect your own," Watterson succinctly explained. One sees this phenomenon, she added, in many other professions, including the law enforcement community and among the priesthood. She wasn't prepared for this unwritten code of honor, but now she realizes this phenomenon is implicit within any "club." There is also an implicit threat of intimidation within a profession that works against whistleblowers. Masserman appeared to have the power to silence those who suspected there was something sinister about him.

Watterson pointed out to us a fact about the story we had inadvertently gotten wrong. We had observed that Masserman's insurance company had settled two malpractice suits against him "without his consent." We had received this information from the cloth edition of *You Must Be Dreaming*, which we had both read as part of our research. It turns out that a lawyer connected to the case had deliberately given Watterson erroneous information. In both malpractice cases Masserman *had* in fact given his consent to his insurance company to reach an out-of-court settlement—a correction Watterson made in the paperback edition of the book.

Asked for an update on Barbara Noël's life following the publication of *You Must Be Dreaming*, Watterson told us that she has not heard from her for several years. Their close working relationship became strained when they were publicizing the book together. Watterson tried to be deferential in responding to interviewers' questions, but she had the sense that Noël loved the idea of being an author and may have felt upstaged by the professional writer. After one radio show when the host, fascinated about some historic aspect of the case, directed too many questions to Watterson, Noël refused to do any more joint appearances and cut off contact with her.

Our Interview of Brenda Solomon

After interviewing Kathryn Watterson, we spoke with Brenda Solomon. We had sent her an early draft of this chapter, before our Watterson interview, and then a later version that included the interview. Much of what Watterson said surprised Solomon, particularly Watterson's willingness to interview Jules Masserman at his apartment. "I would never have gone to his apartment," Solomon told us, having learned from her involvement in the women's movement to be wary of potentially dangerous situations.

Brenda Solomon saw Jules Masserman only once, when she was the co-chair of the Illinois Psychiatric Society Ethics Committee that investigated the complaint against him. Solomon had heard of Masserman's name and reputation, partly because, like him, she lived in Chicago, but she didn't know much about him. She suspects that she was asked to co-chair the ethics hearing precisely because she knew nothing about the case. "I was truly a neutral person." She had no experience serving on ethics committees, no experience with any kind of litigation. She sensed that the Masserman hearing would be controversial, a "hot potato," a case on which others in her situation might hesitate to serve.

Solomon agreed to serve on the ethics hearing because of her strong commitment to the Equal Rights Amendment, a constitutional battle—designed to guarantee equal rights for women—that was waged unsuccessfully throughout the 1970s and early 1980s. She knew women who had sexual relationships with male therapists, despite the fact that little was said or written about this issue in the 1980s. She also knew

311

women who had been victims of father incest. "I was aware that these things were going on." She never doubted her ability to keep an open mind about the question of Masserman's innocence or guilt. It did not take Solomon long to believe Barbara Noël's testimony. Amytal did not undercut the patient's credibility. Because the hearing occurred over a quarter of a century ago, Solomon can't remember whether she reached the conclusion of Masserman's guilt before or after she learned of the existence of other complainants. She never doubted, however, that he was guilty of sexual assault against Noël.

What Solomon most remembers about the hearing was how intimidated she felt by Masserman's wife and lawyer. "He said very little—he seemed like an old, shriveled up man." She was never sure, based on his silence throughout the hearing, whether he was aware of what was happening. But Mrs. Masserman attempted to dominate the hearing. "She was very aggressive, interrupting all the time. . . . She was a very large, bombastic, aggressive woman." Solomon remembers thinking that Masserman was "clever" to have a female lawyer, trying to show that he wasn't prejudiced against women. Solomon does not know whether Christine Masserman believed her husband was innocent or guilty. As an analyst, Solomon is familiar with disavowals and personality splits. Regardless of what Mrs. Masserman knew, Solomon is convinced that she was trying to protect her husband's and her own reputation.

Brenda Solomon's involvement with the Masserman case changed her life, propelling her into a world with which she had little experience. A 2012 recipient of the Helen Meyers Traveling Psychoanalytic Scholar Award, Solomon has taught ethics courses for the past 20 years, though surprisingly the Masserman case is not part of the curriculum. Learning from our interview with Watterson about Masserman's early research on cats was unsettling. "I had no idea about his history with cats." In fact, Solomon was so troubled by his research that the night before our interview, she dreamed of Masserman—a dream, she added, that was deeply disturbing.

Masserman's Legacy and Illegacy

What shall we finally say about Jules Masserman? He was unquestionably a supremely gifted person who excelled in three careers: a consultant to several state and federal institutions; a university professor, researcher and administrator; and a private practitioner of neurology, psychiatry and psychoanalysis. He had a fourth career as well: psychiatry's ambassador to the world. Midway through his 900-page tome, *The Practice of Dynamic Psychiatry* (1955), he writes about the importance of versatility to the psychiatrist. It's clear that he's writing about himself:

> An acquaintance with the poetic introspections of ancient and current mythologies and religions, a respect for the consummate wisdom of man's languages and literature—or for that matter, a feeling for the various joys of building a boat, wielding a tennis racket, playing a cello or flying a plane—all these and an infinity more of personal experiences may be more clinically valuable than yet another foray into Fulton, Ferenczi, Fenichel or Freud. In fact, it may half-seriously be contended that a psychiatrist should be barred from practicing in an office that does not have picture windows through which he can contemplate distant hills, marine horizons, panoramas of a teeming city or other dynamic vistas of the vast physical and complex social realities of life away from his padded couch and outside his sound-proofed doors. (502)

Given, then, Masserman's extraordinary talents and contributions, how can such a person have committed such despicable deeds, betraying the ideals of psychiatry to which he had devoted a lifetime? This remains the unanswerable question.

Christine McGuire Masserman died in 2001 at age 83. An obituary published in the *Chicago Tribune* on November 27, 2001 mentioned that she married Jules Masserman in 1942. "Mrs. Masserman defended him vigorously when his career in practice ended amid accusations by former patients that he had sexually abused them." Jules Masserman died in 1994 at the age of 89, professing his innocence to the end of his life. His death spared the American Psychiatric Association from the dilemma of whether to impose additional sanctions on the man responsible for one of the worst scandals in its recent history.

PART 2

NONSEXUAL BOUNDARY VIOLATIONS

CHAPTER 7

Psychotherapeutic Profiteering

Although we have devoted the first six chapters of this volume to sexual boundary violations committed by psychotherapists, such violations, serious as they are, represent only one class of boundary violations and the less serious, even minor, phenomena called "boundary crossings" known to occur during psychotherapy. In fact, boundary crossings may at times be both intentional and therapeutic, whereas boundary violations, which are considered deviations from good therapeutic practice, *are* usually harmful in one way or another. As Gutheil and Gabbard put it, "we should adopt the convention that 'boundary crossing' . . . is a descriptive term, neither laudatory nor pejorative. An assessor could then determine the impact of a boundary crossing on a case-by-case basis that takes into account the context and situation-specific facts, such as the possible harmfulness of this crossing to this patient. A violation, then, represents a *harmful* crossing, a transgression, of a boundary" (190).

Building on Gutheil and Gabbard's distinction between boundary crossings and boundary violations, Kenneth S. Pope and Patricia Keith-Spiegel agree that boundary crossings may be positive, neutral or harmful. They offer several practical suggestions in deciding whether a boundary crossing will have positive or negative effects. Like Gutheil and Gabbard, Pope and Keith-Spiegel argue that a therapist must carefully consider all of the clinical implications before engaging in a boundary crossing. Other authors have pointed out that boundary crossings are defined as deviations from a largely psychoanalytic model of psychotherapy; in other forms of therapy, strict avoidance of all boundary crossings could be inappropriate and even harmful. Ofer Zur notes that certain boundary crossings can be helpful, particularly in non-psychoanalytic treatments. Given the enormous variety of possible missteps that can occur in psychotherapy, it is reasonable to assume that such missteps are quite common and most frequently are harmless.

There is no question, however, that certain kinds of nonsexual missteps by therapists would be judged by almost all observers as clearly harmful, and therefore are correctly called boundary *violations*. In this chapter we describe examples of boundary violations that had disastrous effects for either the patients, the therapists, or both. While most boundary crossings and violations are never publicized, these examples were widely enough known after they took place, including having been written about in the press, to provide us with sufficient information to tell their stories. We then turn to a prominent therapist's involvement in what has been called the "commercialization of psychoanalysis." We conclude the chapter with a discussion of an unintentional boundary violation by one of the most honorable psychoanalysts of his generation.

We should mention briefly Freud's boundary crossings in his 1909 case history *Notes Upon a Case of Obsessional Neurosis*, better known as the story of the Rat Man. It is the only case study where we have Freud's extended diaries and verbal exchanges with a patient. These notes, 59 pages long and published in 1955 in volume 10 of the *Standard Edition* under the title "Original Record of the Case," offer a fascinating insight into the inner lives of both analyst and analysand. The notes reveal that Freud sent the Rat Man a postcard during analysis, signed "cordially," which the Rat Man felt was "too intimate" (293). On another occasion Freud fed the patient when he was hungry. Freud remarked later in his notes that in the Rat Man's transference he thought that "I made a profit out of the meal I had given him; for he had lost time through it and the treatment would last longer" (314). Robert J. Langs observes in "The Misalliance Dimension in the Case of the Rat Man" that "deviations in technique and extensions of the patient-analyst relationship beyond the usual boundaries—alterations in the frame—evoke extremely significant and intense responses on a fantasied and behavioral level in all patients" (228).

Insider Knowledge in Psychoanalysis

Psychotherapists are privy to all sorts of information from patients' lives that are not directly related to the problems for which the patients are being treated. Therapists cannot help being influenced by what they hear. "It is impossible to know how often psychotherapists may benefit in some way from information they receive in the course of work with clients," Koocher and Keith-Spiegel observe in *Ethics in Psychology and the Mental Health Professions*. "The use of such information does not necessarily constitute ethical misconduct. For example, a client who reports distress about an unreliable automobile mechanic may lead the therapist to avoid using that business. However, that same sort of information is generally available to many people by word of mouth and would not lead to personal gain at the expense of others" (177–178).

Such considerations might apply, for instance, if, based on confidential information, a patient discloses to a therapist that a certain stock is likely to rise or fall sharply in the near future. According to Schlesinger and Appelbaum,

> While the fear that one could slip insidiously into sexual exploitation is often raised as a major objection to touching as a support of the patient's sense of safety, we must recognize that purely verbal interactions are also open to the same objection. Sexual seduction and other forms of exploitation can effectively be accomplished with words alone (cf. Cyrano de Bergerac). Many recent legal suits and ethics hearings have centered on the misuse of information derived from therapist-patient exchange, including "insider trading" offenses. Clinicians have been known to take advantage of patients' confidence by involving them in fraudulent schemes or by inducing excessive dependency. The risks in psychotherapy and psychoanalysis are not solely sexual, and it may be useful to broaden the catalog of risks in the interest of gauging them all appropriately. (133)

Given the fact that, except with insider knowledge, no one is able to predict the future movement of stock prices, a psychotherapist who secretly follows the patient's hunch by investing accordingly should probably be considered a fool in need both of a financial advisor and some personal work on countertransference issues, not to mention an education about boundary crossings. On the other hand, if one supposes that a patient has disclosed to the therapist insider information on the assumption that such information will remain confidential, and the therapist acts on this information for his or her own investment profit, then that therapist has not only violated a boundary but has also probably committed a criminal act.

Exactly such an event took place in 1984 when the Connecticut psychiatrist Morgan F. Moore bought 9000 shares of a company called Posi-Seal International. He bought the shares after hearing during therapy sessions with the wife of a Posi-Seal executive that the company was about to be acquired by a division of Monsanto Corporation and what the acquisition price would be. Moore made a profit of $27,000 (about $62,000 in current dollars) from the transaction when he sold the stock after the public announcement. The Securities and Exchange Commission (SEC) charged Moore with insider trading as well as "a breach of duty arising from a relationship of confidence and trust." Moore reached a settlement with the SEC. Without being charged with a crime or admitting to a civil wrong, he was required to "disgorge" his $27,000 profit and pay an additional $27,000 to the SEC, a total amount in present dollars of more than $120,000 (*New York Times*, March 4, 1986). Moore apparently felt unfairly treated by the government. According to a May 25, 1988 entry in the *Congressional Record*, he is "now semi-retired, living in Brookfield, Conn." Asked about his feelings toward the SEC, he replied, "I don't want to stir up the feds. I trust them about as far as I can throw them" (12290).

The Stock Speculator: Robert H. Willis

Unnoticed at this time, a similar event had transpired in New York City involving a much higher profile patient, Joan Weill, her psychiatrist, and her husband, the financier, philanthropist and company president, Sanford Weill. This story is of interest not only because of the missteps it illustrates but also because of the dire consequences for the psychiatrist involved: federal criminal and civil charges, a large malpractice suit and an action by the State of New York to revoke or suspend his medical license.

Although he was at a relatively early stage of his career at the time, Sanford Weill was already on his way to becoming a wealthy and powerful member of the American financial services industry. Later he went on to an even more successful career, eventually becoming the head of Citibank, a position that he left two years before the 2008 near collapse of the bank along with the rest of country's financial system. Weill's particular strengths were both a colossal work ethic and a determination to build financial institutions through mergers that could create profitable synergies offering a range of products. He played, for example, a significant role in the 1999 repeal of the Glass-Steagall Act, the 1933 law that prohibited banks from taking depositors' money and then risking the deposits by acting like investment banks. While some have blamed the financial collapse in part on Weill's passion for mergers and megabanks, others have taken the opposite view since the institutions that led the collapse were not banks and were not subject to Glass-Steagall in the first place.

Some time prior to 1981, Joan Weill started treatment with Robert H. Willis, a psychiatrist with a private office practice at 4 East 89th Street in Manhattan, a pre-war "doorman" apartment building designed by Frank Lloyd Wright and tucked behind the Guggenheim Museum on the city's prosperous upper east side. Willis, 43 years old at the time he began treating Joan Weill, was associated with Mount Sinai Hospital. He had sterling credentials, having graduated from Brown University in 1960, Tufts Medical School in 1964, and completed his psychiatric training at Yale in 1969. While an undergraduate at Brown, Willis roomed with Martin Sloate, who went on to become a stockbroker in New York.

We do not know when Joan Weill's treatment began or the reason she consulted Willis. In 1981 her husband, who was at the time 48, was Chair of Shearson Loeb Rhodes, which under his management had become, through a series of 15 mergers between 1960 and 1981, the second largest brokerage in the United States, second only to the monster firm Merrill Lynch (Stone & Brewster, 119). Weill was engaged in confidential discussions for another possible merger of Shearson with American Express Company, which at that time was trying to become a full services financial firm. Weill had discussed this possible merger with his wife, and she in turn had mentioned these conversations with Willis. The psychiatrist saw the possibility of using this information to make a profit for himself through the trading of Shearson stock which, he believed, would rise when the merger was announced.

"Pass It On"

Willis contacted Martin Sloate, his stockbroker and college friend. In the first half of April 1981 Sloate, acting on behalf of Willis and his family, purchased 2100 shares of Shearson stock. In that same month, the broker bought an additional 2,200 shares of Shearson stock for himself. Sloate also disclosed the impending merger to a "friend and customer," Kenneth Stein, who then purchased through Sloate's firm another 2,600 shares for himself. The stock was trading at that time around $35 a share. When the merger was made public on April 21, 1981, the estimated value of the Shearson stock was $56 (Cole, 1981, SEC v. Willis, 1993). "Willis sold or tendered his Shearson shares during the period April 22, 1981 through June 16, 1981." According to press reports, Willis made a profit of $75,000 on the transaction (nearly $200,000 in current dollars). Sloate and Stein also sold their shares in Shearson after the announcement. Sloate made a profit of about $3,700 on the transaction. None of these transactions became public knowledge until years later, and if Willis hadn't eventually returned for another bite of the apple, they might never have become known to his patient, Joan Weill, or to the authorities. This fact raises the possibility that other such "insider information" violations might have been (or even now are) taking place on the parts of therapists whose missteps will never come to light.

The next five years were difficult for Sanford Weill, as Monica Langley points out in *Tearing Down the Walls*, her 2003 biography of the banking legend. Although the merger of Shearson with American Express had taken place, Weill's hope to become President of American Express as part of the new arrangement was not realized. Instead, he was given the relatively hollow title of "Chairman of the Executive Committee." Two years later he did achieve the status of President of American Express, but he then found that his power was severely limited. He resigned from American Express and Shearson in 1993 as a result of his failure to establish a new power base. through a proposal, partly funded by Warren Buffet, to take over Fireman's Fund Insurance Company, a failing American Express Subsidiary. Weill then became known as "the most high-powered unemployed executive in the U.S." (Loomis).

Taking his secretary from Shearson, along with Jamie Dimon, his second-in-command at American Express, with him, Weill set up an office of his own. He expected that he would soon be hired at another firm that he could then use as a new base to become a dominant player in the financial services arena. His new office was in a building housing the prestigious Four Seasons restaurant. Weill was at that time worth more than $50 million and could "put his money and moxie into building another financial empire" (Langley, 90). He offered Dimon an annual salary of $100,000 from his "own pocket." The two of them sat around in adjacent offices waiting for the phone to ring. It rang at first, but then stopped. Weill became increasingly despondent, drinking more than most seriously employed people would during daily sumptuous sounding lunches at the Four Seasons. He referred to the restaurant as his "company cafeteria." A startled visitor described Weill as having gone from looking "stocky" to looking "bloated" (103). Although he was by no means rendered dysfunctional by this career setback—during this period he took the lead in the renovation of Carnegie Hall—one can well imagine that his career frustrations spilled over into his personal life, particularly his marriage.

During this period, and with no knowledge of Willis' earlier behind-the-scenes profiteering from her therapy sessions in 1981, Joan Weill remained in treatment with Willis. Her husband pursued a number of career opportunities during this time, none of which worked out. His luck seemed to change in 1986, when he saw the opportunity to exploit the weakness of the financially troubled Bank of America, the country's second largest bank, which had suffered enormous losses due to failing loans in Latin America. Weill became involved in confidential discussions with Bank of America board members, floating the idea of a takeover of the bank with a $1.5 billion cash infusion. Weill's expectation was that he would become CEO (106–107). Because Bank of America was headquartered in San Francisco, such a transaction would have meant a relocation of the Weill family to the West Coast, a potentially disruptive move that concerned Joan Weill and which, understandably, she mentioned to Willis. In a proposal to the bank's board, Weill not only agreed to put $10 million of his own funds into the financing deal but also suggested that his plan eventually could increase the price of Bank of America stock from $13 a share to $20–$22.

Joan Weill discussed the potential transaction with Willis between January and April 1986. According to a subsequent court opinion, Willis then committed what was later discovered to have been a second breach of *fiduciary responsibility*, that is, a therapist's legal and ethical duty to act in a patient's best interests:

In January 1986, Willis communicated to Sloate that Weill was attempting to take the top position at Bank of America, that Weill had the support of friends in the financial world, and that the source of the information was a patient who was a member of the Weill family. This communication was in breach of his fiduciary duty to Mrs. Weill. The information that Willis conveyed to Sloate about Weill's Bank of America plans was material and nonpublic at the time. Sloate responded that this story was ridiculous since Bank of America was never going to make Weill its CEO. Sloate knew or should have known that Willis breached a fiduciary duty he owed Mrs. Weill by disclosing to Sloate information concerning Weill's plans to take over Bank of America that Mrs. Weill had confided in Willis. (*SEC v Willis*, 620–622)

Willis began buying Bank of America stock on January 14. During the next several days he made a series of purchases in quantities of 500 to 2,000 shares per day, reaching a total of 13,000 shares by February 6, an investment of $171,130 (almost $400,000 in current dollars). In addition, Martin Sloate bought 8,500 shares of Bank of America stock for his own account in similar small daily amounts between January 22 and February 11. According to court records, 11 of Sloate's customers purchased Bank of America stock or call options between January 22 and February 20. Weill, who had been frustrated by his negative reception by the board, "went public" on February 20. Stories about his interest in the bank were in the news, and the stock price jumped about two points. In the two days following the public announcement, all the shares held by Willis, Sloate and Sloate's other customers were sold for a profit of about $2.00 per share. As the *New York Times* reported on May 18, 1990, Willis made a profit of $27,475. Ultimately, Weill's proposal to the Bank of America board was rejected, resulting in much ado about nothing. But Willis paid a steep price for his psychiatric profiteering.

CHAPTER 7: PSYCHOTHERAPEUTIC PROFITEERING

Probably none of these financial transactions would have come to public attention had it not been for the stock market collapse the following year, in October 1987. As a result of the collapse, Sloate's customer, Kenneth Stein, who had been an active trader and fund operator, was wiped out, and Sloate's brokerage filed a $1 million lawsuit against Stein for money he owed the firm. Recall that Stein had been Sloate's customer who had been tipped about the earlier 1981 Shearson trades. Knowing about Sloate's inside source, Stein wrote a letter to him threatening to "blow the whistle" on him and his firm, presumably in retaliation, unless the suit against him was dropped. As a result of a tip from Stein to the authorities, an investigation of Sloate's business dealings took place, and Willis' role in both the 1981 Shearson trades and the 1986 Bank of America trades became known.

Criminal and Civil Charges

In a story appearing in the *Philadelphia Inquirer* in 1991, Barbara Demick described Willis as a psychiatrist with "offices on Manhattan's Upper East Side" and Joan Weill, his patient, as a "New York socialite married to a prominent Wall Street executive." In early 1986, Demick continued, Weil's husband "told her he was planning to raise about $1 billion to invest in the company that owns Bank of America, the San Francisco banking giant." Demick then parodied the sequence of events that led inexorably to Humpty Dumpty's great fall:

The wife confided in her therapist.
The therapist told his stockbroker.
The stockbroker told his next-door neighbor in Scarsdale.
And he told his brother-in-law.

327

And he told a handful of friends who were members of his country club.

They told others.

Like a chain letter run amok, the information was rapidly disseminated among friends and acquaintances: Pssst. Pass it on. If you're looking for a hot stock, buy Bank of America Corp.

Before long, dozens of people were buying it, the government alleges. And, in one of the more bizarre insider-trading cases ever brought, the therapist was indicted.

Willis' indictment on 46 counts of securities and mail fraud took place in July 1989. He pled guilty to two of the counts in 1991. In upholding the indictment, the court held that even though Willis had no direct connection to the company, and despite his claim that Joan Weill had neglected to tell him explicitly that information about her husband's business was confidential, he had violated his fiduciary responsibility to his patient. "It is difficult to imagine a relationship which demands a higher degree of trust and confidence than the traditional relationship of physician and patient," the judge stated (*United States v. Willis*, 272). In addition to the criminal charges, Willis also faced civil charges that he settled for $136,000. Although the criminal charges could have brought a sentence of ten years in prison and $500,000 in fines, he ultimately was sentenced in 1992 to five years probation with 600 hours of community service to be performed each year (a total of 3,000 hours, about 11 hours a week). He was fined an additional $150,000. Given the highly critical view of Willis taken by U.S. District Judge Miriam Cedarbaum, the sentence was described as "surprisingly light." The judge admitted that although she had "serious misgivings" about not sending Willis to prison, she believed that he had accepted full responsibility for his actions by cooperating with the government and making restitution.

She said, however, that she could not ignore the "aggravated nature of this crime" ("Inside-Trading Psychiatrist," January 8, 1992).

Willis's troubles did not end there. In the same year as his guilty plea, he was socked with a $5 million malpractice lawsuit by Joan Weill, who claimed that beyond breaching the confidentiality of her sessions with him, he had also committed "medical malpractice and fraud." According to the *New York Times*, "her lawsuit said she had suffered 'great personal distress and anguish' and 'acute personal embarrassment'" ("Psychiatrist is Sentenced"). Because the Weills most likely did not need the money such a lawsuit might bring them, they were willing to endure the additional embarrassing publicity over the lawsuit to seek redress for what must have been for Joan Weill the shattering loss of a trusting relationship with Willis accompanied by an unspeakable feeling of betrayal.

Finally, because he had pled guilty to a federal crime, the medical licensing authorities in New York State charged Willis with professional misconduct. In a negotiated settlement in 1992, Willis' medical license was suspended for one year, but the suspension was stayed, meaning that his practice would not be affected at all. He was fined an additional $10,000 and ordered to perform 500 additional hours of community service. In both the licensing proceeding and the criminal sentencing, Willis lawyers brought in letters from grateful patients testifying to his dedication to their care, willingness to make house calls, and his waiving of fees for indigent patients. The courts and authorities took account of the interruption of Willis' long term treatment relationships in structuring the penalties he faced to avoid further compromising his professional practice through either an actual license suspension or a jail sentence.

Martin Sloate was punished as a result of both his involvement in Willis' stock transactions and the transactions he carried out on his own behalf. Criminal charges of insider trading resulted in a fine of

$161,000 in a proceeding in which Sanford Weill had testified against him ("Broker Fined in Insider Trading"). In addition, Sloate was the subject of an SEC investigation. Although the SEC staff proposed that Sloate should be permanently barred from the securities industry, the SEC concluded that in light of his "lengthy and otherwise unblemished career" in the securities industry, a five-year suspension would be in the public interest.

Sanford Weill went on to rebuild his career through a new round of mergers, ending as Chair of Citigroup, the company formed by the merger of Weill's Travellers Group and Citicorp in 1998. He finally stepped down as Chair in 2006, just two years before the entire structure nearly collapsed, at which point the federal government had to rescue Citigroup.

Another Stock Speculator: Mervyn Cooper

The Weill-Willis case was not the first of its kind. Two less well known cases are also noteworthy. In 1994 Mervyn Cooper, a social worker specializing in marriage and family therapy, was treating an executive at the Lockheed Corporation. A year earlier, Cooper was listed as President of the American Psychotherapy Association, a now-defunct organization that had bestowed questionable credentials on psychotherapists ("Board Certified Professional Counselor"). During their sessions Cooper learned of merger talks taking place between Lockheed and the Martin Marietta Corporation. Cooper contacted a friend, Kenneth E. Rottenberg, and the two agreed to purchase $7,000 worth of Lockheed call options with $2,000 from Cooper and the rest from Rottenberg. The account would be opened in Rottenberg's name alone to conceal the connection among Cooper, the therapist, and a Lockheed employee. As Jack Searles reported in the *Los Angeles Times* on January 2, 1996, they agreed to split their profits in proportion to their contributions to the scheme. Short-term, out-of-the-money call options are usually inexpensive but have a huge potential to appreciate if the underlying stock jumps. They also carry considerable risk should nothing happen and the options expire. Warned of these risks at the brokerage, Rottenberg told the branch manager that he was not concerned about a loss because Lockheed would be involved in a "significant business deal within a week." He advised other brokerage employees to purchase similar options. Ultimately, when the merger of the corporations to form the new Lockheed Martin was announced, Cooper and Rottenberg ended up with a profit of $177,000 on their $7,000 investment (*New York Times*, December 14,1995).

Cooper and Rottenberg were each fined $20,000 and sentenced to 1,000 hours community service for their crimes. In addition, Cooper was required to pay $110,000 to the SEC; Rottenberg paid $50,000 (*SEC v. Cooper and Rottenberg*, December 11, 1995). Cooper also faced revocation of his license by the California Board of Behavioral Science Examiners. Cooper's lawyer stated that his client would not contest a license revocation (Wilcox).

And Another: Alan Brody

In 1996, the Maryland psychiatrist Alan Brody heard from a patient, a company official of Penril Data Networks, Inc., that Penril was about to spin off a division to its shareholders and sell the rest of its business to another company in a $120 million stock deal. Within 15 minutes of the end of the session, Brody began purchasing Penril stock, ultimately acquiring 15,000 shares, leading to a profit of $38,000 when the deal was announced. As Marcy Gordon reported in the *APNEWS Archive*, the

SEC required Brody to pay back the entire $38,000 plus an additional fine of $38,000 plus interest. "The patient had established a relationship of trust and confidence with Dr. Brody, and had a history of confiding in Dr. Brody with respect to all aspects of his personal and professional life for the purpose of undergoing professional treatment," the SEC stated in its court filing.

The examples of "insider trading" of stocks we have provided here are clear instances of boundary violations and therapists' misuse of confidential information obtained from patients. By contrast, Koocher and Keith-Spiegel's example of a therapist who stops using an unreliable automobile mechanic because of a patient's statement does not constitute an ethical violation. But there are many situations that fall into a gray zone where the distinction between benign action and a boundary violation is not clear. For instance, if a reliable patient reports that the food at a particular restaurant is terrible, it would not be a violation for the therapist to avoid that restaurant. On the other hand, if the therapist had already made a reservation to dine in that restaurant, and then was informed by the patient of the terrible food, would it be a boundary violation for the therapist to cancel the reservation based on the information gained from the patient in a confidential session?

Suppose a therapist owns stock in a company and hears from a patient confidential information about a competing business indicating that it has made a breakthrough in a product that will harm the therapist's company's business. Would it be a boundary violation if the therapist sold the stock in the company based on the patient's information? Probably. To avoid such possible conflicts, therapists with patients who work in positions where such information might come up in confidential sessions would be well advised to avoid ownership of individual stocks. These therapists could, for example, confine their own stock investments to large mutual funds or index funds.

The Commercialization of Psychoanalysis: George Pollock

Relating an anecdote from a time in his life when he was serving as the Project Director of the Freud Archives in 1981, after his rift with the establishment had transformed him into the "bad boy" of psychoanalysis, Jeffrey Moussaieff Masson wrote the following description of a meeting he attended during a Congress of the International Psychoanalytical Association in Helsinki:

> . . . as the representative of the Archives, I was also included in a meeting that did a great deal to open my eyes to the political realities of psychoanalysis. I ought not to have been shocked, but I was. As I've indicated earlier I knew of the practice of soliciting money from patients, but this was the first time I was directly involved. About twenty analysts, most of them holding some official position or other, had gathered together to discuss the funding of the new chair of psychoanalysis at the Hebrew University in Jerusalem. A million dollar endowment was needed. How to get it? The solution, said one prominent analyst from Chicago, was easy and had been used several times before. "I would ask each of you to compose a list of your wealthiest patients, with their names, addresses and phone numbers. We will then circulate this list within this group. The next stage is for some of us to contact these people, without of course, telling them how we have their names, and asking them if they wish to donate money for the chair." This was, by any standard I knew, unethical behavior, but nobody in the room voiced any objection.
>
> When I complained to [Kurt] Eissler, he surprised me by defending the action. "Why should not people who have benefited

from analysis use their money to help other people to benefit?" Well, I couldn't see anything wrong with that, provided they thought of the idea on their own. But to have their analyst surreptitiously hand over their name to an outside source was still, in my books, unethical, and it was taking advantage of knowledge (the financial state of the analysand) that was privileged and confidential.

"The whole thing stinks, if you ask me," I told Eissler.

"Well, it's done in all fields, and Freud did it within psychoanalysis as well. You know all the wealthy patients who benefited in the early days of psychoanalysis." (*Final Analysis*, 187)

It is likely that the "prominent analyst from Chicago" to whom Masson refers in this passage was George Pollock, who at that time was President of the Chicago Psychoanalytic Institute. Pollock had also served as President of the American Psychoanalytic Association and, a few years later, was to serve as President of the even larger American Psychiatric Association. In 1988, according to his *curriculum vitae*, Pollock belonged to no fewer than 89 associations and societies (Sabshin, "George H. Pollock"). Pollock, as we shall see, knew a great deal about psychoanalytic politics, particularly about raising funds from wealthy patients.

It is well known within the healthcare field that grateful wealthy patients or their families routinely make significant contributions to medical institutions such as hospitals, medical colleges and research foundations. In fact, it is common to solicit donations from wealthy patients. There is considerable debate, however, about the ethics of such solicitations. Contemporary thinking on this issue recognizes the ethical conundrum faced by physicians whose patients might be approached. The current view is that physicians should not make such solicitations themselves of their own patients for the following reasons: undue pressure on patients to contribute; possible expectations of preferential treatment from donors; and concerns about patient confidentiality and trust.

Nevertheless, the growing reliance on such donations has led in recent years to an intensification of such efforts. To allow this fundraising practice to continue, the federal healthcare privacy rules permit hospital "development" personnel to access certain information from patients' medical records without patient consent, provided such practices are disclosed in advance and the patient does not "opt out." Authorities in the field have, nonetheless, urged that solicitation of contributions should be founded on the patient's having affirmatively consented to such solicitations; the act of soliciting consent has, in itself, ethical implications (Prokopetz and Lehmann). An empirical study of 20 physicians who were recipients of "grateful patient" donations at Johns Hopkins showed that such physicians were "aware of, and in some cases troubled by the ethical concerns related to this activity" (Wright et al., 651). Using new software created for the purpose, hospitals do "wealth screening" on newly admitted patients based on zip codes. The hospitals provide those from affluent zip code areas with a number of perks not offered to other patients, such as daily newspapers and flower and snack baskets. According to Richard Thompson, the actual medical care such patients receive is supposedly the same as that given to all other patients, but he includes the following quote by Ralph Waldo Emerson: "You can easily judge the character of a man by how he treats those who can do nothing for him."

In psychotherapy, particularly in psychoanalysis, the issue of "grateful patient" donations is even more problematic because of the intense transferences associated with such treatments. Raising funds from wealthy patients may have shocked Masson in 1981, but it is not a new idea for psychoanalysts. Gabbard and Lester report several early boundary violations of this nature. They point out that

Freud's behavior in this regard was at times "reprehensible" (83). He exploited the generosity and/or masochism of wealthy patients through gifts given to support the psychoanalytic enterprise and even to give himself the opportunity, as he put it, of "playing the rich man with regard to children and relatives."

This issue has appeared in only a few articles in the professional psychoanalytic literature. David Forrest suggested in a 2011 article that psychotherapy patients of voluntary faculty members (i.e., of practitioners who themselves could not benefit from such donations to a medical facility) could be sent a letter by their own psychiatrist advising them if they wished to make a contribution directly to the "Development Officer" of the department; the patients should not mention such a donation within the therapy. In a response, a journal editor wrote:

"Do You Love Me or My Money?"
From a fundraising point of view, it is of course more logical to solicit wealthy patients whose donations can make a substantial difference in funding. However, long clinical experience has shown that many wealthy patients are especially sensitive in their lives and relationships to fears of being financially manipulated and exploited by others: when present, this inevitably plays an important role in their transference reactions in the clinical situation.

These reactions become more problematic and difficult to manage precisely in situations where the analyst asks for a donation and then declares the topic off limits to analytic exploration and understanding. Although an ethicist may opine that this position is useful in trying to eliminate any semblance of coercion, it unfortunately cannot address what seems to me to be an important issue for the treatment of such individuals. (Stine)

In a 2007 article published in *Psychoanalytic Psychology*, Douglas Kirsner has documented a striking example of VIP treatment of a wealthy patient-donor by the psychoanalyst Ralph Greenson, whom we discuss in Chapter 9. Kirsner (480–481) describes a weekend trip that Greenson, who lived in Los Angeles, took to New York solely for the purpose of interviewing a prospective date, a lonely 60-year-old man whom Greenson had located by answering a personal ad on behalf of a wealthy patient, Lila Annenberg Hazen. The two had one date, but the relationship did not work out. Hazen was evidently disappointed because she soon turned against Greenson and cut off funding for a foundation she had set up on his behalf and through which much of the funding for the Anna Freud Centre in London and the Child Study Center at Yale had been channeled. Hazen's estate in 1986 was about $430 million in contemporary dollars.

The Chicago Psychoanalytic Institute

To understand the cultural environment in which the notorious boundary violation committed by George Pollock took place, it is important to understand the unique characteristics of the Chicago Psychoanalytic Institute. As recounted by Kirsner in *Unfree Associations*, the Institute was founded in 1932 by a group of émigré European analysts who aligned themselves not with the Psychoanalytic Society in Chicago but with the Berlin Institute. The first director of the Institute was Franz Alexander, who himself had been the first analyst trained at that institute. Alexander remained in the position of director for *24 years*. In that period he made himself widely known throughout the United States both in psychoanalytic and psychiatric circles through many publications, innovative and controversial proposals to modify psychoanalytic treatment, and a strong interest in psychosomatic disorders. In later years, the Chicago Institute became widely known for its additional contributions to psychoanalysis as well as for some of its less laudable graduates, such as Jules Masserman and Zane Parzen, whom we have discussed in earlier chapters.

The Institute under Alexander was structured in the image of the Berlin Institute, with a "lay" Board of Directors appointed by Alexander, rather than the more common arrangement of a board consisting mainly of elected or appointed members of the psychoanalytic society. Many Board members of the Chicago Psychoanalytic Institute were Alexander's former analysands (Kirsner, 211). The Institute was highly authoritarian: the real power belonged to the director and to "the Staff," an in-group of 20 analysts appointed for life by the director (112). The autocratic governance structure mirrored the "machine politics" well known in the city of Chicago itself (118), resulting in a kind of "corruption" in which patronage was distributed by the director. Unlike the founder of the Chicago Psychoanalytic Society, Lionel Blitzsten—who was an advocate of the strict ego psychological version of Freudianism—the founder of the Chicago Psychoanalytic Institute, Alexander, was an innovator, scientist, and reformer. Kate Schechter observes in her 2014 book *Illusions of a Future* that Blitzsten and Alexander were rivals, but the two psychoanalysts managed to coexist, each with his own set of followers.

The administration of the Chicago Psychoanalytic Institute paralleled Chicago patronage politics, according to Kirsner. "Like the Mayor of Chicago, the director of the Chicago Institute was undeniably 'the boss.' A vital feature of the position was political—to keep the various factions from being too dissatisfied. Until Pollock left there was always a strong and powerful leader of the Chicago Institute who had, owing to the institute structure as well as personal temperament, been dominant and oligarchic rather than democratic" (119).

George Pollock became the director of the Chicago Psychoanalytic Institute in 1971. Forty-nine years old, he was an energetic advocate of psychoanalysis and psychoanalytic research and a forward-looking catalyst for change. Schechter notes that Pollock, frustrated in his efforts to be appointed chair of the Department of Psychiatry at the University of Illinois, decided instead to transform the Chicago Institute into a miniature university (126). He disbanded "the Staff," instituted an "organized faculty," and created an elected "Psychoanalytic Education Council" on whom he bestowed various "Professor" titles. Pollock maintained control over teaching in the Institute through his power to appoint committee chairs of various key committees, to dominate the Education Council, and to appoint his former, and even current, patients to the Board. He also instituted a two term limit for the position of director, a position which he renamed "president" to correspond with a typical University structure.

The Chicago Institute had more training analysts than any other institute. The title was given to about 58 of the 86 faculty members, a proportion far higher than at any comparable institute. The "Training Analyst" title was believed to mean something important at other institutes, was widely coveted, and was often the entree into the institute's in-group. By contrast, "training analyst" was a meaningless honorific at the Chicago Institute and was freely dispensed by Pollock as a reward for loyalty to his regime. Those on whom the honor was bestowed had few if any responsibilities but were free to flaunt the title of "Training Analyst at the Chicago Institute" on the national stage.

Probably the most unusual aspect of the Pollock regime was his prodigious fundraising. The Institute became fabulously wealthy through grants, donations and fees. All faculty members were paid for their services (most faculty members at other institutes volunteer their time for teaching and administrative duties). As the Institute grew, its budget ballooned until it became "the richest [psychoanalytic training] institute in the country" (Kirsner, 127). By 1976 the budget for the Chicago Institute reached $760,000, a gigantic sum compared to the budgets of the similarly sized Philadelphia Institute for the same year ($75,000) and the smaller Boston Institute ($3,000) (299, n.11). Under Pollock's domination and fundraising, the Chicago Institute budget reached $2 million per year. One faculty member told Kirsner that what had happened was "'a commercialization of psychoanalysis'" involving the "enforcement of a structure that took the emphasis away from intellectual pursuits toward fundraising, promotion campaigns, handling the media, and budget considerations" (127).

Schechter (148) describes Pollock's construction of a "publishing empire" centered on a journal, *The Annual of Psychoanalysis*, which contained at least one article by Pollock in nearly each of its annual volumes for a period of twenty years. The Institute published the *Annual* using Institute funds and then, to create the aura of a successful publication, covertly used additional Institute funds to buy up multiple copies of the *Annual*. When Pollock was replaced as Institute Director, his successor found a closet filled with volumes of the *Annual*. It was also discovered, from Institute balance sheets suppressed by Pollock, that the budget was "dramatically in the red" (215, n.32).

While serving repeated terms as Director of the Chicago Institute, Pollock expanded his power. President of the Illinois Psychiatric Society and the Chicago Psychoanalytic Society, he was active on the national stage as well: President of the American Psychoanalytic Association (1974–1975), Treasurer and then President of the American Psychiatric Association (1987–1988) and President of the American Academy of

Psychoanalysts. He also conducted a seminar at the University of Illinois Medical School. He had wide interests, read constantly, had a library of 40,000 books and subscribed, according to a 2003 obituary, to 300 academic journals (Osterman). These obituary numbers, however, strain credibility. Were these books and journals part of Pollock's personal library and subscriptions, or were they part of the Institute's impressive library and journal subscriptions that he created? Pollock's view of himself, and perhaps the view he conveyed to his family who might have contributed this information to the press upon his death, blurred the distinction between himself and the Institute. As Kirsner notes, "One of the problems was the extent to which Pollock seemed to identify himself with the institute implying that his interests and institute's interests necessarily coincided" (129).

Falling from Grace

Pollock's enormous fundraising successes, unbridled ambition and lust for national recognition created an ethical blind spot that had the potential to lead him astray—and finally did. His "fundraising" conduct with a patient in his private practice of psychoanalysis in Chicago ultimately led to the unraveling of his career.

Pollock had been treating in psychoanalysis an elderly wealthy woman, Anne Pollock Lederer, starting in 1969 and continuing until 1980 (Hidlay). Unrelated to George Pollock, she was the daughter of E.J. Pollock, who had served in the 1930s as vice president and controller of the then mighty Chicago based Sears, Roebuck & Co., retiring from that position in 1939 (Furlong). Upon her father's death, Mrs. Lederer received a significant inheritance from him. Married to a Chicago physician, she was widowed in 1973. It's likely that the deaths of her father and husband allowed George

Pollock to play an even more important role in her life. In 1980, four years before her death at age 78, Pollock transferred her care to two other psychiatrists, perhaps because she could no longer travel to the Institute to see him. According to the records connected to this transfer, Pollock wrote to these colleagues, "Incidentally, I do hope you are charging her a full fee for your house calls and visits. She can well afford it" (Hidlay). Though she wasn't his patient any more, Pollock continued to prescribe medication for her until 1983. During the years prior to 1980, Mrs. Lederer had established a trust fund that paid Pollock $50,000 per year (about $210,000 per year in current dollars) starting in 1978 and continuing until 1993. In addition, she gave Pollock's family, beginning in 1978, $30,000 per year ($110,000 in current dollars). Between 1969 until her death, Mrs. Lederer donated $601,000 to the Chicago Institute (about $1.2 million in current dollars).

Finally, in 1980, she created the Anne P. Lederer Research Institute to which Pollock was for a while a paid consultant. When her "longtime attorneys" raised objections to her setting up the research institute, Mrs. Lederer dismissed them and in their place hired attorney Leonard Schienfeld, a friend of Pollock (Hidlay). During the time she was Pollock's patient, Mrs. Lederer, who was said to have been quite lonely, served on the Board of the Chicago Psychoanalytic Institute as well as holding a job in the Institute's library. She also had been a frequent dinner guest of two employees of the Institute, the Institute librarian, George Miller, and his wife, who was also employed by the Institute as Miller's secretary (Schechter, 157). Pollock, who was an expert in problems of the elderly and the mourning process, later claimed that, despite seeing her five days a week for over a decade, her treatment was not "psychoanalysis." Instead, he asserted that he was providing her a substitute family in the Institute.

During the years of Pollock's treatment of her, Anne Lederer slowly became estranged from her only child, a son named Francis L. Lederer,

II. Following his mother's death, Francis Lederer filed a lawsuit against Pollock, claiming that the psychoanalyst had exercised undue influence over his mother and that he had used that influence to extract from her money to which Francis would have otherwise been entitled. About $5 million was at issue. In fact, however, Francis was not only the recipient of $200,000 from his mother's estate but also upon her death received a several million dollar trust that had been set up for his ultimate benefit by his maternal grandfather. In court filings, Pollock's lawyers described Francis as "a greedy and guilt-ridden son who never had a good relationship with his mother."

"Will contests can be oh so ugly," reported James Warren and his colleagues in the *Chicago Tribune* on September 6, 1988, "and a tussle involving a prominent Chicago psychiatrist and a millionaire virtually cut out of his wealthy mother's estate is as unseemly as any." The lawsuit struck the journalists as the stuff of melodrama, or soap opera, as their title suggests: "'As Will Turns': A Real-World Soap." The title was perhaps inspired by Pollock's lawyers, who characterized the allegations as a "distorted, twisted exercise in fiction." In the sworn pretrial testimony, "potential witnesses have said that Mrs. Lederer considered Pollock to have taken the place of her husband after his death in 1973. Pollock advised her on all facets of her life, from what to eat to where to live and what attorneys to hire to revise her will. He gave her gifts, sent her flowers and phoned her almost daily, the witnesses said" (Warren, et al.).

Francis Lederer's attorney, Kevin Murnighan, did everything he could to impugn George Pollock's integrity. "She gave him her mind and he took her pocketbook." Murnighan added, "Dr. Pollock junked his ethical principles and psychoanalytic duty and became the decedent's friend, business adviser and recipient of lavish gifts. Because her mind was troubled and because she voluntarily opened it to him in trust, Dr. Pollock was able to control Mrs. Lederer." An expert witness, Larry

Strasburger, a psychiatrist at Harvard Medical School, testified that the medication Pollock prescribed for Mrs. Lederer was given in amounts leading to her becoming "psychologically habituated and physically dependent" on it (Warren, et al.).

Pollock's lawyers for their part pointed out that Mrs. Lederer's decision to leave much of her money to a charitable cause was simply following family tradition. The lawyers noted, furthermore, that Francis Lederer had received $6 million from his grandfather's trust and an additional $2 million irrevocable trust from his mother. As a result of these assets, Francis hadn't held a job for the past 17 years.

Following the empanelling of the jury, which took four full days, the lawyers made their opening statements. The third and last lawyer to speak, Robert Tepper, representing Pollock, pointed out that Mrs. Lederer came to regret leaving her son the $2 million irrevocable trust, which had passed outside the estate. "She later decided it was a mistake to make the trust irrevocable and told people the only thing her son wanted from her was her money." Francis's lawyer raised an immediate objection, and at that point Cook County Judge Frank Petrone, after a conference with the attorneys, ruled that the remark was prejudicial and declared a mistrial on November 2, 1988, sending the jury home (Perkiss). Two days after the mistrial, the press reported without elaboration that the suit had been settled for "what's said to be $1 million" (Warren et al.). The Associated Press gave additional details on November 15. According to Francis's lawyer, the settlement of $1 million was in fact paid to him from the funds Mrs. Lederer left to the research institute. The annual trust payments to Pollock and his family were left undisturbed. The resolution of the lawsuit cost Pollock and his family nothing ("Settlement Ends Lawsuit").

Pollock resigned from all of his official positions, including directorship of the Chicago Institute, but he continued to practice in

Chicago. His term as President of the American Psychiatric Association ended in 1988 as well. A laudatory piece published in the *American Journal of Psychiatry* in 1988, at the end of Pollock's tenure as APA President, failed to mention the lawsuit (Sabshin). Additional details of the story came to light in 1995, when it was reported that the Illinois Department of Professional Regulation, the state's licensing body for physicians, had sent a complaint to Pollock alleging that his receipt of funds from the trusts created by Mrs. Lederer violated the Medical Practice Act. Pollock responded by filing a lawsuit against the Department based on a claim that the five year statute of limitations had expired, a claim that the trial court sustained. The Department appealed the decision to the Illinois Court of Appeals, which reversed the trial court and remanded the case to the trial court for further proceedings (*Doe v. Department of Professional Regulation*, *AMA News*, February 13, 1995). The Department of Regulations database indicates that Pollock's license was renewed for a final time in 1997 and expired in 2002, so evidently it was not revoked. Pollock died on December 12, 2003 of heart disease, at age 80. Rachel Osterman's obituary published in the *Chicago Tribune* related Pollock's many accomplishments but made no mention of the events of the Chicago Institute debacle.

"The End of the George Pollock Tenure as Institute Director"

How did Pollock's colleagues at the Chicago Institute view the scandal? Most of our information comes from the transcript of a May 27, 2009 meeting at the Chicago Institute for Psychoanalysis that was convened to reflect on "The End of the George Pollock Tenure as Institute Director." Without naming the people who spoke at the meeting, Kate

Schechter quotes from this transcript in *The Illusions of a Future*. We have received a copy of the same transcript from the Chicago Institute and also quote from it, without naming the participants. To avoid confusion, we use Schechter's pseudonym, "Dr. B.," for the unnamed Chair of the Chicago Institute's Ethics Committee.

The May 27, 2009 Chicago Institute meeting is fascinating for what it reveals both about Pollock and his colleagues. The moderator began by noting the large attendance, which shows that "you agree that this is an important topic." The moderator then announced that the discussion would be taped, "so don't say anything that you don't want to have on the tape." Someone wondered aloud whether any attorneys were present, suggesting, if so, the need for caution. The answer was a qualified yes: "You could have your attorney sitting next to you and check with your attorney about what you say, yes." Despite being taped and the possible presence of lawyers, the discussion was remarkably spontaneous and uninhibited, with the members venting to themselves, seemingly unconcerned about posterity.

As Dr. B. recounted, a colleague had reported to him "a disturbing story" he had heard "from the couch [i.e., from a patient] that there was some unethical behavior going on in George's practice." Another colleague, whose two sons were lawyers, reported that a legal periodical, *The Law Bulletin*, had described a lawsuit filed against Pollock related to the same accusation (Kirsner, 131). Dr. B., burdened by strongly conflicted feelings about Pollock, decided to bring the issue to him in private. Pollock stonewalled, as Dr. B told his colleagues on May 27, 2009. "So when I confronted him with this information, he denied it. He said, 'B., it's not true.' I was appalled at his lack of honesty. And so I didn't know quite what to do. I knew what the procedure was supposed to do, but here was the head of our Institute, somebody that I admired, somebody that I respected, and I didn't know what to do next." Deeply troubled by this situation, Dr. B. then began a series of meetings with other members of the Institute's Council. The Board of the Institute, consisting largely of Pollock's ex-patients, refused to act. "We were disturbed. We were unhappy. We didn't know what to do. We were puzzled. And so we tried to follow the procedure, but we were overwhelmed." Refusing to resign, Pollock hired the prominent Washington, D.C. attorney Robert Bennett to defend him.

During his opening remarks, Dr. B. seemed to be speaking to history, and he could not resist a Shakespearean allusion. "George Pollock was a very, very complex person. He was a good man, a kind man, an intelligent man, and a good analyst, and a good contributor to the field and his own research. I feel a little bit like I'm Mark Antony. But he was too ambitious. Power grew on him." Dr. B. was highly ambivalent toward Pollock, unsure whether he wanted to praise or bury him. A few moments later Dr. B. described how upset members of the faculty were when they learned about Pollock's lack of honesty; in Dr. B.'s words, they "went berserk"—and then, when someone (a "male voice") at the meeting asked him to define the word, Dr. B. responded, "Berserk. They were—one of them could not tolerate to remain in the meeting any longer. He was shouting and making lots of noise and disagreeing with the various people who were talking." Either the same or another member asked, "Was he trying to shout down the facts that you were presenting?" "No," answered Dr. B. The questioner continued, "People were denouncing Pollock, you're saying," to which Dr. B. replied, "Yeah. They were denouncing Pollock." Dr. B. ended his statement by repeating that he loved Pollock and then, using confusing syntax, suggested that Pollock was either like or *not* like Nixon and Bill Clinton.

Tellingly, as might be expected of an ambitious person who falls in love with a position of power in an Institute with a history of one-man domination, Pollock knew how to stay in control. One member pointed out how, under the guise of democratization, Pollock centralized his own power shortly after arriving at the Institute. By the end of his second term, "he had created an administration that was tightly in his own hands. He rewarded his supporters and punished any critic. And at the end of the second term, he posed the idea of a third term, to which the council acquiesced, and the board approved it. Significantly, he had appointed his former patients to be on the board so that he had a loyal set of supporters that would approve whatever he would present."

One member compared the Pollock story to the "inexorable quality of a Greek tragedy," dramatizing the theme that power corrupts. (Dr. B. had earlier quoted Lord Acton's statement that power corrupts; absolute power corrupts absolutely.) The comparison resonated in Dr. B., who interjected, "when we look at George, we have to look at ourselves because all of us, every one of us is capable of doing the same thing. The fact that we don't is what's different. But we are capable." Despite this realization, most of the members were horrified by Pollock's actions and his determination to remain in power. When a member described how he and three others reluctantly confronted Pollock, they were taken aback by his response: he looked at each one and said, "You remember the favor I did for you?" Upon hearing this, a male voice exclaimed, "Whoa," followed by a female voice: "Wow." Pollock's leadership strategy was to make everyone beholden to him. One infers from the discussion that many faculty members during the Pollock era were the beneficiaries of his patronage and protection. None of them was willing to blow the whistle until Francis Lederer's lawsuit brought unwelcome notoriety to the Institute. Praising those who confronted Pollock as "courageous," one member confessed that "we all lived in fear of him." The same person believed the Institute acted correctly in confronting him but that "we were all complicit and corrupt and were all sorts of things with his reign, and we were in lots of ways, and we need to deal with that, too."

A member pointed out that when Pollock left the Chicago Institute, he used the Lederer Foundation money to secure an appointment at a university where "[indiscernible] was chairman." Someone couldn't resist muttering, "Yes. Yeah. Another crook." Another member began to mention a specific person, stopped himself with the words, "Speak nothing but good of the dead," and then continued, referring to an important faculty member who was "breathing fire toward George because George appointed everybody and everything. There was no democracy in the Institute."

Analyzing the Analyst

One would expect someone at a psychoanalytic institute to place Pollock on the couch, and this is what happened. An analyst asked, "Is it that the ego expands so much that anything that you do is all right, essentially? You don't have to face a kind of a shaming or guilt-ridden superego because it's not present anymore. You are justified in what you're doing because of your own grandiosity, in a sense. This would be one way of thinking about this." Another member remembered asking why Pollock needed to be the president of so many organizations and being told, "Well, he was always a favorite child," an explanation that struck the member as running counter to current psychology: "If one is a favorite child, genuinely, there is a time when enough's enough, that you actually can get filled up." Dr. B. affirmed that Pollock was a "favorite child, actually. In his family." Another member had "some speculative ideas as to what motivated George." "[T]he first event that led him to wish to dissolve the staff and create a council [at the Chicago Institute] was the trauma of his not having been appointed professor and chairman of the Department of Psychiatry at the University of Illinois. He was very intent on getting that. But Mel Sabshin got the job. And that was a very, very painful, a painful event in his life." No one at the meeting questioned whether this event, which most people might consider disappointing but not traumatic, was sufficient to explain the degree of Pollock's ethical blindness.

One of the most striking moments in the discussion came when a member recalled Pollock saying to him about Anne Pollock Lederer, "I saved that woman's life. If that woman had not been in treatment with me, she would be dead by now." That belief became Pollock's excuse or justification for exploiting her.

There were other psychoanalytic speculations. One member suggested a "deep injury which led to a split," resulting in insatiable grandiosity. Another person agreed, adding that "to his dying days, George insisted that he was being mistreated and abused by the powers that be." The same person believed that Pollock had a "vertical split," a charismatic, generous side and another side that was "totally blind to what he was doing." Of all the interpretations offered during the meeting, the most ingenious was an Oedipal one involving George Pollock's relationship with Anne Pollock Lederer. "She was like his mother. Her maiden name was Pollock. He was her son Pollock. And it was this Oedipal thing, and he felt he, you know, he was the Oedipal child with the Oedipal victory and so on and so forth, and it's just perfectly obvious."

Offering an interpretation based on Freud's investigations of group psychology, one member opined that Pollock was "ideal to be a tool of the group, to do what we wanted doing." As the leader, Pollock raised money for the Institute and prevented it from being split by factions, as happened at other psychoanalytic institutes. After Pollock left, this person implied, the Chicago Institute lost much of its stability and respect for tradition. The speaker was obviously miffed by subsequent events; he had been asked not to teach anymore because he was too old.

Reading the transcript, one senses deep sadness and regret among his colleagues over the Pollock scandal and a desire to make sure that the "George situation" would never happen again. The members of the Chicago Psychoanalytic Institute engaged in painful soul-searching, and however silly some of their interpretations may strike us, they were genuinely trying to understand their complicity in one of the most serious scandals in the history of psychoanalysis. One of the paradoxes of George Pollock, everyone seemed to conclude, was that he was brilliant in many ways but ultimately not brilliant enough to recognize his blind spots. The members believed at the end of the meeting that there was now momentum for genuine ethics reform both within the Chicago Institute and the profession. The meeting concluded with the hope that another follow-up session would take place in the fall discussing the need for reform. We do not know if such a meeting took place.

Exploitation of Wealthy Elderly Patients

George Pollock wrote in a 1988 book review that psychoanalysis of the elderly was a legitimate therapy, notwithstanding Freud's stated belief to the contrary. The daily appearance, year after year, of Mrs. Lederer and her black housekeeper in the Institute's waiting area raised eyebrows among other faculty members, although none spoke out at the time, probably out of fear of retribution from Pollock. His "treatment" strategy of providing a family setting within the Institute for this lonely woman clearly seems to have been a form of "therapy" not properly called "psychoanalysis" and perhaps related to her wealth. It is hard to imagine that such an approach would have been taken with a patient of mere middle-class means, not to mention a widow living in poverty. According to Tueth, "The major risk factors for victims of elder exploitation include being over 75 years, being female, social isolation, frailty, and cognitive impairment. Associated factors include living with the abuser, being unmarried, and being financially independent" (106).

An even more bizarre example of exploitation of a lonely and wealthy elderly woman by physicians and their institution came to light in recent years. As Dedman and Newell describe in their "truth is stranger than fiction" 2014 book *Empty Mansions: The Mysterious Life of Huguette Clark and the Spending of a Great American Fortune*, Clark (1906–2011) was the heiress to an enormous fortune of hundreds of million dollars. As a child she had lived in the largest mansion in New York City, 962 Fifth Avenue, containing 121 rooms for four people. Later in life she became a recluse in an enormous apartment on Fifth Avenue. Huguette Clark appeared to be eccentric rather than mentally ill. When she was taken by ambulance to Doctors' Hospital in 1988, however, she looked like a "bag lady" with advanced non-metastatic cancerous lesions on her face that required extensive surgery for excision and repair. Dedman and Newell describe Doctors Hospital as a "fashionable treatment center for the well-to-do, a society hospital, a great place for a face-lift or for drying out" (229).

Following treatment, Clark then—*by choice*—remained in the hospital *for the rest of her life*, more than two decades. What makes this a psychiatric scandal, an example of psychotherapy off the tracks, is that she was evaluated by a psychiatrist who determined that she was *not* mentally ill despite her bizarre decision to remain in the hospital and be treated as a mental patient. Another time a doctor asked Huguette to see a psychiatrist, "not because he thought she was mentally ill but because he thought talking with another doctor might help persuade her to return home. She declined to discuss it, and neither the doctor nor the hospital ever mentioned it again" (233). Dedman and Newell conclude that no one will ever know why people regarded Huguette as "peculiar." Speculation ranges from being the daughter of an older father, her sister's or mother's deaths, her great wealth, a childhood trauma, or autism or Asperger's (356). Is Huguette an example of underdiagnosis or overdiagnosis, undertreatment or overtreatment? The questions add to the ambiguity of the story.

During this time her apartments and three huge estates remained vacant, as they indeed had been during most of her life prior to hospitalization, except for caretakers. She appeared to be highly intelligent, had a variety of interests, and was described as being kind and generous. She declined to leave the hospital to return to her home, although while in the hospital she supervised, at a distance, expensive renovation projects of her home. She spent the rest of her life in her small hospital room, wearing a patient gown and one or more sweaters, cared for by a devoted private duty nurse who worked 12 hours a day, seven days a week. Huguette Clark almost never ventured outside; she usually had the shades of her room drawn, hiding the view of Central Park her hospital room commanded. While in the hospital, her hospital expenses, along with the costs of her various donations, contributions, and artistic activities, amounted to about $400,000 per year.

The hospital was well aware of this extremely wealthy patient who, though rarely ill, eventually accumulated a hospital medical record of over 10,000 pages. During inspections by the hospital accrediting agency, her record was hidden by the hospital staff to prevent questions being raised about the prolonged hospitalization of a physically healthy woman. The hospital administration devised a plan to encourage her to contribute her fortune to the institution, and when the hospital found itself in financial trouble, increased the pressure on her. Finally the hospital was faced with a buyout by a real estate developer who wanted to demolish the building and replace it with an apartment development. To rescue the hospital, the board turned to Huguette Clark for a $100 million gift or, alternatively, with a plea for her to buy the building to save her room. Although facing the threat of having to relocate to another hospital, she refused to make the contribution or purchase: her reaction to the request was "that's a lot of money." She eventually was transferred to Beth Israel Hospital, where she lived out the rest of her life in a bleak hospital room with a view of a wall, a roof and a large air conditioning unit. She died at age 104.

The Hazard of Delegated Omnipotence: Kurt Eissler

Confidentiality breaches following a patient's death sometimes verge on boundary violations, such as Martin Orne's releasing of Anne Sexton's therapy tapes, as we discuss in *Confidentiality and Its Discontents*, or Ralph Greenson's "defense" of Marilyn Monroe following her death, as we discuss in Chapter 9. Psychotherapists are trained to avoid boundary violations, but sometimes they find themselves in vexing legal, ethical, and moral quandaries for which they are not prepared and which result in boundary violations through no fault of their own.

Such was the case described by Kurt Eissler, one of the most distinguished and scrupulous analysts of his age. Born in Vienna in 1908, he came to the United States and authored many books and articles. As the *New York Times* noted in its obituary on February 20, 1999, Eissler "founded, directed, and defended" the Sigmund Freud Archives, which is part of the Library of Congress, "and then handpicked a successor," Jeffrey Moussaieff Masson, a Sanskrit scholar and psychoanalyst, "who ended up plunging the archive into a sea of trouble." Eissler was 90 when he died.

Long before becoming one of the most controversial figures in psychoanalysis, Eissler described a different type of predicament in his 1955 book *The Psychiatrist and the Dying Patient*. The case study reads almost like a novel, filled with unexpected twists and ambiguous character motivation. He makes no effort to minimize the embarrassing situation in which he found himself ensnared when he tried to help a terminally ill woman manage her complicated financial affairs. Shortly before her death, she signed a will bequeathing him a great deal of money. Despite his ethical decision not to accept the inheritance, the will was contested after her death, leaving him in an awkward, untenable situation. Eissler almost takes pleasure in the dilemma, realizing it gives rise to a fascinating story. The patient has been identified through public court records as Edith Manischewitz, the wealthy widow of Max Manischewitz, who at the time of his death had been the first vice president of the Manischewitz Matzo Company. He was in turn the son of the founder of the iconic company, Rabbi Dov Behr Manischewitz, who started the bakery in 1888, the first industrialization of the production of matzo using machines (Estate of Edith Manischewitz). We are indebted to Peter Rudnytsky and Peter Swales for this identification.

The patient was a thin, pale woman in her early 60s who was married to a successful but controlling advertising executive. She suffered from a number of problems including anxiety, depression and psychosomatic (mainly gastrointestinal) symptoms. The patient had, in addition, a "bizarre character with strong tendencies toward dependency and acting out" (201). The couple was wealthy, but money appeared to exacerbate her problems: she was permitted to make no decisions for herself, which led to a fake, superficial existence. "She gave the appearance of a highly sophisticated fashion doll dressed up with extremely good taste" (199–200). Childless, she had taken a relative into her house with the intention of adopting her, but the growing ambivalence in the surrogate mother-daughter relationship later ruled out adoption. The relative married and moved away from C— to O—; she was the one who asked Eissler to help the patient. He never names the patient or the relative, though the latter's husband, Mr. X, soon becomes the antagonist in the story.

Eissler initially felt that it was "inadvisable" for him to treat the patient, fearing that the patient's husband would regard him as an "intruder who threatened to upset the almost slavish dependency of his wife" (202), but the psychoanalyst overcame his reluctance. Treatment appeared to help, allowing her to gain insight into her husband's manipulative, exploitative character. "In dealing with people he was said to use a technique which unavoidably led to their devaluation. He gave them exorbitant gifts; if they were accepted, he felt entitled to claim that the recipient was corrupt and accessible to bribe. Yet if the gifts were refused, the declining party was unmasked as unrealistic and inadequate in judgment" (202).

To nearly everyone's surprise, the patient proved to be a "woman of good judgment" after her husband's death, demonstrating her ability to handle her legal and financial affairs. Her improvement was soon imperiled, however, by the worsening of her physical health, and she underwent two surgeries. She rallied, and when her quasi-daughter asked her to move to O—, the patient felt her old conflicts emerge and asked Eissler for advice, telling him that he had become indispensable to her. Believing that an analysis of her transference feelings toward him was impossible because of her age, he advised her to see another psychiatrist for a month to prove he was not indispensable. She agreed and later conceded that Eissler was right. She moved to O—, and the case seemed to be over. Ten months later, the patient's reappearance alarmed Eissler. She looked severely ill despite the fact that two physicians had examined her and found nothing physically wrong. She bitterly reproached Eissler for allowing her to move to O—. He insisted that she have another physical exam with an internist, and to his horror, he discovered she was terminally ill with inoperable cancer.

One of the case study's major unintended ironies is Eissler's belief, shared by most of the physicians of the mid-20th century, that dying patients should not be apprised of the true nature of a fatal illness. Eissler's rationalization for not informing her about the serious prognosis is that telling her the truth would have precipitated "severe psychopathology." Rereading the case study a half century later, one is reminded of the patriarchal nature of medicine that existed for centuries prior to the present era, in which ethics affirm patient autonomy. According to Reuben Fine, Eissler's book was intended as a strong endorsement of the patriarchal position (198). Eissler's patient is merely told that her "benign disease" would require protracted treatment and hospitalization. "She thanked me profusely for having saved her life because I had insisted on a further physical workup and asked that she be permitted to call on me if she should later desire to do so. I protested her belief [that I had saved her life] and promised to fulfill her request" (208).

A Reluctant Executor

Like many in her situation, the patient nevertheless suspected she was dying. She told Eissler that if this was indeed her situation, she would change her will and leave part of her money, which she had allocated in an earlier will to her quasi-daughter in O—, to other relatives who were more in need of financial assistance. To test Eissler, she demanded to know the truth of her medical condition. Realizing that some physicians and lawyers might censure him for his decision, he continued to promote the illusion of her eventual recovery, convincing himself that her mental health was of paramount importance. Again sensing the truth, two weeks before her death the patient changed her will, without Eissler's knowledge, leaving Eissler a "considerable legacy" and making him executor of the will. She died in her sleep, Eissler informs us, and then adds, in a statement fraught with irony, that she believed to the end that he had saved her life.

There's never any question that Eissler thought he was acting in his patient's best interests. Nor is there doubt about his integrity. He realized immediately that he could not accept the bequest and instead asked the patient's lawyer to distribute his share of the will to the other legatees or to charitable organizations. He reluctantly agreed to serve as the executor of the will only because he was told that there would likely be an "outbreak of family quarrels" if he refused. This is the boundary violation of the story, as Eissler came to realize, as well as an example of what might be called the hazard of "delegated omnipotence," which caused him to believe that it was within his power to "fix" the situation and prevent a dreaded family quarrel, a well-meaning goal but hardly the task of a psychoanalyst. Eissler's decision provoked an angry letter from Mr. X, who challenged his honesty, but the latter seemed reassured when Eissler declared his refusal to accept the legacy. Mr. X later claimed, however, that the patient was not competent when she changed the will because she was operating under the spell of "transference." That's where the ambiguities of this case history lie.

Transference, we recall, is a central issue in sexual boundary violations, where either a patient or therapist accedes to the other's demand for sex. Transference clouds one's judgment, creating a situation where the patient, believing he or she is "special," is likely to do anything the therapist requires for the continuation of treatment. Transference may play a similarly powerful role in nonsexual boundary violations, leading patients to act in ways that may be counter to their best interests. Mr. and Mrs. X felt that the dying patient, under the sway of transference induced by psychotherapy, acted in a way that went counter to *their* own best interests. Eissler makes several noteworthy observations about transference, some of which are stated wryly. "If a psychotherapist or psychoanalyst does not handle transference in a therapeutically correct way, he may nevertheless increase his clientele, but he will not cure his patients, and therefore he must be considered a poor therapist despite the success he may have in his social group" (228). There's nothing wry, however, about his insistence that the austerity therapists impose on a patient must be equally valid for themselves.

Part of the uniqueness of Eissler's story is that he understands and even to an extent identifies with Mr. X's accusations against him. Janet Malcolm briefly discusses Eissler's case study in her 1984 book *In the Freud Archives*, where she refers to Mr. X as an analyst (73), but there's no mention of this detail in the case study; rather, he is characterized as a "professional man of impeccable reputation and comfortable means" (235). Eissler transmutes the complainant, whom he knew socially, into a formidable adversary with an intimate understanding of the complexities of psychoanalysis. Like a novelist, Eissler imagines a complainant accusing a therapist of harboring unconscious aggression toward a patient who later commits suicide. "Can you swear that you never dreamed of this patient's death or never wished his death in your unconscious? Did not the patient perhaps notice from your mien or a gesture that you regretted ever having taken him into treatment?" To which Eissler can only respond in this hypothetical dialogue: "What analyst could really swear that he had never had an unconscious death wish against a patient who later committed suicide?" (223). Eissler's imaginary complainant may remind us of the Grand Inquisitor in Dostoevsky's *The Brothers Karamazov* or the narrator in Kafka's "In the Penal Colony," who concludes, perhaps anticipating psychoanalysis as an ally, that guilt, in this case, the analyst's guilt, is "never to be doubted."

Eissler's story remains a cautionary tale of the unintended consequences of even benign boundary violations. To begin with, he argues that wealthy patients pose peculiar problems for therapists. "Automatically—almost like a reflex—the wealthy patient then tries to make the psychiatrist abandon the relatively firm and distant therapeutic attitude by the offer of gifts, that is to say, by bribery. When the psychiatrist proves himself inaccessible to bribery, this may amount to an unbearable frustration and the patient may quit the treatment using one or the other excuse" (212). By extension, as we shall see in the next two chapters, famous patients, such as actors, actresses, politicians and celebrities, pose similar problems for therapists, who may be seduced or trapped into boundary violations. Eissler warns of the dangers of therapists who opportunistically exploit a patient's transference, and he demonstrates why professional ethics must be more stringent in psychotherapy than in other professions.

Dying patients pose different problems for the therapist. In retrospect, Eissler confesses that he should never have accepted executorship of the will even with the understanding that he would not be paid for the service. The moment the patient died, he adds, he should have ended all involvement with the case.

Working with highly needy, dependent patients may lead to other boundary violations. Eissler admits that when the patient's negotiations with her deceased husband's business partners broke down, he drafted a letter for her that had a beneficial effect, averting a "financial and psychic catastrophe" for her. He concedes, though, that he took a great risk in writing the letter, especially since he had never met the recipient of the letter. Eissler acknowledges near the end of the case study that he might have erred in helping his dying patient, a mistake motivated not by greed or material self-interest but by therapeutic ambition, which he concedes is the "arch-enemy of psychoanalysis." Without a degree of ambition, he remarks, he would not have been able to help the patient, but he fears that he was "inordinately ambitious" in his treatment of her. "No hurdle was too high for me to take; when the patient was in a calamity I always was at hand to help her out" (238).

Eissler never uses the word *countertransference*, but therapeutic ambitiousness could be a part of a therapist's countertransference: the desire for fame, success, honor, or power. Ambition might cause an analyst to conform to an idealized superego version of himself or herself as a helpful person in the conventional sense, which can conflict with the more realistic goal of being helpful by acting as a competent psychoanalyst. In one of his few statements on the subject, Freud warns analysts in "Recommendations to Physicians Practising Psycho-Analysis" (1912) that "therapeutic ambition" is dangerous (115). Michael Guy Thompson observes that therapeutic ambition "is difficult to recognize. When we commit it, it's usually because we only want to help. On a narcissistic note, we may simply be too eager to 'cure' every patient we treat" (271).

Eissler ends the story with a self-mocking irony. Whereas he always believed that the patient was satisfied with his treatment of her, he now faults himself for never having given her the opportunity to express her unconscious aggression toward him. "With particular finesse, under the guise of a special favor, she made me the victim of an ambivalence which must have dated far back in our relationship." By making him her beneficiary, Eissler adds, twisting the knife further into himself, the patient "had succeeded beyond the grave in gratifying her ambivalence toward me"—and perhaps her relatives (239–240).

CHAPTER 8

Gregory Zilboorg: The Svengali— or Rasputin—of Psychoanalysis

Boundary violations have momentous consequences for patients and sometimes for therapists, who may lose their licenses, but seldom do boundary violations have an impact on an entire profession. Historically, most professional organizations have remained silent about a transgressive therapist, embarrassed by the negative publicity. Occasionally, however, a therapist's transgressive boundary violations will have portentous consequences for a profession, particularly when it is beset by ideological differences and personal rivalries. This helps to explain why Gregory Zilboorg's story is so important to the history of psychoanalysis.

Gregory Zilboorg (1890–1959) is among the most charismatic and controversial characters in the history of the psychoanalytic profession; it is difficult to think of anyone who comes even close to matching him.

For a reader with a taste for boundary violations, Zilboorg's career is a magnificent banquet. Yet, in a published obituary, the noted psychoanalyst Franz Alexander, who in fact had been Zilboorg's analyst, described him with probably as much positive spin as he could muster: "With Gregory Zilboorg's death, American psychoanalysis lost one of its most colorful personalities. He was a sensitive psychologist, a man of many gifts and broad cultural interests, a master of the written and spoken word. In his personal contacts he exercised a magnetic influence. His personality was full of inner contradictions, hence he was often misunderstood, but also admired" (380). Alexander then adds three details about Zilboorg's supposed professional training: He received his M.D. from the Psychoneurological Institute in Leningrad; then he came to the United States where he received a medical degree at the Columbia University College of Physicians and Surgeons; and finally he received his psychoanalytic training at the Berlin Psychoanalytic Institute (381).

A Questionable Background

However, more recent research has cast doubt on the factual accuracy of Alexander's statements. As Mark Leffert suggests in his erudite review, "The Psychoanalysis and Death of George Gershwin: An American Tragedy" (published in the *Journal of the American Academy of Psychoanalysis and Dynamic Psychiatry* in 2011), Zilboorg "simply could not have had the medical degree he repeatedly claimed to have been awarded [from the Psychoneurological Institute in Leningrad]" because that Institute offered none of the courses required for a medical degree in Russia." Leffert's research on Zilboorg's background, on which we have relied, shows that he could not have graduated from the Berlin Psychoanalytic Institute either, because its rigorous curriculum at that time took a full three or four years to complete, and Zilboorg was in Berlin for only one year. It is possible, however, that Zilboorg attended lectures at the Institute for a year as what would be called today an auditor (426–427). In short, much of the information in Franz Alexander's obituary of Zilboorg is suspect; even the fact that it was written by Zilboorg's analyst, Franz Alexander, strikes one as highly unconventional. Alexander's positive spin becomes more remarkable in light of the serious ethical charges he brought against Zilboorg 18 years earlier, when the New York Psychoanalytic Society was roiled by an unprecedented investigation of one of its own members.

Despite his questionable background, Zilboorg quickly rose to prominence in the New York psychoanalytic and psychiatric communities. After graduating from Columbia's medical school in 1926, Zilboorg worked for five years at a private psychiatric hospital in New York, and then in 1931 he opened a private practice in psychoanalysis in New York. He served as eventual chair of the Education Committee of the New York Psychoanalytic Institute. He later became the Chair of the American Psychiatric Association's Committee on the History of Psychiatry. He was a Clinical Associate Professor of Psychiatry at New York Medical College and the New York State University Medical College. In addition, he was the Chair of the Section on History and Cultural Medicine of the New York Academy of Medicine (*Notes and News,* 477). Oddly, despite his prominence as a New York psychoanalyst, there is no evidence that Zilboorg ever applied for or received a license to practice medicine in New York.

In the brief space of three years after opening his office, Zilboorg had become the "fashionable analyst to see in New York, treating prominent patients drawn from the worlds of theater, literature, music, and finance" (Leffert). Farber and Green describe Zilboorg as a "flamboyant showman who wore a black cape and sported an enormous handlebar moustache" (62). That moustache, which curiously is nowhere in evidence in portraits of Zilboorg in the archives of the George Eastman House in Rochester, New York, was dubbed the "lunatic fringe" by the Hollywood producer Carleton Alsop, who later became a CIA spy in Hollywood (Farber and Green, 62). A mere 14 years after graduating from Columbia University's medical school, Zilboorg was hobnobbing in New York society as an invited guest at the opening of the 1940 Philharmonic season (*New York Times*, 1940). He was among a select group of invitees along with such notables as Tallulah Bankhead, Ethel Barrymore, and Mr. and Mrs. Lawrence Rockefeller at a 1941 cocktail reception in honor of Gloria Swanson at the New York Museum of Modern Art (Museum of Modern Art, July 26, 1941).

Svengali-like

Other descriptions of Zilboorg are equally evocative. "A flamboyant refugee from the Russian Revolution, Zilboorg was a short, dark, Svengali-like figure who mesmerized the Warburgs until adoration turned to disenchantment. His colorful past cloaked him in a mysterious aura. He had been secretary to the labor minister of Kerensky's cabinet, was a Cordon Bleu chef, a photographer, a polyglot fluent in eight languages, a medical doctor, and the author of a major history of psychiatry" (Chernow, 333). Chernow is not the only scholar who described Zilboorg as Svengali-like. Katharine Weber uses the same allusion in her 2011 memoir *The Memory of All That: George Gershwin, Kay Swift, and My Family's Legacy of Infidelities*. An acclaimed novelist and memoirist who teaches creative writing at Kenyon College, Weber is the granddaughter of the songwriter Kay Swift. Weber never met Zilboorg, who died when she was four years old, but her memoir, along with an article she wrote for the *New York*

Times in 1998 and an article in *American Imago* in 2015, provide us with important information about him. "He published many distinguished contributions to the field of psychoanalysis, and he won a literary prize for his English translation of a 1921 Leonid Andreyev play, 'He, the One Who Gets Slapped.'" Five years later, Zilboorg published for the first time in any language an English translation of the Russian dystopian novel, *We*, by Yevgeny Zamyatin. Publication of the novel had been banned in the Soviet Union. *We* is considered to have inspired the later 20th century dystopian novels *1984* by George Orwell and *Brave New World* by Aldous Huxley.

Some of Zilboorg's colleagues held him in high esteem. In his discussion of "Early American Historians of Psychiatry: 1910–1960," George Mora tells us, parenthetically, that he had the "personal pleasure of knowing [Zilboorg] quite well" (59). Those who could not appreciate Zilboorg's many talents, Mora implies, were envious. He was a "man both greatly admired and resented by contemporaries because of his tremendous ability to love (as evidenced by the warmth he conveyed to his family and friends)" (61). Other colleagues were wary of him. A.A. Brill, a patriarch of the New York Psychoanalytic Society, characterized Zilboorg as "a flamboyant and explosive personality . . . who had created endless trouble in the New York Society." Another New York Psychoanalytic Society leader, Smith Ely Jelliffe, depicted Zilboorg as being of the "rule or ruin" variety (N. Hale, 138). Still another New York Psychoanalytic Society leader, Abram Kardiner, could not abide Zilboorg but was nevertheless intrigued by his many contradictions, as Kardiner reveals in his *Reminiscences*, an extended oral history interview transcribed and available at Columbia University's Rare Book and Manuscript Library:

> I didn't like him, but I was fascinated by him. I knew that he couldn't be trusted one inch, insofar as loyalty, consideration,

friendship or anything like that was concerned, and I knew that he was a dazzler, but he was a mighty convincing dazzler. He could tell you a story with any kind of ingredients. He'd make them up as he went along. He had the ideal gifts for a first class phony. But in addition to that, he was really very bright. He had a great deal of intelligence, and when I would argue with him, "Why do you need these shenanigans which would be appropriate if you were a stupid fellow, but you have great intelligence"—"I can't help it," he said, "this is my character and I've got to live it this way" (169A)

Such negative characterizations of Zilboorg appear in several biographies of his patients. In her biography of George Gershwin, Joan Peyser quotes a former Zilboorg student stating that he was "a very difficult man. He was considered by the professional community to have had psychopathic qualities. He took advantage of his patients, socialized with them more than other analysts thought he should, and did not hesitate, for example, to give patients advice. . . . While it is true that he was very brilliant, his colleagues found much of what he did abhorrent." A physician who held Zilboorg responsible for his wife's suicide said, "He was brilliant, dangerous in both simple and complex ways, vicious and exploitative. He did whatever was necessary to create a relationship with his patients which invariably did him some good, financially or otherwise" (218–219).

A Prolific Author and Leading Light

A Renaissance man, Zilboorg was described by colleagues as a genius (Braceland, 671). He wrote many books, including *The Medical Man and the Witch During the Renaissance* (1935); *History of Medical Psychology*

(1941); *Mind, Medicine and Man* (1943); *Sigmund Freud, His Exploration of the Mind of Man* (1951); and *Freud and Religion: a Restatement of an Old Controversy* (1958). A reviewer in the *American Journal of Psychiatry* described *History of Medical Psychology* as the "most ambitious and comprehensive review of the history of psychiatry that has appeared in English," a "very scholarly book . . . [that] represents a vast deal of reading and research." Zilboorg was widely admired by historians of psychiatry, being himself a leading light among them (C.B.F.).

Zilboorg was also a minor figure in New York's avant-garde entertainment and art scene, participating as one player in a public chess match against a blindfolded chess master, and refereed by Marcel Duchamp, at the opening of a chess themed art show at a surrealist art gallery. Despite his orthodox Jewish roots in Russia, when he arrived in the United States Zilboorg became a Quaker. He was a man of catholic taste—and then he literally converted to Roman Catholicism later in life.

From Each According to His Ability

Despite his earlier experiences in pre-Soviet Russia, Zilboorg remained throughout his life a political liberal of the far left. He was active in left wing causes during the 1930s, freely conveyed his views to his rich clientele, and, as one might imagine happening in analytic treatment conducted in that manner, converted some of his conservative wealthy patients to his political point of view. Zilboorg's fees were evidently geared to his patients' incomes. In the Great Depression era, when typical analytic fees were four dollars per session ($65 in current dollars), and when Freud was charging $10 an hour (Kardiner, 15), Zilboorg asked, and evidently received, $75 ($1,200 in current dollars) per session and even more from his most affluent patients. Zilboorg charged Marshall Field, one of the richest men in America, the higher fee (Madsen, 222). In his Gershwin biography, Howard Pollack quotes an unnamed person as having described Zilboorg as "someone who 'maintained a high theoretical disdain for money, but enjoyed a high income.'" George Gershwin paid Zilboorg more than \$3,000 (\$52,000 in current dollars) in 1935 alone. Gershwin reportedly said, "He finds out how much you make and then charges you more than you can afford" (Pollack, 208). Lillian Hellman, another Zilboorg patient who felt that he had been of great help to her, nonetheless commented about him, "'He was an old fashioned Socialist who hated inherited wealth as undeserved, and many of his patients were people like that.' In other words, since Zilboorg's patients had inherited their money, it was legitimate that Zilboorg had bilked them of it, not for mercenary reasons, but for the sake of a political principle" (Gallagher, 93).

Zilboorg was among a handful of psychoanalysts who treated wealthy patients. These analysts fared extremely well in the 1930s, earning on average twice as much as other New York physicians during the dark depression days, when medical fees in New York City were actually below those in the rest of the country (N. Hale, 118). After Lillian Hellman's death, a psychoanalyst friend of hers, Milton Wexler (Ralph Greenson's partner), remarked that "the only thing Zilboorg had cured Hellman of was a good deal of money" (Gallagher, 93).

Boundary Violations with the Warburgs

Zilboorg's psychoanalytic practice was suffused with what today would be considered an outrageous and startling lack of boundaries. Bettina Warburg, of the fabulously wealthy Warburg banking family and herself a psychoanalyst who eventually became a leader and probable financial backer in assisting European analysts to relocate to the United States in the 1930s, was in analytic treatment for four years with Zilboorg, who was her training analyst at the New York Psychoanalytic Institute. Zilboorg's analysis of Bettina Warburg linked him to the Warburg family in a relationship that would blossom in a most unnatural way.

Zilboorg's boundary violations addressed in this chapter began at least as early as his relocation close to Bettina Warburg's residence. While serving as her training analyst, he purchased and moved into a house across the street from the Warburg home on 70th Street in Manhattan. Geographical closeness facilitated familial closeness. Zilboorg eventually became so entwined with the Warburg family that Katharine Weber referred to her "mysterious quasi-relative" as "Gregory" (136).

Zilboorg ingratiated himself with the Warburgs and their family problems. Of German-Jewish descent, the Warburgs were one of America's most prominent families, distinguishing themselves in banking, science, the arts and philanthropy. In 1916, Bettina Warburg's brother, James Paul Warburg ("Jimmy"), despite his family's disapproval, and "in a spirit of revolt against parental authority" (Chernow, 185), married Kay Swift, a non-Jewish New Yorker of great musical talent and a strongly independent disposition. In 1925 she met George Gershwin, who became a frequent visitor to the Warburg home. A friendship based on their common interests developed, and their relationship eventually turned into a long affair. Kay Swift Warburg became intent on but conflicted about the possibility of divorcing her husband, Jimmy Warburg, to marry Gershwin.

On her sister-in-law Bettina's suggestion, Kay Swift consulted Zilboorg, who in 1932 took her into analysis, presumably to help her resolve her ambivalence about the divorce. To complicate her situation, her husband, Jimmy, and her lover, George Gershwin, both eventually also went into analysis with Zilboorg. "Analysis with Zilboorg drove

Kay into a deeper quagmire," Katharine Weber writes in *The Memory of All That*:

> Now she found herself married to one man she loved, deeply involved with another man she loved, and having a strange and unwanted sexual involvement with her psychoanalyst, who pressured her to stay in the marriage and to maintain the status quo. When after some ten months of this she told him she was determined to divorce Jimmy and simplify her life also by terminating this analysis, Gregory threatened her with exposure of her darkest secrets, telling her that if she left him, if she followed through on this plan, he would tell things to both Jimmy and George, now both in treatment with him as well, which would make both of them want nothing more to do with her and would probably also result in her losing custody of her children. (195)

Swift was startled when Zilboorg began discussing Gershwin's sessions with her during her own analytic hours (Peyser, 218). During the last six months of her analysis, she and Zilboorg became sexually involved, not for romantic reasons but because he claimed it was an element in her treatment (Rimler, 81). According to Katharine Weber, "for some inexplicable reason" Kay Swift "felt obligated to have sex" with Zilboorg, "on the analytic couch, during their sessions, for which she paid fifty dollars each time." Swift confided to Weber that Zilboorg was "the only man with whom I ever had sexual intercourse to whom I was not physically attracted" (147). Swift told Weber that after having unwanted sex with Zilboorg, she would write a check for her analytic fee and cry. "He would pocket the check and tell her to 'stop the damned eye-pissing'" (199). In late 1934, Swift went to Nevada and received a divorce from Jimmy Warburg;

afterwards, she ended treatment with Zilboorg. Because both her ex-husband and Gershwin were Zilboorg's patients, however, the analyst sometimes became a weekend guest at the Warburg family's summer home, Bydale, in Greenwich, Connecticut.

In time, according to Weber, Kay Swift came to see Zilboorg in an entirely negative light. She believed that Zilboorg turned her former husband, who remained in analysis with him, against her, "planting the image of her as foolish and promiscuous, and cultivating in her ex-husband what would become a lifelong hostility and scorn for Kay which he transmitted to his children." Years later, Jimmy Warburg minimized the importance of his time on Zilboorg's couch, although he remained in analysis for eight or nine years. Throughout this time, Zilboorg was a fixture at the Warburgs' homes on East Seventieth Street and at Bydale. Zilboorg was also the analyst of Jimmy Warburg's second wife, Phyllis, for 17 years. In Kay Swift's view, Zilboorg's influence was "malevolent" (Weber, 195). Writing to a friend about her analysis with Zilboorg, Swift could not understand why she had allowed herself to believe in him. "I wonder now why I took such a lot of unadulterated bull from him, and conclude that he simply made a whip of my own sense of guilt and beat me with it on all occasions" (Weber, 255).

The odd relationship between Zilboorg and the wealthy Warburg family continued into the 1940s. Weber's father described to her a curious encounter with Zilboorg in 1946 during a Sunday lunch at Bydale when her parents were not yet married. "There, a supremely uncomfortable gathering consisted of Sidney [Kaufman, Weber's father] and Andrea, Jimmy and Phyllis (on the verge of divorce), and Zilboorg. Sidney and Zilboorg spoke Yiddish together over the smoked salmon, insulting their host (who couldn't understand them and probably didn't enjoy hearing Yiddish spoken by either his analyst or his future son-in-law) for his lack of bagels and *menschlichkeit*" (Weber, 196).

Vicki Ohl observes in her 2004 Kay Swift biography *Fine &
Dandy* (the title is an allusion to Kay Swift's 1930 Broadway musical,
the first major musical comedy written by a woman) that Swift later
wrote a thinly disguised fictionalized account of her life in the West,
Who Could Ask for Anything More! The title reveals Swift's disdain for
psychoanalysis. "Western men," Swift proclaims, "have attained that
exhilarating quality for which people in the East pay psychiatrists huge
sums of money." Swift's criticism of those who seek psychiatric help,
Ohl remarks, "was undoubtedly fueled by her own disastrous experience
with psychoanalysis under Dr. Gregory Zilboorg in 1934" (140).

Bettina Warburg referred several relatives and acquaintances to
Zilboorg while she was in analysis with him, but eventually like Kay
Swift, she too lost confidence in him. As Weber observes in *The Memory
of All That*, Bettina Warburg broke off her training analysis when she
discovered that Zilboorg was, as she related many years later to her
great-niece, "a crook" (351, n.9). Bettina failed, however, to convey her
misgivings to her relatives. Weber notes that Bettina never warned
her brother, sister-in-law, or cousin Eddie (Edward Warburg), to
whom she had recommended treatment with Zilboorg. Eddie Warburg
spent 26 years of "costly analytic entanglement" with Zilboorg. "Eddie
never forgave her for recommending Zilboorg and never revealing her
subsequent misgivings" (195).

Involving Himself in His Patients' Lives

One way Zilboorg involved himself in his patients' lives was by sharing
his interest in photography with them. He was an avid and skilled
photographer, in particular a Leica enthusiast. Two of his portraits of
Henry Sigerist, a Swiss medical historian and long time friend, were

chosen to be shown at the 1935 International Leica Exhibition at Rockefeller Center. In the late 1930s, Zilboorg's images were published in several influential photography magazines, including the May 1938 issue of *Camera*. While Gershwin was still his patient, Zilboorg presented him with a Leica identical to his own and interested the composer in photo processing. Zilboorg's basement darkroom in his home became a haunt in which Gershwin, Kay Swift and her adolescent daughter, Andrea (Katharine Weber's mother) developed and printed their photographs (136).

Weber offers in her memoir the details of a storied trip Zilboorg made to Mexico in the mid-1930s with an "unusual entourage" that consisted of three of his analysands: Gershwin, who was in analysis with him in 1934 and 1935; Marshall Field, the "department store heir"; and Eddie Warburg. The trip demonstrated not only the lack of boundaries that permeated Zilboorg's clinical practice but also his ambition and negative countertransference. Zilboorg, who feared encountering Bolsheviks in Mexico, carried a loaded pistol at all times. To exclude and humiliate Gershwin, who had confided to his analyst the fear of being left out of conversations, Zilboorg spoke Spanish, which the composer didn't understand, with the Mexican painters they met. Worst of all, Weber adds, Zilboorg "conducted analytic sessions with each of his three patients and then presided over breakfasts with them during which he often made humiliating references to their private matters" (Weber, 209; Rimler, 118–119).

The Center of Attention

During the trip to Mexico with Zilboorg, George Gershwin met the famed artist David Alfaro Siqueiros. Later, when Siqueiros was in New

York, Gershwin commissioned him to paint his portrait, but requested that he be shown seated at the piano during a concert. The result, Weber remarks in her *Times* article, was a 6' x 8' painting titled "George in an Imaginary Concert Hall," which was unveiled at a reception at the Waldorf-Astoria hotel. One of the most unusual features of the painting is that it is drawn from a position behind the stage looking out toward the audience. One thus sees Gershwin at the piano and behind him, the audience. The presumed subject of the painting is, of course, George Gershwin, but perhaps the most stunning detail is Zilboorg's central position in it. The first two rows consist of Gershwin's family and friends. As if to confirm Zilboorg's belief that he was the center of his patients' lives, if not the center of the universe, he is in the first row, along with other Zilboorg patients, and is seated next to Ira Gershwin's wife, Lenore.

© 2019 Artists Rights Society (ARS), New York / SOMAAP, Mexico City

Zilboorg Likely Falsely Accused in Gershwin's Death

Upon moving to California in 1935, Gershwin ended his regular sessions with Zilboorg. According to Leffert, Gershwin was not in analysis with Zilboorg when the composer's fatal brain tumor became evident in 1937.

Leffert contends that Gershwin's life could have been saved as late as June 1937 if he had received an accurate diagnosis at that time, or, for that matter, if Zilboorg had made an appropriate neurological referral in 1934. Leffert admits, however, that "here we are, of necessity, left to speculation supported by data." He adds that "very little is known about what took place in these evaluations that were done on Gershwin and the physicians who performed them" (421). It remains unclear whether, during his analysis with Zilboorg, Gershwin was suffering from symptoms related to the tumor, which was likely present, possibly in a non-malignant form. The analysis had ended a year and a half before Gershwin's condition took a steep downhill course.

Gershwin biographer Joan Peyser, in a letter to the editor published in the *New York Times* on October 4, 1998, quoted Dr. Paul Brauer as admitting that although Zilboorg was brilliant, his colleagues found much of what he did "abhorrent. In the 1950s the New York Psychoanalytic Institute defrocked him." Peyser then added,

> To me, Zilboorg's most heinous crime was providing Leonore Gershwin, Ira's wife, with the rationale for the neglect of her brother-in-law's symptoms that friends and associates had found alarming. (Moss Hart later told his wife, Kitty Carlisle, that at a dinner party Gershwin kept putting his fork in his ear, apparently unable to locate his mouth.) Zilboorg's diagnosis was neurotic depression. In the early 1990s, postoperative microphotographs of

the brain tumor that killed Gershwin were studied by two leading neurosurgeons. Both men agreed that the composer had for years suffered from a slow growing cystic astrocytoma that even then could have been treated.

Even at the time of Gershwin's death, Zilboorg was blamed by some members of the composer's circle (Bach, 154). In his memoir the playwright S. N. Behrman describes Gershwin's shocking decline during the final days before he was hospitalized in California. Intolerant of psychoanalysts in general, Behrman implicitly blamed Gershwin's analysts. "I had a special antipathy for George's New York psychoanalyst. He was boorish. Years later when I read Sir Ernest Jones's life of Sigmund Freud, I came upon Freud's own fear of the psychoanalysts who might succeed him. He called them 'wild analysts.' I thought at once of this analyst" (255). Zilboorg, on the other hand, claimed that Gershwin had called him for advice from California when his symptoms became apparent. According to Zilboorg, he told Gershwin the symptoms were most likely organic rather than psychological. "There is some reason to question this because Zilboorg and his wife both went out of their way after Gershwin's death to deny that the doctor had played any role in a misdiagnosis" (Rimler, 143). Gershwin had been admitted to Cedars of Lebanon Hospital for three days around June 23, about two weeks before his death, at which time he "was examined by one specialist after another. All of them except one concluded that the illness was emotional." The neurologist who suspected a brain tumor recommended a spinal tap to rule out this possibility, but Gershwin refused (158).

The playwright Moss Hart, at the time a patient of Zilboorg at the enormous fee of $100 per hour (Bach, 129), or $1400 in current dollars, possibly equal to a quarter million dollars per year, at first defended Zilboorg. Soon thereafter Hart became disillusioned with

Zilboorg and left him to start analysis with Zilboorg's rival in the New York Psychoanalytic Society, Lawrence S. Kubie. Kubie was similarly seen as captivated by his patients' celebrity and pedigree. Kubie was a "money snob and a celebrity snob," according to a former patient, who added that Kubie "was a star fucker and I was onto him like that" (213). Kubie's autocratic ways caused Hart to refer to him as "Herr Doktor." One wonders if other celebrity patients followed suit after Gershwin's death, leaving Zilboorg financially strapped, which might help to explain his reckless behavior described later in this chapter.

In Zilboorg's defense, it must be added that even after Gershwin's medical condition became florid in June 1937, most of the physicians who examined him, according to the biographer Edward Jablonski, did not attribute his symptoms to a physical cause (318). The one exception was Eugene Ziskind, who twice suggested a diagnostic lumbar puncture. Ziskind is described in Leffert's article and in Gershwin biographies as a "neurologist," but the obituary in the *Los Angeles Times* on November 14, 1993 refers to him as a psychiatrist and, in fact, as having been the chair of psychiatry at both UCLA Medical Center and Cedars of Lebanon Hospital. Ziskind performed a neurological examination on Gershwin that was normal.

It is possible that during Gershwin's time with Zilboorg, when the tumor was in a much earlier stage and any symptoms were much more subtle, even had Zilboorg made a referral, the diagnosis would still have been missed just as it had been by the numerous physicians late in the course of the illness (Wood, 241). Additionally, had Gershwin agreed at the beginning of June, 1937 or later in that month to the lumbar puncture, which would have been diagnostic, there was a significant life-threatening risk from the test itself. Typically nowadays, before a patient with evidence of increased pressure inside his or her skull is the subject of a lumbar puncture, an MRI or CT scan of the brain is made because in such cases the risk of a fatal outcome from the test itself is increased. No such imaging techniques existed at that time, and the plain x-rays of Gershwin's head that were available at that time showed no significant abnormalities.

Zilboorg's Leftist Politics

Zilboorg involved himself deeply not only in his patients' hobbies, cultural interests and vacation travels but also in their business activities. One involvement in particular led to eventual difficulty. Zilboorg influenced many of his upper-class patients to identify with and adopt his left-leaning political views. His radical views and activities aroused the attention of the witch-hunting House Un-American Activities Committee (HUAC) in 1951. HUAC identified him as among 245 of the sponsors of the 1949 "Scientific and Cultural Conference for World Peace March" that had been affiliated with from five to ten Communist front organizations. Zilboorg was upstaged in this regard in the Committee's report by Albert Einstein, who was listed as having been affiliated with "eleven to twenty Communist-front organizations."

PM

One of Zilboorg's patients who appears to have moved to the left in his political views was Ralph McAllister Ingersoll, a descendant of a prominent and proper Connecticut family. Ingersoll was known in the 1930s as "the editorial genius behind *Time*, *Fortune* and *Life*" within the Luce publishing empire (Daly). Prior to working for Luce, Ingersoll had served as managing editor of the *New Yorker*, shaping that magazine during the five years following its inception in 1925. By the late 1930s, Ingersoll planned to leave the Luce enterprises and to found a new daily left-leaning pro-labor newspaper in New York City called *PM*. He also adopted a more proletarian name, plain Ralph Ingersoll, far removed from his social register-Hotchkiss-Yale background.

PM was to be unique in that it would not accept any advertising and would be supported entirely by subscriptions and daily sales. Ingersoll made a decision to strike out on his own despite a $1 million stock offer from Luce to remain with *Time*, Inc. for five additional years. Instead, with the help of his attorney brother-in-law, he formed a new corporation, Publications Research, Inc. with the purposes of both the planning for the new publication and the raising of funds to capitalize it (Hoopes, 168–169, 176). As we shall see, Zilboorg was involved in this business endeavor with Ingersoll. Publications Research was funded in part by a $25,000 loan from Daniel Gilmor, a "young radical" who happened to be the organizer of a communist study or lecture group of which Ingersoll was a member, along with other members of the New York intelligentsia. Gilmor also became part of the planning of *PM*, along with the writers Lillian Hellman and Dashiell Hammett.

When Ingersoll told Zilboorg that he joined this group, the analyst "broke up the session with his roar of laughter. 'You! You . . . they think of you as Party material? You, the totally perfect bourgeois—mind, body, and soul! Those simple minded idiots!'" (Hoopes, 175). Zilboorg, a committed left-wing socialist but dedicated anti-communist who had been a minor employee of the Kerensky government, believed he was still a marked man in the eyes of the communists. Zilboorg told Ingersoll that he could never accept "a true communist" as a patient. "It would stir up too many savage emotions" (176). Evidently, Zilboorg weaned Ingersoll away from the communists. The connection with Gilmor was broken, and the future *PM* was saved from a rumored communist taint, although Ingersoll insisted that the communist point of view should still be represented in *PM*'s pages. (234)

Ingersoll sought out funding for *PM* through the sale of shares of another new corporation, "The PM Newspaper Inc." Each share cost $100,000 (about $1.7 million in current dollars.) Marshall Field, another Zilboorg patient who had turned to the left during his analysis, purchased two shares as did the wealthy John Hay Whitney. Zilboorg claimed that he had "engineered the meeting" between his patients Ingersoll and Field "on the theory that the psychic ills of both men could be cured with the founding of a progressive newspaper" (Madsen, 230). It is possible, however, that neither knew at that time that they had each been Zilboorg's patients. According to Field, he and Ingersoll did not discover they were "brother alumni of the Zilboorg office" until some time after *PM* had begun.

Early in the planning of *PM*, Zilboorg had originally advised Ingersoll, who was his patient during this entire period, not to take the risk and to return to the Luce employ. As Ingersoll recounts, Zilboorg interrupted one of his sessions, "sat me down across the desk from him, saying that he wanted, this day, to talk to me more as a friend than as doctor to patient, although, I must understand the advice he was going to give me would be consistent with what he would also prescribe as my psychiatrist" (Hoopes, 190). Zilboorg's premise in giving this advice— that the wealthy people who had promised Ingersoll support would not in the end come through and thus would betray him—turned out to be incorrect, and Ingersoll went forward with his plan. With the needed funding in hand, Zilboorg then joined Ingersoll in the planning of *PM*. This occurred while Ingersoll was still in analysis with Zilboorg.

Zilboorg's correspondence reveals additional evidence of his involvement with Ingersoll and *PM* outside of *but during* Ingersoll's analysis. On June 11, 1940, just before the actual launch of *PM*, Zilboorg wrote the following letter to his friend, the medical historian Henry Sigerist (Bickel, 96):

Dear Henry:

"Black Hamlet" [a book] will be returned to you in a couple of days.

When are you starting on your trip? I wanted to see you very much before you start, in order to talk over *PM*. I want to arrange that you, Ingersoll (the publisher) and I get together and talk things over—particularly the Medical Department.

As always,
Gregory

Zilboorg was clearly involved at a minimum in the planning of medical columns for *PM*. Sigerist replied on June 12, 1940: "I should greatly welcome the opportunity of meeting Intersoll [*sic*]. I really feel that *PM* can fulfill an extremely important function in the medical field." A week later Zilboorg replied, confirming the meeting with Sigerist and Ingersoll the next day. The planned meeting had to be postponed a few days, but it did take place. "It was a most delightful evening with you and Ingersoll," Sigerist wrote to Zilboorg on June 24, "and I am glad I had an opportunity to see the plant. I am very confident as to the future of *PM*. The idea is sound, the paper meets a definite need and therefore must be a success. It will be a great pleasure for me to cooperate by supplying the editors with materials on health and medical conditions in the country, and I am getting ready for the trip" (97).

Thus, the correspondence indicates that Zilboorg conducted a business meeting in his office after office hours with both one of his psychoanalytic patients and a personal friend whom he was involving in a business arrangement with the patient. Zilboorg accompanied them on a tour of the printing plant in which the paper was to be produced. Zilboorg had been involved in renting facilities for *PM* within the plant of the *Brooklyn Eagle*, another newspaper of that era.

Beyond all this, apart from writing a few articles under a pseudonym, Zilboorg's involvement in *PM*'s editorial policies is unclear, as Jack Alexander noted in an article published in the *Saturday Evening Post* in 1941. During the early days of *PM*, following its June 1940 launch, Zilboorg often appeared in the paper's editorial offices. Alexander compares Zilboorg's presence to that of the "evanescent" Cheshire Cat. "Thus does the psychoanalyst go through cycles of appearing and then disappearing into thin air" (103) in connection with *PM*. Carl Rollyson, Lillian Hellman's biographer, describes Zilboorg as "enmeshed in the production of *PM*" along with his patients Field, Ingersoll and Hellman, as well as Hellman's lover, Dashiell Hammett. Rollyson characterizes Zilboorg as "a formidable figure whose advice [his patients] could not easily dismiss."

PM's Demise

Despite its early success, within a few months *PM* was near collapse. As a result of its no-advertising policy, an unrelated but serious management blunder, its heavy spending on first class resources and its disappointing sales, the publication had burned through most of the cash raised in the initial financing. By October the paper was sinking. Sigerist insisted that Zilboorg deliver the following message to his patient. "Next time you see Ingersoll," Sigerist wrote on October 15, 1940, "tell him to have an eye on his Circulation Department. It seems to be so thoroughly disorganized that it almost looks as if somebody were sabotaging there.

Just a few cases to show you what happens." Sigerist then enumerated the publication's failure to fulfill its subscription commitments to him and several acquaintances (Bickel, 99).

The prospects would have been bleak for *PM*'s survival had not Marshall Field stepped in to save the paper. Field bought out the other shareholders for 20 cents on the dollar and then bankrolled the paper himself (Madsen, 237). Each shareholder would then have lost about $80,000 in the venture (about $1.3 million in current dollars). Referring to Zilboorg's possible role in advising Ingersoll and participating in the management of *PM* at this time, Jack Alexander observed that some of the original stockholders had made Zilboorg their "personal devil and talk of him as if he were a Svengali" (103). Field was characterized as "either a naive good guy mixed up with odd people or a brainwashed victim of Comrade Gregory Zilboorg."

Mr. "X"

In December 1940, Dr. Zilboorg began treating a patient, referred to as "Mr. X" in published accounts and variously described as a writer for *PM* or as a publicist connected in some way with the paper. There seems little doubt that Zilboorg's connection with *PM* led to the patient's selection of Zilboorg for his treatment. Because Mr. X was seen five times a week using free association and dream analysis (Levy Memorandum, 1), it is reasonable to assume that the patient believed he was in psychoanalysis with Zilboorg.

Seeing Zilboorg for only a few months, from December 1940 through part of April 1941, Mr. X came to believe that the analyst was exploitive. Mr. X claimed that Zilboorg asked him for special favors related to the patient's position, such as getting for Zilboorg second row tickets to a Joe Lewis prize fight, getting a radio from a manufacturer that Mr. X represented, and obtaining special film developing tanks. While this was going on, *PM*'s prospects were in doubt despite Field's financial rescue, and Mr. X was concerned about his own financial future in the face of the possible loss of other accounts. Finally, in addition to Mr. X's psychoanalytic sessions, Zilboorg offered to act as a business consultant to his patient for an additional fee of $5,000 ($80,000 in current dollars) for the following year. Zilboorg also requested that Mr. X pay him the full year's fee in advance for this advice because, Mr. X testified, Zilboorg told him he was short of cash and needed the money immediately to pay his taxes. Mr. X partly complied with that request by giving Zilboorg $1,000 in cash as a first payment on the $5,000. Mr. X then became alarmed by Zilboorg's conduct and asked a friend for advice. As a consequence of this advice, Mr. X broke off his treatment with Zilboorg and contacted Franz Alexander in Chicago. Alexander, who had been Zilboorg's analyst, advised Mr. X to write to Zilboorg requesting a refund of the $1,000. Alexander also suggested that Mr. X see a different New York psychoanalyst to continue his treatment.

Franz Alexander

As we discussed in chapter 1, Hungarian-born Franz Alexander (1891–1964) was one of the most influential early psychoanalysts. The first student at the Berlin Institute for Psychoanalysis, he was awarded a prize by Freud for the best clinical essay published in 1921. With his former student Hugo Staub, Alexander published in 1929 the first psychoanalytic study of criminology, *The Criminal, the Judge and the Public*, which was translated into English by Gregory Zilboorg. Alexander remained director of the renowned Chicago Institute for

Psychoanalysis for 25 years. In 1931 he became the first professor of psychoanalysis at the University of Chicago, making him the first professor of psychoanalysis in the United States (Schechter, 78). Martin Grotjahn observed in 1966 that whereas Freud disturbed the sleep of the world, the controversial Alexander "disturbed the sleep of the psychiatrists and psychoanalysts. This is not easily forgiven" (390).

Professional Charges and a "Confession"

Alexander, clearly dismayed by Mr. X's charges against Zilboorg, also contacted the New York Psychoanalytic Society, and it was agreed that he and Dr. David Levy of the New York Society would meet with Zilboorg at the coming meeting of the American Psychoanalytic Association in Richmond in May 1941 to discuss Mr. X's accusations. At that meeting, Levy and Alexander confronted Zilboorg with Mr. X's accusations. Zilboorg's response, according to Levy and Alexander, was a confused mixture of agreement with and denial of the charges. Zilboorg admitted eventually that Mr. X's accusations were the "substantial truth." Alexander and Levy considered that statement to be Zilboorg's "confession" to the charges. Hopeful that the matter could be resolved on the spot with no publicity, Levy and Alexander offered to drop any further action on two conditions: first, that Zilboorg resign from all administrative positions at the New York Psychoanalytic Society and Institute; and second, that he reenter a personal psychoanalysis so that he could better understand and avoid in the future what they believed was "unprofessional conduct." Zilboorg agreed to both demands.

To understand the implications of what Alexander and Levy had demanded of Zilboorg, it is important to realize the enormous struggle that was at the time taking place in the New York Psychoanalytic

Society. The storm clouds of that struggle had gathered throughout the 1930s as immigrant European psychoanalysts, mostly men of Jewish origin, relocated to New York to escape the advance of Nazism in Europe. Although there were undoubtedly other background issues relating to the economics of practice and access to psychoanalytic patients in that pre-war era, the manifest or surface conflict had to do with the Institute's training program. The dispute focused on whether the program would teach a strict "Freudian" version of psychoanalysis, emphasizing unconscious fantasy as a reflection of largely sexual conflicts, or whether other points of view, including an examination of the cultural forces that contribute to neuroses, would be taught as well. The debate was so heated that it eventually led to major defections from the Society and Institute. Significantly, Zilboorg, as chair of the powerful Education Committee of the Institute, was at that point in his career a major proponent of the classical view, while Levy had a leadership role among the "culturalists."

An even more pointed controversy within the New York Society and Institute was the inclination of a minority of the members to raise doubts about Freud's "libido theory." The libido theory, which Freud distinguished from his "clinical theory" (a body of ideas about actual patients and their treatment) and which he called part of his "metapsychology," an attempt to tie the mind to the body, had taken on the aura of a near-religious belief system among the conservative members. Libido theory postulated "psychic energy" that was invested in different parts of the body during infantile development leading to variations in personality development. Expressing doubts about the theory was near heresy to the theory's adherents. Among the doubters were Abram Kardiner, David Levy and John A. P. Millet. Kardiner notes in *My Analysis with Freud* that the creator of psychoanalysis never used libido theory in Kardiner's own analysis (69). Freud entrusted

Helene Deutsch to travel to Berlin in 1924 to evaluate the libido theory innovations being made by Karl Abraham, and when Kardiner asked Freud what he thought of the new Berlin technique, he was told, "I do not know, and I am not ready to give any opinion about it" (83). Deutsch returned with a positive evaluation, but Kardiner never tells us whether Freud reached a decision. It's clear, though, that Kardiner had no use for the libido theory—or for other aspects of psychoanalytic theory that were inaccessible to empirical investigation.

Zilboorg, who had earlier been in some difficulty within the Institute and in fact had temporarily been suspended from teaching, was able to recover his standing by developing an allegiance to the libido theory. Just as he had first become a Quaker and then a Roman Catholic, he became a libido theory zealot. In the words of a former student, Zilboorg "drilled into us his newly found enthusiasm for the libido theory, the successive stages of libidinal organization, the Oedipus complex, repression, and the theory of instincts" (Millet, 556). Levy himself claimed that he was not so much a "culturalist" as a critic of the New York Psychoanalytic Society's refusal to open up its range of courses to allow presentation of such views. As chair, Zilboorg had become "particularly indignant at anyone who criticized his integrity or that of the committee" (Frosch, 1052).

Investigating Mr. X's Charges

Upon their return to New York from the Richmond meeting, Levy realized that Zilboorg had no intention to follow through on the agreed upon penalty. Levy, therefore, filed a complaint against Zilboorg on behalf of the patient. The Board of Directors of the New York Psychoanalytic Society believed it had no choice under the bylaws but to investigate these serious charges. In what must have been an extremely costly endeavor, the Board held a series of five formal hearings sessions between October and December 1941 during which Zilboorg, Levy and the Board were each represented by a total of up to seven lawyers, one lawyer for the Board and at times three lawyers each for Levy and Zilboorg. The Board's investigation of Zilboorg was unprecedented. Never before in the history of the New York Psychoanalytic Society had it considered disciplining one of its own members. A stenographer recorded testimony that generated a transcript 752 pages long. The meetings were held in the evenings, some lasting from 8 p.m. until 3 a.m. The testimony came from, among others, the patient, Zilboorg, Zilboorg's secretary, and Levy. Much of the hearing time was taken up by verbal jousting among the lawyers in disputes as to what evidentiary rules would apply to these high stakes but obviously non-judicial proceedings. We are grateful to Nellie Thompson, PhD, research psychoanalyst and curator of the A.A. Brill Library, New York Psychoanalytic Society & Institute, for providing us with a copy of the transcript of the special meetings. Some of the transcript appears in Mark Leffert's article, from which we have quoted, as well as in John Frosch's article "The New York Psychoanalytic Civil War" published in the *Journal of the American Psychoanalytic Association* in 1991.

The First Hearing Session. Friday Evening, October 31, 1941

With the attack on Pearl Harbor only five weeks away, a tempest was developing in the New York Psychoanalytic Institute. The first thunderclap took place in the form of the opening hearing on the evening of Friday, October 31. Present were the nine members of the

Board of Directors of the New York Psychoanalytic Society; their lawyer, who chaired the hearing; the patient and his two lawyers; Franz Alexander from Chicago and David M. Levy, a member of the Society and also at that time the President of the American Psychoanalytic Association; two lawyers representing Alexander and Levy; Zilboorg and his two lawyers; and a court reporter.

The lead lawyer representing Levy and Alexander was Murray C. Bernays. Born Murray Cohen in Russia in 1894, Bernays immigrated to the United States with his parents. He graduated from Harvard College and was attending Columbia Law School in 1917 when he married Hella Bernays, a niece of Sigmund Freud and the daughter of Freud's sister Anna. In an unusual twist, shortly after the marriage he had his last name legally changed to Bernays. When the couple divorced in 1924, after having two sons, he retained the Bernays name, thus continuing his link to the Freud family. ("Bridegroom Takes the Name of His Bride", "Murray Bernays, Lawyer, Dead; Set Nuremberg Trials Format").

The 8 p.m. hearing began with legal wrangling. Zilboorg's lawyer argued that the charges should be dismissed immediately due to the lack of a formal letter of complaint signed by a member of the Society, as required by the New York Psychoanalytic Society bylaws. The wrangling continued for two hours, at which point Zilboorg and his lawyers walked out of the hearing in protest (Special Meeting. 37). The taking of testimony finally began and continued for several hours. Each witness was placed under oath, giving the proceeding the aura of a trial. Mr. X, the patient and complainant, was the first to testify. He described himself as the highly successful head of a firm that had been failing due to his increasing alcohol use. He feared that as a result he would lose his business. He consulted Zilboorg, who recommended five times a week psychoanalysis. The agreed on fee was about $400 per session in current dollars. Zilboorg requested that Mr. X pay him weekly in cash on the basis of Zilboorg's claim that only in this way would the patient know he was paying for the analysis (55). Arrangements to pay for psychoanalysis in cash are sometimes for the purpose of evading taxes (Bateman and Holmes 210).

Mr. X admitted quickly in his testimony that he became attached to Zilboorg, felt dependent on him, and was in awe of the analyst while in his presence. Mr. X implied that he was pleased in the beginning to honor Zilboorg's requests for front row championship prize fight tickets, to which Mr. X had access, for a radio at wholesale cost and for Mr. X's wrist watch, which Zilboorg admired (50). Zilboorg would accept the watch, however, only if Mr. X provided a cordovan strap for it. After a couple months, Mr. X started to feel annoyed and exploited by Zilboorg's requests (56). Nonetheless, he continued to feel gratitude toward Zilboorg because the analyst made what Mr. X viewed as helpful suggestions for the promotion of *PM*, to which Mr. X served as a consultant. Zilboorg urged Mr. X to pass along his suggestions to Ralph Ingersoll, the editor of *PM*, thus communicating to one of his patients through another (56–57). Mr. X made clear in his testimony that although his business was successful at that time, he feared that his abuse of alcohol would hurt his work.

Finally, Zilboorg asked Mr. X how much he thought Zilboorg could earn per year if he were to work in Mr. X's profession. After Zilboorg named some higher figures, they both agreed that Zilboorg could be confident of earning $5,000 per year (about $80,000 in current dollars). Zilboorg then proposed that Mr. X should employ him at that rate for the next year to help Mr. X save his business while at the same time continuing the analysis (63). Zilboorg proposed that they could meet at a second hour each day, after his regular office hours, to discuss business matters. Mr. X suggested that he would need to discuss this proposal with his business associates before making such a commitment, but Zilboorg asked him, instead, to keep the arrangement confidential (69). The analyst also requested that Mr. X pay him the entire amount in cash so he would not have to pay taxes on the $5,000. He wanted Mr. X to pay all the money in advance, by March 1, because Zilboorg said he had a cash crunch and needed to pay his income taxes, due on March 15. Mr. X's confidence in Zilboorg was shaken; he felt that Zilboorg was burdening him with the analyst's own problems.

After Mr. X was excused from the stand, it was Alexander's turn to testify. He related how he and David Levy met with Zilboorg in Richmond, Virginia, as described above, as well as his meeting with Mr. X in Chicago. Alexander testified that he was stunned by Mr. X's story, but he was convinced, then and now, that the patient was neither psychotic nor bore a grudge against Zilboorg. Alexander asked Mr. X to return the next day to give additional details. After enlisting Levy's help, Alexander then felt compelled to confront Zilboorg with Mr. X's charges. "I don't know whether the method was good or not," Alexander testified, "but I can tell you the purposes. The main purpose was to prevent the repetition of such a thing, that Zilboorg should not repeat such an act again, whatever the act might be. That was the main purpose. The second was to save psychoanalysis if possible from an unnecessary scandal and save future patients from possible scandal. We discussed the thing in great detail. Third, to save Zilboorg as much as he can be save[d], that is, treat him constructively as that he might not do again anything which might involve him and the organization in difficulties" (128).

After Alexander was excused from the stand, it was Levy's turn. Under oath, he denied he was motivated by Institute politics, although he admitted that he had differences of opinion with Zilboorg. He flatly denied that Zilboorg had exhibited any evidence of being "shocked" at the Richmond meeting. Levy thought the meeting with Zilboorg had been polite and collegial; Zilboorg seemed to appreciate that Levy and Alexander sought to spare him from undue publicity by handling the matter in private. Finally, Levy said, Zilboorg had actually thanked him and Alexander for their consideration at the end of the meeting. Alexander stated that Mr. X's narrative during that evening's hearing was in almost every detail the story that Mr. X had related to him earlier in Chicago. The session ended at 2:30 a.m. following testimony from Alexander and Levy.

The Second Hearing Session. Friday Evening, November 28, 1941

A second hearing on the Zilboorg matter was scheduled, again for a Friday evening, this time at 7:30 PM, probably because the first hearing had ended so late. This session, however, stretched into the small hours of Saturday, adjourning at 3 a.m. Again there were present ten members of the Board of Directors, the Board's lawyer, plus Levy and Zilboorg, each accompanied by two lawyers. Zilboorg and his lawyers had walked out of the first session, but they decided to attend the second session, after having read the transcript of the earlier session, so that Zilboorg would have a chance to respond to the Levy-Alexander account.

After several errors in the transcript of the previous hearing were corrected, the business of the hearing resumed with Dr. Levy being cross-examined by Dr. Zilboorg's lawyer. Overall, the lawyer's strategy was to discredit Dr. Levy by pointing out minor inconsistencies in his memory of events, as well as to demonstrate that Levy had a political motive, which Levy denied, for trying to discredit Zilboorg (194). Rather than accepting the Levy-Alexander claim that their meeting with Zilboorg in Richmond was intended to resolve the matter without publicity, thus sparing Zilboorg, the Society and the profession from embarrassment, Zilboorg's lawyer attempted to characterize their actions as "vigilante justice" by imposing their own penalty on Zilboorg, a punishment that in the lawyer's view could be not supported by the bylaws of the Society. Zilboorg's lawyer also attempted to discredit and disqualify Alexander on the grounds that most analysts would take the view that an analyst should not "testify against" a former analysand (224).

One of the oddest moments of the testimony was when Levy was asked several hypothetical questions about bringing up an analyst for disciplinary action. "Did you know," Levy was asked, "that Dr. Freud shook hands with the patient when he entered the room and when he left the room?" "Yes," Levy replied. "Do you feel that shaking hands may set up a moral transference? Do you think that shaking hands might lead to a transference that would lead the analyst to get something out of the patient that he otherwise would not get?" Levy replied again with a one-word answer: "No" (245).

The hearing then turned to Zilboorg, who was invited to make a statement. He began by acknowledging that he received the gifts mentioned from the patient. Zilboorg then made a provocative comment: he was willing to talk as doctor to doctor, and as analyst to analyst, but he did not want to be interrupted by the lawyers in attendance. "I do not like lawyers, and this includes my lawyer, too. They are here merely to be tolerated and as guides accepted in legal form" (250–251). After conceding he accepted gifts from his patient, Zilboorg thought his remarks would be sufficient, apparently hoping that the matter would then be dropped. But being invited to go on, he launched into a lengthy personal statement, in turn submissive, sarcastic, aggressive and self-justifying.

Zilboorg's appeals to the Board had a highly dramatic quality; he portrayed himself as the victim not only of the two analysts but also of the patient. "How can you listen to these accusations against me? You, my colleagues, you alone can understand me. You know how ethical I am, how painstaking in my conduct. How they have vilified me. They reduced me to tears. They took advantage of my weakness, my cowardice. They put me on the rack. They forced me to accept degrading terms. They conspired against me. How can you believe them? It is all a malicious plot. I am completely innocent." (Frosch cites this passage [1053], but we are unable to locate it in our copy of the transcripts of the Special Meetings.)

The main thrust of Zilboorg's argument was that he had seen the patient only 30 times between the start of the relationship on December 17, 1940 and their last appointment on February 17, 1941. He portrayed the patient as a disturbed alcoholic who was extremely unreliable, missed numerous appointments, and appeared at some appointments either with a severe hangover or under the influence of alcohol. Zilboorg added that the patient was subject to fugue states or memory lapses. Zilboorg readily admitted his passion for prizefights and even offered his own psychoanalytic interpretation of his enjoyment of the sport. "You will remember how the Educational Committee or the Board of Directors once agreed to interrupt a meeting at ten o'clock, because I wanted to hear the broadcast of a prize fight, and one time we ended the session in Dr. Kubie's home to listen to a similar broadcast. That is my sublimation of my murderous instinct" (284). A few moments later, Zilboorg offered a psychoanalytic interpretation of Mr. X's need to give gifts. "It is my opinion that he gave me the thousand dollars as an unconscious, impulsive, spontaneous way to homosexual ejaculation" (302). The interpretation was so preposterous that it remained unchallenged by any of the speechless lawyers or psychoanalysts present. Zilboorg denied that Mr. X was in psychoanalysis and contradicted the patient's assertion that he had some sessions while lying on the analytic couch. In general, Zilboorg's portrayal of the patient stood in stark contrast to the impressions gained by Levy and Alexander and seemed inconsistent with the patient's self-presentation in the first hearing.

After attempting to undercut Mr. X's reliability and integrity, Zilboorg then sought to do the same with his two accusers, Alexander and Levy. Recalling Alexander's statement in Chicago, "Gregory, you are under a great emotional strain," Zilboorg testified that he regarded the remark as "strange": "I know Alexander so well and I know some of the weaknesses of Alexander, and he knows that I know, and I spent with him so many times when he exposed his personality in so many ways to me, that he should ask me to come to him for analysis was queer" (311). Zilboorg added that Alexander told people whom he disliked that they were "very sick." Zilboorg believed that Alexander, Levy and a third unnamed psychoanalyst ("accomplices") had plotted in Richmond to "frame" him (316, 324). Only at a later hearing did Zilboorg identify the third analyst as Abram Kardiner (626).

Zilboorg then stated that Alexander had a grudge against him because he had raised objections to Alexander's foreword to a book. In a long, rambling diatribe against a "gentleman whose name you all know" but who is a "psychoanalytic quack" engaged in "wild analysis," Zilboorg referred to a "psychoanalytical novel" written by this person for whom Alexander inexplicably wrote a ten-page foreword to the second edition. Zilboorg never mentioned the author's name, but he referred to the novel's title: *The Spectacle of a Man*. It's never clear why Zilboorg detested the novel or its author, John Coignard. There's nothing in the novel, first published in 1937 and then reprinted in 1941, or in Alexander's foreword, that explains Zilboorg's strange animus, despite his testimony that *The Spectacle of a Man* is a "spectacle of Alexander indeed" (315).

Zilboorg next addressed in his testimony the consistency of Mr. X's story to Alexander. One of the "outstanding symptoms of paranoia," Zilboorg told the board members, is "consistency," and the "basis of consistency is not sufficient to establish the truth" (320). We don't know how the board members felt about Zilboorg's observation, but some of them may have noticed the consistency of his own hostility toward Alexander, as was evident in his next statement. After disclosing in Richmond the consistency of Mr. X's story, "Alexander looked me straight in the eyes and smiled. I would rather not discuss reasons, but whenever Alexander is in his best sadistic form he smiles. I saw it on many occasions" (320).

Zilboorg's expressions of hostility toward his accusers continued for the rest of the hearing. "I never considered Levy friendly to me; my impression was that he was quite hostile to me because he always supported the various dissident doctors whom I opposed" (326). Describing Levy's later attempt to shake hands with him, which others might interpret as a gesture of friendship, Zilboorg remarked, "I couldn't; I couldn't thank the gentleman for turning the knife in my heart" (332). He concluded his testimony, as the clock approached 3 a.m., with the words, "I consider that I was held up, framed-up, by a pernicious man whom I consider sick, and another man who is as honest as you can make them, but almost as foolish in his moral sadism as possible—I mean Levy" (337). At the end of the testimony, an apparent Board supporter of Zilboorg suggested that the hearings should end there and then, but the Board in a brief executive session decided to have another hearing in which Zilboorg could be cross-examined by Levy's lawyer, Murray Bernays.

The Third Hearing Session. Friday Evening, December 12, 1941

The third session heard testimony from Bertram Lewin, to whom Alexander had referred Mr. X for additional treatment after the patient's consultation with Alexander. According to Lewin, he saw the patient starting in May 1941 for a total of 41 psychoanalytic sessions (out of 61 scheduled) from May until the patient ended the analysis in September 1941. Lewin confirmed Zilboorg's observations that the patient was seriously alcoholic, having arrived for some sessions with a severe hangover, and having been unreliable in keeping appointments. On the other hand, Lewin did not confirm that the patient was schizophrenic or otherwise delusional. On his attorney's advice, Lewin did not directly answer questions as to the patient's supposed propensity for violence. Lewin saw no evidence of "blocking" or "negativism" (388). He felt that the patient formed a strong attachment to him; significantly, the patient never offered him a gift (376). Lewin treated the patient using strict ("artis legis") psychoanalytic technique (361) that was his custom with every patient. Lewin also disclosed that he had several phone conversations with Zilboorg about the patient during the treatment. In answer to a direct question from Zilboorg as to whether he was seeing the patient, Lewin lied and said he was not. This "white lie" was justified, Lewin stated, on the grounds that he was acting as the patient wished, that is, not disclosing to Zilboorg that Mr. X was seeing another analyst. The patient failed to appear for an appointment scheduled for August 1, the last appointment before Lewin's vacation, leaving him uncertain about Mr. X's intention to continue the analysis on the next appointment date, September 3. The patient finally reappeared for a single session on September 15, after which he wrote a note to Lewin ending the treatment.

Zilboorg, rather than his lawyer, then conducted a cross-examination of Lewin. Zilboorg attempted to make certain statements about the patient in the guise of questions for Lewin, but these questions were cut off by the Board lawyer. Aside from the fact that Lewin agreed with Zilboorg's statement that Lewin had described the patient as occasionally violent, the cross- examination revealed little.

The second and last witness of the evening was heard in what was significantly more revealing testimony. Virginia Schoales, the assistant to

Ralph Ingersoll, the publisher of *PM*, offered a picture of a confused and conflicted set of relationships among Ingersoll and Mr. X, both of whom were Zilboorg's patients, Zilboorg, and herself. According to Schoales' testimony, Mr. X, the head of a successful public relations firm, worked as a publicist for *PM*, but in that role he failed to satisfy Ingersoll, largely as a result of worsening alcoholism. Ingersoll suggested that Mr. X see Zilboorg, and Mr. X complied. Schoales was not surprised that Mr. X had given gifts to Zilboorg because she had observed that Mr. X habitually pressed gifts on other people as well. Mr. X mentioned his analysis with Zilboorg to her on several occasions, but his feeling about the analysis seemed to vary from hope and idealization, on the one hand, to hopelessness and futility, on the other. Finally, on February 24, Ingersoll "fired" Mr. X, who then demanded that *PM* pay him $5,000 to terminate his contract.

Schoales reported that Mr. X told her that Zilboorg had threatened to sue Alexander and Levy (499), to whom Mr. X felt gratitude, for libel after the Richmond meeting. She also mentioned that Mr. X had given a written statement of the facts to Levy's lawyer to support their defense in the event that such a suit actually occurred. Mr. X's gratitude soon turned to anger, however, when he realized that his statement to Levy was being used to bring charges against Zilboorg at the New York Psychoanalytic Society. Feeling aggrieved, Mr. X had agreed only reluctantly to testify. At times he said that he'd like to shut down his business and work permanently for *PM*; at other times he complained that he had to turn down potential clients whose politics conflicted with *PM*'s pro-labor stance. Finally, Zilboorg had told Schoales his version of the facts behind the charges since Ingersoll, his other patient, was out of the country and would be returning when Zilboorg himself would be out of the country. Zilboorg was anxious that Ingersoll hear his version first because he anticipated that Ingersoll would be upset when he heard Mr. X's claims. The hearing adjourned at 1 a.m.

Franz Alexander's Statement

Back in Chicago, Alexander received a request from the Board to attend its next session so he could be questioned further. Instead he sent a letter (Alexander to Board, December 16, 1941), revealing that he did not wish to testify further because he could not add to his earlier testimony. Having read Zilboorg's earlier testimony and clearly stung by his former analysand's accusation of bearing malice toward him, Alexander wrote that he saw no point in trying to defend himself against the "obviously irrational accusations of a desperate man who tries to discredit the witnesses with ad personam arguments" (1). Alexander implied that in retrospect he had gone too far in trying to help Zilboorg by keeping the entire matter confidential and by trying to work out an agreement among himself, Levy, and Zilboorg. He described Zilboorg's account of the Richmond meeting as a "mendacious" distortion of what actually took place. Alexander believed that he and Levy were trying to save Zilboorg for the profession while at the same time protecting the reputation of the New York Psychoanalytic Society and the profession as a whole. Reflecting on the matter prior to the Richmond meeting, Alexander recognized that he bore a great responsibility. "It became clearer and clearer to me that the very foundations of psychoanalytic practice are threatened if patients are not fully protected in their wholly dependent and helpless attitude toward their analyst" (2). He dismissed Zilboorg's objection to writing the foreword to *The Spectacle of a Man* as "too fantastic and infantile an idea to be considered by any sensible person" (4).

Alexander also wrote an article, "The Qualifications of a Psychoanalyst," which he enclosed with his statement. Read at the Richmond meeting as a paper, the article contained a section on integrity. "We must admit that there are few professions which give more opportunity for the exploitation of other people's weakness than psychoanalysis. The patient developing a transference regresses to the helpless attitude which the little child has towards his parents. . . ." Freud pointed out the sexual temptation. Only in extremely neurotic analysts is this a real danger. Much more common is the financial temptation which can be so well supported by self-deceptive rationalizations" ("The Qualifications of a Psychoanalyst" 5–6). Despite the statement, the Board still requested that Alexander attend the December 19 hearing in New York, which he did accompanied by his Chicago lawyer.

The Fourth Hearing Session (Part 1). Friday Evening, December 19, 1941

The fourth hearing session convened at 8 p.m. with even more people present. Added to those who attended the previous session were Alexander, his Chicago lawyer, and Karl Menninger, the incoming President of the American Psychoanalytic Association—all in all a total of 14 psychoanalysts and six attorneys. The session began with more legal wrangling and then proceeded with Zilboorg's being called to testify further. In a long soliloquy, after insisting on commenting on the letter submitted by Alexander, Zilboorg continued his attacks on his former analyst, on Levy, and on Mr. X. Zilboorg's answers to specific question about the alleged $5,000 proposal and the actual $1,000 payment were again a mixture of sarcasm, denial, and claims of persecution by Alexander. "He wanted to eunichize me professionally, and then make a good professional man out of me. A cruel person—he says I make him out to be a cruel person who wants to harm me. I am not making him out a cruel person who wants to harm me. I am returning the compliment. He is very sick, and he hates to see a son rise one hair above his father" (535).

There are moments in the testimony when Zilboorg sounds like a character in *Crime and Punishment* or *The Brothers Karamazov*. Asked to refrain from repeating himself because of time constraints, he responded wearily that he had been struggling with these accusations for the last nine months, adding, "I was bringing in matters which have nothing to do with matters by which Alexander tried to blacken his personality. I made a slip of the tongue. He tried to blacken my character; I believe that" (538). Zilboorg then referred ominously to a scandal at the Chicago Psychoanalytic Institute that Alexander had tried to contain, a scandal that he "wished on the New York Society, of which we have been suffering for the past three years" (540). During these moments Zilboorg implied that he would reveal if necessary damning information about Alexander's character. Many of Zilboorg's replies to questions were a critique of the question as opposed to an answer. He was asked more than once to avoid repetition of his earlier testimony. Zilboorg continued to deny that he had confessed to anything at the Richmond meeting with Alexander and Levy. The questioning went on for four and a half hours, at which point it was interrupted to allow Menninger to address the Board.

Karl Menninger

After explaining that he had requested the privilege of addressing the Board, and pointing out with obvious irritation that he had been kept waiting outside the hearing room for four and a half hours, Menninger chastised all concerned in the proceeding on the grounds that what was taking place, word of which clearly had gotten around both within psychoanalytic circles and in gossip among patients and others interested in the field, was more harmful to the profession than any act being considered in the hearing. "I understand that Dr. Zilboorg is accused of having behaved in such a way as to hurt psychoanalysis. I want to assure you that nothing could hurt psychoanalysis like the prolongation of this inquiry and the creation of the criticism that it is causing" (614). Menninger urged that the proceeding be terminated. He then grandiosely claimed that since this appeared to be a personal squabble between Zilboorg, on the one hand, and Alexander and Levy, on the other, he would be able to settle the matter quickly if he was allowed to meet privately with the three of them. "You can settle it in five minutes, I believe, if you will let me talk to Dr. Levy and Dr. Alexander, to whom I have spoken a few minutes, and to Dr. Zilboorg, if you will let me talk to these men and get the damn lawyers out of this room, I can settle this thing, and I can settle it in a way that will be satisfactory to the Board, I believe, because this, after all, is our problem" (616). (Is this reminiscent, we cannot help wondering, of the underlying meaning of the word *omertà* as used within La Cosa Nostra?)

These comments were given serious consideration until Levy's lawyer pointed out that Levy was not available, having been called to Washington in connection with the emergency war mobilization taking place at that time. In response to the December 7 attack on Pearl Harbor, the United States had declared war on Japan one day later, and on December 11 the United States had responded to declarations from Germany and Italy by declaring war on those two countries as well. The anxiety present throughout the country must have been felt within the hearings as well. This likely accounts for much of the increasing testiness and contentiousness of those who gave testimony, as the transcript of the hearings demonstrates. Annoyed by a member's statement that it was presumptuous for Menninger to believe that the Board of Directors was motivated by "petty animosities," Menninger left the witness stand but not before darkly declaring that he had defended "more than one of the men in this room from similar things. I want to repeat that, because I think it is significant" (623). In other words, Menninger implied, those in psychoanalytic glass houses shouldn't throw stones. With no positive response to his pleas, Menninger was excused and left the hearing.

Menninger sent Adolf Stern, a Board member, a letter on December 30, 1941 expressing dismay over the Zilboorg hearings. "Because I feel that such things are extremely harmful to psychoanalysis, I had hoped to use my personal and official influence to bring this to a speedy conclusion. I was sorry not to have been able to convince the executive committee of the possibility of doing this. I must say that I deeply deplore the handling of the complaints of a patient lodged with the officials of the New York Society, and in doing so I do not wish to reflect in any way upon the sincerity and integrity of any of the members" (Menninger 353). Menninger repeated his statement, made during the hearings, that "This is not, in my opinion, an appropriate way to deal with such complaints" (353), though he never suggested a better way of dealing with complaints of ethical violations.

Menninger's desire to protect psychoanalysis may have been commendable, but in urging a cover-up of serious allegations against a prominent analyst, he failed to grasp the historic importance of the case. The Board's investigation of Zilboorg was not about a "personal squabble" but an attempt to protect a patient from an unscrupulous analyst. How could Menninger expect psychoanalysis to remain an honorable profession if grave allegations of wrongdoing were cavalierly dismissed? How could he expect to avoid legal controversy and outside interference if psychoanalysis did not discipline its own members? Menninger failed to realize that gossip begets gossip when covered in a cloak of silence. He also failed to realize that patients must be protected from unprofessional analysts. One of the most disturbing aspects of the Jules Masserman scandal, as we discussed earlier, was the mental health community's refusal to comment on much less censure the actions of one of its most powerful leaders. Part of this refusal, as Kerry Novick suggested to us (personal communication, January 20 2016), involves the refusal to deidealize analytic forefathers.

After Menninger's departure, Alexander was then called to testify over the objections of Zilboorg's lawyer. Under oath, Alexander was asked a single question by his own lawyer: Were all the statements in the letter he had submitted to the Board in the hope of not testifying true? He answered in the affirmative (629). Zilboorg had instructed his lawyer not to question Alexander further, so he was then dismissed. With everyone exhausted, the hearing was adjourned at 2 a.m. Saturday morning.

The Fourth Hearing Session (Part 2). Sunday Afternoon, December 19, 1941. Zilboorg Is Cross-examined.

The hearing reconvened on Sunday afternoon of the same weekend with Zilboorg as a witness being cross-examined by Bernays. The Committee deemed out of order questions asked by Levy's lawyers as to whether Zilboorg had engaged in a business relationship with other patients, such as Ralph Ingersoll. Another question deemed out of order was Zilboorg's involvement with *PM*. This question could have established the plausibility of Mr. X's charge that Zilboorg had offered to serve as a business consultant to him in exchange for a $5,000 annual fee. In fact, information that Zilboorg was a shareholder in Publications Research, Inc. during Ingersoll's analysis, and the likelihood that, as rumored, he had been involved with Ingersoll and others in the planning of *PM*, was never entered into the hearing. The truth was that Zilboorg was already listed in public records among the owners of *PM* through his partial ownership of Publications Research, Inc. (Roth, Statement of Ownership). After the near bankruptcy of *PM* at the end of its first three months of publication, and Marshall Field's decision to buy out the other shareholders, Publications Research, Inc. had become a partial owner of *PM* as part of its refunding. The owners of Publications Research, Inc. thus had become partial owners of *PM* itself and were so listed in the paper's ownership statement (Ingersoll).

Two Memoranda

The Levy Memorandum

At the conclusion of the hearings, the lawyers for both parties, Zilboorg and Levy, submitted extensive summary memoranda to the Board. Part I of the Levy memorandum was a 50-page presentation of the Levy-Alexander version of the Richmond story. The memorandum reiterated Zilboorg's "confession" and argued that the discussion that had taken place in Richmond among the three men was neither hurried nor pressured. Zilboorg had admitted to all the points in the accusations, the memorandum continued, and during the two-and-a-half hour meeting he was clear-headed and completely rational. In essence, the Board's decision depended on who was more trustworthy about the Richmond meeting, Levy and Alexander, or Zilboorg? The Levy-Alexander memorandum attacked Zilboorg's portrayal of Alexander as in essence a "perjurious conspirator," as being an "offense against common sense" (14). Showing that Levy and Alexander had little to gain by distorting the facts while Zilboorg had a great deal to lose by admitting to their account, the memorandum concluded, "Both stories cannot be true. The man-on-the-street would have no trouble in determining which to believe" (16).

Levy's lawyers appended to their memorandum a "Part II" titled "Personal Statement, and Some Psychological Observations concerning Dr. Zilboorg's Testimony, Prepared by Dr. Levy" (51-66). Admitting that he, Levy, actually did "have a stake in the matter," the memorandum argued that Levy's account of what took place at the Richmond meeting must nonetheless be considered in the light of Zilboorg's highly emotive and colorful denials during the hearings. The memorandum then went on to pick apart Zilboorg's contention that Levy and Alexander had cooked up a "plot" against Zilboorg. It was absurd to believe, the memorandum continued, that his former analyst, Alexander, had set out "to destroy him." In a footnote, the memorandum affirmed that Levy had acted with the minority group within the Institute even when he disagreed with the minority position because he considered the important issue to be "academic freedom" as opposed to undue "orthodoxy" (58). The Levy Memorandum ends with a rhetorical flourish. "Dr. Zilboorg used cajolery. He complimented the attorney for the Board. He represented the members of the Board as his colleagues who alone could understand. At times he sobbed and pleaded. At other times he was sarcastic and vituperative. He used all the methods of the theatre. These were all devices to stir up the emotions of his audience and distract their attention from the issue." (66).

The Zilboorg Memorandum

On the other side, Zilboorg's lawyers submitted a memorandum that was much more aggressive and legalistic, conveying a clear impression that legal action (presumably a lawsuit) might ensue should the matter be decided against Zilboorg. They argued, first, that the New York Psychoanalytic Society and its Board had no jurisdiction to reprimand Zilboorg based on the particular reading by Zilboorg's lawyers of the Society's bylaws. Second, Zilboorg's lawyers asserted that although he had denied having proposed to enter into a business arrangement with the patient, and also denied the improper receipt of any gifts, even if he had committed these acts, the Society had no written code prohibiting them. His lawyers pointed out, moreover, that physicians in other fields do enter into such interactions with patients. Zilboorg conceded that the Society might consider such acts as unprofessional conduct by a psychoanalyst; nevertheless, the Society would need to adopt a code stating the unprofessional acts for which an analyst could be sanctioned. To punish Zilboorg in this situation, his lawyers claimed, would be equivalent to a "bill of attainder" [*sic*], i.e., to punish a member under a law created after the fact. Zilboorg's lawyers then added that he denied he was "psychoanalyzing" the patient, and that Levy and Alexander had failed to prove the contrary. Because the Society existed to further *psychoanalysis*, Zilboorg's treatment of the patient, presumably psychotherapy, was not within the purview of the Society. Zilboorg was in their view no more accountable to the Society for his medical non-psychoanalytic psychotherapy practices than he would be accountable for treatment he rendered to the patient for a "common cold."

Zilboorg's lawyers then repeated his contention that Mr. X was an alcoholic and untrustworthy; therefore, his testimony could not be considered reliable. They concluded with the claim that Zilboorg had not had a fair hearing based on the technicality that the complaint to the Board had been submitted by Levy, not by the patient: Mr. X. had stated through his lawyer that he did not wish to file a complaint against Zilboorg. Levy, on the other hand, denied being the complainant since he had received the complaint directly from Mr. X's lawyers. Without a named complainant, Zilboorg's lawyers argued, the Board could not proceed against him.

The Board Renders a (Non-Binding) Verdict

Upon the conclusion of the hearings, and a review of the extensive memoranda submitted by lawyers representing both sides, the ten member Board voted by seven to three in favor of a motion to recommend to the Society that it adopt a resolution of reprimand against Zilboorg. Each faction of the Board submitted to the Society membership a six or seven page report explaining its position. These reports were read aloud at a special meeting of the Society in January 1942. Zilboorg declined to speak on his own behalf other than to state that he wished to renew all the objections stated in the hearings and in his lawyers' memorandum. He also pointed out that any action against him by the membership would be "illegal."

Phyllis Greenacre, a Board member, was convinced that the charges against Zilboorg were true, since she was the friend of a fellow analyst who had a sexual relationship with him during her training analysis with Zilboorg. Greenacre recalled during an interview decades after the event that her friend had spoken in defense of Zilboorg at the meeting. She attributed her friend's unexpected behavior to unanalyzed positive "transference" (Scull, 290-291). Greenacre's years-later revelation of Zilboorg's additional sexual boundary violation is not the only example of such charges against him in addition to his misconduct with Kay Swift. Wilhelm Reich, as part of an attempt to defend himself against charges of sexual misconduct, compiled "a long list of alleged psychoanalytic indiscretions (whether it is accurate or not is impossible to tell)," which included this item: "Zilboorg slept with Elizabeth Badgeley, also a patient" (Turner 465-466, n.71).

The Members of the Society Decide the Issue

The actual decision of the Society stemming from the charges against Zilboorg would have to be made at a meeting of the members of the New York Psychoanalytic Society. The minutes of that March 3, 1942 meeting convey the impression to us that the membership's position on the issue had been established prior to the meeting. Abram Kardiner, a member of the same dissident group as Levy, walked out of the meeting before the ballots were distributed. "What went on behind the scenes, I do not know," Kardiner stated in his *Reminiscences*, "only I do know this: it was at this trial, and when I saw what happened in the end, this was the last time I set foot into the New York Psychoanalytic Society. This was no place for me, for the simple reason that it was obviously being operated as a racket" (185). Following discussion of a motion to reprimand Zilboorg, a vote was taken. Sixteen members of the society voted in favor of reprimand, but 39 voted against, thereby exonerating Zilboorg. A member then moved that a vote of sympathy to Dr. Zilboorg should be taken, to which there was no objection. The Society extended its sympathy to Zilboorg by a unanimous vote.

Suing the New York Psychoanalytic Society?

Would Zilboorg have sued the New York Psychoanalytic Society if its members voted to reprimand him? If he threatened to sue Alexander and Levy, as Virginia Schoales reported, it's likely that he would have sued the entire organization or individual members who voted against him. Gabbard and Lester assert without providing documentation that Zilboorg in fact had threatened to sue the Society if the vote didn't go in his favor. "Presenting himself as a victim of vicious and predatory behavior by his colleagues, Zilboorg stirred considerable sympathy. When the issue came up before the full membership of the New York Psychoanalytic Association, Zilboorg threatened to sue every member of the organization who voted for his censure" (85). Nellie Thompson (personal communication, July 7, 2015) told us that she hasn't seen any evidence of such a threat by Zilboorg, though she admitted that the lack of evidence doesn't indicate the absence of a threat. Nor did she know whether Kubie's call for a secret ballot was motivated by the fear of a lawsuit against particular members. Even before this entire process was underway, the minutes of the June 20, 1941 special meeting of the Board of Directors refer to statements made by Levy and Mr. X regarding the Zilboorg case and add: "After discussion it was decided that special counsel be retained to advise the Board and the Society in connection with the matter." The motion, which was unanimously passed by the board, may simply imply that the Society was preparing to begin its investigation of a member's alleged misconduct, but it may also suggest that the Society had to protect itself from a possible later charge that it was conducting an illegal investigation.

At least one member later regretted his vote. Nellie Thompson (personal communication, July 7, 2015) observed to us that "while it was true that Kubie did support Zilboorg, I'm convinced that he later changed his mind about Zilboorg's guilt. In a letter written to Jacob Arlow many years later in which he recalls his long and close friendship with Bert Lewin (who did not support Zilboorg), he makes reference to a disagreement they had which, however, did not damage their relationship. He then writes that he now thinks Lewin was right in this matter."

One can only speculate how the New York Psychoanalytic Society would have voted if its members had additional information about Zilboorg's behavior. *Quite apart from his relationship with Mr. X*, Zilboorg's career reveals an astounding number of sexual and nonsexual boundary violations with the Warburgs, the betrayal of his patients' confidential self-disclosures in analysis, and involvement with his patients' personal and professional lives. Zilboorg was one of the earliest therapists to attempt to discredit a patient's testimony by stigmatizing the patient for having a mental illness, a strategy used by nearly every mental health professional involved in a case of criminal litigation or malpractice.

Zilboorg and Menninger

Zilboorg never acknowledged any wrongdoing either before or after the Society's vote. Nor did Menninger believe that the New York Psychoanalytic Society should have conducted the investigation. Menninger's letters to and from Zilboorg indicate that each saw the other as a trusted political ally. Zilboorg continued to portray himself as a victim. "They seem to have followed the advice of the Queen in *Alice in Wonderland*," he wrote to Menninger on January 6, 1942: "First sentence and verdict afterwards." Zilboorg then poured contempt on his fellow analysts. "If, as it undoubtedly will, the matter is brought up before the Society, the whole thing will speed through eighty mouths—many of whom are as good analysts as you and I are Chinese scholars" (355).

In a letter written to Menninger on January 23, 1942, Zilboorg puts the best spin on the case. "They, I understand, state that I did not exploit the patient, that I showed no bad faith, etc., but that as a result of a countertransference I committed technical errors which were to the detriment of the psychoanalytic movement and that therefore I am to be reprimanded" (356). In his March 11, 1942 letter, written a week after his official exoneration, Zilboorg describes Levy as a "moral sadist of the first order" and Alexander as a person who "committed an immoral act which is now a precedent and which is potentially and actually injurious to psychoanalysis." Zilboorg then invokes a Biblical analogy to characterize his situation. "To permit this precedent to stand without comment means to reverse the fundamental principles of psychoanalysis and guide the hand of Abraham in order to cut off Isaac's head more efficiently" (361). Zilboorg hints in the next paragraph about filing charges against Alexander. "I suppose there are many reasons why such countercharges against Alexander before the American [Psychoanalytic Association] might not be advisable. On the other hand, could such a thing be left alone, as if it never happened?" (361).

For his part, Menninger sought to defuse Zilboorg's anger. There is no need to adopt a resolution stating that it is unethical for an analyst to testify against a former analysand, Menninger wrote to Zilboorg a few days later: "in the first place, this is already an unwritten law which most of us would not think of violating; and, in the second place, it is too soon after the New York going-ons to do anything about it as it might be interpreted as having been engineered by you, which would make even some of your friends irritated, feeling that you were pursuing your victory; and, third, we already have enough trouble for this May meeting without adding this to it" (362). Menninger's reference to some of Zilboorg's friends being "irritated" was probably a veiled reference to himself!

Keepers of the Orthodoxy

Shortly after the vote was taken, Levy submitted his resignation from the New York Psychoanalytic Society. The immediate reason for his resignation, he wrote, was that he was "unable to stomach" the Society's refusal to take disciplinary actions against Zilboorg (Frosch, 1053). Kardiner was also outraged, and in a critique of his contemporaries that has proven prophetic, he complained about the rigid dogmatists who had stifled empirical research. "Attempts at innovation were

414

discouraged by those who had established themselves as Keepers of the Orthodoxy, who had a vested interest in maintaining their power and influence, and could only do so by freezing the field in its existing mold, thereby automatically disqualifying any innovation" (*My Analysis with Freud*, 121).

Momentous Consequences

It's conceivable that the outcome of the Zilboorg case had an unanticipated momentous effect on the future of psychoanalysis in the United States. Before the membership vote, a dissident group of analysts had contemplated leaving the New York Society for theoretical and academic reasons but had taken no action. After the membership vote, the dissident group made its fateful decision to form a new Society, as George E. Daniels observed in an article published in the *Bulletin of the Association for Psychoanalytic Medicine* in 1971–1972:

> The circumstance, however, that had as much as anything to do with separating off the group that later formed the Association for Psychoanalytic Medicine grew out of the investigation by a special committee of the New York Society of charges brought against one of its members for unprofessional behavior. The committee recommended censure of this member and the report came before a meeting of the full membership. Due to political maneuvering, the recommendation was defeated and the whole issue whitewashed. The disgust about this type of maneuvering was a symptom of the general dissatisfaction with and [*sic*] strongly political and pseudo-scientific attitude that prevailed at this time in the New York Psychoanalytic Society. This circumstance was responsible for

the elaborate machinery set up by the Constitution and By-Laws to deal with such contingencies.

There were no doubt additional reasons for the formation of the Columbia University Center for Psychoanalytic Training and Research, as Nellie Thompson (personal communication, July 7, 2015) has suggested to us, including the tensions between Sandor Rado (and his supporters) and the other members of the New York Psychoanalytic Society, as well as David Levy's adamant opposition to lay analysts. But we now see that the precipitating event behind the formation of the Columbia Institute was the New York Psychoanalytic Society's membership vote in favor of Zilboorg. As Kardiner remarked in his *Reminiscences*, "The trial of Zilboorg was also the signal that the right wing was definitely in the saddle, and then they began to really ride roughshod over Rado and myself and the rest of the characters who were making trouble for the psychoanalytic movement as a whole" (187).

Just two months after the Zilboorg vote, a meeting was held in Levy's apartment to organize the new Society that was to be called the "Association for Psychoanalytic Medicine." Ultimately, the formation of this new psychoanalytic society in New York led to the creation within Columbia University of a new institute for training psychoanalysts. The following year the members of the new association sent a letter to the president of the New York Psychoanalytic Society that expressed their "distaste for further participation in the affairs of the Society" and their intention to "withdraw from its activities though not to resign from it" (Daniels). With the departure of the dissidents, the New York Psychoanalytic Society and Institute fell under the complete control of the strict "Freudian" forces. Libido theory became the institutional religion. As the most influential institute in the country, it set a pattern of extreme conservatism in the psychoanalytic movement for decades.

Nevertheless, 13 years after the founding of the Columbia Institute, Kardiner, Karush and Ovesey, then at Columbia, shook the psychoanalytic world by their heretical paper "A Methodological Study of Freudian Theory: II. The Libido Theory." Their paper, however, was not accepted by any psychoanalytic journal and was instead published in a psychiatric journal in 1959, the *Journal of Nervous & Mental Disease*. The article foreshadowed the doom of libido theory, as one of us, Paul Mosher, noted in a 1998 article, "Frequency of Word Use as Indicator of Evolution of Psychoanalytic Thought." Mosher examined the number of times the word *libido* appeared in the six core psychoanalytic journals indexed in the CD-ROM made available in 1997 by Psychoanalytic Electronic Publishing (PEP), a joint venture of the American Psychoanalytic Association and the Institute of Psycho-Analysis (London), of which Mosher is a Founding Board Member. "Libido" starts out at about the same frequency as "self" in the 1920s and then declines steadily every decade thereafter to reach a very low level in the 1990s (581). The observation recalls Joseph Schachter's wry comment about the history of psychoanalysis: "discarded theories— like old generals—didn't die, they just faded away (10)." Mosher, Schachter, and Arnold M. Cooper have all remarked on the demise of the libido theory, an indication that the Kardiner, Karush, Ovesey article succeeded in redirecting psychoanalysis away from one of its early but least productive theories.

Zilboorg was never directly sanctioned for his conduct, but eight years later, in 1950, the New York Psychoanalytic Institute declined to reappoint him as a Training Analyst (Leffert, 437) for reasons that are unknown. Zilboorg claimed that he was not reappointed for ideological reasons, as the following amusing story by Kardiner suggests. "Long after I was persona non grata in the New York Psychoanalytic Society, Gregory Zilboorg met me at a meeting of the American Psychoanalytic

Association once, and hailed me with the greeting, 'Now we are brothers.' 'What have we in common?' said I. 'Oh,' he said, 'I have been thrown out by the Holy Trinity [an allusion to Heinz Hartmann, Ernst Kris and Rudolph Loewenstein] because they don't agree with my ego psychology,' and so on" (*Reminiscences*, 177).

Did Zilboorg believe that he was thrown out for maintaining heretical views? Did he believe that Alexander's allegations of misconduct against him were motivated by countertransference hatred arising from Alexander's analysis of him many years earlier? Or was his charge against Alexander an unorthodox legal defense, concocted by Zilboorg and his lawyers, part of a strategy to defend Zilboorg by attacking his accuser's credibility?

Hostility and Its Discontents

Nearly 20 years after the hearings and the membership vote exonerating him, Zilboorg seemed still to be preoccupied with his conviction that Alexander's participation in the accusation and hearing was due to Alexander's hostile state of mind toward him. In an article titled "Emotional Engagement of Patient and Analyst," Zilboorg first discusses problems that can arise from a positive countertransference but then, referring to the hateful feelings an analyst can develop toward a patient, he slyly names his former analyst and nemesis:

> It is different and more difficult when we come to hostility. Barring exceptional cases in which hostility seems unavoidable and justified, it is difficult if not impossible to have our hostility toward a patient appear to us in the cloak of objectivity. . . . Under "normal" circumstances hostility toward a patient can be kept in check only if

repressed into the unconscious. Thus it may appear on the surface as a mild depressive complaint that there is a very difficult patient at hand, it may appear in the form of a rather intensive interpretation of the patient's narcissism, but almost never as true hostility. This hostility being repressed might have a cumulative effect; *years later it might even appear in the form of a legal or quasi-legal prosecution of a former patient.* Rare as such cases are, they are very instructive; they demonstrate how brittle yet how intense is a relationship based on unconscious hostility. Under no other circumstances do human relationships suffer to such an extent. Franz Alexander many years ago in Berlin aptly spoke of this joining in battle of hostilities which is involved in psychoanalysis as *die Narzissmen reiben sich*—the reciprocal friction between (or among) narcissisms. (146; underlining added, italics in original)

What shall we say about this extraordinary passage? Zilboorg claimed during the hearing that Alexander had a "very strong personal animosity" toward him, "half of which is deeply unconscious, and I have good reasons to believe that the other half is conscious" (Special Meeting, 596–597). It's unlikely that this was true of Alexander, but it's undeniably true of Zilboorg, whose hostility was not limited to his former analyst. Zilboorg's long history of sexual and nonsexual boundary violations with his patients, along with his history of exploitation and manipulation, suggests massive hostility that was seldom repressed.

Alexander doesn't suggest anything untrue in his Zilboorg obituary, but we wonder why he was so generous to the man who accused him of treachery during the New York Psychoanalytic Society Board Meetings. Perhaps Alexander had Freud's Latin aphorism in mind in his 1915 essay "Thoughts for the Times on War and Death": *"de mortuis nil nisi bonum"*—Of the dead, [say] nothing unless good—(*SE*, vol. 14, 290). Alexander knew that an obituary is an opportunity to pay respect to the dead, yet his respect for Zilboorg paled in comparison to his lifelong respect for psychoanalysis. Surely he knew that in the final analysis Zilboorg did a disservice to their chosen profession. Just as, according to Katharine Weber, Zilboorg threatened Kay Swift with exposure of her darkest secrets if she left analysis and refused his demand for sex, so did Zilboorg ominously threaten to reveal something terrible about Alexander's character. Zilboorg's pattern of acting out repeated itself, as we have suggested throughout this chapter. It's likely Alexander's obituary reflects the belief that he was acting in the best interests of psychoanalysis, perhaps endorsing Menninger's assumption that the public should learn nothing about the profession's personal squabbles. In the long run, however, it would have been better for Alexander either to acknowledge in the obituary Zilboorg's ethical transgressions or to decline writing an obituary. Why praise a man in death whose actions in life endangered a patient's welfare?

Another obituary, published in the leading American psychiatry journal, lauded Zilboorg unconditionally and with no reference at all to the problematic nature of his career aside from suggesting that his critics suffered from envy of Zilboorg's many talents. "When he died 17 September, 1959, American Psychiatry lost one of its most brilliant, stimulating and colorful figures. . . . Whereas in the arena of psychiatric meetings he reacted with unbelieving and hurt surprise to those who challenged him, in the [personal and family] situations mentioned above his genius became apparent and a brilliant, warm, understanding and kindly man emerged." (Braceland, 671–2).

The Criminal, The Judge, and the Public

One of the most bizarre aspects of the Alexander-Zilboorg relationship was the book they worked on together ten years before

Alexander's participation in bringing forward the charges against Zilboorg. The title of that book in retrospect could not have been more ironic: *The Criminal, the Judge, and the Public: A Psychological Analysis*. Zilboorg and Alexander must have been keenly aware during the New York Psychoanalytic Society's disciplinary hearings that they were reenacting the book's title, with the former as the defendant and the latter as judge. Published in 1931 and reprinted in 1956, the book was co-authored by Alexander and his former analysand, the Berlin lawyer Hugo Staub, and translated into English by Zilboorg. *The Criminal, the Judge, and the Public* is seldom cited by contemporary psychoanalysts and almost never by criminologists, but it offers a fascinating insight into how Alexander and Zilboorg must have felt during the hearings. Zilboorg first brought up the book during the November 28, 1941 meeting, noting that he never confessed to any of the charges to which Alexander claimed he confessed during the Richmond meeting. Zilboorg then adds that as he was leaving the Richmond meeting, he noticed that "Alexander—his conscience occasionally disturbs him—did not look at me. He is the man who wrote *The Criminal, the Judge, and the Public*, which I translated, in which he pleaded for a psychological understanding of those we judge. And here he rejected psychological explanations and wanted only cold facts, wrist watch, prize fight tickets, in the manner of those dry jurists who he at one time attacked so eloquently" (328). Zilboorg implies here that Alexander's refusal to view Mr. X as "not even a little psychiatric" not only misled Alexander into accepting the patient's false allegations against Zilboorg but also contradicted the spirit of *The Criminal, the Judge, and the Public*. Alexander is thus acting as a district attorney, Zilboorg insists, not as a psychoanalyst—and we recall Zilboorg's earlier statement that he doesn't like lawyers who, he believes, falsify the truth.

Two Russian Gregories: Zilboorg and Rasputin

Several scholars have compared Zilboorg to the fictional Svengali, but we suggest that he also resembles a shadowy historical figure—another Russian Gregory!—Grigori Rasputin, the mystical faith healer who became a trusted friend to the last Tsar of Russia. Said to possess miraculous powers, the charismatic Rasputin, like the charismatic Zilboorg, who was involved with the Kerensky government, was highly ambitious, cunning, and self-aggrandizing. Both men exerted hypnotic control over others. Rasputin's influence with the Russian Imperial family paralleled Zilboorg's involvement with his patients' lives, an entree into the worlds of high finance, industry, publishing, and the arts. Brilliant and dangerous, both men came to symbolize a fascination with power in all its incarnations, including lust. Just as Rasputin came to be one of the most hated and feared people in Tsarist Russia, so was Zilboorg despised by many of his colleagues. Both were considered by friends and foes alike to be geniuses— evil geniuses. Both succeeded for a time in outwitting their enemies. Zilboorg was not murdered, as Rasputin was, but eventually he lost much of his authority when he was "defrocked" by the New York Psychoanalytic Society, a belated recognition that his colleagues should have stripped him of his power a decade earlier.

CHAPTER 9

The White Knight and The Damsel: Ralph Greenson and Marilyn Monroe

The White Knight

Romeo Greenschpoon and his twin sister, Juliet, were born in Brooklyn, New York in 1911 to an immigrant Russian-Jewish couple who had achieved modest success in their new country. Romeo's father, initially a pharmacist, went on to medical school and became a physician. His mother, described as intelligent and ambitious, was a pianist; she became an artist manager and member of the New York art world. Young Romeo became fascinated with the arts. "Surrounded by New York's divas and impresarios, Romeo's head was filled with the romance of the stage, but he'd often escape to the misty black and white silhouettes up on the screen at Brooklyn's grand movie house, and lose himself in the romantic travails of the actresses with their translucent complexions" (Schneider,

22). In late adolescence he changed his first name from Romeo to "Ralph R.," but both before and after this change he was known to his friends as "Romi." In the story we are about to tell, young Romeo's name is fraught with irony in his role as the white knight rescuing a damsel in psychiatric distress.

Becoming Ralph R. Greenson

After studying medicine in Berne, Switzerland from 1931 to early 1933, Greenschpoon travelled to Vienna where he became a student of psychoanalysis while completing a psychiatric residency (Solnit, 512). He entered analysis with Ernest Stekel, a psychoanalytic renegade, and he interacted directly with Freud in psychoanalytic meetings. In 1936, Greenschpoon—by then married to his lifelong partner, Hildi, whom he had met in Switzerland—moved to Los Angeles to set up a practice in psychoanalysis and to begin a four-year second analysis with Freud's disciple Otto Fenichel. Known for his entertaining manner and storytelling, Greenschpoon started writing articles for psychoanalytic journals, publishing papers in both 1936 and 1937 under the name Ralph R. Greenschpoon. Subsequently, he changed his last name and was known thereafter as Ralph R. Greenson. He began a close friendship with the writer and social scientist Leo Rosten (no relation to poet and playwright Norman Rosten), who took him to social gatherings that included notable Hollywood personalities.

Greenson's psychoanalytic practice was largely comprised of patients who were film industry luminaries. In Los Angeles he became known for his ability to teach and write. He was an adept public speaker and loved to entertain at his home. After serving a stint as an Air Force psychiatrist, working at a military hospital with active duty personnel suffering from what today would be called PTSD, he resumed his practice in Los Angeles. Leo Rosten's novel *Captain Newman, M.D.* was loosely based on Greenson's experiences during World War II. The novel was later made into a 1963 film of the same name, with Gregory Peck playing the role of the military physician.

From the early 1950s, Greenson shared office space with Milton Wexler, one of the first American "lay" (non-medical) psychoanalysts. Wexler was trained as a lawyer, but he gave up the practice of law to earn a doctorate in psychology at Columbia University. He joined the staff of the Menninger Clinic in Topeka, Kansas, where he gave his schizophrenic patients unusual round-the-clock care. To avoid interrupting their treatment, he took some of them on vacation with his family. "'He was an organizing force in their life,' said his daughter, the neuropsychologist Nancy Wexler. 'A lot of people got better'" (Poser, 242—245).

Greenson and Wexler both became known for their involvement with the artistic and movie- making communities and for their treatment of film stars. Each also blurred boundaries in their involvement with their patients' artistic lives, contributing to film scripts and socializing with former patients. They created a discussion group to focus on new techniques for treating schizophrenia. Rejecting the use of traditional analysis, Greenson and Wexler theorized that patients suffering from this devastating illness lacked the "psychological structures" needed to participate in psychoanalysis. Greenson and Wexler instead focused on the "real relationship" between the therapist and the patient. Although this controversial form of treatment was far from psychoanalysis, Greenson maintained his primary identity as a psychoanalyst. He became the most prominent psychoanalyst in the western part of the United States due to a combination of showmanship, scholarship and charismatic teaching (Poser, 239). In addition, he earned the reputation as the "center" of world psychoanalysis through his friendship with Anna Freud. He was also known to be thin-skinned with a "lifelong tendency to irrational fits of anger" (Spoto, 529).

The Damsel

The life of Norma Jeane Mortenson has been told and retold through an estimated 100 biographies and as many as 1,000 publications about her. Her fame as the movie actress "Marilyn Monroe" made her arguably the best known twentieth-century film star. Partly as a result of the mystery surrounding her death in 1962 at age 36, Marilyn Monroe has become a cult figure with an enormous following. The story of her life has been written and rewritten by nearly everyone who knew her, including her former husband Arthur Miller; her friends; her maid and seamstress; and by Norman Mailer, who later retracted his sensationalized claims.

Among the doorstop-size biographies of Marilyn Monroe by professional writers, investigative reporters and academics, the most reliable appear to be those written by Anthony Summers (1985), Donald Spoto (1993), Barbara Leaming (1998), J. Randy Taraborrelli (2009), Keith Badman (2010) and Lois Banner (2012). Such biographies have become so numerous a half-century after her death that there is even a book written about the biographies themselves: *The Many Lives of Marilyn Monroe* by Sarah Churchwell (2005). According to Churchwell (7), quoting Victor, "More books have been written about Marilyn Monroe than any other entertainer. The most conservative estimates are in the low hundreds; more accurate guesses exceed the six hundred mark, and at least half a dozen new Marilyn books are published every year in the English Language alone" (Victor, 36). There are numerous films about her; semi-fictional accounts of her life; and books with precisely spelled out dialogs written by memoirists who claimed to recall conversations decades after her death. Spoto's biography is probably the most widely respected, although he minimizes the extent of her psychopathology and is unaware of the seriousness of the problems that Greenson faced in treating her. Taraborrelli, on the other hand, is more sensitive to the extent of her disturbance, but he overestimates the severity of her drug use in the early stages of her career.

Readers find themselves in a quandary when trying to understand Marilyn Monroe's life and persona. The picture drawn in one biography is strikingly different from that drawn in another biography. What is factual in one biography is fanciful in another. The more biographies one reads, the more one feels a sense of futility about the possibility of knowing the truth of her life. In the account that follows, which focuses on Marilyn Monroe's relationship with her last psychoanalyst, Ralph Greenson, along with her legacy affecting psychoanalysis, we have tried to rely on consensus statements and primary sources. Greenson's notes regarding his treatment of Monroe are locked away in the archives of UCLA and cannot be seen until 2036. Greenson and his family were, however, not completely silent about the case during her treatment and in the years following her death.

The unknowability of Marilyn Monroe's early life is not that different from the impossibility of reconstructing an accurate—not to be confused with an agreed-upon—account of the early life of a patient in a psychoanalysis. The early life account, co-constructed in an analysis by the analyst and the patient, is a mixture of "the real truth"; a "new truth," that is, the remodeling of early memories that occur in all of us; and additional revisions of memory within the patient brought about by the analysis itself. All of these accounts are influenced by the analyst's theoretical views and countertransference. An additional factor with Marilyn Monroe is that she fictionalized some of the accounts of her early life, apparently to gain public sympathy. This is not surprising because like any superstar, she was obsessed with her public image. Her self-created persona was that of a helpless sexual creature who would be alluring to the powerful men who rescued her (Spoto, 128).

The future actress was born in 1926 in the charity ward of a Los Angeles hospital to a (probably) unmarried mother, Gladys Baker, who left her in the care of others for most of her childhood. Most biographies portray the mother as suffering from a deteriorating mental condition, but even the nature of that condition is in doubt, and assertions that she suffered from schizophrenia have been challenged. The young Norma Jeane Mortenson (sometimes "Norma Jean," sometimes "Mortensen," sometimes "Baker") lived for a number of years with a strict church-going family, the Bolenders, who steeped the child in religious values and morality. She was then taken, briefly and abruptly, at the age of seven to live with her mother. Grace McKee, Gladys Baker's friend, often visited the child, and McKee eventually became one of the most important people in Monroe's life. Both women worked in the Los Angeles movie industry, were "free wheeling" in their personal lives, and created an environment that was markedly different from the one Norma Jeane had with the Bolenders. The following year, 1934, her mother was hospitalized with a serious mental disorder, and the care of Norma Jeane fell to McKee.

Gladys Baker and Grace McKee were not only immersed in the film industry for employment but were also obsessed with movie stars. McKee was particularly fixated on Jean Harlow (born Harlean Carpenter). "In nine films released during the next two years [1930–1932] (most notably *The Public Enemy*, *Platinum Blonde* and *Red Headed Woman*), Jean Harlow's overt sexuality, her shockingly dyed and cinematically lighted platinum-colored hair and her shimmering screen image made her endlessly fascinating" (Spoto, 37). Convinced that Norma Jeane was destined to become a film star like Jean Harlow, McKee supposedly brainwashed the future actress to believe this was her destiny. She began to teach Norma Jeane how to use cosmetics to enhance her appearance; over time, the future Marilyn Monroe became obsessed with her looks. Norma Jeane had three successive mother figures, each with a decidedly different outlook. By contrast, she had no constant father figure in her life. Her attempt to find a stable relationship with a powerful man who would take care of and protect her became a dominant theme in her personal life.

A "radiantly beautiful girl," Norma Jeane began her career as a model, but her ambition, like that of most young Los Angeles models, was to become a movie actress. Nearly every photographer who saw her early in her modeling career noted that she had an unusual talent for posing for a still camera. She thrived in front of a lens, and her relaxed, upbeat appearance, with only a hint at first of sexuality, made her a great success as a model. Astute, driven and hardworking, she appeared on a magazine cover in 1945 at the age of 19. By spring of the following year, she had been on the cover of no fewer than 33 magazines, an "immediate and stunning" outcome (Spoto, 94–95). Sexuality was her entry ticket to a world of movie producers, photographers and agents. By July 1946 she was granted a screen test at 20th Century Fox movie studios, again dazzling the cinema professionals who saw her perform.

Becoming Marilyn Monroe

The following month, on the suggestion of a Fox executive, she changed her name to "Marilyn Monroe." She received an immediate six month contract and weekly salary from the studio, but she failed to be selected for any film roles. Despite the fact that salaried potential actors were not required to appear at the studio unless they had actual movie roles, she attended the studio every day, asking questions and trying to learn everything she could about cosmetics, lighting and costumes. The contract was renewed for an additional six months during which time she continued to receive a salary and was given two minor parts in films. At the end of the second six months, however, the contract was not renewed, and she had no further paychecks. She then began to attend on a regular basis the Actors Laboratory, a workshop where serious stage actors and writers from New York met in Los Angeles to train actors and exchange ideas. By 1949, in need of money to allow her to continue participation in the Actors Laboratory, she secretly posed for a series of nude photographs, an act of desperation that ultimately launched her career.

Monroe had also been supporting herself through prostitution, primarily for meals, until she was taken in by a generous philanthropic couple, John Carroll and Lucille Ryman, who offered her a free apartment and other support. To gain their sympathy, she "said she had been raped at nine and had sex every day at the age of eleven, all of which she later admitted was untrue. It was a way of getting us to take her in, to keep her off the streets of Hollywood, and it worked" (Spoto, 128). She constantly sought reassurance from Carroll and Ryman that they would not abandon her. They were the first of a series of married couples (Greenes, Strasbergs and Greensons) who eventually took her into their family to rescue the "waif," as she portrayed herself. Having no experience living for any length of time in a family of her own, she involved herself repeatedly in relationships of this kind, including with her final psychoanalyst, in an attempt to recreate the childhood she never had but for which she always longed.

The pictures from the 1949 nude photo shoot surfaced on a calendar in March 1952, threatening to cause a scandal that would swiftly end

Monroe's career. Instead of denying that the photos were of her, she admitted the truth, telling an interviewer, to gain sympathy, that she needed money at the time (she was paid $50). The studio in turn constructed a story of the actress's impoverished childhood in which she had been shuffled through a series of foster homes. The nude photos and fictional account explaining them helped catapult the actress to fame. The following year, 1953, the first issue of *Playboy Magazine,* composed in Hugh Heffner's kitchen, carried the 1949 nude photos, with no payment to Monroe, and her career took off. This sudden cultural change leading to the acceptable public celebration of sexuality was a major opening shot in the launch of the "sexual revolution."

How and why was Marilyn Monroe different from the other sex goddesses of the age? Her biographers have attempted to answer these questions. Her best biographers can only fall back upon paradoxes. "What was at the hidden center of the phenomenon that was Marilyn Monroe?" Anthony Summers asks, and then notes that "Behind the hyperbole and the hysteria there was a child who grew to be a woman, who was a symbol of love yet essentially lonely, who died famously but in folly at the age of thirty-six." Summers also points out that the "private person read philosophy and planned gardens, yet drowned in drugs and alcohol" (4). Taraborrelli offers a different explanation, emphasizing her fear of the mental illness that ran through her family. "Because her grandmother and mother were committed to insane asylums Marilyn lived with the constant threat of impending madness" (xv). Taraborrelli observes that although the public viewed her mood swings and unpredictable behavior as mere eccentricities, the "difficult emotional tug-of-war she endured for much of her life, ignored by almost everyone, may have been her defining characteristic" (3). The creation of her persona as Marilyn Monroe may have been her greatest role. "Indeed, the star that some people saw toward the end of her life was but a shell game—a well crafted presentation of someone who had disappeared years ago ... that is, if she ever really existed" (6).

Marilyn Monroe's Religion: Psychoanalysis

Arthur Miller, Monroe's third husband, regarded her, as he wrote in his 1987 autobiography *Timebends*, as a "born Freudian": "there were no accidents of speech, no innocent slips; every word or gesture signaled an inner intention, whether conscious or not, and the most innocuous-sounding remark could conceal some sinister threat." By contrast, Miller observed ruefully, he had always erred in the opposite direction, "canceling out hostilities around me for the sake of getting on with life, a habit that had already created some serious misunderstandings between us" (242).

Some of these marital misunderstandings involved the value of psychoanalysis, to which Monroe had given herself wholeheartedly, and about which Miller remained deeply ambivalent. He wrote sympathetically about Monroe's psychoanalysts, particularly Marianne Kris and Ralph Greenson, and about his own analyst, Rudolph Loewenstein, a "Freudian of great skill" (320). The playwright believed, nevertheless, that psychoanalysis encouraged an introspection that paradoxically kept Monroe imprisoned within herself. "Psychoanalysis was too much like talking *about* something rather than doing it, which was the only thing she had ever believed in anyway —her life had all been put up or shut up" (458).

At a minimum, Monroe was seen by six different psychoanalysts during her career, including Abraham H. Gottesman, Margaret Herz Hohenberg, Marianne Kris, Anna Freud, Ralph Greenson and Milton Wexler. There may have been others psychoanalysts as well. In an interview with Rachel Shteir published in *The New Yorker,* Ilonka Venier Alexander stated that her grandfather, Franz Alexander, told her that he had treated Marilyn Monroe, though curiously, she doesn't mention this detail in her 2015 biography *The Life and Times of Franz Alexander.*

Monroe's first experience with psychoanalysis probably occurred when she saw Gottesman in Los Angeles in the early 1950s. There is no information about this treatment except for a number of cancelled checks written to him included among memorabilia listed in public auctions. Gottesman was a member of the Los Angeles Psychoanalytic Society and a member of the Los Angeles Psychoanalytic Institute's faculty. Most biographical accounts of Monroe's psychoanalysts, other than Badman's (41), fail to comment on her treatment by Gottesman.

By 1954 Monroe had established herself as an internationally known film star and sex symbol. She had appeared in 19 films, including *Don't Bother to Knock (*1952), *Monkey Business* (1952), *Niagara* (1953), *Gentlemen Prefer Blondes* (1953), *How to Marry a Millionaire* (1953), *River of No Return* (1954) and *There's No Business Like Show Business* (1954). Tired of "dumb blonde" roles, Monroe turned her back on her contract with Fox Studios and moved to New York City to pursue a career as a serious actress. On the last day of 1954, Monroe and photographer Milton Greene formed "Marilyn Monroe Productions," a production company intended to give her more control over the films in which she starred and to bring her a greater financial return for her work. In pursuit of that goal, she enrolled in the Actors' Studio, which was at that time under the leadership of Lee Strasberg, a disciple of Constantin Stanislavski, who developed a style of acting that came to be called the "method." As Taraborrelli explains, Lee Strasberg's notion of method acting, inspired by Stanislavski, required an actor to use "'sense memory,' drawing from his own past experiences. The concept was that in doing so the actor would create a character with more depth and interest" (262). Strasberg, an aficionado and also a patient of psychoanalysis, a trendy pursuit among people in the arts at that time, urged students of method acting to undergo psychoanalysis to connect with the emotional aspects of their personal history, which they could then use to recreate the emotions of the characters they were portraying.

In 1955, Marilyn Monroe began her involvement with the first of the four psychoanalysts who were to play a major role in the remaining eight years of her life. Margaret Hohenberg, a classical psychoanalyst and a member of the prestigious New York Psychoanalytic Society, had been recommended by Milton Greene, Monroe's friend and business associate, who himself was at the same time Hohenberg's patient. The analyst had been "approved" by Lee Strasberg. Hohenberg was described as "a Brünnhilde type, a 57-year-old Hungarian immigrant complete with tightly wound braids and a Valkyrian bosom" (Kashner). One might question the propriety of Hohenberg's decision to take into treatment a business partner of a current patient. The misstep eventually led to Monroe's decision to end her treatment with Hohenberg when the actress's business relationship with Greene cooled.

Early Symptoms of Mental Illness

Marilyn Monroe entered psychoanalysis at the suggestion of Lee Strasberg, but as Taraborrelli notes, although she could have seen Hohenberg only once a week, she visited the analyst three to five times a week (Schwartz, 484–485), an indication that she may have felt "ill-equipped to handle her own life" (Taraborrelli, 266). She was also telephoning the analyst for advice. There were other possible reasons for Monroe's deepening involvement with psychoanalysis. She had a strong family history of mental disorder, possibly schizophrenia, a troubled childhood and a history of drug use, most significantly an addiction to barbiturates. Both her mother and her maternal grandmother experienced auditory hallucinations ("voices"), and both died in mental institutions. Her mother was given a diagnosis of "paranoid schizophrenia," a severe mental illness that tends to occur earlier in life among men, but typically begins in women in their late 20s or early 30s.

As early as 1949, Monroe complained to her drama coach, Natasha Lytess, that she was hearing voices and asked Lytess if she too could hear them (Taraborrelli, 154). The voices were more troubling than ever while she was making *Gentlemen Prefer Blondes*. Drugs, probably barbiturates prescribed by studio physicians to help calm her down, brought her temporary relief. Later, as described in anecdotes told by her friends, she complained that she was being followed by FBI agents, spied on, and served poisoned food in certain restaurants by waiters who could read her mind (Taraborrelli, 373). The intensity of her deepening dependence on Hohenberg, while perhaps to be expected in many psychoanalytic treatments, appears in retrospect problematic, presaging the risk of an unmanageable form of regression, a problem that appeared later with full force in her relationships with her subsequent psychoanalysts.

In addition, Monroe's dependence on others can be seen in her unusually pronounced attachments to a series of acting coaches, including Natasha Lytess and Paula Strasberg. When filming, she insisted on the presence of Lytess and later Strasberg on the set. She would often ignore the film director's advice in favor of her acting coach's. This atypical conduct predictably resulted in serious conflicts between her private female acting coaches and the male directors under whom she worked. Unable to "conquer" these directors by seducing them, she instead resorted to mother-figures for protection.

Barbiturates

Seldom used now, barbiturates were extremely popular prior to the development of less dangerous sedative drugs beginning in the 1960s. Barbiturates were especially common in Hollywood, serving as the "tranquilizers" of the day. They were used both to treat daytime "nervousness" and night time insomnia. According to Kolb and Noyes (1959), co-authors of a standard psychiatric textbook of that era, the increased use of barbiturates potentially resulted not only in acute intoxication but also in addiction. "Acute intoxication with barbiturates accounted for 25% of all fatal acute poisoning cases brought to hospitals and more deaths are caused by barbiturates, either accidentally ingested or taken with suicidal intent, than by any other poison." Unlike other types of narcotic drug addictions, physicians were responsible for a high proportion of barbiturate addiction. "*The physician should therefore remember that in prescribing barbiturates he assumes a heavy ethical responsibility. There is a possibility that these drugs may create a dangerous type of addiction. Especial care should be exercised in prescribing them for emotionally unstable persons. Simple insomnia alone is rarely a valid indication for the use of barbiturates*" (571; emphasis added). Those who become addicted to barbiturates display one or more symptoms: "the patient is confused, often drowsy and depressed, shows poor judgment and impaired intellectual functioning and a regression in habits. Frequently he is emotionally unstable, morose, quarrelsome, and if irritated by minor incidents or fancied insults may be assaultive. *Some addicts become hostile and develop mild paranoid ideas.*"

Treatment of barbiturate addiction, Kolb and Noyes warn, is problematic. "Even a gradual reduction in barbiturates [for an addicted person] carries a certain risk. Patients should therefore be under constant supervision and observation during withdrawal *which should be carried out in a hospital.*" Contrary to popular belief, barbiturate addiction is more serious than morphine addiction. "Abstinence from morphine is less dangerous than abstinence from barbiturates and morphine causes less mental and emotional disturbance (572–573; emphasis added). Addiction develops as a user's body becomes less responsive to the drug's effects over time, thus requiring larger doses to achieve the same effect. Those who are in control of their own dosage gradually increase the amount of the drug they are taking. Unwanted side effects of the drug, as described above, may increase with increasing dosages.

Marilyn Monroe's drug use began early in her adult life, starting probably with Dexedrine-like drugs, "uppers," often employed as appetite suppressants for weight control. She proceeded to use combinations of amphetamine-like drugs with barbiturates intended to control the jitteriness caused by the amphetamines alone. She then progressed to the use of barbiturates alone for daytime relaxation and nighttime sedation. "Bunny Gardel, who did Marilyn's body makeup on numerous pictures, knew her from her earliest days at Fox. By the early fifties, 'She used to come to the dressing room and put down a plastic bag, and you never saw so many pills in one bag. There would be uppers, downers, vitamins, and God knows what in the bag'" (Summers, 85). Monroe was hospitalized at least twice for withdrawal from barbiturates, but on each occasion she soon resumed the use of such drugs. As her drug use increased, she developed the habit of puncturing holes in barbiturate capsules and pouring the powdered contents into a glass of water to obtain a more rapid effect.

Although psychiatrists gradually recognized in the 1950s the dangers of barbiturates, the risks were not yet fully appreciated by the medical profession as a whole. Hollywood physicians employed by the studios casually prescribed such drugs to calm high strung stars and executives. The use of barbiturates during the day could in itself lead to insomnia unless additional doses were taken at night.

Realizing that Hollywood success depended on her on-screen appearance, Marilyn Monroe was obsessed with getting a good night's sleep before each day of filming. Frantic over the need for sleep, she not only dosed herself with barbiturates at bedtime but also took measures to block out any light from her bedroom, including having heavy black material stapled over the windows. In the morning she was often stuporous or was sometimes unable to wake up in time to appear at the studio. When she finally arrived, she would remain in her dressing room for hours, either asleep again or fussing desperately with her makeup and hair. Production on her films was therefore frequently behind schedule, and she was notoriously late for filming sessions. Despite all these difficulties, including panic until filming began, a magical transformation took place when the cameras started rolling. That magic depended upon her increasing reliance on barbiturates. Not only did she require higher doses to get the desired effect, sleep, but she was subject to increasing side effects, including morning drowsiness, anxiety and nighttime confusion. This pattern—fear of not sleeping, which would harm her on-camera appearance the next day, and continued use of barbiturates for insomnia, especially when filming was in progress or following a disruption of an important personal relationship—continued to the day of her death.

Increasing Personal Difficulties

During the period from 1954 to 1959, Marilyn Monroe married for the second and third times, each marriage ending in divorce. The second marriage, to the New York Yankees baseball superstar Joe DiMaggio, lasted a mere nine months and the third, in June 1956, to playwright Arthur Miller, lasted for five years. During the third marriage she experienced three failed pregnancies including one ectopic (tubal) pregnancy that required abdominal surgery.

While in England filming *The Prince and the Showgirl* with Laurence Olivier, Monroe became so distraught that her frantic phone calls to Margaret Hohenberg brought the analyst to England to calm the actress. Such an unusual action for a psychoanalyst, clearly a "boundary crossing" no matter how well intended, signaled more boundary issues to come, though not generally involving Hohenberg. One cause of Monroe's increasing distress was her discovery of an entry in Miller's diary expressing contempt for her. The incident later appears in Miller's 1964 play *After the Fall*, where the protagonist's guilt-ridden acknowledgment of his complicity in his ex-wife's suicide is now viewed, despite the playwright's denials in *Timebends*, as Miller's replaying of his tormented marriage with Monroe. Another reason for her growing distress was her perception at that same time that Olivier and his British theatrical colleagues were treating her with contempt too.

Hohenberg recommended that Monroe consult with Anna Freud, who was then living in London and treating children. Monroe had five visits with Anna Freud, whom some biographers, unaware of Monroe's earlier treatment with Gottesman, incorrectly refer to as the actress's second psychoanalyst. Much of our information about Anna Freud's treatment of Marilyn Monroe comes from the actor and journalist Detlef Berthelsen, whose 1991 book *La Famille Freud au Jour le Jour* is based on his interviews of Paula Fichtl, the long-time maid and housekeeper of Sigmund Freud and Anna Freud. One day in August 1956, Berthelsen observes, Anna Freud took Monroe to the clinic's Kindergarten, where the actress felt at ease, even playing with the children. Interestingly, Monroe told Anna Freud that when she was 21 she had read Sigmund Freud's *The Interpretation of Dreams*; she was especially fascinated by his descriptions of dreams about nudity.

"Compulsive nudity," writes Berthelsen, "the need to undress in public, was a symptom that Marianne Kris had noted about Marilyn. Marilyn's diagnosis is written on a card that still exists today at the Anna Freud Centre. The coded summary reads 'Emotional instability, exaggerated impulsiveness, constant need for external approval, inability to be alone, depressive tendencies especially concerning rejection, paranoia with schizophrenic elements.'"

Monroe and Anna Freud played a game of marbles on a table, Berthelsen continues, each facing the other. "Eventually, Marilyn started flicking the marbles, one by one, toward Anna. From a child psychoanalytic point of view, Anna interpreted the gesture as a 'desire for sexual contact.' In fact, an analyst who worked with Marilyn later [presumably Kris] confirmed she had a fear of men." Anna Freud believed that her brief treatment of Monroe was a success. Paula Fichtl stated that patient and analyst "parted on good terms"—such good terms, Berthelsen adds, that a few months later "a check of a sizable sum arrived at Maresfield Gardens; it was signed by Marilyn Monroe" (155–156; translated by Julie Berman).

Monroe was at that time 30 years old, in the middle of the age range during which the risk for a woman of the onset of paranoid schizophrenia, particularly one with such a strong family history of the illness, would be of the greatest concern. It is impossible to know the extent to which her eventual breakdown was caused by genetic factors, conflicted relationships, environmental stress, drug addiction, or psychoanalytic treatment. Many biographers attribute her increasing instability and mental deterioration from this point to the attempts by her psychoanalysts and Lee Strasberg to help her uncover her painful past, a speculation that we find unconvincing. But other aspects of her therapy may have contributed to her problems. It is not unheard of for the deterioration of a patient whose illness is following an unstoppable downhill course to be blamed on the doctor, and certainly this could have been the situation in Monroe's case.

Borderline Personality Disorder

It is not our purpose to attach a diagnostic label to Marilyn Monroe, but we do want to note in passing that a contemporary diagnosis of someone exhibiting her behavior might be borderline personality disorder, defined in the latest edition of the *Diagnostic and Statistical Manual of Mental Disorders*, published by the American Psychiatric Association, as a "pervasive pattern of instability of interpersonal relationships, self-image, and affects, and marked impulsivity, beginning by early adulthood and present in a variety of contexts." Of the nine diagnostic criteria listed for borderline personality disorder, five of which are necessary for the diagnosis, Marilyn Monroe appeared to have met *all nine* criteria:

1. Frantic efforts to avoid real or imagined abandonment.
2. A pattern of unstable and intense interpersonal relationships characterized by alternating between extremes of idealization and devaluation.
3. Identity disturbance: markedly and persistently unstable self-image or sense of self.
4. Impulsivity in at least two areas that are potentially self-damaging (e.g., spending, sex, substance abuse, reckless driving, binge eating).
5. Recurrent suicidal behavior, gestures, or threats, or self-mutilating behavior.
6. Affective instability due to a marked reactivity of mood (e.g., intense episodic dysphoria, irritability, or anxiety usually lasting a few hours and only rarely more than a few days).
7. Chronic feelings of emptiness.

8. Inappropriate, intense anger or difficulty controlling anger (e.g., frequent displays of temper, constant anger, recurrent physical fights).
9. Transient, stress-related paranoid ideation or severe dissociative symptoms. (*DSM–5*, 663)

In an article published in 1983, the psychoanalyst Richard Chessick took exception to the diagnosis of borderline personality in the Marilyn Monroe case and argued instead for the diagnosis "narcissistic personality disorder." Chessick's grounds for denying the borderline diagnosis would not stand in the light of current thinking, although he is correct that she also showed many pronounced and undeniable signs of having a narcissistic personality. It is worth noting that the categorical personality diagnoses suffer from great overlap and that estimates of the incidence of narcissistic personality disorder in patients with borderline personality disorder is about 33%.

Marianne Kris

After the demise of the production company she had founded with Milton Greene, Marilyn Monroe decided to end her treatment with Margaret Hohenberg. On the advice of Anna Freud or perhaps Arthur Miller, she began psychoanalysis with Marianne Kris in 1957. A childhood friend of Anna Freud, Kris had relocated to New York in the 1930s, becoming a classical psychoanalyst and a member of the New York Psychoanalytic Society. The analysis continued intermittently for the next four years, with long interruptions during Monroe's film making stays in California. Her life situation and mental condition deteriorated during this time, partly, perhaps, because her marriage to Miller was falling apart. The cause and effect relationship is uncertain. Monroe's deterioration might have been the cause of the failing marriage instead.

Monroe's analysis with Kris was highly unusual, filled with major boundary crossings. The following anecdote describes a visit by Kris and some friends to the Miller apartment at a time when Monroe's behavior was becoming erratic, largely because of her growing dependency on drugs. The account, which appears in Taraborrelli's biography, comes from Barbara Miller (no relation to Arthur), who was about 12 when the visit took place. "I was a big fan of Marilyn Monroe's," Barbara Miller writes, "and couldn't wait to meet her. She was a lot heavier than I thought she'd be, but still she was very beautiful. She came swooping into the living room to greet us in a floral-printed caftan that was just lovely. She had her hair long, to her shoulders--very blonde. I remember she had the most delicate hands with tapering fingers, her nails painted red. She was very nice, but seemed I guess tipsy would be the word." When the adults expressed a preference for soft drinks over alcoholic drinks, the actress smiled, stating, "I generally don't like to drink alone, but I'll make an exception today." She then called out the name of their maid. When no one appeared, she called again. Finally, she screamed out, "Arthur, where is the goddamn maid?" Monroe "shook her head and rolled her eyes." She then announced that her secretary was out and that Arthur was "somewhere trying to write" but was "having a hard time."

Barbara Miller recalls that Kris "studied Marilyn carefully" and said, "Dear, is there someplace where you and I might talk? I'd like to speak to you alone." The patient did not meet the psychiatrist's suggestion kindly. "I think we've done enough talking, Doctor, don't you? I'm fine, really I am. All I need is a Bloody Mary if I could just get the goddamn maid to come in here. Jesus Christ." Kris's next statement, "You don't seem fine," only made the situation worse. Her eyes blazing, Monroe snapped, "Why can't you leave me alone? I've had it with you. I'm sick of going over and over and over the same things. I'm not going to do it anymore." She then walked out of the room, leaving her guests in "stunned silence."

Ten minutes later Arthur Miller appeared, looking contrite, and conveying his wife's apologies. "She's not been well. It's just been awful, and I hope you'll accept our sincere apologies and come back another time." Miller then asked Kris to call him later about an urgent matter, to which the analyst agreed. As the visitors awkwardly left, Monroe suddenly appeared with a tray of drinks. "Wait," she exclaimed, and offered them drinks. "Wouldn't you like to sit down and talk?" Barbara Miller recounted that Monroe was a "totally different person," smiling and cheerful, with no memory of what had happened. She hugged everyone goodbye and told Kris that she would call her the next day. Barbara Miller recalled that no one said anything in the cab on the way home. "Everyone just sat and stared straight ahead" (304–305).

Marilyn Monroe's health continued to decline when her divorce from Arthur Miller became final in January 1961. In February she confided to her friend and masseur Ralph Roberts her close call with suicide, when she almost jumped out of her living room window. "I squeezed my eyes shut at the open window, clenched my fists. I remembered reading somewhere that people who fall from heights lose consciousness before they hit the ground. Then when I looked down, I saw a woman walking along the sidewalk near the building awning. She was wearing a brown dress and . . . *I knew her*" (Taraborrelli, 344).

I Did a Terrible Thing"

Monroe's self-care during this time was impaired, and she was rapidly losing weight. Apart from leaving to see Kris each day, she stayed in her darkened bedroom, listening to popular romantic recordings and trying to calm herself with drugs. She seemed to be sinking into melancholia, a particularly dangerous form of severe depression. Hearing about her near-suicidal leap, Kris finally decided that a hospital admission would be necessary, both to protect her life and address her addiction to barbiturates. Apparently aware of Monroe's fears of being locked in a mental hospital like her mother, Kris told her that she was simply going to the hospital for a rest. During a three-day hospitalization in the highly respected Payne Whitney Psychiatric Hospital, Monroe became distraught, believing that her isolation in a bare locked room was different from the "rest" that her analyst had promised. Desperate, Monroe called on DiMaggio to rescue her. With Kris's help, he was able to arrange her discharge from Payne Whitney. She was picked up by Kris and Ralph Roberts, who described their trip from the hospital to the actress's apartment. "How dare you betray me!" Monroe shouted at Kris. "I trusted you. How could you do that to me? And you didn't even visit me? What is wrong with you?" According to Roberts, the actress was "like a hurricane unleashed. I don't think Dr. Kris had ever seen her like that, and she was frightened and very shaken by the violence of Marilyn's response." After dropping Monroe off at her apartment, Roberts drove the analyst home. "There was a lot of traffic, so we inched down the West Side Highway overlooking the river, and Dr. Kris was trembling and kept repeating over and over, 'I did a terrible thing, a terrible, terrible thing. Oh God, I didn't mean to, but I did'" (Taraborrelli, 353–354).

At her apartment DiMaggio recognized that his former wife was seriously ill and arranged for her to be rehospitalized immediately but under less threatening conditions. He did not want the hospitalization to evoke her fear of insanity, as she understood her mother and grandmother's illness, and feared for herself. She was admitted to the Neurological Institute at

Columbia Presbyterian Medical Center for a three week stay in a private room on a floor reserved for private psychiatric patients under the care of the Columbia Psychiatric Faculty. During her stay she was a patient of Dr. William A. Horwitz, a specialist in the treatment of depression and at the time the Assistant Chair of the Department of Psychiatry (Horwitz, personal communication to P. Mosher, 1961; W. Harris, personal communication to P. Mosher, 2015). Horwitz was a kind and considerate physician who was recognized as a "psychiatrist's psychiatrist" (Kolb, "William Horwitz"). He was not unfriendly to psychoanalysis: indeed, he was married to a prominent analyst. Horwitz claimed that he had as patients in his practice the largest number of severely depressed psychoanalysts of any psychiatrist in the United States. He believed that the delusional ideation he saw in ill psychoanalysts, all of whom had presumably been psychoanalyzed, was no different from the delusions he observed in other patients. This observation led him to question whether psychoanalysis could bring about fundamental changes in character (Horwitz, personal communication to P. Mosher, 1960).

Feeling betrayed by Kris, Monroe later broke off treatment and never forgave her. Nor did she contact Kris again. Some writers have criticized Kris for hospitalizing her patient in a deceptive way, but at the time Monroe's situation was grave. The combination of borderline personality disorder, possible bipolar disorder, drug addiction, collapsing life circumstances and a history of previous suicide attempts adds up to a dangerously high level of risk. It is possible that Kris's intervention, although it led to an abrupt termination of their treatment relationship, saved Monroe's life, if only in the short term. Biographers recount previous incidents, not atypical for persons with borderline personality disorder, in which Monroe had taken potentially fatal drug overdoses and then summoned help. The result each time was a narrow escape from death. This pattern of behavior indicates a patient at high risk; if by chance the rescue does not occur, the outcome could be fatal, either intentionally or not.

Finding Jesus: Ralph Greenson

Kris had suggested in January 1960, after Monroe became overwrought following an argument with her acting coach Paula Strasberg during the filming in California of *Let's Make Love,* that the actress should consult with Ralph Greenson. He first saw her for a consultation in her bungalow at the Beverly Hills Hotel, apparently on an urgent basis. He observed her to be heavily sedated, with slurred speech and poor reactions. "She seemed remote, failed to understand simple conversational sallies, and rambled on incoherently." Given her faith at that time in psychoanalysis, which she referred to as her "religion," she wanted to go straight to the couch for Freudian therapy. Alarmed by her condition, Greenson decided instead on "supportive therapy" rather than psychoanalysis. He saw her for a few sessions aimed at reducing her drug use. According to Summers (188), he discovered that she was taking large amounts of several drugs obtained by doctor shopping, including phenobarbital, sodium pentothal, and Amytal. "She habitually took several of these drugs intravenously" (188). Greenson diagnosed her as a "borderline addictive personality." The label "borderline" had a different meaning in those days, although the combination of these terms in the 1960s would clearly convey a picture of someone who was seriously ill.

Back in New York, while she was still seeing Kris, Monroe had continued to have daily phone conversations with Greenson, calling him sometimes several times a day. She also saw him on her frequent trips to Los Angeles. Returning from one such trip in a euphoric state, she effused to her maid and confidant, Lena Pepitone, "I've finally found it. I've found a Jesus for myself." She believed her messianic analyst was giving her a new life. "He's doing wonderful things for me. He gives me courage. He makes me smart, makes me think. Now nothing bothers me. I'm so happy" (Pepitone and Stadiem, 183–184). Monroe regarded Greenson as the best psychoanalyst she had come across; each admired the other. The quoted passages from *Marilyn Monroe Confidential*, "co-authored" by Pepitone and Stadiem in 1979, are most likely reconstructions of conversations that might have taken place years earlier between the maid and actress. Critics have pointed out that in personal appearances, Pepitone had a limited command of the English language whereas Stadiem was a graduate of Columbia University and Harvard Law School. Their book resembles an historical novel, like Michel Schneider's *Marilyn's Last Sessions: A Novel*. Nonetheless, despite this reservation, the following prescient dialogue appears in Pepitone's account:

> Evidently, when Marilyn was in Hollywood, she saw this man every day.
> "What would you do if he took a vacation," I asked her.
> "I'd call him wherever he was."
> "And what if you couldn't reach him?"
> "I'd be in trouble."

Heroism or Bravado?

Greenson's more sustained but intermittent treatment of Monroe did not begin until June 1960, one month before the filming of *The Misfits*. Why did he agree to take her on as a patient? Seven other psychiatrists in the Los Angeles area had declined to accept her as a patient due to her history of previous suicide attempts and the fear that she "might succeed in a bid to kill herself while under their care" (Badman, 41). The suicide rate among patients with borderline personality disorder is 400 times higher than among the general population, and the risk for a patient with this disorder as well as drug addiction and a history of previous suicide attempts is probably much higher than that. Psychotherapists' reluctance to take on suicidal patients is well known among both the public and the profession. For reasons that have never been properly addressed, the mental health professions, along with people in general, have a culture of "shaming and blaming" psychotherapists who experience a patient suicide, unlike, for instance, the culture of medical specialties such as oncology and cardiology, where the death of a high risk patient is less commonly blamed on the practitioner. Irvin Yalom points out in *The Gift of Therapy* (2002) that "approximately 50 percent of senior therapists have faced the suicide, or a serious suicide attempt, of a current or past patient" (253). In addition, suicides are the most common cause of malpractice lawsuits against psychiatrists.

Was Greenson's involvement with Marilyn Monroe an act of heroism, an attempt to save the life of a person he viewed as condemned to death by the inevitable unfolding of her illness without a professional's attempt to save her? Or was his involvement an act of bravado fueled by his well known narcissism and influenced by the fact that the patient was the world's most recognized film star as well as perhaps the sexiest person alive? These two possibilities are not mutually exclusive.

For a man like Greenson, Monroe was a countertransference trap waiting to happen. She had a way of positioning herself in relation to powerful men as a helpless lost waif (a word that Greenson actually chose in describing her), which would clearly elicit in these men fantasies of greatness and power. For example, the American portrait photographer Philippe Halsman described the experience of working with Monroe this way: "She was extremely easy to photograph, because she completely subordinated herself to you, becoming remarkable putty in your hands. There was no subterranean duel for supremacy going on, as happens with so many models. She gave you a feeling of great power in your own superiority. There she was, adoring you, absolutely smitten; and, oddly enough, every man in the room got the same feeling" (Hattersley, 66).

Nearly ten years earlier, Judd Marmor, also a Beverly Hills psychoanalyst, had published in a 1953 issue of the *American Journal of Psychiatry* a paper titled "The feeling of Superiority: An Occupational Hazard in Psychotherapy." Marmor described the way in which certain psychotherapists are particularly vulnerable to daily projections onto them of their patients' wishes for an omnipotent protector. The therapists eventually come to think of themselves as having competencies, even "magical" powers, lacking in their colleagues. Given the fact that Greenson was already thought of among colleagues as being self-inflated if not grandiose, and that for years his patients had projected onto him their "delegated omnipotence," it is easy to conclude that he imagined himself succeeding with a patient whom his colleagues, some of whom had turned her down, regarded as not only untreatable but also as a potential suicide.

Realizing that he was dealing with a highly disturbed patient, and after relying on the advice of his office partner, Milton Wexler, Greenson decided to launch an "experimental" treatment that consisted of what would be called in other circumstances an array of serious or even bizarre boundary crossings and violations. Current thinking emphasizes a therapist's responsibility to maintain firm boundaries in the treatment of borderline personality disorder, but Greenson's handling of Monroe's case was exactly the opposite. In fact, Hopkins has described Greenson's approach as a "maverick technique" (658, n.15). Aside from the risky possibility of the therapist's developing a sexual relationship with a patient, which hardly anyone believes occurred in this instance, Greenson, with the best of intentions but working in an era before much was known about the disorder, appears in hindsight to have made every possible error one could imagine.

The novelist Michel Schneider speculates that Greenson saw Monroe as a "fatal attraction" whom he thought he could control. "His greatest enemy was boredom and when Marilyn suddenly appeared in his wearily familiar sky, shining with her incredible white brilliance, she represented an escape from the monotony of his practice he could never have hoped for" (26–27). Schneider saw the Greenson-Monroe relationship as emblematic of the larger relationship between psychoanalysis and the film business, each succumbing to the other's madness. "Like all *coups de foudre* and lasting unions, the two professions' encounter was based on confusion: the psychoanalysts were straining to hear the invisible, while the filmmakers sought to put on the screen what couldn't be articulated in words" (16–17).

Rescue Fantasies

We believe that Greenson was in the grip of a "rescue fantasy," a complicated problem in which therapists' narcissism seduces them into believing that they have the ability, perhaps even a special power, to effect a radical cure of a patient's distress rather than achieving more realistic goals. A fulfilled modest goal may be life transforming, but a therapist motivated by a rescue fantasy may not settle for a treatment that leaves a patient with considerable limitations. In Monroe's case, Greenson must have seen himself as trying to save the career, and indeed the life, of a severely ill drug addict who was perhaps the most legendary film star of the 20th century.

Greenson prescribed dangerous medications for Marilyn Monroe well beyond the usual dosages. He also attempted to provide her with relief from her loneliness and despair by using his family as a surrogate home for her. By doing so, he hoped she could experience what a normal family life would be like, in contrast to her chaotic childhood. He must have believed that this unusual therapeutic treatment would stabilize her, break her drug addiction, and make it possible for him to conduct a classical psychoanalytic treatment with her. He never pretended to himself or others that his treatment of her was psychoanalysis.

The Specifics of Greenson's Treatment of Marilyn Monroe

Greenson began seeing Marilyn Monroe on a daily basis, sometimes twice a day. The sessions lasted much longer than the standard 50-minute hour. Some sessions lasted as long as five hours. He made an unusual financial arrangement with her, stating that he would bill her for only one session a day regardless of how much time he spent with her on that day. His justification, he told her, was that he didn't want her to believe he was spending all that time with her simply for the money. The sessions were held in his home or at her apartment (or later at her house). Sometimes therapy sessions occurred in both places on the same day, as Greenson noted in the following statement, which is available on the Internet ("Marilyn Monroe Timeline"):

RALPH R. GREENSON. M.D
436 NORTH ROXBURY DRIVE
BEVERLY HILLS CALIFORNIA

July 15, 1963

Miss Wolf
Gang, Tyre, Rudin & Brown
6400 Sunset Boulevard
Los Angeles, California

Dear Miss Wolf:

    The following is an itemized account explaining
the bill for professional services which I sent to the estate
of Marilyn Monroe for the sum of $1400. I shall list below
the date and place where the psychiatric interview took place:

Sunday, July 1	Patient's Home	
Monday, July 2	Office	
Tuesday, July 3	Office	
Wednesday, July 4	Patient's Home	
Thursday, July 5	Office	
Friday, July 6	Office	
Sunday, July 8	Patient's Home	
Monday, July 9	Office	1962
Tuesday, July 10	Office	
Wednesday, July 11	Office	
Thursday, July 12	Office	
Friday, July 13	Office and Patient's Home	
Monday, July 16	Office	
Tuesday, July 17	Office	
Wednesday, July 18	Office	
Thursday, July 19	Office	
Thursday, July 20	Office	
Monday, July 23	Office and Patient's Home	
Tuesday, July 24	Office	
Wednesday, July 25	Office and Patient's Home	
Thursday, July 26	Office	
Friday, July 27	Office	
Monday, July 30	Office	
Tuesday, July 31	Office	
Wednesday, August 1	Office	
Thursday, August 2	Office and Patient's Home	
Friday, August 3	Office	
Saturday, August 4	Patient's Home.	

Explanation: All office visits lasted a minimum of 1½ hours.
All visits to the home were approximately 2 hours in duration.
On those days on which it was stated that the patient was seen

RALPH R. GREENSON. M.D
436 NORTH ROXBURY DRIVE
BEVERLY HILLS CALIFORNIA

both at the office and at her home, it means there were two
separate visits on that particular day. I had arranged
with Miss Monroe that her fee would be $50. per hour.
However, since she needed a great deal of extra time and
since I did not want her to think I gave her extra time
or made extra visits for monetary reasons, I decided that
I would charge her $50. for every day that I saw her pro-
fessionally. The sum of $1400. therefore represents the
fact that I saw her professionally on 28 days from July 1
through August 4, 1962.

Very truly yours,

Greenson also became involved with Marilyn Monroe's professional and personal life. He convinced her to dismiss her attorneys and to hire instead his brother-in-law, Mickey Rudin, as her attorney. Rudin also represented at least one other Greenson patient, Frank Sinatra, who had an affair with Monroe while both of them were Greenson's patients. The analyst became involved in coaching her acting and in discussing with Fox Studios problems that arose from her absence from work. Greenson attended meetings with Fox executives to plead her case. He convinced Monroe to hire Eunice Murray, the divorced wife of a psychoanalyst colleague, as a live-in housekeeper. Murray, whose family home Greenson had purchased, reported to him in secret on the actress's activities. Greenson also tried to persuade Monroe to end her relationships with several people on whom she had become dependent, including Ralph Roberts, her long standing masseur, close friend and confidant.

There were virtually no boundaries in the Greenson-Monroe relationship. After therapy sessions at his home, he would invite her to stay and have dinner with his family. He asked his daughter, Joan, to pick up Monroe's medications at a pharmacy and deliver them to her home. He urged his daughter, wife, and son, Daniel to befriend the actress and spend time talking to her. She felt free to drop by his home at almost any time and with little notice, even accompanied by friends. She attended parties and "musical evenings" at Greenson's home. He frequently spoke with her by phone between sessions, including during the night when she had trouble sleeping. When she fell apart and he was called on an emergency basis while in Switzerland on a trip, he immediately left his wife there and flew back to Los Angeles even though he had arranged coverage for her while he was away. The absence of boundaries in the patient-therapist relationship implied an absence of professional detachment.

Greenson's children initially maintained a public silence regarding their family's relationship with Monroe, but they chose to speak out regarding their involvement with her in connection with an auction in which they were putting up for sale some of the actress's memorabilia in their possession. Their comments appear in Christopher Turner's "Marilyn Monroe on the Couch," published in *The Telegraph* on June 23, 2010, 47 years after her death. Greenson described Monroe to Kris as a "perpetual orphan," and he enlisted his family to help her. According to Turner, Joan Greenson described Monroe as "fragile, artistic, intuitive and fun-loving." In an unpublished memoir she sent Turner, Joan Greenson, who was an art student at the time, said that Monroe would give her "sisterly advice about men and about life"; other times, "it seemed like I was the older one and more experienced, and I would give her sisterly advice." Daniel Greenson, who became a psychoanalyst like his father, was a medical student when he became acquainted with Monroe at his parents' home. "Until she came along," Daniel Greenson told Turner, his father "was assiduous in not saying anything about who his patients were." Monroe was the only person Daniel Greenson met who was in treatment with his father at the same time. Greenson's children both acknowledged that their father's treatment of Monroe was foolhardy but believed he was motivated to help her. "My father's heart was in the right place," Daniel Greenson told Turner, "but his mind wasn't."

In his memoir *Marilyn: An Untold Story*, the poet and playwright Norman Rosten relates an incident he and his wife, Hedda, witnessed at Greenson's home, where Monroe had invited them to listen to chamber music. Surprised by the invitation, and never having been in analysis himself, Rosten asked Monroe whether such a visit was allowed. "'He's a great person and has a wonderful family,' she said, leaving my question unanswered. 'You'll like them all and vice versa.'" Rosten described Greenson and his family as gracious and wonderfully informal. "Marilyn fitted in easily. One could sense her complete relaxation here, as though this were a second home (a warmer foster home, the thought flashed through my mind)." When Rosten asked Greenson how Monroe was doing in therapy, the analyst replied:

It may seem odd to you the method I am using to treat her, but I firmly believe that treatment has to suit the patient and not vice versa. Marilyn is not an analytic patient, she needs psychotherapy, both supportive and analytical. I have permitted her to become friendly with my family and to visit my home because I felt she needed actual experiences in her present life to make up for the emotional deprivation she suffered from childhood onward. It may seem to you that I have broken the rules, but I feel that if I am fortunate enough, perhaps some years from now, Marilyn may become a psychoanalytic patient. She is not ready for it now. I feel I can tell you these things because she considers you and Hedda her closest friends and there must be somebody with whom I share some of my responsibilities. By the way, I have spoken to Marilyn and she has given me permission to talk to you in general terms about herself. (98–101)

Norman Rosten describes another incident on his final day in Los Angeles when he and Monroe browsed through Beverly Hills galleries. She impulsively purchased for $1,000 ($7,800 in contemporary dollars) a small bronze Rodin statue of a man and woman embracing. Her cheerful mood suddenly darkened as she contemplated the statue on their drive back to her home in her chauffeured limousine. "We'll stop off at my analyst," she abruptly told Rosten. "I want to show him the statue." The decision troubled Rosten, who told her it was wrong to pay such a visit unannounced. "Whereupon Marilyn stopped at her house, phoned him while I waited in the car, and triumphantly returned with the news that we had permission to drop by. She leaned forward inside the car and called out with a giggle, 'On to my doctor!'" Greenson greeted them courteously, and Monroe, after placing the statue on the sideboard adjoining the bar, "stridently" turned toward him and asked what he thought of her new purchase. "He replied quietly that it was a striking piece of art." Unsatisfied with his reply, she kept touching the bronze statue and asked belligerently, "What about it? What does it mean? Is he screwing her or is it a fake? I'd like to know." Referring to what appeared to be a bronze spur attached to the casting, she asked, "What's this? It looks like a penis." After a "sober examination," the three of them decided it wasn't a penis. "Marilyn kept repeating, her voice shrill, 'What do you think, Doctor? What does it mean?'" Rosten ends his vignette with the statement, "A hidden drama was exploding" (113–115).

Rosten's account is reminiscent of Monroe's public outburst toward Marianne Kris in her previous analysis when the actress was alarmed by the threat of abandonment as her marriage with Arthur Miller deteriorated. Rosten doesn't mention the possibility that his own impending departure later that day may have triggered this curious incident. Both incidents show the childlike *real relationship* that Monroe had developed with her psychoanalysts.

Joe DiMaggio came to believe that his former wife regarded her analyst as a surrogate father. Because of her fragile health, DiMaggio decided to spend Christmas of 1961 with her. She informed him that they were going to have dinner with the Greensons. It did not take long for DiMaggio to conclude that she acted as if Greenson was her "long-lost father" and that his family had become a replacement for the one she had never had. According to Taraborrelli, "Joe DiMaggio would say that he had a sick feeling in the pit of his stomach" (390).

Malignant Regression

Although he was not the first to use the term, the British psychoanalyst Michael Balint referred to "malignant regression" in *The Basic Fault* (1968). Using medical language to describe tumors, he noted that the regression occurring in a psychoanalytic treatment may take on two different forms, one benign, of little danger, the other malignant, potentially deadly.

Regression in psychotherapy has been recognized from the beginning of the twentieth century. Without becoming embroiled in the controversies surrounding this phenomenon, we may observe that each person has a tendency to re-experience certain feelings, originally occurring in early childhood, in present-day situations, particularly those involving dependence on another person. These feelings, including love, hate, fear and desire, vary from person to person. Such feelings expressed toward a psychotherapist may become the key to understanding important aspects of a patient's early life and current personality. To benefit from the experience of regression in psychotherapy, patients must be able to maintain a second view of the situation, often called "the observing ego," which will allow them to step back and to view what is happening from the outside, and thus to learn from the experience rather than being absorbed into it.

To assist the patient in maintaining this double view, a therapist attempts to avoid boundary violations that will gratify the patient's inner wishes and heighten the sense of being "taken care of" beyond what is reasonably expected of a therapist in a professional relationship. Going beyond that point may propel certain patients into a state in which infantile wishes become confused with present reality, resulting in the patient's inability to distinguish between the two. Most experts believe that it is important for therapists treating patients suffering from borderline personality disorder to maintain firm therapeutic boundaries, even if this means significant frustration for the patient and a risk to the continuation of the therapy. For these patients, there is a greater risk that gratification of their wishes may trigger *malignant regression*. If this occurs, a patient's subjective need for her therapist may feel so intense that she loses sight of the fact that such feelings are an artifact of the therapeutic situation, replicating her deep attachment to a mothering figure in infancy. Patients may spiral downward into a state where they genuinely cannot face life without the therapist's constant reassurance. They may feel an intense panicky need to have constant contact with the therapist day or night, and they may experience infantile rage toward the therapist when these needs are frustrated. Feelings of intense love and hatred toward the therapist, mixed with unbearable fears of abandonment by the therapist, are part of this descent.

Some therapists become intensely involved with their borderline patients, spending an inordinate amount of time worrying about them, thinking about them, and talking about them. In their 1987 textbook *Effective Psychotherapy with Borderline Patients*, Waldinger and Gunderson repeatedly commented on this problematic relationship. One therapist remarks: "There have been very few human beings in my life with whom I have been as intensely involved as I was with this woman." The analyst's intense involvement with a borderline patient can itself be seen as a countertransference response to the patient's projection onto the therapist of the image of the all-good mother that the therapist then feels pressured to play out (Gorkin). The analyst's attempt to enact the role of ideal mother is fraught with difficulties because of the patient's fears of engulfment, the danger of malignant regression, and the increased probability of the analyst's anger and withdrawal as his or her best caretaking is found wanting by the patient. Balint points out that patients will "feel better, appreciative, and grateful" as long as their needs are gratified by the therapist. The danger occurs when patients' needs cannot be met. "If the expectations are not or cannot be met, what follows is unending suffering or unending vituperation or both. Once this situation has established itself, the analyst will find it very difficult to resist its power, to extricate his patient and himself from it, and still more difficult to terminate the relationship" (140). Sometimes such therapy ends tragically.

Having Monroe around the house wasn't always pleasant for Greenson's family. They accepted his odd treatment of her as reasonable, given his prestige as a psychoanalyst, and the actress was both pleasant and helpful around the house. Nevertheless, Greenson's wife complained that it was difficult to be with Monroe because of her emotional volatility. Greenson's family felt that they were "walking on eggshells." Additionally, when Monroe was not staying at Greenson's home, she made frequent phone calls to him at all hours of the day and night. When Greenson and his family were away on trips, the pattern of frequent phone calls continued, even intensified. Not mentioned in accounts of this relationship is the likely strain Monroe's presence placed on Greenson's marriage.

Regression and Dependency

Greenson encouraged Monroe to sever her connections with those people who he believed were responsible for her drug dependence. The plan may have been well-intentioned, but it heightened her childlike dependence on him. He became increasingly aware of the extent of her illness. He told colleagues, according to Taraborrelli, that she had begun "to exhibit strong and growing signs of borderline paranoid schizophrenia, just like her mother and, possibly, her grandmother before her." Three psychiatrists told the biographer that years earlier Greenson had confided to them, separately, his belief that she was suffering from borderline paranoid schizophrenia. "He was very specific," one of the doctors told Taraborrelli. "He was concerned, very much so. He felt it would get worse as she got older unless it was treated in a specific way.

He also said that Marilyn knew and that she was looking into ways to treat it herself, and that he was trying to discourage that. He didn't want her out there medicating herself, but he suspected that this is what was going on behind his back." He tried prescribing the powerful antipsychotic drug Thorazine but changed his mind when he became concerned about a side effect, perhaps weight gain, that she experienced while taking it. She, however, then continued to seek out Thorazine from other physicians (372–379).

Soon Greenson began to fear that he would never be able to break her drug dependency. As a celebrity, she always seemed able to find a doctor who would prescribe additional drugs including barbiturates. "Doctors had gone along with her demands for new and stronger sleeping pills even though they knew perfectly well how dangerous this was," Arthur Miller lamented. "There were always new doctors willing to help her into oblivion" (Taraborrelli, 335). "I'm not sure how to monitor someone like her," Greenson admitted to Anna Freud. "She's very crafty" (Taraborrelli, 371).

Monroe's condition continued to deteriorate in early 1962. She was involved in a new film project, *Something's Got to Give,* which Greenson had advised her to undertake to complete her contract to Fox Studios. Her eroding self-confidence, however, along with increasing drug use and physical illness, made it impossible for her to appear for filming sessions. The studio was so worried about her inability to appear on the set that they hired Greenson as a consultant. He was beginning to feel the strain of her deepening dependence on him, as Summers observes. "Marilyn's anchor, to the extent that she had one at all, was Dr. Greenson. She saw him almost every day. As crisis followed crisis, and as Marilyn threatened to fall back wholly on drugs, his sessions with her would last four or five hours." He later wrote that he had become a "prisoner of a form of treatment that I thought was correct

461

for her, but almost impossible for me. At times I felt I couldn't go on with this" (269). He saw her seven days a week, but he felt he was making her psychological problems worse, perhaps because of his countertransference. Realizing she could not tolerate any negative feelings arising from his behavior, Greenson feared that the only way she could achieve peace was through death, an unsettling thought. Even more unsettling is the likelihood that he wished for her death.

Folie à Deux

To our knowledge, no one has written about a possible link between malignant regression and *folie à deux*, a French expression for "madness shared by two," or shared psychosis. Greenson was not psychotic, but he must have worried about the consequences of his decision to involve himself in nearly every aspect of Marilyn Monroe's life. They seemed to share the delusion that neither could live without the other. Eventually, Greenson ended his work with other patients to work *solely* with Monroe.

On Greenson's advice, in early 1962 Monroe purchased a home about one mile from his and in the same architectural style. He hoped that owning a home for the first time in her life would give her a base of security that could replace the security she seemed to experience by spending social time at the Greenson home. A tug of war seemed to be developing during this time between DiMaggio and Greenson, at the time the two most important men in Monroe's life, with the winner gaining control over her. She did not want a permanent residence in the Los Angeles area, a feeling that DiMaggio shared.

In early March, when negotiations about the proposed new Fox film *Something's Got to Give* were in progress, Monroe appeared in public to receive the Golden Globe Award. According to her friend Susan Strasberg, Monroe showed up at the dinner "drunk, barely in control, her voice slurred—and she wore a dress so tight she could hardly move" (Spoto, 497). "For once, the silence in the room betokened not admiration or awe but, even in Hollywood, shock."

For the past few days, Monroe had been living in an upstairs bedroom at the Greensons' home, supposedly while waiting for her new house to be ready. DiMaggio had arrived in Los Angeles to assist her in moving to her new house, and upon learning that she was residing with the Greensons, he proceeded there. His arrival was described by a Greenson supervisee (later interviewed by Spoto) who happened to be at the house. The young doctor thought it was odd that Marilyn Monroe was upstairs, "in residence," as she had often been during the previous year, and now under sedation for emotional collapse. According to Spoto, at that time the supervisee believed—as he continued to believe many years later—that the arrangement was "out of line for a prominent training analyst who was supposed to be teaching students both the proper frame in which to help people and the proper professional identity to keep in working with patients."

The situation became odder when DiMaggio arrived at Greenson's home and found his former wife upstairs. "Learning that Joe had arrived she wanted to see him. But Greenson forbade them to meet. He asked Joe to remain downstairs to talk with him, and after a while Marilyn began to make a minor fuss upstairs—like a person confined to a hospital against her will who wanted to see her family or her visitors. Nevertheless, Greenson insisted on detaining Joe, and Marilyn was eventually close to a tantrum." Then came the oddest moment of all. "Joe excused himself and insisted that he was going to go up to see Marilyn, and Greenson turned to me and said, "You see, this is a good example of the narcissistic character. See how demanding she is? She has to have things her way. She's nothing but a child, poor thing" (Spoto, 500). The supervisee never said anything to Greenson,

463

but the event distressed him for years, and he lost respect for his former mentor. Spoto adds, "No professional expertise is required to recognize the classic signs of projection, for it was obviously Ralph Greenson himself who had to exert control and whose narcissistic personality demanded that he have his way with her."

Greenson's mother-in-law, who was living in Switzerland, suffered a stroke in February 1962, and Hildi Greenson asked her husband to accompany her to Europe. Fearing the effect of his separation from his now extremely dependent patient, Greenson postponed a decision for as long as possible, but he finally agreed on a five-week visit, beginning in May. He decided to combine the visit with a speaking engagement in Tel Aviv. One can easily imagine that Greenson's hesitation to leave his patient under these circumstances was a source of family tension. His decision to leave Monroe for several weeks surprised and annoyed Greenson's friend Henry Weinstein, whom the analyst had maneuvered into place as the producer of *Something's Got to Give*" in place of David Brown, the studio's original producer for the film. Discovering Monroe comatose at home one day in mid-April when she failed to appear for an appointment, Weinstein became aware of her deteriorated condition. He described her then as having been in a "barbiturate coma" (Spoto, 508). Hildi Greenson greatly anticipated the Switzerland trip, "perhaps as much for the chance to put some distance between her husband and the patient to whom he was inordinately and inextricably attached; by this time, anyone who knew patient and therapist also knew that she had become virtually his career. Greenson admitted to a close friend that "Hildi was afraid to leave me home alone" (515).

The Greensons left on May 10, 1962, and Monroe's condition worsened, perhaps because of the analyst's absence. Such a separation of a borderline patient and a psychotherapist could even in the best of circumstances have a disturbing effect, but in the case of a highly unstable patient who has regressed to a state of extreme emotional dependence on her therapist, the effects could be devastating. Greenson later wrote about some of the measures he and Monroe took to avoid her complete collapse while he was away. First, he arranged coverage by his office partner, Milton Wexler, who already knew through his "supervision" of Greenson of the problem. Second, Greenson asked his children to look after her while he was away. Third, he gave Monroe a prescription for Dexamyl, a combination of a barbiturate and the stimulant Dexedrine. This drug, no longer sold, could be dangerous, especially for a barbiturate-addicted patient like Monroe. Greenson later wrote that the drug was "an attempt to give her something of me to swallow, to take in, so she could overcome the sense of terrible emptiness that would depress and infuriate her" (Spoto, 515). Greenson was unaware, however, that she had several sources for a variety of barbiturates and other drugs, including Demerol, a narcotic.

A White Knight

Monroe discovered her own way to rescue herself, albeit temporarily. She found an amulet, a magical good luck charm in the form of a white knight from a chess set, which she said made her think of Greenson. She resolved to carry it everywhere during his absence to protect her from overwhelming anxiety. Greenson described this phenomenon in a clinical vignette in a 1974 paper, "On Transitional Objects and Transference." The patient he describes can easily be identified as Marilyn Monroe.

> I told an emotionally immature young woman patient, who had developed a very dependent transference to me, that I was going to attend an International Congress in Europe some three months thence. We worked intensively on the multiple determinants of her clinging

465

dependence, but made only insignificant progress. Then the situation changed dramatically when one day she announced that she had discovered something that would tide her over my absence. It was not some insight, not a new personal relationship, it was a chess piece. The young woman had recently been given a gift of a carved ivory chess set. The evening before her announcement, as she looked at the set, through the sparkling light of a glass of champagne, it suddenly struck her that I looked like the white knight of her chess set. The realization immediately evoked in her a feeling of comfort, even triumph. The white knight was a protector, it belonged to her, she could carry it wherever she went, it would look after her, and I could go on my merry way to Europe without having to worry about her. (493–494)

Greenson saw one symbolic meaning of the white knight but missed another symbolic meaning. Called Romeo when he was born, Greenson was the white knight, the therapist-savior who would rescue his Juliet, the damsel in psychiatric distress. The boy who loved to lose himself as a child in the romantic travails of beautiful actresses now had an opportunity as a man to make his messianic dreams come true. Motivated by rescue fantasies, he would succeed where others had failed.

At the time of his departure for Europe, Greenson suggested that Monroe dismiss Paula Strasberg, her long-time acting coach. Instead, Monroe fired her housekeeper, Eunice Murray, Greenson's friend. Monroe's undeniably hostile act of defiance toward Greenson must have indicated the rage she was feeling for his "abandonment" of her during this perilous time in her life. Firing the housekeeper may have also been Monroe's concession to the friends who were urging the actress to end her relationship with Greenson.

During this time Monroe failed to appear for several filming sessions for *Something's Got to Give*, and the film was falling behind schedule. The film was in trouble for other reasons, including frantic daily revisions of the script. The entire Fox studio was sinking into financial ruin, partly as a result of rocketing costs from the simultaneous project *Cleopatra* starring Elizabeth Taylor, Monroe's much more highly-paid Fox Studio rival. Although the costs of Monroe's film were a mere fraction of Taylor's, Fox was actively considering shutting down the former. Some biographers believe that the studio sought a way to blame the shutdown on Monroe to collect on the film's insurance.

Monroe received a breach of contract notice from the Fox office on May 17, implicitly threatening legal action if she failed to appear for filming sessions. According to Spoto, two witnesses recalled that her response was "undisguised justifiable outrage," blaming the entire situation on her absent analyst. "How could Greenson have blithely left her for Europe?" She was furious that her "team," as she called the three men at Fox: her producer Weinstein, her analyst Greenson and her lawyer Rudin failed to protect her (519).

On the same day, May 17, nine days after Greenson's departure for Europe, Monroe was scheduled to fly to New York to sing "Happy Birthday" to President Kennedy at a birthday celebration to be held in Madison Square Garden two days later. The thought of the performance terrified her. There is some evidence that she believed Jack and Jacqueline Kennedy would soon be divorced and that he would marry the actress. Mrs. Kennedy did not attend her husband's celebration, an indication perhaps of her displeasure over Monroe's appearance. How do we interpret Monroe's belief, if indeed that's what it was, that the President of the United States planned to marry her? Was the idea merely wishful thinking or delusional, as is seen in some patients with "erotomania," a delusional belief that one is loved by a person of high status? On the other hand, there might have been a quasi-realistic basis for Monroe's belief. She had already been married to one of the greatest baseball superstars in history—and then one of the greatest American playwrights.

With the white knight concealed in her dress, which must have been awkward for her because the dress was almost transparent, so tight that it had to be sewn onto her, Monroe delivered an iconic, erotically charged and seductive version of "Happy Birthday" aimed at Kennedy to enormous acclaim from the audience and Kennedy's embarrassment. At the conclusion of the celebration, the President thanked the various performers at the gala and then offered his wry comment on Monroe's performance. "I can now retire from politics after having had Happy Birthday sung to me in such a sweet, wholesome way."

In the days following the gala, Monroe was in a continuing rage about Greenson's abandonment of her. She continued to work on the film, but the wheels for her dismissal were turning behind the scenes. She celebrated her 36th birthday at the end of the June 1 filming session in a brief party put on by the crew and her friends, but at which the film's director conspicuously failed to appear. She then returned to her lonely home. According to Spoto, she told friends in telephone calls that evening that she was enraged at Greenson, on whom she had been "conditioned to rely completely." She felt she had no defenses against the axe that was "about to fall" (526).

She must have felt that the axe had indeed fallen one day later when, "weeping uncontrollably," she telephoned Greenson's children, who had been told by their father to respond to her calls. "They entered Marilyn's bedroom where they found her indescribably lonely and depressed, then giddy and disoriented—the classic signs of Dexamyl overdose" (Spoto, 527). They called Milton Wexler, who came immediately and found not only a drugged patient but also a significant collection of a variety of prescription drugs on her nightstand. Clearly the situation was out of control; she had been obtaining drugs without Greenson's awareness. Wexler took all the drugs he saw on the nightstand and left. Because he was not a physician, he was perhaps unaware of the possible problems arising during a sudden withdrawal from the various medications she might have been taking.

Greenson describes in the same paper from which we quoted above the panicky transatlantic telephone calls from her while he was in Europe. "The patient had lost the white knight and was beside herself with terror and gloom, like a child who has lost her security blanket. A colleague of mine [Wexler] who saw her in that interval said that all his interventions were to no avail and he reluctantly suggested that I cut short my trip and return. I hated to interrupt my vacation and I doubted whether my return would be beneficial." His return proved to be surprisingly helpful. "I no sooner saw her than her anxiety and depression lifted" (494). He suggested later that he and the patient worked through the meaning of the white knight to the patient's benefit. We suspect the truth was otherwise.

We agree with Spoto that "the contradictions in Greenson's conduct must be faced in all their complexity." Greenson did what therapists in his situation are trained to avoid: he enacted the role of savior and made himself central in a patient's life (528). The spectacle of a psychoanalyst flying across the world from Switzerland to Los Angeles in response to an emergency call from a patient would be unusual enough, probably *unprecedented*; but the fact that Greenson was the *second psychoanalyst* in the span of six years to fly across the ocean in response to an emergency call from the same patient makes the event more astounding. Hohenberg, we recall, had flown to England from New York in response to Monroe's crisis during the filming of *The Prince and the Showgirl* in 1956.

A Damsel with Two Black Eyes

Furthermore, it is clear that Greenson was sorely aggrieved by this event. His use of the word "hated" to describe how he felt about interrupting his vacation seems, intentionally or not, to convey his countertransference feelings at that juncture. Arriving in Los Angeles

469

on June 6, he immediately drove to Monroe's home where they had an encounter that developed into a physical altercation. Two biographers, Spoto (532) and Badman (176), both believe that Greenson became violent and struck her in the face hard enough to blacken her eyes. At her insistence, Greenson then drove her in his car to the office of Dr. Michael Gurdin, a plastic surgeon whom she had consulted on an earlier occasion. Gurdin's office notes describe her as under the influence of drugs with slurred speech and hesitant to speak. Greenson, instead, answered most of Gurdin's questions. The plastic surgeon found her to have facial bruises (in common language, two black eyes) that could have resulted from either a fall or having been struck in the nose. According to Greenson, she fell in the shower, although there was no shower in the house in which she was living.

There is another reason why it was unlikely that Monroe's facial injuries were caused by a fall. Because the studio was considering dismissing her from *Something's Got to Give* as a result of her absences from the set, replacing her with another actress, it would have been in her interest had the injury been disclosed to the studio. This would be a plausible explanation for why she couldn't return to the film until her face healed. Instead, Greenson made no such disclosure to the studio even though he was holding meetings with studio executives guaranteeing her return. Greenson preferred to hush up the incident rather than offer an explanation. The credibility of the biographers' accounts is heightened indirectly by the fact that the physical encounter between Greenson and Monroe was by no means the only such event in the history of psychoanalysis. Analysts working with difficult patients have sometimes slipped into a countertransference trap from which they were unable to extricate themselves. Astonishingly, it was Greenson's office partner and consultant for the Monroe case, Milton Wexler, who in 1964, two years after Monroe's death, was accused by a patient of slapping her in a fight. According to one account, Greenson, hearing the screaming from the adjoining office, ran into the office and "wrestled Wexler to the ground and pulled them apart" (Kirsner, *Unfree Associations* 154). A committee of leaders in the Los Angeles Psychoanalytic Institute believed the accusation was credible and related it to the same kind of "great closeness" between the analyst and the patient that had occurred in the Greenson-Monroe case.

As Kirsner reports (307), this was not the first instance in which Wexler was involved in a physical struggle with a female patient. Wexler described the event in a 1951 article. Assaulted by a patient, he immobilized her and then felt a "strong resentment" that compelled him to take more forceful action. "I fulfilled my promise to meet force with force. I can say this about our struggles together: With but one exception, never did any of our vehement verbal and physical battles end without peace-making and affectionate exchanges of devotion; rarely did she omit to thank me for putting an end to the threatening and overwhelming forces which had seized control of her" (159). The accusation against Wexler led to a political battle within the Institute, from which he eventually withdrew. It appears that the only reason he was not disciplined by the Institute was because of his ability as an attorney to find procedural flaws in the ethics investigation. With the help of his historian daughter, Alice Wexler, he and she emphatically denied the Institute's accusations. Kirsner concluded from his own investigation of the case that the charges against Wexler were accurate (274, ff.).

The studio was informed that Monroe would not be able to return to work for the next few days, but despite Greenson's reassurances to studio executives that she would return, she was fired from the picture the next day. Fox filed a $500,000 lawsuit against Monroe. Unknown to them at the time, she had only two more months to live. A Fox Studio memorandum describes the next events. On June 8, unaware of the

OFF THE TRACKS VOLUME 1

lawsuit that was not made public until later that day, Greenson met with Fox Studio executives (Spoto, 533). He had two difficult tasks: concealing Monroe's injury until the bruises healed, and reassuring the executives that she would return to work on the film. In response to the studio's doubts that she would return to work, Greenson said he "would be able to get his patient to go along with any reasonable request and *although he did not want us to deem his relationship as a Svengali one, he in fact could persuade her to anything reasonable that he wanted*" (534, Spoto's italics).

An Intriguing Parallel

The following two months were a whirlwind of confusion and stress. Greenson saw Monroe daily, either at his office or at her home. Sometimes he saw her twice a day, for sessions lasting usually ninety minutes but occasionally up to five hours. Ironically, Greenson's behavior weirdly echoed the increasing time that Josef Breuer devoted to his treatment of "Anna O." (Bertha Pappenheim), a case which, despite its disastrous outcome, led to Freud's creation of psychoanalysis. "The Case of Fraulein Anna O.," written by Breuer and appearing in *Studies on Hysteria* (1895), co-authored by Breuer and Freud, has been called the "founding myth" of psychoanalysis. "Even for a talented and compassionate physician," remarks Gillhooley, "Breuer's treatment of Anna O. was unusual and truly exemplary. As devoted as Anna had been to the care of her father, Breuer became as intensely devoted to her, for long stretches of her treatment seeing her twice a day. One researcher estimates that Breuer put over a thousand hours into his treatment of Anna. This was unheard of in late-nineteenth-century Vienna" (93). Like Breuer with Anna O., Greenson became consumed by his treatment of Marilyn Monroe, devoting countless hours to her, unable to break her spell over him.

Beyond the malignant regression experienced by both Anna O. (Balint, 139, 149–150) and Marilyn Monroe, there are two further eerie connections. Both Breuer and Greenson attempted to allay their patients' mounting anxiety, and possibly to extricate themselves from awkward situations, by prescribing a calming agent. Both physicians coincidentally chose chloral hydrate, now an antiquated but occasionally still used drug first introduced to medicine in 1869 and the first artificially synthesized sedative-hypnotic drug in medical history. The second even stranger link between the two cases is that in the casting of the 1960 film *Freud: The Secret Passion*, director John Huston wanted to enlist Monroe to play the part of Anna O. Greenson conferred with Anna Freud, who disapproved of the idea of such a film, and when he conveyed this information to Monroe, she wrote a letter to Huston declining the part:

The Beverly Hills Hotel

November 6, 1960

Dear John,

I have it on good authority that the Freud family does not approve of anyone making a picture of the life of Freud—so I wouldn't want to be part of it, first because of his great contribution to humanity and secondly my personal regard for his work.

Thank you for offering me the part of "Anna O." and I wish you the best in this and all other endeavors.

Yours,

Marilyn

The Beverly Hills Hotel
AND BUNGALOWS
BEVERLY HILLS · CALIFORNIA

November 5, 1960

Dear John,

I have it on good authority that the Freud family does not approve of anyone making a picture of the life of Freud — so I wouldn't want to be apart of it, first because of his great contribution to humanity and secondly, my personal regard for his work.

Thank you for offering me the part of "Annie O." and! I wish you the best in this and all other endeavors.

Yours

Marilyn

PERSIAN ROOM · LANAI RESTAURANT · POLO LOGGIA & PATIO

After her firing, Monroe began a public campaign to revive her career, worried that she might never make another film. She granted a number of interviews to journalists and posed for still photo shoots with eager photographers from *Vogue*, *Cosmopolitan* and *Life* magazines. The intensity of the campaign was based on a combination of her enormous popularity and the public's hunger for photos and magazine articles about her. In the meantime, her co-star in *Something's Got to Give*, Dean Martin, who had a clause in his contract giving him a veto over the selection of his co-star, refused to continue the picture without her. Eventually, Fox agreed to rehire Monroe and doubled her salary; a new contract was completed on August 1, following negotiations in which Greenson and Rudin participated.

Although Greenson sought to wean Monroe from her heavy drug use, she continued to obtain barbiturates and other sedative drugs from different sources without his knowledge or that of her internist, Hyman Engelberg, to whom her analyst had delegated responsibility for her medications. Biographers disagree sharply about her activities at this time. Some claim that she underwent an abortion in July. Others biographers claim she had a sexual relationship with either President John F. Kennedy or his brother, Robert Kennedy, the Attorney General (or possibly both) and that, embarrassed by her performance at the President's birthday party, the Kennedys were breaking off their relationship with her. Still other biographers allege that she had decided to end her treatment with Greenson and remarry DiMaggio, who had been the only reliable figure near the end of her life (Summers, 296; Spoto, 549). Based on later statements from Summers and Spoto, it is plausible that she was caught in a clash between DiMaggio and Greenson, each urging her to break off her relationship with the other (Heymann, 366–367). DiMaggio had submitted his resignation from his job, which required considerable travel, effective July 31, 1962, in anticipation of their scheduled second marriage (Spoto, 249).

From professional bills found in her files, it appears that during May, June and July of 1962, Monroe had also been consulting by telephone with Margaret Hohenberg, the New York analyst whom she had been seeing prior to her treatment with Marianne Kris. Monroe may have been consulting with Hohenberg in anticipation of ending her treatment with Greenson and returning to New York. It's not clear whether Greenson knew about her telephone sessions with Hohenberg. Monroe's chaotic personal life heightened her anxiety and insomnia, further increasing her consumption of sedatives. Greenson had a marathon five-hour therapy session with Monroe at her home on Saturday, August 4, 1962. Her tragic death occurred a few hours after that session, just four days before her scheduled wedding date with DiMaggio.

Death

Reimagining and retelling the story of Marilyn Monroe's death has become a major industry. Reports of phone conversations with her by a variety of friends and acquaintances at the end of July and early August inconsistently described her as lucid, cheerful, drugged, and depressed. The number of published accounts and video "documentaries" of her death probably exceeds the number of full biographies that have and continue to be written. Many of these accounts portray her death as murder by sinister outside forces. Speculation over her "murder" has centered on the Kennedys, CIA, FBI, Greenson, certain organized crime figures and the fired housekeeper Eunice Murray. Conspiracy theories abound with elusive sightings around her house on her death day, stolen recordings from "bugs" planted in her home by government agencies and/or private investigators, and mysterious trips to a hospital by ambulance where she was pronounced dead and then returned to her house to cover up what happened. An entire entry on Wikipedia is devoted to the "Death of Marilyn Monroe."

She was found dead during the night of August 4 or the early hours of August 5. Drug overdose is the best explanation of her death. Huge amounts of both barbiturates and chloral hydrate were found in her blood at the autopsy. It appears that both Greenson and Engelberg had prescribed sedatives for her in the days before her death. The two physicians were not in communication with each other at that time, partly due to some problems in Engleberg's personal life that made him difficult to reach. The content of Greenson's five-hour therapy session with Monroe at her home on the afternoon of August 4 is not known. An investigation by the Los Angeles Coroner attributed the death to "an overdose of sedative drugs, a probable suicide." A CBS news video on April 20, 2006, reviewed additional evidence gathered since her death and raises the provocative question: "Was it suicide or was it murder?" Biographers such as Alma Halbert Bond suggest that loneliness was the driving force behind the death. "For Marilyn Monroe, as for many others, the only companion to accompany her to the grave was her loneliness" (251), an interpretation that implies suicide. But there is a third highly plausible possibility: an accident.

During the 1960s psychiatrists became more aware of the potential of barbiturates to cause accidental deaths in patients using barbiturates for sleep. Significantly, the passage discussing acute barbiturate poisoning in the 1978 ninth edition of the same book's 1958 fifth edition from which we quoted earlier describes acute barbiturate intoxication as occurring "frequently in those with suicidal intent and sometimes as an accidental occurrence in some who are using such agents for insomnia. In the latter instance, in partially confusional states from previous doses that have failed to provide hypnosis [i.e., sleep], the patient automatically takes excessive amounts. Again, accidental overdosage may be observed in persons suffering severe anxiety who self-administer additional doses when the prescribed amount has failed to bring relief" (Kolb, *Modern Clinical Psychiatry*, 674).

We speculate that the struggle between Monroe's friends, including Joe DiMaggio, to whom she was to be remarried in four days, and Ralph Greenson, who had been attempting to sever her contact with friends, might have been the trigger of the agitation she had been experiencing. The battle between these two forces might account for Monroe's five-hour session with Greenson earlier that day. Her unresolvable ambivalence toward Greenson as a result of his role in her malignant regression must have been unbearable. In her view, she needed Greenson to survive, but she believed he had abandoned her during the time of her greatest need to be with his wife in Europe. Upon returning, he then physically injured her during a heated argument. It's possible, perhaps likely, that he had devoted those five hours to an attempt to persuade her to cancel the plans for her marriage, something she refused to do because at that time in her life DiMaggio was the only person she felt she could rely on. Near the end of her life she had emotionally substituted DiMaggio as her anchor and fantasied protector in place of the formerly idealized Greenson. Her love for Greenson had turned to burning resentment. At least two of her acquaintances reported her stated intention to free herself from Greenson (Spoto, 558).

Years earlier, Susan Strasberg had observed Monroe's pattern of drug taking when the actress was a frequent overnight guest at the Strasberg apartment in New York. In one disturbing scene, she found Monroe dazed and confused. Unable to stand in the apartment hallway, Monroe crawled across to the Strasberg's bedroom door. "She finally raised her hand, and began to scratch on it like a puppy that's been locked out. 'Lee . . . Lee,' she whimpered. I decided that if my parents didn't hear her, I had to help her. I couldn't stand seeing her like that. Just as I started toward her, the door opened and my father appeared. He was half-asleep. But he lifted her up and carried her back to Johnny's room [Strasberg's brother's bedroom, which the actress used when visiting]. She'd taken too many pills again. She would forget and take more and then remember too late" (90–91). This pattern of drug taking closely resembles that described in the excerpt from the Kolb textbook. The regressive nature of Monroe's relationship with the Strasberg family, a forerunner of her more intense attachment to the Greensons, is illustrated by another vignette reported by Susan Strasberg. One night she passed the open door of Johnny's room and saw her father in pajamas "sitting on the side of the bed, holding Marilyn cradled in his arms." He was softly singing a Brahms lullaby, the same lullaby he had sung to his daughter when she was a little girl. "Her eyes were closed, her head lay trustingly on his shoulder. A slight smile softened her lips" (90).

According to Spoto, Greenson had stopped prescribing Nembutal for her, and he also had asked Engelberg to refrain from prescribing Nembutal without his permission. "They were to monitor the drugs each was providing. But the previous day Engelberg wrote Marilyn a prescription for Nembutal without Greenson's knowledge." Supported by the autopsy data and toxicology results, Spoto reasonably concludes that when Greenson left Monroe's home, with the actress still in an agitated state, he instructed Eunice Murray to administer to her an enema containing chloral hydrate, a technique used in the pre-tranquilizer era to bring about rapid sedation of agitated patients in hospitals. The use of enemas was a commonplace then among actresses, including Monroe as a means of weight control, although they were not commonly regarded as a method of drug administration (586). Removing the liquid from chloral hydrate capsules and adding it to an enema would have been a simple task for Murray. However, the interaction of the Nembutal that Monroe had been taking during the day and the chloral hydrate in the enema proved fatal. If Greenson had been consciously aware of the amount of Nembutal she had taken, he would not have ordered the chloral hydrate. Rudin recalled Greenson saying on the night of Marilyn's death, "'God Damn it! Hy [Engelberg] gave her a prescription I didn't know about!' John Mier recalled a similar, incomplete statement [by Greenson]: 'If only I'd known about the other prescription" (Spoto, 586).

Following Monroe's death, the "body desired by millions belonged to no one" (Spoto, 594). Monroe's funeral was arranged by DiMaggio, who invited 30 guests including Monroe's close friends and the Greenson family. Many biographies reprint a photograph of a shaken looking Greenson and his family at the funeral. Allan "Whitey" Snyder, her make-up artist and long time friend, who was all too aware of her obsessive need to look her best in public, made her up for this last public appearance. Pointedly, DiMaggio did not invite any members of the Hollywood set: neither the press, executives, producers, writers, nor the performers with whom she had worked. For years thereafter, he had flowers delivered to her grave weekly.

Arthur Miller

Marilyn Monroe's third husband, Arthur Miller, did not have flowers delivered weekly to her grave, as her second husband did. Instead, he wrote about her first in his play *After the Fall* and then in his autobiographical *Timebends*. He implies throughout *Timebends* that she was intoxicated by death and that nothing, including psychoanalysis, could release her from its fatal spell. "Beneath all her insouciance and wit, death was her companion everywhere and at all times, and it may be that its unacknowledged presence was what lent her poignancy, dancing at the edge of oblivion as she was"

(242). No Freudian, Miller nevertheless believed that the "branching tree of her catastrophe was rooted in her having been condemned from birth—*cursed* might be a better word—despite all she knew and all she hoped" (436). Only by living at the peak, "only in the permanent rush of a crescendo was there safety, or at least forgetfulness, and when the wave dispersed she would turn cruelly against herself, so worthless, the scum of the earth, and her vileness would not let her sleep, and then the pills began and the little suicides each night" (436).

Greenson's Reaction

Greenson was overwhelmed by Monroe's death, experiencing a maelstrom of feelings of loss, failure and humiliation over the death of his most famous patient. These feelings were probably complicated by rage. It's likely that he had, consciously or not, a death wish toward her as their relationship became more and more unmanageable. He knew that the relationship was damaging his personal and professional life. At the same time, he seemed to feel both guilt and anger toward the others whom he implicated in Monroe's death, notably Hyman Engelberg and, oddly, Robert Kennedy. "We made some mistakes," the grief-stricken Greenson admitted to the press. "And if you really want to know what happened to Marilyn, why don't you ask Robert Kennedy" (Jay Margolis, 167). He made a similar remark during a recorded phone call with a reporter in 1964. Kirsner discovered a letter in the Anna Freud archive in the Library of Congress, written by Greenson on August 20, 1962, that reveals the depth of his despair:

This has been a terrible blow in many ways. I cared about her and she was my patient. She was so pathetic and she had had such a terrible life. I had hopes for her and I thought we were making progress. And now she died and I realize that all my knowledge and my desire and my strength was not enough. God knows I tried and mightily so, but I could not defeat all the destructive forces that had been stirred up in her by the terrible experiences of her past life, and even of her present life. Sometimes I feel the world wanted her to die, or at least many people in the world, particularly those who after her death so conspicuously grieved and mourned. It makes me angry. But above all I feel sad and also disappointed. (Kirsner, "Do As I Say," 478)

Greenson was amazed by the number of people who were devastated by her death. He decided to travel to New York for a few days, both to escape from the press, which was insensitive to his grief, and to talk to his analyst and colleague, Max Schur, who had been Freud's physician. "I can say certain things [to him] which I cannot say to anybody here" (Margolis, 166). On January 20, 1963, Anna Freud sympathetically wrote back to him, telling him about her own patient who had taken cyanide two days before she returned from a visit to the United States a few years earlier. "One goes over and over in one's head to find out where one could have done better and it leaves one with a terrible sense of being defeated. But, you know, I think in these cases we are really defeated by something which is stronger than we are and for which analysis, with all its powers, is too weak a weapon" (167).

Nor did the passing of time mitigate Greenson's grief. Seven years after her death he was still describing himself as devastated. "I don't know if I will ever get over it really and completely" (Farber and Green, 107). Marilyn Monroe's death was a turning point in his life. "He went through a long period of soul-searching and reassessment, taking on fewer private patients and immersing himself in his teaching and writing. He even decided to grow a beard in a conscious effort to change his physical appearance." Asked by a colleague about the significance of his beard, he responded, "I wanted to be somebody else" (110). From that point on Greenson's personal and professional life seems to have gone downhill. Characterized as "depressed and disillusioned," he continued to work until at least 1970 at which time another patient, the 35-year-old actress Inger Stevens, committed suicide with an overdose of barbiturates. According to Hyman Engelberg, Greenson "seemed to want to get away from himself. . . . His friendships waned and he became something of a recluse. I saw less and less of him as time went on, partially, I suppose because I left the medical office we shared, and moved to a new address. A frail and broken man haunted by his failed efforts to save Marilyn Monroe, Ralph Greenson died in 1979. Frankly, I don't think there's anything that anyone, including Ralph Greenson, could have done to rescue Marilyn. One way or the other, she had made up her mind by this juncture to end her life" (Heymann, 367).

In "Special Problems in Psychotherapy with the Rich and Famous," an unpublished essay dated August 18, 1978 and now in Greenson's locked archive at UCLA, the analyst, according to Spoto, "described the end of his relationship with this special client in a passage immediately following a lightly veiled disquisition on Marilyn, her background and her problems." It's not clear how Spoto gained access to the locked archives, though we don't question the accuracy of his reporting. "Rich and famous people," Greenson wrote, "believe that prolonged psychotherapy is a rip-off. They want their therapist as a close friend, they even want their wife and their children to become part of the therapist's family. . . . These patients are seductive." The rich and famous, Greenson continued, "need the therapist twenty-four hours a day," and they are "insatiable." Greenson's bitterness toward these patients is palpable. "They are also able to give you up completely in the sense they are doing to you what was done to them by their parents or servants. You are their servant and can be dismissed without notice" (Spoto, 559). Apart from enigmatic remarks to the press and a statement to the coroner during the investigation mentioning Monroe's sexual encounter with a high government official, Greenson remained publicly silent about the case for several years. Eventually, though, events gave him an excuse to speak to the press. Once he began speaking in public, he couldn't stop.

Conspiracy Theories

Given the enormous notoriety of Monroe's death, which made headlines around the world, rumors began to circulate about sinister plots to murder her and her alleged sexual involvement with the Kennedy brothers, organized crime figures, Frank Sinatra and Greenson himself. These rumors were abetted by well known gossip columnists of the day, most notably Walter Winchell. Monroe's involvement with the Kennedy brothers, which Greenson appeared to confirm after her death, added fuel to the firestorm of conspiracy theories. According to Spoto, the stories arose from a group of sleazy, profiteering writers and investigators who voiced allegation after allegation to form an echo chamber of half truths and outright lies. It is likely that Monroe did have a relationship with John and Robert Kennedy, including on one occasion a sexual encounter with the President. This may have retriggered the erotomania that she experienced earlier in her life, leading to a delusional belief that Jack Kennedy was in love with her and was prepared to leave his wife to marry her. Following her embarrassing public appearance at the President's birthday party, it is likely that Robert Kennedy was instructed to inform her that she should have no more contact with either himself or the President. Telephone logs in the Justice Department record her numerous attempts to reach Robert Kennedy. The calls were intercepted and did not go through to him. This may have been the "rejection" to which Greenson referred when he blurted out Robert Kennedy's name to the press following Monroe's death. In a 1964 recorded phone conversation with the journalist William Woodfield, Greenson again raised Robert Kennedy's name. "I can't explain or defend myself without revealing things that I don't want to reveal. I feel I—I can't, you know—you can't draw a line and say I'll tell you this but I won't tell you that. It's a terrible position to be in to have to say I can't talk about it because I can't tell the whole story. . . . Listen, you know, talk to Bobby Kennedy" (Margolis and Buskin, 168).

Incited by Greenson's remarks, conspiracy theorists confidently alleged that the Kennedy brothers were responsible for Monroe's death. The stories lacked credibility and by 1965, those involved in circulating the rumors proved to be unreliable narrators. The whispers about Robert Kennedy and the "Kennedy-killed-Monroe" fiction characterized by Spoto as "malicious gossip" became shouts after Robert Kennedy's assassination in 1968 (602). Those shouts became deafening when in 1973 Norman Mailer published *Marilyn*, an attempt to recount her life in a pseudo-novel format. In his final chapter, Mailer used material from Fred Lawrence Guiles' earlier book, *Norma Jean*, written before the Kennedy assassination and subsequently discredited. Guiles had written about an affair Monroe supposedly had with an unnamed "lawyer and public servant with an important political career." Mailer named Robert Kennedy as the person involved. Mailer had his "bestseller," as Spoto cynically observes, by being the first to suggest that Robert Kennedy was involved with her death. Mailer then offered the even more outlandish theory that government agents might have had her killed to frame the attorney general (603). Mailer made these accusations in *Marilyn* while

OFF THE TRACKS VOLUME 1

at the same time hiding behind conjecture. "If she could be murdered in such a way as to appear a suicide in despair at the turn of her love, what a point of pressure could be maintained against the Kennedys. So, one may be entitled to speak of a motive for murder. Of course, it is another matter to find that evidence exists."

Mailer's "biography" was published as a large slick coffee-table volume with many photographs of the actress. The book became a perennial bestseller and is rumored to have been the second most widely sold book Mailer wrote, surpassed only by *The Naked and the Dead*. *Marilyn* cost $19.95, about $100 in contemporary dollars. Pauline Kael's judgment of the book, which she reviewed in the *New York Times*, was summed up in her title: "A Rip-Off with Genius."

Breach of Confidentiality

Greenson was well aware of the ethical obligation not to speak out about a patient, but he felt compelled to join the public conversation about Monroe, justifying the breach of confidentiality by claiming that he wanted to protect her reputation. But it's likely he had other reasons for speaking out, including trying to undo his own contribution to the Robert Kennedy rumors. Greenson may have also been annoyed that Mailer was exploiting the name of a patient over whom the analyst still felt a sense of ownership. Greenson's attempt to repair the situation did not go well.

In a seven-part series of articles published in the *Chicago Tribune* between June 8–19, 1973 and then widely syndicated, Maurice Zolotow, a show business biographer who had published the first full-length biography of Monroe while she was still alive, attempted to refute Mailer's unsubstantiated charges. Zolotow claimed that he had done what Mailer had not done: he had interviewed the people involved in the final days of Monroe's life, including Eunice Murray and, most notably, Ralph Greenson. Zolotow's articles explained the known circumstances of Monroe's last days, building up a mystery as to what actually happened and then ending in the seventh installment with the following editorial blurb: "In today's report, the last in the series, the mystery is solved."

Zolotow's article went well beyond a comment on her death and included a passage, evidently based on his Greenson interview, where the analyst felt the need to defend himself from criticism of his treatment of Monroe. "Apparently what Greenson was doing was affording her a foster home. He must have thought that giving her such an experience—of relating with his wife and daughter—would help her grow up emotionally, and for a while the therapy seemed to be successful." Zolotow's use of the phrase "affording her a foster home" implied that Monroe was at times living in the Greenson home, a statement supported by evidence. Tellingly, Greenson's reference to Monroe's relationship with his "wife and daughter" omits the fact that she also had a relationship with his son, Daniel (Turner, "Marilyn Monroe on the Couch"). According to Summers, "Danny Greenson, Joan's twenty-four-year-old brother, had not expected to get on with Marilyn. He was a student, politically radical by contemporary standards, and he expected 'a rich Hollywood bitch.' Instead he found himself drawn to a woman who was 'in no way put on or artificial, with a real warmth.' Marilyn, in her black wig, went along with Danny when he was apartment hunting. They talked politics, and he found her sympathetic to his leftist opinions" (205). Greenson concealed this information from Zolotow, perhaps because of the criticism it would evoke from the psychoanalytic community.

As far as we know, the American Psychoanalytic Association never commented on Greenson's treatment of Marilyn Monroe. Nor has the

487

case been discussed in detail, as we have, as an example of a boundary violation. In a footnote in *Psychiatry in Law/Law in Psychiatry*, Ralph Slovenko refers to Greenson's "totally antianalytic approach to therapy" (619, n.1), a statement that is hyperbolic but not completely incorrect.

Greenson was careful to avoid denying that Monroe had a sexual relationship with John Kennedy, but he told Zolotow that at the time of her death, "I can assure you that, contrary to Norman Mailer's speculations, Marilyn did not have any important emotional involvement with Robert Kennedy or any other man at this time." Greenson then offered his conviction that Monroe's death was due to an "accidental overdose," apparently referring to the fact that she had been consuming Nembutal capsules during her final day, and that the combination of the Nembutal and the chloral hydrate enema he prescribed resulted in her death.

The Zolotow article was accompanied by a sidebar titled "What must I do?" (2). The sidebar began by noting that in the prior month, May 3, 1973, the American Psychoanalytic Association issued a "stern policy paper stressing the need for a patient's complete privacy." The policy paper was a response to public disclosure of the 1971 burglary of Daniel Ellsberg's psychoanalyst's office, an event that had not become known until it came to light in an April 1973 trial. The sidebar then mentioned that Greenson wrote to the Secretary of the American Psychoanalytic Association asking that the Executive Council respond to the following question. "What is the analyst's responsibility or limitation concerning privacy when a patient dies, and books are written about her death which vilify her or are full of inaccuracies and falsehoods which are damaging to her memory?" Is it the analyst's duty to keep quiet, Greenson asked, or should the analyst expose the inaccuracies of a book as long as they do not relate to confidential matters? One of Greenson's sentences is particularly revealing. "Should he defend her against accusations which are false and demean her, even tho they touch on confidential subject matter, but the confidential subject matter is false? [sic]." Greenson then pointed out the danger of remaining silent or speaking. "By keeping quiet, he simply permits the fallacies to continue, even to multiply. Yet speaking out may be looked upon as a breach of confidentiality, altho the patient in question has been dead for more than 10 years." Greenson ended the letter by suggesting that "perhaps unscrupulous authors depend on our ethical silence and take advantage of it." The sidebar concluded, "As of this writing Dr. Greenson has not received an opinion from the Committee." At this point Greenson was on ethical thin ice because of his disclosure to Zolotow of confidential information about the analyst's treatment of Monroe. The confidential information, which was unrelated to the subject of the article, was printed in Zolotow's widely syndicated series.

Mailer was at the same time widely criticized over his "lurid speculation" in the final chapter of his book about Monroe's death. "Mailer and his publisher, Grosset and Dunlop, were accused of crassly exploiting the tabloid gossip about Monroe and the two Kennedy brothers so they could cash in on the reputations of three deeply admired American legends who were conveniently dead and in no position to defend themselves" (Wallace and Gates, 253). In July, Mailer appeared on a CBS *60 Minutes* segment titled "Monroe, Mailer and the Fast Buck." Mike Wallace conducted an aggressive interview with Mailer, asking, "Why did you write the book?" To which Mailer replied, "I started to write it as—to do a preface, to pick up a sum of money. I needed the money very badly. And then what happens. I fell in love with the material" (254). As Wallace confronted him about his substandard work on the book, Mailer admitted that he had not actually interviewed anyone for his book; had relied on secondary sources and gossip; and attributed his uncharacteristic carelessness to the pressure on him to produce enough words to fill the book by a deadline. Mailer estimated the "odds" that Monroe had died of an accidental overdose at 10 to 1, but he also claimed that there was a 50–50 chance that Robert Kennedy had been at her house that night. Wallace countered that latter assertion by interviewing Eunice Murray, an eye witness whom Mailer had neglected to interview supposedly because she was "in hiding." In fact, Murray was listed in the phone book and had never hidden from anyone. Murray told Wallace that she and Monroe had been alone in the house the entire evening up to the time Monroe died (255–256).

Why did Greenson feel that he had to discredit Mailer's book when others effectively discredited it? Mailer was not bound by confidentiality; Greenson was. Greenson's outrage over Mailer's book had as much to do with defending his own reputation as defending Monroe's. Astonishingly, Greenson tried again to clear the air (and his name) by giving *another* press interview, this time to a reporter from the *Medical Tribune* (Sandler, 1973). Greenson complained to the reporter that Zolotow had promised before publication to show him both the proposed article and a transcript of his taped interview with him, so that Greenson could remove "confidential material." Greenson claimed that Zolotow "did not live up to the terms of the interview." Greenson's motive in speaking publicly, he explained to the *Medical Tribune* reporter, was to "protect Miss Monroe's memory and I also want to protect psychoanalysis and I feel this [article by Zolotow] damages it—and unwittingly I was an accomplice in that stupidity.... I made one mistake and that was to trust Zolotow."

Greenson then revealed what was possibly his primary motive in this final public statement in *Medical Tribune*: defending *himself* and his odd treatment of Monroe, a point at least as important to him, it appears, as his wish to protect "Miss Monroe's" memory. "I have been dragged through the mud. I knew when I began treating Miss Monroe that I was taking on something that was going to cause difficulty for me and for my professional life. But I never dreamed it would get to this point." Greenson conceded that he had taken a risk treating her because of her past suicide attempts. "Nevertheless, I felt sorry for her. I felt that if people like me are not willing to treat such a person, who the hell should—a beginner?" Greenson was particularly anxious to refute the rumors arising from Zolotow's statement that the analyst provided Monroe with a "foster home," implying that she had slept over at his home. Conceding only that Monroe was a frequent visitor, Greenson once again rejected the "distortions" in Zolotow's article, concluding that "they're not fair to me and, above all, they are not fair to her." Greenson's statement is both self-serving and inaccurate. There is at least one eyewitness report that Monroe lived in the Greenson home for a brief period; moreover, among the Monroe artifacts auctioned off by the Greenson children in 2010 was one of her nightdresses (Turner, "Marilyn Monroe on the Couch").

A Controversial Will—and Monroe's Legacy to Psychoanalysis

Monroe was not a conventionally religious person, but she acted as if to her, psychoanalysis was her religion. In fact, she said on more than one occasion that "psychoanalysis [or Freud] is my religion" despite the facts that she had been raised a Christian Scientist and had converted to Judaism prior to her marriage to Arthur Miller. During the filming of *Gentlemen Prefer Blondes*, her co-star, Jane Russell, brought her to a Christian group meeting to show Monroe how Christianity might help her overcome extreme anxiety before film appearances. "For her part Monroe gave Russell a book on Sigmund Freud. 'Neither of us converted the other,' according to Marilyn" (Spoto, 232), but they remained good friends. Like many religious adherents, Monroe resolved to leave some of her estate to her "religion," psychoanalysis.

Monroe began writing a new will near the end of 1960, when she was finalizing her divorce from Arthur Miller. She signed the will on January 14, 1961, one month prior to her hospitalization at Payne Whitney. Contrary to what one might expect for a great film star, Monroe had relatively little money as a result of having been employed by Fox Studios under a "slave contract." For many years she received "woeful business advice" and paid the highest tax rates. She was also financially burdened by an "unruly assortment of landlords, friends, charities, hairdressers, make-up men, secretaries, housekeepers, decorators, drama coaches, physicians, psychiatrists, attorneys and accountants" (Badman, 57). She left in the will a modest sum of $100,000 (about $800,000 in current money) for the support of her institutionalized mother and for Mrs. Michael Chekhov, the widow of her famous early acting coach.

More importantly, as it turned out, Monroe left 75% of the "residue" of her estate to Lee Strasberg and 25% to be administered by one of her psychoanalysts, Marianne Kris, and "to be used by her for the furtherance of the work of such psychiatric institutions or groups as she shall elect." Had Monroe known of the coming rupture of her relationship with Kris one month later, it is doubtful that she would have designated Kris in the will. This bequest proved to be a goldmine because it entitled Kris to distribute one fourth of the royalties from *all* of Monroe's films as well as the royalties from other Monroe images, such as still photos owned by her estate, for the benefit of an iconic psychoanalytic institution.

The following year, Monroe was thinking seriously about death, and she decided to change this will in the summer of 1962. Events, however, conspired against her. Summers states that Monroe wished to cut the Strasbergs out of her will because of her belief that they had taken advantage of her. "With a remarriage to DiMaggio pending, she probably intended to substitute him as a primary legatee" (297). The last year of Monroe's life, darkened by the specter of mental illness, was heartbreaking to her friends, Wilson notes. "Some of them actually thought she should be 'put away'" (286). According to Rudin, shortly before her death "Marilyn was constantly talking to him about changing her will. 'I avoided the subject,' Rudin told me—and there was eloquence in his glance when he mentioned that there is a well established legal principle that anybody making a will must be of sound mind. 'After all, was she of sound mind?' A terrifying thought, of course, but wasn't Marilyn Monroe already mad? If she was, then of course Mickey Rudin couldn't participate in making a new will" (Wilson, 297; Summers, 297). The 1961 will was not changed, however, largely because Rudin, fearing she was mentally ill, kept procrastinating.

Had she written a new will, it seems likely that Monroe would also have removed the bequest that gave Marianne Kris control of 25% of the residue of her estate. Dismissing or ignoring her wish to change her will could have implicated both Rudin, Monroe"s lawyer, and Greenson, his brother-in-law, in a conflict of interest because during this time, Greenson was involved in funneling money of other wealthy patients to the Hampstead Clinic in London, renamed the Anna Freud Centre in 1982 (Kirsner, "Do As I Say" 478-484). Kris intended to designate the Anna Freud Centre as the recipient of the bequest from Monroe. Nevertheless, at the time no one imagined the value of Monroe's estate, and there is no concrete evidence of a conspiracy. Monroe's will became a source of controversy for other reasons, and it was in probate for *40 years. Forbes* Magazine identifies Monroe as the third highest money-maker in its annual ranking of "The Top-Earning Dead Celebrities," with an income of $27 million in 2011." She slipped to sixth place in 2014 but still brought in another $17 million in that year.

According to the terms of the 1961 will, following Monroe's death, funds from residuals began to flow to the Anna Freud Centre. Over the years, the bequest resulted in millions of dollars of support for the work of that institution, which is dedicated to the psychoanalytic assistance of children. According to Peter Fonagy, CEO of the Anna Freud Centre, it received about 4.1 million pounds in licensing support between 1991 and 2003. The Centre received another 1.2 million pounds upon the sale of its share of the proceeds in 2013, resulting in a total of at least 5.3 million pounds. During this period the pound averaged about $1.84, so the value of the bequest would have been about $8 million.

In 1980, 18 years after Monroe's death, Marianne Kris died, leaving the 25% interest in the estate that she controlled to the Anna Freud Centre. Two years after Kris's death, Lee Strasberg also died, leaving his entire estate, including his 75% interest in the Monroe estate, to his second wife, Anna Strasberg. By 1980, the Monroe estate through inheritances was in the hands of Anna Strasberg (75%) and the Anna Freud Centre (25%) (Anderson). To formalize their joint interest in the estate, Anna Strasberg and the Centre formed a corporation, Marilyn Monroe, LLC., with Strasberg holding the controlling interest but with a provision that both parties had to agree to further uses of Monroe's name or image.

During the 1980s, tension developed in the relationship between the Anna Freud Centre and Anna Strasberg, and finally exploded in 1989. The Centre felt that Strasberg—who was evidently trying to be protective of Monroe's legacy as she believed that her deceased husband would have wished—was reluctant to license and capitalize on Monroe's image. Strasberg maintained that their agent, Roger Richman, had failed to negotiate sufficiently lucrative licensing deals on behalf of the estate. Some of these deals could have allowed souvenir manufacturers to produce Monroe porcelain dolls and plates as was being done at the time with the likeness of Elvis Presley, and the manufacture in Japan of toilet paper with Monroe's image on each sheet. To help resolve the dispute, a Surrogate Judge, Marie S. Lambert, appointed Anna Strasberg as the executor of the estate. The judge opined, however, that the estate should be more aggressive in cashing in on Monroe's image, adding that she herself was a collector of souvenir plates. "'Right now there's stuff that's hot,' the judge said" (Margolick).

In 1996 Anna Strasberg dismissed Richman and formed an alliance with an aggressive Indiana marketing company, CMG Worldwide, headed by Mark Roesler, then known as "the king of the dead-celebrity business." Proceeds from the estate accelerated significantly as CMG began widespread licensing of Monroe's image and name. That increased revenue created new legal problems, however. Those who had photographed Monroe had bequeathed the rights to those photos to their heirs, and the heirs had been licensing the photos for various uses, but they had not been paying Monroe, LLC. for the use of Monroe's image. CMG along with Monroe, LLC. filed a lawsuit against these photographers' estates in 2006 (Koppel). In a complicated series of lawsuits, two cases involving the ownership of rights to Monroe's image and name ("the Right of Publicity") reached a federal appellate court (*Milton H. Greene Archives, Inc. v. Marilyn Monroe LLC.*). The issue was whether Monroe was a resident of New York or California at the time of her death. (A law in California makes it possible to pass along one's right of publicity to heirs; no such law exists in New York.) A federal appellate court ruled that because the Monroe estate had argued successfully over the years that the actress had died a New York resident, the estate was not obliged to pay California estate taxes; therefore, the estate could not change its position. Marilyn Monroe's image and name were thus in the public domain. The court decision ended in these often quoted words: "We observe that the lengthy dispute over the exploitation of Marilyn Monroe's persona has ended in exactly the way that Monroe herself predicted more that fifty years ago: 'I knew I belonged to the Public and to the world, not because I was talented or even beautiful but because I had never belonged to anything or anyone else'" (10237). In the following year the Anna Freud Center sold its remaining rights to the Monroe estate to CMG Worldwide, and so after more than 60 years the relationship between Marilyn Monroe and psychoanalysis came to an end.

All in the Family

Ralph Greenson's son, Daniel, who as a medical student went apartment hunting with Monroe in 1962, graduated from the U.S.C. School of Medicine in 1964, two years after her death. He went on to become a psychoanalyst, joined the American Psychoanalytic Association and established a practice in San Francisco. In December 2000, one of his patients, Lisa Lancaster, whom he had treated from 1992–1999, filed a complaint against him to the San Francisco Psychoanalytic Institute. The complaint alleged that Greenson "had committed violations of the Principles [of ethics] during the course of his treatment of her, including 'sexual and nonsexual boundary violations' and breaches of confidentiality regarding other patients" (*Lancaster v. American Psychoanalytic Association*, 2002). Following two reviews by the Association's Ethics Committee and a further review by an Appeals Committee, the latter voted to uphold the finding of the former that Daniel Greenson had committed major and repeated violations of its principles, including sexual and nonsexual boundary violations, breaches of confidentiality and exploitation of the patient's transference relationship. The Appeals Committee also upheld his expulsion from the American Psychoanalytic Association. The organization's Executive Council ratified the decision of the Appeals Committee on May 16, 2002 (*Lancaster v. American Psychoanalytic Association*, 2002).

Remembering the Past

What shall we finally say about Greenson's treatment of Marilyn Monroe? He was not the first to believe that the therapist must devise a new approach for each patient. Jung implies this throughout his autobiographical *Memories, Dreams, Reflections*, as does Irvin Yalom in *The Gift of Therapy*, where he argues that *the therapist must strive to create a new therapy for each patient* (34). But at what point does an experimental treatment become a series of boundary violations, and when does the claim that one is engaging in an experimental treatment become a mere rationalization for such violations? Are boundary violations defined in the context of a particular version of psychotherapy, such that a boundary violation in one form of psychotherapy might become the standard practice in another form, or is there a broader standard that would apply to any form of psychotherapy? These are the questions we have raised throughout our discussion.

In Greenson's defense, Kirsner suggests that his approach "can be seen in terms of the experimental approaches of the time that were demonstrated to be misconceived only later" (*Unfree Associations*, 153). Leo Rangell, a classical analyst and lifelong critic of Greenson, was far less forgiving. "This was seductive behavior, not therapeutic behavior." Rangell added that a glamorous movie star must be treated "gingerly and unseductively" (Farber and Green, 108–109). In a different context, Emanuel Berman wrote that there is a crucial difference between "critically evaluating experimental treatment methods and stigmatizing them in toto as boundary violations. To keep psychoanalytic treatment alive, and to render it more effective, we need innovative experiments. *Such experiments may require attempts to reassess our conception of boundaries. . . . Defining innovative approaches as boundary violations may delegitimize them and support barren conservatism"* (570).

The Spanish-born philosopher George Santayana was not thinking of boundary violations when he observed that "Those who cannot remember the past are condemned to repeat it." We cannot help wondering how Daniel Greenson failed to heed the cautionary tale of his father's treatment of Marilyn Monroe. Did Daniel Greenson learn from his father that boundary violations in psychoanalysis are acceptable? That he was the exception to the rules? Might the son not have gone off the tracks if his father had been censured for his unorthodox treatment of Marilyn Monroe? We cannot answer these questions, but we can point out the damage one of Daniel Greenson's analyands experienced as a result of his transgressions. In a paper presented at the "Wounds of History" conference in New York in 2013, Sue von Baeyer reported how she felt when she learned that Daniel Greenson, her training analyst at the San Francisco Center for Psychoanalysis, had committed a sexual boundary violation. She was thwarted in her efforts to engage the psychoanalytic community to discuss the significance of these transgressions. She also experienced, in the words of Muriel Dimen, "feeling tainted by the refusal of training analysts from her institute to take her into treatment" (367).

Ralph Greenson died of heart disease at the age of 68. It's not likely that we will learn much more about his life, and his treatment of Monroe, until his archives at UCLA are open to the public in 2036.

Acknowledgments

We are grateful to the many people who were kind enough to read one or more chapters of *Off the Tracks*. They include Ralph Fishkin, Peter Fonagy, Glen Gabbard, Thomas G. Gutheil, David Hamilton, Susan Harris, Jules Kerman, Jay S. Kwawer, Luba Kessler, Douglas Kirsner, Malkah Notman, Kerry Novick, Robert Pyles, Judith Schachter and Nellie Thompson. We're especially grateful to Malkah Notman, Brenda Solomon and Kathryn Watterson for their willingness to be interviewed.

We would not have been able to conduct our research without the invaluable help of the Interlibrary Loan staff at the University at Albany. Special thanks to Timothy Jackson, Angela Persico and Glen Benedict for fulfilling hundreds of our interlibrary requests.

We wish to acknowledge our thanks to David A. Olson, Oral History Archivist at Columbia University's Rare Book and Manuscript Library, for his help in allowing us to read Abram Kardiner's *Reminiscences*, a transcript of his 1963 oral interview. We are grateful to Beth Lander, College Librarian at the Historical Medical Library, The College of Physicians of Philadelphia, for her help in allowing us to read Walter Freeman's unpublished Autobiography. A Wood Institute Travel Grant paid for our research expenses at the College of Physicians of Philadelphia.

We are grateful to Professor Peter L. Rudnytsky for his constructive criticisms. We appreciate his suggestions for revision, many of which we have implemented. We believe that his criticisms have strengthened the two volumes; we alone are responsible for whatever problems remain.

Finally, we are grateful to the entire staff of IPBooks, including Arnold Richards, Larry and Tamar Schwartz, copyeditor Carol Skolnick and cover artist Kathy Kovacic.

A Note about Double Authorship

Unlike most double authored books, in which one author writes some chapters and the other author writes the remaining chapters, both of us have contributed equally to every chapter in the two volumes. Consequently, *Off the Tracks* is truly collaborative. To emphasize this, Jeffrey Berman is the lead author of volume 1, and Paul Mosher is the lead author of volume 2—though the lead authors could have easily been reversed. There are stylistic differences between the two of us—one of us is an English professor, the other a psychoanalyst—but it's impossible for us to separate one's ideas from the other's. "Blessed are the forgetful," quipped Nietzsche, "for they get the better even of their blunders."